ORGANIZED WOMANHOOD

ORGANIZED WOMANHOOD

Cultural Politics
in the Pacific
Northwest,
1840–1920

By Sandra Haarsager

University of Oklahoma Press : Norman and London

Library of Congress Cataloging-in-Publication Data

Haarsager, Sandra, 1946–
    Organized womanhood: cultural politics in the Pacific Northwest,
    1840–1920 / by Sandra Haarsager.
        p. cm.
    Includes bibliographical references and index.
        1. Women—Northwest, Pacific—Societies and clubs—History—19th
    century. 2. Women—Northwest, Pacific—Societies and clubs—His-
    tory—20th century. 3. Women in politics—Northwest, Pacific—
    History—19th century. 4. Women in politics—Northwest, Pacific—
    History—20th century. I. Title.
    HQ1904.H33   1997
    305.4'06'0795—dc21   97-12710
    ISBN 0-8061-2974-3 (cloth)   CIP
    ISBN 0-8061-3001-6 (paper)

Text design by Cathy Carney Imboden. Text is set in ITC Caslon No. 224
with Franklin Gothic display.

The paper in this book meets the guidelines for permanence and dura-
bility of the Committee on Production Guidelines for Book Longevity of
the Council on Library Resources, Inc. ⊗

1 2 3 4 5 6 7 8 9 10

WOMEN'S CLUB COLLECT

Keep us, oh Lord, from pettiness;
Let us be large in thought, in word, in deed.

Let us be done with fault-finding
And leave off self-seeking.

May we put away all pretense
And meet each other face to face,
Without self-pity and without prejudice.

May we never be hasty in judgment
And always generous.

Let us take time for all things;
Make us to grow calm, serene, gentle.

Teach us to put into action our better impulses,
Straightforward and unafraid.

Grant that we may realize it is
The little things that create differences,
That in the big things of life we are as one.

And may we strive to touch and to know
The great common human heart of us all.

And, oh Lord God, let us forget not
To be kind!

—Mary Stewart, 1904

CONTENTS

PROFILES OF LEADERS

PREFACE

This book begins with the "organized womanhood" movement itself and ends with the movement's connection to our own times. Where possible, I incorporated the words of the clubwomen themselves about their beliefs, actions, and motives and of those who advised, criticized, blamed, and praised them. Clubs and clubwomen (like denominations and congregations) had rich, subtle variations, and changes in their environment over time altered them further. The movement and its methods were as varied as the locales, terrains, towns, and personalities of the Pacific Northwest.

Women's clubs were also fluid organizations. They changed direction, focus, and even category depending on their leaders or the perceived needs of members or communities, some after a few meetings and some after a decade of meetings. When I began this project I had no idea how pervasive or varied this social movement was. Even small towns like The Dalles on the Columbia River had as many as a dozen women's clubs.

This history is divided into ten chapters interspersed with profiles of selected leaders. Leadership, as with any large-scale social movement, is critical to success. Although I chose several leaders to profile, the list of remarkable women in the Northwest who were candidates is much longer.

The club movement and its connections to other social movements, such as maternal associations, are the focus of chapter 1. The history of the first women's club in each state in the region is also described. The first regionwide organization was the Women's Christian Temperance Union (WCTU). Its rapid rise and fall in the Northwest is recounted in chapter 2. The WCTU, although not exactly successful with its extensive legislative agenda and cultural politics that took it far beyond prohibition, brought women together and into the legislative process at the city, county, and state levels. It also left the Northwest dotted with reading rooms that clubs immediately following the WCTU turned into the cultural institution called the public library.

The rise of the national club movement, the connections between men's and women's clubs, and the professionalization of the movement are some of the issues explored in chapter 3. The use of culture for self-development also reinforced the rituals of club life. Some stemmed from men's clubs, some from ideas about education and refinement, while others were unique to club life. Chapter 4 explores how patterns and rituals, from parliamentary procedure to using club colors, unified the women and their clubs.

Arts historian Lawrence Levine argues that elites responded to class and ethnic instability, especially in the cities, by using the arts to manage social problems. In providing artistic opportunities and exposure, they also remade cultural institutions "to convert the strangers so that their modes of behavior and cultural predilections" emulated their own.[1] In the cultural politics of the Northwest, the presence of the arts and cultural institutions also validated towns and cities as legitimate, permanent, and at least mature, if not sophisticated. For cities and enterprises dependent upon eastern capital, this image took on economic as well as social importance. The crowning achievement of many Northwest clubs was the creation of local libraries, giving the private act of reading a public space that also directed behavior. In these ways culture took on distinctly political overtones, the focus of chapter 5.

Chapter 6 recounts how clubs moved from studying literature and building libraries to lobbying for social change, using the major cities of the Northwest—Portland, Boise, and Seattle-Tacoma—as case studies. It also looks at issues of race and ethnicity in the expansion of the movement. The clubs and their complex relationships with working women, including their role in establishing landmark protectionist legislation, are described in chapter 7. Chapter 8 considers the club movement's active role in other social movements, especially suffrage and the long campaigns to win it.

Because the Northwest was so new, clubwomen had wider opportunities to enact regional visions through organizations of their organizations. Gaining the right to vote heightened their influence. Their concerns, achievements, and conflicts appear in the agendas of the Oregon, Idaho, and Washington State Federations of Women's Clubs, described in chapter 9. Finally, chapter 10 evaluates the movement's legacy of social programs and services that were formalized in the modern welfare state, analyzes the de-

cline of the movement, and connects it to contemporary issues a
century later.

One of the problems in writing about a movement's cultural
history is the inevitable gaps in available records; another is not
having enough pages to chronicle in detail all that happened in a
large-scale social movement like this one. Both are flaws in this
history of the women's study clubs in the Pacific Northwest. However, the appendix details alphabetically some specific clubs and
activities in Northwest locales during this period.

I would like to acknowledge those who made this project possible. First is the John Calhoun Smith Fund at the University of
Idaho, for its financial support of the archival research that went
into this book. I also want to acknowledge and thank the staffs at
archives throughout the Northwest and at the Bancroft Library at
Berkeley for their help in finding minutes and other records. I am
grateful to those at the University of Oklahoma Press, particularly
senior editor Kimberly Wiar, for their professionalism and support, and to historian Susan Armitage, who reviewed an earlier
version of this work. And last, I would like to thank my family—
Dennis, Anna, and Andrew—for once again putting up with my
long hours in front of a computer screen or peering from behind
piles of notes and books. Most of all, I want to acknowledge the
thousands of women in Idaho, Oregon, and Washington who
banded together to make themselves and their cities better (and
the faithful secretaries they elected who recorded what they did).

ORGANIZED WOMANHOOD

INTRODUCTION

The *Women's Club Collect* by Mary Stewart, written at the height of the women's club movement, appeared in hundreds of club yearbooks that laid out a club's annual plan of work. The collect, usually a short prayer attached to a particular day or season, came from Anglican and Catholic church traditions. The club collect reflected what women saw as their season, their time to come together to create a collective vision.[1] Its sentiment set forth a creed for women's club activism and reflected what members felt they got from their clubs. From scattered beginnings in the nineteenth century, the woman's study club movement mushroomed into a major social force before the turn of the century, spreading education, culture, and changes in the legal and political system like spores on the wind.

Collectively, the women used what they called "organized womanhood" to redefine not only women's roles but also the state and its relationship to citizens. In the Northwest, women played a far greater political role in the settlement of the region than current histories suggest. Initially, women's clubs offered a forum where educated women interacted, which became settings for community policymaking as clubs evolved from social to civic to political organizations. They represented the interests of women then broadened those interests into larger social movements.

Women's efforts to structure institutions for social betterment through voluntary associations have gone largely unheralded and unrecorded, as historian Anne Firor Scott and others have noted.[2] Whether a club's stated purpose was study, philanthropy, reform, or improving conditions for women and children, its unstated purpose was twofold: to create a framework giving women access to public life and to wrest community priorities from the imperatives of economic development, especially in the West. Clubs mediated the private and public spheres and provided a means to create or process social change, especially changes in the legal, economic, and political status of women and children. They also kept culture present as a counterbalance to male-dominated political and economic institutions, through the arts, through civility (enforced through ordinances if necessary), and for personal expression.

Attention to women's history has given new meaning to the old category called "the state," shedding light on the intersection of public and private life, historian Kathryn Kish Sklar notes. The history of women gathered in voluntary societies makes the history of social welfare policies come alive with struggle and change, dissolving old paradigms. In the past, efforts at reform and the shift from private to public programs for social welfare were lumped under ideas of social control or attempts to force the state to assume responsibilities once held by the family. That no longer sufficiently explains "complex interactions among class interests, social problems, and state initiatives."[3] Cultural politics and the history of social welfare during this period, especially at the state and regional levels, integrate women's history into other descriptive frameworks, such as urban history, regional history, political history, legal history, and even the history of professionalization and of the arts. The traditions of limited government in the United States left openings for female reformers, who expressed their ideas (and made them acceptable) by attaching them to the values of the home.

This thread of domestic values and cultural politics ties the end of the nineteenth century to the end of the twentieth. Ideas about welfare, entitlements, and family values swirl around the culture, doing battle with ideas about limited government and individual rights. The results of women's club activism and Progressive era reforms in government reach over the decades. Directly and indirectly, women shaped policy as they shaped their communities, especially at the local and state level, then later at the national level. The issues that engaged them ranged broadly, from education to public health to recreation to the arts.

In the Northwest, hundreds of club initiatives at the local, state, and regional levels informed public policy. Those who shape the culture through its attitudes and rhetoric also shape public responses. That is where clubwomen in the Northwest had their most significant impact, from public libraries to worker protection. Recognizing this interaction between male-dominated and female-dominated political cultures is critical in assessing histor-

ical outcomes.[4] It is here that this book is situated, as a regional
history of women's cultural politics through study clubs and their
other organizations and what their practical politics wrought in
the Northwest.

Women also used clubs for identity formation, both as women
and as part of a group bounded by class, by culture, even by the
movement itself. Women isolated in nascent towns without services or amenities especially needed this association. Clubs created a female space outside the home and church where none had
existed before; they took women who were timid and apologetic
speakers and recast them as local orators and parliamentarians,
or at least made them more confident in expressing their opinions. Women who found their voices through study and club ritual soon found causes to talk about.

There was a chain in the Northwest linking the WCTU, the
study club, and civic activism, forged in a compression of time
and events as its development unfolded. Their legacy enabled the
Northwest to lead the nation in giving women the right to vote, in
improving women's legal status, in passing landmark labor legislation and other measures well before the rest of the nation took
those steps. The cadre of leaders that emerged from the club
movement became leaders of other social movements such as suffrage and consumer rights.

From Literature to Lobbying

The women in the Northwest often began meeting to study literature. Soon many groups, some within a matter of months, turned
from the study of literature to the study of what they called
woman's condition or current social problems and then from
study to action on problems or deficiencies in their own communities or states. Clubs empowered women to question some of the
assumptions that bounded women's lives or to use those assumptions subversively as reasons to change conditions around them.
They also offered opportunities for education and self-development denied many women, an important and neglected facet of
clubwork. Early club leaders overlapped organizations.

The initial leaders of the important Women's Christian Temperance Unions in the Northwest founded later study clubs and
helped lead suffrage movements in Idaho, Washington, and Oregon. Their leadership was vital, and clubs gave them both plat-
forms and causes. Many of them and their followers were in turn

influenced by the national leaders who came to the remote Northwest. That list included Susan B. Anthony, Frances E. Willard, Carrie Chapman Catt, Florence Kelley, and General Federation of Women's Clubs leaders like Ellen Henrotin of Chicago. National suffrage leader Catt lived for a time in Seattle and founded one of that city's most influential and active clubs, coming back as a national suffrage leader. This Seattle club too began life as a small study club, but soon engaged in cultural politics and lobbying for changes in public policy.

The Pacific Northwest experience points to several themes besides women's role in expanding the state. One is that club activism linked self-improvement to civic improvement. It legitimated activism by tying it not only to the domestic ideal, but also to concepts of progress and modernism in the region, with its rapidly expanding population. Another theme is that women had their own imagined West, quite different from the West of the dime novels or the gold-seekers. Their West is found in their narratives, their papers, their club programs, their ideals and goals. Their West had spaces for women, homes, and community values expressed through social policies and cultural institutions.

Another theme is that study clubs used their research and unique rituals to form their own interpretive community. Because members depended on literacy and reading for self-improvement and empowerment, it is no coincidence that most public libraries in the Northwest and in much of the nation were the legacy of women's clubs. Because women needed a voice and the ability to speak in public settings, clubs emphasized research, presentation, and discussion skills that empowered women in subsequent civic work. Their fusion of ideas about literacy and democracy also filled their ideas about culture, behavior, and professionalism. Clubs often engaged in a power struggle over what the dominant culture of the region should look like, in its arts, politics, laws, and services, and how women fit into it.

Women and Western History

In the course of writing this book, I traveled to the Bancroft Library archives at the Berkeley campus of the University of California. I looked forward to reviewing the original notes local historians left about the Northwest, which were used to compile Hubert Howe Bancroft's multivolume history of the West. Anticipation turned to disappointment when I found the records contained nothing about women, even the wives of the men who built the West. The notes offered numerous accounts of men who built banks, railroads, grain elevators, herds, and other economic enterprises. Not only were women absent, but the wives of these builders who shared their lives seemed not even to have names. On library shelves throughout the Northwest I found thick subscription histories, rich with details. Only rarely did they contain references to any of the women who influenced the course of the communities in the Northwest.

I should not have been surprised. Until recently, historians writing about the development of the West excluded women and women's roles in their tales of pioneers, frontier development, extraction industries, and transportation networks. History has been viewed through the lens of the political and economic structures that mirrored the governance and commerce of the West.

Also, part of the mythology of the West is the ongoing fascination with the pioneers and their journey. For many, especially the women, the historical record seemed to end once they reached their destination. Accounts at the time and those written later typically focus first on the journey then on the hard work of carving out mines, mills, homesteads, farms, and towns from the "untamed wilderness." They tell of urban development and calamities, like the fires that devastated Seattle and Spokane, of heroes putting their stamp on the land and making it economically productive, literally making deserts bloom and forests fall or turning rock into gold.

The issue of gender in western history until recently had been relegated to certain "types." Categorical assumptions about gender in western frontier mythology—woman as helpmeet, mother, "gentle tamer" of the West, excluded from enterprise, professions, industry—have kept women's contributions to the history of the West in a subordinate position.[5] References to women, if there were any, were through their husbands' names and deeds. For instance, over the decades even fine journals like the *Oregon Historical Quarterly* carried in their indexes many more entries on wolves and wool than on women. Other journals seldom included any articles on women at all, except for occasional pioneer profiles or pieces about suffrage campaigns. Women even were denied their active role in most accounts of the successful suffrage campaigns in the Northwest, which were dismissed as something men did to increase a new state's political power, a fluke, or an effort to bring more women into the state.

Yet I know from work in other archives and from other histori-

ans that women collectively exercised political as well as other
forms of power, despite deficiencies in their economic, legal, and
political status. That is the case especially if power is defined as
"any action, formal or informal, taken to influence the course of
behavior of government or the community," as Paula Baker defines it in arguing for recognition of women's roles in urban politics.[6] Power also comes with the ability to shape the values and
beliefs that constitute a culture, which women have always had in
varying degrees and certainly put to use in the tumultuous decades on either side of 1900. Though unheralded, women through
collective action created many of the social and cultural institutions we now take for granted as part of the built environment in
the West.

The "new" western historians talk of the West as a place and
the Northwest as a unique region within that place. This sense of
place that defines the West continues to be the site of disputes
over its fundamental nature and whose story, from what perspective, gets told. The dissension is in part over an idealized West derived from Turnerian ideas about the moving American frontier
fostering a democracy characterized by tough, unfettered, and
unlettered pragmatists in a place with boundless resources and
optimism, a place where America's destiny was realized. Not
everyone subscribed to that vision of the West, even in the nineteenth century. Many women imagined a West that included institutions, communities, services, and a sense of culture that be-
lied tales of the Wild West.

As a region, the Northwest—here defined as the states of Washington, Oregon, and Idaho—is physically a land of contrasts and
extremes. It is arid and forested, rugged and fruitful, developed
and wild. The federal government became and remains the major
landholder, and federal land policies and irrigation projects made
extensive settlement possible.[7] The region's natural resources,
difficult topography, production capabilities, great distances, and
local networks influenced the nature of its communities. So did
the nature of its people, in this place of often clashing cultures
and ethnicities. Those differences and differences of class often
fractured powerful connections based on gender or locale. Historian Patricia Limerick in *The Legacy of Conquest* warns against
projecting "a sentimentalized hope for women's essential solidarity into the past." The history of the West is in its struggles over

power and hierarchy "not only between races but also between classes, genders, and often groups within the white majority," historian Donald Worster writes.[8] The history is also found in the struggle for common ground and alliances to bridge those differences within groups.

ORGANIZED WOMANHOOD IN THE NORTHWEST

Women in the nineteenth century built strong female support networks within the confines of the domestic sphere. Before the club movement, social connections were largely determined by kinship or neighborhood and by religious, political, and class sympathies, especially for women. When families left for the West, that subculture of female friends and relatives was strained if not sacrificed. It was difficult to reconstruct in places where women found themselves isolated by distance or privation, especially after relocating to transient mining camps or irrigation tracts that defied attempts to establish a sense of community. As historian Susan Armitage notes, "frontier individualism was forced upon these women: they had to be more self-reliant and less communal than they had been before."[9] However, along with hopes for a new life they brought traditional sex-role standards and cultural expectations.

After the difficult initial years of settlement, women used their self-reliance to join other women in voluntary association to improve themselves and their raw communities through what they themselves began to label "organized womanhood." The lines between benevolence and self-improvement blurred. Initially the cause of temperance brought some women together, especially in towns where saloons outnumbered other kinds of businesses (which included most towns). Later others wanted to recreate the kinds of clubs they had left behind in the Midwest or New England. One woman in Spokane, at the eastern edge of Washington, went so far as to advertise in the newspaper for like-minded women to join a Sorosis Club similar to the one she had left in Illinois. Once organized, the clubs sought subjects to study and causes to promote. They found many. The clubs varied as did the causes, although certain similarities linked them.

Past work on the women's club movement has tended to lump the clubs together, without much attention to time frames, programs, structure, or regional variation. Some writers describe women's club activism as an urban development, a response to finding near their doorsteps the slums, inadequate services, disease epidemics, overcrowding, crime, and prostitution linked to cities and industrialization.[10] Clubs in the West had a different starting point from clubs in other locales. The West lacked the social, cultural, economic, and political development of the East, as well as its more stable, hierarchical social divisions and its large industrialized cities. Many of the towns in the Pacific Northwest were sagebrush plains, riverbends, or forested hills only a few years before or during the phenomenal expansion of the national women's club movement in the closing years of the nineteenth century. The compression of time and the transient and unformed nature of the communities of the Pacific Northwest meant that their new clubs turned more quickly to meet immediate community needs, from creating sidewalks to shepherding traveling libraries.

Clubwomen were not simplistic "civilizers" whose passive presence "tamed" male behavior. Theirs was a bold attempt to aggregate and use power to order their world and create spaces in it for women inside and outside the club, literally and figuratively. Clubwomen took up what later generations termed "quality of life" issues, from the arts to public health to the environment to education. In the early years in most places in the West, the women found malleable communities, sometimes hostile and lawless, and tried to make them conform to their collective perceptions of what communities should offer and should be while protecting their status as women.

The first significant club network webbing the Pacific Northwest was the Women's Christian Temperance Union. Within the space of little more than a decade, many initial leaders of the WCTU in the Northwest left it to found study clubs and lead suffrage campaigns, a pattern of rapid change and shared leadership that did not occur to this extent elsewhere in the country. The WCTU fostered organized womanhood in the Pacific Northwest, developing among members a sense of connection, of personal and collective identity, of community service, and of power. By 1890, less than a decade after its founding in each state, the WCTU had an extensive network of unions throughout all the states in the Pacific Northwest, scattering dozens of departments and reading rooms along the way.

The Culture of Clubs

Today the word *club* carries connotations of a rigid class system or of racist or sexist enclaves that include a few and exclude others. *Club,* like its French companions *clique* and *coterie,* carries implications that run counter to egalitarian ideals of democracy, despite the openness of some clubs.[11] This traditional conception of clubs, stemming in part from men's social clubs and lodges, affected the nature of women's clubs. In their rituals, elitism, networking, and social reinforcement, women's clubs had some significant connections to their predecessors, but they also worked against that model, particularly in the somewhat less class-oriented Northwest where all were relative newcomers.

The word *club* carried different connotations for the women who participated. Many, like the Sub Rosa study club bubbling up in the desert development called Mountain Home south of Boise, initially were nervous about even claiming the word for their activities, fearing they would be seen as too brash and bold or imbued with the worst characteristics of the men's clubs. Women's club life, however, reflected a new idealism. In women's club life, the path of study and culture toward social uplift, education, and refinement countered prevailing and more masculine images of competitiveness, materialism, and acquisition in the pursuit of happiness and construction of communities. This ideal also reinforced a dualism—woman's claim on the spiritual and moral realm and man's claim on utility and the marketplace.

There were many kinds of clubs and club activism. Some were conservative, while others were radical. Some (many in the Northwest) began as one type of club and became another. Some stayed small, while others had hundreds of members. The clubs all shared certain commonalities and rituals, however, making it easier for diverse groups come together in federations.

Culture, the Arts, and Cultural Politics

Cultivation of the arts, a traditional enhancement of the quality of life, was also used to mark education and status. In most of the West, cultural institutions and artistic traditions were absent and had to be created, fostered, and justified. Women sought cultural continuity and connections with other women in the face of change and the limitations of frontier life.[12] They also sought outlets for their own artistic talents and interests. Clubs often gave them both. Furthering the arts was an aspect of intellectual life clubwomen envisioned as essential to the domestic ideal. Americans as a group often mistrusted the arts, suspicious of whatever seemed to have no utilitarian purpose or evoked images of a European aristocracy or decadent cities, Karen Blair notes in her work on women's arts associations.[13] That was evident too in the mythology of the West, which celebrated visions of hardy pioneers taming the land and subduing the "savages" with toughness and ingenuity, with little time or energy left for anything "impractical."

However, as settlements grew into small cities, as families replaced transient men, ideas of refinement—always women's special domain—gained new attention and status near the turn of the century. For women in a struggle to create an identity for the West to counter its raw nature and frontier image, the arts, from literature to exhibits, became particularly important. Beyond the issue of image, women inculcated the arts as "uplifting," a path toward the higher and better, in themselves as well as in society. The arts also became indicators of status in a turbulent time when traditional class lines were shifting nationally as in the West. Boosters in cities like Spokane, Boise, and Lewiston, male and female, bragged about the distinction of having opera house theaters (Spokane claimed to have the biggest stage west of the Mississippi).

Among the women's clubs in the Northwest, those that focused on the fine arts tended to be more exclusive in membership. However, they were relentless and largely successful in their efforts to bring the arts to all citizens, whether through large traveling art exhibits like those organized by a club in Pocatello, Idaho, or by bringing performers and concerts to town quarterly as did the Ladies' Musical Club of Seattle.[14]

THE POLITICS OF CULTURE

Culture also has a broader meaning. It is used in these pages to reflect the characteristics that set one group of people apart from another. They include traditions, priorities, values, institutions, and social relations and expectations, as well as concepts of gender, codes of behavior, and so on. A culture's construction resides in shared forms of discourse and systems of meaning, or else communication is not possible. Cultural politics then is found in the struggle over the power to define, establish, or alter a culture or a dominant set of beliefs and values, such as those that fit a group's vision of the ideal community. There are many partisans in this struggle and the "sides" and boundaries are in flux like national or personal alliances. Power can be shifted by making a new kind of discourse or ideology dominant or by taking the dominant discourse and its shared meaning and using it subversively in a contest over what cultural theorist Michel Foucault calls the terrain of meaning. Whose story gets told, how, and where is one of the outcomes of that struggle, and that makes club programs, relations, and rituals significant.

Culture, when expressed as a set of shared values, ideals, and standards, makes the actions of individuals intelligible to the group and the actions of the group intelligible to the individual. Wearing club colors like a uniform, or using parliamentary procedure to decide upon a plan of work, presented a code of identity to each member. Relying on a unique set of systems and traditions, all clubs were held together by a sense of individual and collective identity as well as purpose. That sense of collective identity, whether expressed in ideas of maternalism or manifest destiny, in times of change is stretched to cover the changes and incorporate them into the cultural fabric. Where it will not fit, the fabric tears. Attempts to mend the ruptures and make it whole, by restating, reforming, and reimposing traditions, cause new tensions. For women's clubs, the role of women and the nature of community and governance are perennially at the core of that tension, in the Northwest no less than elsewhere.

THE PURSUIT OF KNOWLEDGE

Literacy, the act of reading, and the transmission of culture through the written word in the form of research, reports, and books were another kind of ritual central to the women's study club mission. Reading rooms, traveling libraries, and public libraries were the club movement's material manifestations, in community after community. Choosing and circulating books for others to read, as part of club programs or in library collections, is in itself a political act, one the women never failed to appreciate although they would never have considered it political. Literacy is conceived as a skill, but it also represents attitudes and mentalities, as theorist Harvey Graff says about the tradition of literacy. As a technology "for communications and for decoding and reproducing written or printed materials," writing or reading alone is not an "agent of change." Its impact "is determined by the manner in which human agency exploits it in a specific set-ting."[15] Clubwomen promoted the skill of literacy, but they also wanted to exploit it as an agent of change through libraries and texts made accessible to all residents.

The production of knowledge—in its content, form, disciplines, and distribution—is indeed a political action. Clubwomen used books, libraries, study, and lecturers to carry forward cultural and social ideals through texts and the practice of reading and analy-sis. They saw the process of transmitting culture and transferring knowledge never as confining or controlling, but as liberating and progressive. They proffered equal access to the latest information about topics from child care to health care and sought to elevate tastes from dime novels to classic literature.

Women worked valiantly and with little reticence for this cul-tural goal throughout the Pacific Northwest. For instance, leaders of Boise's Columbian Club, in building the library collection cir-culated in boxes around the state, felt no shyness about button-holing men as soon as they stepped down from the stage or rail-road car, seeking donated books. Others went door to door or held endless fundraisers. Books had become important cultural arti-facts, symbolic for women who had little access to higher levels of education (although it should be noted that most men, for other reasons, had limited access to higher education as well).

That women valued and revered books and the reading of them was not unique to women's clubs. It was apparent in the autobio-graphies of many women who became prominent in the last quar-ter of the nineteenth century. For many women, Barbara Sicher-man writes, "books acquired an almost magical status, books in general as well as particular books."[16] The link between literacy and libraries as beneficent agents of democracy, equality, and progress was assumed. It no longer is. Literacy can and has been used as a barrier to maintain social structure and order as well as to democratize and liberate. Literacy can be a cause of social change or a consequence of it, depending on who benefits and the social conditions.

Changes in technology and distribution made reading materials along with commercial goods more readily available in the distant Northwest, bringing in tracts, dime novels, and sensational news-papers. Some feared lurid fiction and the new forms of media might "overstimulate" or contaminate minds, especially the minds of those in the lower classes, who many believed were more susceptible to manipulation. Debates about classic literature and popular literature ensued, and stratification of cultural products was a result. This process played out in the cultural politics of the public libraries. For instance, clubwomen along the Columbia at The Dalles, Oregon, who had the pleasant duty of choosing works for the library they created, also created dissension. To their surprise, their choices dismayed some members.

The connections between library history, the history of literacy, and cultural formation are intriguing and bound up with the women's club movement. The idea of the public library, with access to the best books in an atmosphere of cleanliness and order, was also a means of social control, however benign and instructive.[17] That may have been an underlying motive in offering "the best books," but it is not what most clubwomen raised dollars and volunteered their hours to accomplish. They wanted to share what they had found to be of great personal and cultural value. This is especially true in the Northwest with its limited settings for personal enrichment and social contact outside saloons, those masculine social spaces that barred women and sometimes corrupted men.

As the club movement flooded the Northwest, clubs engaged in a range of concerns affecting women. Besides betterment, the clubs generally worked for what they called "village improvement," through research and study, then through practical projects such as food safety, beautification, libraries, or protection of working women. In this clubs reflected the pervasive faith in progress and American exceptionalism later embodied in Progressive reform and belief that the values of the home were culturally important to the republic. They wanted to bring the benefits of cultural, economic, medical, material, and sociological advances to neighborhoods and communities that sorely needed them and to better themselves (and give women more power) in the process.

Inside their clubs, they believed what their *Club Collect* said, that they were learning to work through their differences toward collective good. They used the methods and findings of the new social sciences and sought realignment of government's priorities toward citizens through consumer regulation, pension programs, public health programs, and reform of the justice system. Many programs, laws, and institutions that in the twentieth century protected Northwest residents had their genesis or enactment as part of the agenda of a club or of clubs coalesced into federations.

Helping Working Women

Many women's clubs in the Northwest, especially through their federations, took up causes for working women, especially wage-earning women in the Northwest's larger cities. In all three states, but especially in Oregon, the federated clubs backed a series of protectionist measures designed to make the lot of the working woman easier and safer. Although many proposals initially failed, some important measures became law and were validated by the U.S. Supreme Court in a landmark labor law decision stemming from a challenge to Oregon's law protecting female workers.

Clubs also traveled other routes to help women who needed to earn money to survive. Some sponsored women's exchanges, selling products made by women, including members in some cases; some ran employment bureaus; a few established boarding homes for single working women or places for "noon rests"; others started clubs and classes designed specifically for working women; many pushed for "mothers' pensions" to support penniless unemployed mothers and widows. These services generally prospered for a while, until times, conditions, and interests changed.

Despite these efforts, clubwomen and working women did not always understand one another. While they accomplished much together and joined forces to pass landmark legislation in the regulation of conditions, wages, and hours, tensions between them began to increase, especially after 1910 in the Northwest. To the exasperation of the more political clubs and leaders, working women did not always appreciate what the powerful women's clubs had to offer them, especially since the clubs believed they had a corner on what was "highest and best." Early cross-class alliances began to break down. Nevertheless, especially in the Northwest, the activist clubs campaigned to improve the lot of working women, from setting the maximum hours they could work to the minimum wages they could be paid. They also helped end the worst abuses of child labor, again turning to government to enact provisions to protect citizens, especially women and children.

The Struggle for Identity and Power

The economic history of the Northwest is the history of mining, logging, and farming more than of manufacturing. Promise of free land and fortunes from gold initially brought immigrants into all parts of Oregon, Washington, and Idaho. Most men who came to the mining camps and frontier settlements without families were more concerned about economic opportunity and enterprise than about schools, benevolence, temperance, or even churches. Those by design or necessity were often left to women, although men too certainly recognized the importance of these institutions. Also, much of the region developed a tolerance for drinking and prostitution as part of a service economy for transient men and profitable businesses for others.

The arrival of mothers and children in these nascent communities led to a struggle over masculine identity, "a struggle involving the sexual double standard, religious commitment, temperance, gambling, men's psychological commitment to the wives and children, and male and female prerogatives within the family," as historian Robert Griswold notes.[18] Women in clubs involved in cultural politics or civic activism were at the heart of that struggle. Also at the center of it were the winning campaigns for suffrage in the West. Successes in the West came long before the first successful campaigns in the East. In the Northwest, suffrage campaign leaders gained political support and savvy and even shared leaders across borders.[19] Getting the vote gave clubwomen and their campaigns more clout, although not nearly as much as some feared and others wanted.

One characteristic of club leadership in the Pacific Northwest was the relatively high level of education many leaders had. Another was the number of professional women who were members and especially officers of the clubs. Club leaders throughout the region often included doctors, teachers, and lawyers. Club leaders were married to entrepreneurs, professionals, or middle managers, few of whom became (or arrived) wealthy. Some of their spouses were also involved in local or state politics, especially in Idaho. These women, some of them profiled in this book, were among the first women to practice their professions or to take to the podium in the region. Many, like Tacoma's Dr. Alice Smith, came to the Northwest to pursue what they saw as greater opportunities to use their skills and fewer restrictions.

Most of the clubwomen—like the Northwest itself—were white and Protestant. Yet the nature of the West, with its multiracial and multiethnic sites in an undeveloped and sometimes inhospitable locale, led to regional differences in club formation. The sparsely settled Pacific Northwest had a proportionately larger foreign-born and more transient population than the rest of the country, leading to less rigid lines in club memberships. The lines with regard to race, however, were more distinct. The controversial issue of African-American membership in the club federations found more support in the Northwest than elsewhere, but still the individual clubs—like other organizations of the time—were segregated. African-American women's study clubs emerged in cities of the Northwest when white women created their clubs, and they proved to be an important force for those communities. Like their white counterparts, they focused on individual betterment and community improvement, stated as "racial uplift." Like the Dorcas Society of Seattle, which found homes or treatment for children rejected elsewhere, the African-American clubs offered services and vital support African Americans could not find elsewhere.

Some clubs reached out to the fast-growing immigrant populations in the port cities of the Northwest. Club projects for immigrants and also for Native Americans in the Northwest ranged from vocational classes to English instruction to women's exchanges. Seattle even had a settlement house initiated by the Council of Jewish Women that involved the support of several clubs. The targets, as elsewhere, were Americanization and assimilation as well as aid and education.

Often these programs and classes were helpful to individuals and groups. Others were meddlesome and invasive. Critics called them condescending or patronizing, like many plans to help the "disadvantaged classes." Where some women welcomed the intervention, support, and education from "Mother's Club" members or Visiting Nurses, for instance, others were offended by their know-it-all intrusions. Nevertheless, these clubwomen generally, if erratically, improved conditions for many of those they sought to help and in some cases ameliorated some of the worst conditions immigrants faced. Direct contact also lessened some of the nativism and prejudice that threatened immigrant populations, especially in the first two decades of the twentieth century, even as they carried the ideals of "Americanization" forward.

"Middle-Class" Women

The women's club movement has long been stereotyped as middle-class if not elite. That oversimplifies a complex movement with diverse membership, even more so in the Northwest, where social relationships and occupational and economic status tended to be a little less hierarchical and less stable. Although the term *middle-class* is ill-defined and problematic, clearly members of women's clubs shared and spread (some would say imposed) a particular set of values and were seldom anywhere near the bottom of the economic or social scale. However, many at all economic levels aspired to membership in the clubs.

Middle-class as a category generally refers to an economic measure, occupational grouping, or movement into a level of society with a particular set of traditional values. It has also taken on a pejorative cast as a label of denigration used by a culturally if not economically elite class. The term needs clearer definition. Although income level is certainly an important social indicator, *middle-class* goes beyond that. It is also a social construct, a point of reference, a shared understanding about "where we came from, where we are or where we want to be," says one writer. "Above all, it's a state of mind and a set of values embedded deep in the heart of America."[20]

Perhaps the term *middle-class* is better understood in the context of revising one's identity to fit into a particular group through a process of self-construction. That constructed reality reflects a set of traditional values, an assumed level of prosperity, and the ongoing struggle to integrate the rapid-fire societal changes that came with the transition from nineteenth-century agrarian values to control by twentieth-century markets and bureaucracies, including changing views of progress.

At the least, lumping middle-class white women together as a cohesive group has some of the same problems as lumping Native American populations together. In the Northwest there seems to have been less economic class uniformity among club memberships than elsewhere, but like clubwomen elsewhere they shared uniformity in some critical values. Self-improvement, civic betterment, city beautification, and other causes embodied those values. Women found "organized womanhood" and cultural politics could make those values material. It also gave them personal and collective power.

Village Improvement and the Female Gaze

Club chronicler Mary Ritter Beard early in the twentieth century described women's growing sense of civic improvement. "Thousands of men may loaf around clubs without ever showing the slightest concern about the great battle for decent living conditions that is now going on in our cities; but it is a rare woman's club that long remains indifferent to such momentous matters," she wrote. "Nor . . . is this movement for civic betterment confined to the greater cities. In thousands of out-of-the-way places which hardly appear on the map, unknown women with large visions are bent on improving their minds for no mere selfish advancement, but for the purpose of equipping themselves to serve their little communities," she continued. "They form local associations. These local associations are federated into state and national associations. The best thought and experience of one community soon become the common possession of all," she added, describing how the clubs shared ideas. "Thus we see in the making, before our very eyes, a conscious national womanhood. Here is a power that will soon disturb others than the village politicians."[21]

Beard might have been speaking about the "out-of-the-way" places in the Northwest that are the focus of this book. While some remained focused on study of literature and fine arts, most clubs to some degree sought to reshape themselves through "social betterment," as they called it, and reshape their communities, using what Beard called "conscious national womanhood" for civic improvement through club education, club projects, and club activism. They left a legacy through their ideas about culture that inscribed the political and cultural landscape of the Northwest, just as fences, railroads, and city skylines inscribed the physical landscape of the West that Bancroft's agents chronicled.

One important question to ask about a political or cultural system is who is marginalized or victimized, how, and why. The East marginalized the West, economically and culturally; women were marginalized by the legal system as part of a union with their spouses and without separate legal standing; children were often marginalized as part of the work force, even as targets of trade in unwholesome milk; families and communities were sometimes marginalized by the process of rapid development and industrialization.

All of those concerns fell under the distinctly female gaze of the women in the Northwest. What they saw was often what men did not see: families victimized by an inequitable economic and legal system, women and children victimized by neglect or abusive male behavior exacerbated by the saloons and ignored by the courts, citizens victimized by a lack of support services and educational opportunities, and communities without amenities of all sorts. That included distinctly female spaces outside the home.

Clubwomen in the Northwest probably did little to change the East-West balance in national affairs despite widespread suffrage in the West. Yet they did much to take women and children from the margins and make them central to social welfare programs. They also helped give them legal standing. Their communities also benefited in many large and small ways, from parks with playgrounds to jails with matrons. That legacy is one consequence of the female gaze upon the structure and systems of the West. The shift from private to public responsibility for social welfare that crystallized in the New Deal and the Great Society is in part the legacy of women's activism in these associations. That activism welled from the bottom up, with the campaigns of thousands of women in hundreds of small community clubs, many of them allied by federations.

Their beliefs and concerns led to expansion of government to serve and control citizens for the public good. But disagreement over what government should do about some old issues—immigration, unwed mothers, welfare fraud, spiraling program costs, crime, welfare's damage to individual initiative, budget shortfalls, and a host of others—soon splintered whatever consensus had existed during those pivotal decades, exacerbated by a reactionary backlash over their successes and direction. The issues remain with us.

When Republicans gained control of Congress in 1994 they promised to end the abuses and dismantle or curtail many of the government's programs in an attempt to address the massive federal debt and provide relief to mandate-burdened states. However, no one seriously advocated an end to club-backed priorities such as wage and hour laws, the minimum wage, social security and disability pension programs, public health protections, consumer protection, prohibitions against child labor, or dozens of other laws and programs. Those provisions are now commonly accepted as legitimate functions of government, as the clubwomen of a century ago had hoped. However, it also must be said that clubwomen would have been astounded, some appalled, at this expansion of government programs and funding and the extent of its intervention into social problems.

ACCOMMODATING CHANGE AND DECLINE

Club priorities shifted over time or sometimes hit barriers, like a tide hitting a seawall, in response to pressures inside and outside

their communities and to the dramatic cultural, social, and technological changes that came between 1875 and 1925. Changes
were accelerated in the West because of the compression of time,
the boom and bust cycles of development, and explosive growth
from 1890 to 1910 and beyond. Homes were changing, work was
changing, the culture was changing, and so was woman's place in
them. The domestic ideal and supremacy of "womanhood" gave
way to technology, professionalization, and bureaucratization.
These came in the form of domestic science, efficiency experts,
social scientists, and changing commerce. In the Northwest, railroads, agricultural technology, urbanization, city utilities, migrations, and mass culture led to wrenching changes. Ironically, some
of the very changes in services, government, and women's roles
that women's clubs had promoted served to diminish their own
power and influence locally even as they gained power nationally.
One of the most far-reaching shifts was the growing employment
of women, a trend that heralded the end of the women's club
movement, even though the movement itself enjoyed some of its
greatest national achievements in the 1920s.

The rise of domestic science, consumerism, and mass culture
marked the decline of domesticity and society's tacit acceptance
of women's innate right to impose domestic values on the public
sphere. Domestic science reflected the Progressive trend of defer-
ring to trained experts and changing the value of educating women
from uplift to professional training.[22] The result was growing faith
in scientific management and declining faith in the ideals and
skills connected to the domestic sphere. By the 1920s consumption had replaced cultural influence as the guiding principle of
the domestic sphere.

Simultaneously, women began abandoning the ideology of the
home as the impetus for restructuring society. Restructuring society soon equated with radicalism. The Northwest's growing if
often overblown share of labor unrest, culminating in the 1919
general strike in Seattle, showered suspicion on any activists promoting major changes. Reflecting the tenor of the times, clubs
began to regroup and reconsider their priorities as *radical* turned
into a noun for name-calling. Even as women enjoyed greater access to education, the professions, the polls, and the podium,
clubs pulled back. The movement faltered, but left behind something significant in forcing redefinition of both government and
gender in the larger culture. That process is never finished, but

what they did colored the course of events in the Northwest and the nation more than a century later.

For all its successes, the club movement had significant short-comings. Clubs failed to incorporate women of color into the movement as a whole. In the Northwest, clubs maintained fewer social barriers, crossed more class lines, and recognized the sisterhood in womanhood, as their memberships and programs for working women and others demonstrated. But with some exceptions, most members did not move beyond the extensions of traditional female roles as caretakers, teachers, and moral guardians. This widespread social movement tended to reflect majoritarian views and was less radical or challenging than it might have been. Clubs fostered conformity more often than challenges or used conformity to challenge prevailing systems. However, they sought equity, rights, and protection for women, although most would have been embarrassed if not appalled to be called feminists.

What they failed to get was credit for what they did. Because the women in these clubs did not possess the formal political power to enact measures or the financial means to sustain their designs, changes spurred or sponsored by the clubs frequently were attributed to others. Conversely, the fact that a club worked toward a particular goal listed among its priorities was no guarantee that the proposal succeeded or that the club's role was primary if it did succeed. Yet in town after town and city after city, women started community institutions, public services, or cultural programs when no one else would undertake them. When municipalities or legislatures did take them over from clubs, they also took the credit. Clubs seeking stable public support for services or legal changes encouraged the shift. This process also moved institutions and programs from the realm of private charity or unregulated markets to public responsibility and support. Thousands of women in thousands of meetings found that their movement made a difference, not only in the nature of the Northwest, but also in their lives.

1

WOMEN COME TOGETHER

The Roots of the Club Movement, 1838–68

At a prescribed hour each morning, each member of the tiny Columbia Maternal Association walked out of her isolated mission in the Pacific Northwest to pray, meditate, and think of her sisters. The Columbia Maternal Association, founded by mutual compact in 1838, was the first women's club in the Pacific Northwest. It surfaced on the remote island outposts of Presbyterian missions at roughly the same time that women elsewhere in the country began to find solace, support, education, and strength in coming together in associations.

The women of the Columbia Maternal Association and their daily meditations marked the tentative beginning of a powerful movement in the Pacific Northwest, a movement that left women and their communities in a different place than they had been. The women wanted to mold themselves to fit an ideal and mold communities that were graced by social institutions offering services beyond those connected to commerce, the predominant model in the formative years of the West. Social costs that followed rapid changes in technology, industrialization, agricultural development, and markets were high as tiny settlements became a web of towns strung over vast distances in the West.

The West, the land of hope, dangled the promise of changed circumstances, even social realignments, like a magnet over iron filings. Leaders of movements, like the missionaries and Susan B. Anthony, brought their campaigns to the Northwest. Nascent women's clubs, like "mite" societies and Civil War sanitary aid societies, followed the Columbia Maternal Association in bringing women together, precursors in the movement that had many forebears. Lyceum lectures and debating societies added to the fecund mix, even in difficult times and settings full of hardship.

Those who moved into the Pacific Northwest, gradually making cities of frontier settlements, were not always part of a westward wave of migration as popularly conceived. For instance, the heavy immigration to the fertile Palouse Hills of eastern Washington and northern Idaho began in earnest in 1877, not from the east but from the west, as Willamette Valley settlers in western Oregon migrated east and north looking for more or better land to claim. Others had preceded them, coming from the same place but looking for gold more than a decade before. Still others came from California.

THE NATURE OF THE WEST

Much of the Northwest was soon dotted with small settlements, clustered together. Farming towns tended to emerge wherever twenty or so families of settlers found they were more than a day's ride to the next town for provisions and supplies. Their needs led to general stores supplied by river and wagon from Portland before the railroad came through. By contrast, mining towns grew explosively to a population of thousands, trailing service businesses behind them, but they turned into ghost towns once the ore played out. The land that became the states of Oregon, Washington, and Idaho, with a combined area of more than 253,000 square miles covering 8 percent of the continental United States, saw rapid development. But the population was small and scattered compared to the vastness of the land. Even in 1990 the Northwest held only 3 percent of the nation's population.

In the decades near the turn of the century the growth of the Pacific Northwest was exponential. Accommodating growth, which in many places went from a handful of clapboard or log buildings to a small city in the space of only a few years, was a major undertaking for communities. Women in particular began to express concern about the nature and direction of that growth. Between 1870 and 1900 the population of the United States increased some 90 percent, from 40 million to 76 million. Between 1880 and 1900 Idaho's small population roughly quadrupled, from roughly 33,000 people in 1880 to 84,000 in 1890 and 123,000 by 1900. Washington increased even faster, nearly sevenfold, from roughly 75,000 in 1880 to 350,000 in 1890 to 518,000 in 1900, finally eclipsing Oregon in population. Oregon, settled first and starting with a much larger population base of 175,000 in 1880, more than doubled its population in twenty years, to just under 314,000 in 1890 and 414,000 in 1900. By 1910 their populations had grown much larger: 326,000 in Idaho, 1,142,000 in Washington, and 673,000 in Oregon.[1]

The nature of this development, much of it in empty spaces touched only by nomadic Native American populations, made the evolution of the region—and women's clubs—quite different from other parts of the country. The population density of the United States in 1920 was 29.9 people per square mile. In Oregon it was 8.2, in Idaho 5.2, and in Washington 20.3 per square mile.[2] Isolation along with mutual dependence affected social development.

The major cities of the three states outpaced the states in growth rates. From 1900 to 1910 Idaho's largest city, Boise, went from 6,000 residents to 17,000; Oregon's Portland went from 90,000 to 207,000; Washington's Seattle grew from 80,000 people to 237,000 and Spokane from 37,000 to 104,000.[3] The pressures of growth and such fast urbanization on provision of even basic services threatened communities with chaos and hardship while they promised progress and development.

Despite the growth and its rich resources, the Northwest's population was a tiny part of the nation's population. The U.S. population of 106 million by 1920 left the Northwest's combined population of about 2.5 million relatively insignificant in the national scheme at little more than 2 percent of the total. However, another population shift had repercussions even in the relatively small and certainly remote parts of the Northwest. In the 1880s 5.2 million immigrants entered the United States; between 1900 and 1910 another 9 million entered, the majority landing in New York City.[4] Some of them headed for the Northwest, sometimes stopping in the Midwest or California on the way.

Many of the initial community problems in the Pacific Northwest differed from problems women faced elsewhere. Where women in established cities worried about crowded schools, spreading slums, or political corruption, women in the new settlements of the Pacific Northwest found dusty streets without sidewalks, nonexistent or inadequate schools, piles of garbage with their attendant flies and rats, inadequate water and sewer systems, dilapidated buildings, transient populations, and towns where saloons outnumbered other types of social amenities and men outnumbered women. They also found places without services or institutions, without concerns for culture, "refinement," or even safety.

That led women to a more intense and material kind of club activism, with more practical and visible results.

Women in the Pacific Northwest

What was unique about the women's club movement in the Pacific Northwest reflected what is unique about the region itself—its natural resource wealth, its great distances, its small, isolated communities, its rapid-fire development from open land to sites for the technological and material changes of the twentieth century. The region's motley collection of residents, invaders all, brought along differing histories and expectations, but most shared an optimism about creating a new society and culture in the wilderness. Initially the missionaries began the long process of displacing the Native American population. They and the thousands who followed staked literal or figurative claims of civilizing the West, justifying this as making the land and their lives productive by the measures of their time.

The creation of communities in the Pacific Northwest required women and children. White men for decades had moved alone through the Northwest, lonely figures on a landscape, as they explored new territory, mapped resources, created a network of military encampments, and established trade routes and trading partners to exploit resources such as fur and timber. Settlements grew from or around forts, and towns from settlements. The urbanization and migration that created what became the region's larger towns brought new social alignments. The arrival of families, the presence of women and children in a permanent population, required creation of stable community institutions such as schools, churches, libraries, hospitals. Women's clubs, whether constituted as philanthropic groups, religious auxiliaries, or service and study clubs, garnered time, attention, and money to build or supplement such projects, to set a place at the community table for the arts, or to provide relief for those hit by hard times or emergencies, within the confines of nineteenth-century ideas about charity for "the worthy poor" and the limits of available resources.[5] In the process they helped bind communities together and set city priorities. With no direct political power, clubwomen nevertheless often engaged in politics and forced social change.

Although women's contributions to the developing economy of the Northwest received little attention, they were vital, whether in sharing in the labor of agricultural production or working for wages to support themselves when single, deserted, or divorced. In the Pacific Northwest some women sold butter they churned and eggs they collected (a few even raised turkeys) or socks made from wool they carded. Others worked for low wages as teachers, domestic help, or clerks. A few were professional women, anxious to hang out a shingle in areas they hoped would be receptive to them, and many of them created organizations. Women who peopled the West often left behind networks of relatives and friends, making their isolation even more difficult and the networking in clubs even more important. The earliest clubs fit certain patterns. From benevolent societies to literary societies to maternal associations, they all had distinct purposes but common benefits.

Benevolent Societies and Reading Circles

When the Northwest was little more than a gleam in Thomas Jefferson's eye, women began forming benevolent societies in the East with an eye on reform. One example was New York's Society for the Relief of Poor Widows with Small Children, founded in 1797 and replicated a few years later in many cities. It took up causes that brought social justice issues before a wider public as members attempted to redress wrongs against women.[6] In Philadelphia in 1795 Anne Parish, a Quaker, urged twenty-three young women to devote one day a week to visiting the poor and needy, thus founding the Female Society for the Relief and Employment of the Poor. Three years later when a disastrous yellow fever epidemic devastated the city, many left, but the women with Parish stayed and fought the disease by raising money, caring for the sick, and comforting the bereaved.[7]

Women's reform work precursors also included the New York Female Benevolent Society, founded in 1833, which rented housing for reformed prostitutes and helped find employment for women.[8] At the national level there was the American Female Moral Reform Society, organized in 1839 out of moral reform societies in the Northeast created during the Great Awakening of the 1830s.[9] As some Northwest women's clubs did later, the society acquired land to build homes for the destitute and in 1847 petitioned legislators for laws taking neglected children or vagrants from their parents. Subsequent efforts included founding an industrial school, caring for children abandoned during the Civil War, and buying communal sewing machines for women to use to earn money.

Sewing machines figured in an early Idaho club's community relief effort as well. In central Idaho's mining towns of Bonanza City and Custer, founded in 1878, women formed a benevolent sewing circle that shared sewing machines, prompted by a need for supplies for hospital care. "Regardless of who owned one, to some extent it was looked on as community property. The aid society was formed due to the lack of hospital facilities."[10]

Other women, stirred by a religious impulse and a seldom-admitted will to power, combined a call to action with a vision of what a community and society ought to be in the new republic. Their concepts of citizenship, charity, order, and equity inspired missionary movements, charitable societies, reforms, and community improvement campaigns. This vision also led them to challenge alcohol consumption and double standards for sexual behavior. In addition to benevolence, through such societies organized women began to seek their own spiritual and intellectual development, especially as more women reached higher levels of education and recognized the value of literacy.

As a result, women also began creating more inward-looking reading circles or literary societies solely for self-improvement and education, although they were greatly outnumbered by benevolent societies, including those stemming from church memberships.[11] Because many saw study clubs as selfish and unwomanly, their existence had to be justified as enabling women to reach even higher levels of selfless service. In this way members began connecting benevolent acts for the community to self-improvement and education for themselves in order to do more, become better, and attain a higher ideal. However, establishing a program for aid and benevolence, or deciding on a course of self-study, required decisions about who was worthy of aid or education and the nature of that aid or education. Through these decisions, women gave themselves an important role to play. They enhanced the culture's recognition of the need to protect home values and therefore women and children. And from each other the women gained support, information, empowerment, and competence.

Women's societies grew in number throughout the nation in the first half of the nineteenth century.[12] In women's clubs from 1822 to 1872 in Rochester, New York, leaders reflected family interests as they reached beyond the domestic sphere, historian Nancy Hewitt found. As in other groups, members were white, Protestant, and middle-class, although they represented a range of views and levels of activism, from cautious to radical.[13]

When women came West, they tended to bring their ideas about organized contact with them to their new homes. The Columbia Maternal Association of 1838 is one example. Another is the Ladies' Protection and Relief Society in San Francisco, founded in 1853, which like its counterparts in the East built a refuge for widowed or deserted women and their children. From the beginning, women's societies took responsibility for creating community institutions, such as orphan asylums, homes for wayward girls and boys, libraries, employment bureaus, homes for the aged, and so on, institutions also dependent on the women who helped create them for subsidies and staffing.[14] It is no surprise then that the women cast their nets for more adequate and stable support, leading them to lobby and petition political officials directly to make these programs community and political priorities.

Dramatic National Changes

In 1860 six of every seven Americans were white and native-born, and 80 percent lived in rural areas or towns of fewer than 2,500 people.[15] From 1870 to 1900, 2.5 million native-born citizens moved from the East to the West, the land of opportunity and manifest destiny, a total roughly balanced by the immigration to the East from overseas. In the 1890s the West began attracting more immigrants than did the East.[16] Between 1870 and 1920 what had been the mostly rural United States became more than 50 percent urban, when urban still meant small cities. In 1850 only eight cities reached more than 100,000 people. By 1920 sixty-eight did, most of them in the East.

The cities of the Pacific Northwest, although they swelled rapidly, remained small compared to the East's older cities, especially those that absorbed the waves of immigration. In the Pacific Northwest, as in the rest of the country, cities initially were compact, dark at night, with few diversions. Between 1870 and 1900 technology wrought massive changes, in city lighting, public transportation, and available diversions—diversions like dance halls that conflicted with the kind of culture many wanted for their communities. Being urban became a matter of mindset and culture as much as a fast-growing cluster of buildings in a rural setting.

At the same time, new technology eased much of the back-breaking drudgery of rural life, and urban life, for that matter. The shift from wood to gas heat, from homemade clothes and food to ready-made, and from home laundries to steam laundries or washers lightened women's hardest burdens. Sewers and basic sanitation greatly improved living conditions, as did public transportation. All these changes gave women a precious commodity—time. Of course, for those families able to afford domestic servants, the shift to more leisure time had already occurred. The prevalence of such servants in households has been exaggerated, however. According to the Census Bureau, only one servant existed for every ten households in 1910, down from a high of 1.3 in 1870. Counter to common belief, home technology played more of a role in freeing women than the availability of servants at the turn of the century, especially in the West. Iceboxes, hot and cold running water, indoor toilets, and other changes also freed women to look toward improving standards for their home, themselves, and the city.

IDEAS OF IDEAL WOMANHOOD

Popular writers like editor Sarah Josepha Hale of *Ladies' Magazine* and later the influential *Godey's Lady's Book* promulgated the domestic ideal and its power. Hale well before mid-century held that woman should be companion to and influence upon man, but to do that and fulfill family roles successfully, women had to have both education and intelligence.[17] Like many, she spoke in complementary dualisms about gender. The strength of man's character was in his physical propensities, his efforts to build and tame, while the strength of woman resided in her moral propensities and sentiments, her refinement, ideas subsequently played out in women's associations. Like other women of the time, Hale saw this not as a limitation but as an elevation of women's status. Increasingly, men engaged in making money and producing products left to women—or women grasped—the responsibility for moral development and protection of morals, a role they quickly assumed. Some used this sense of moral superiority and the separate sphere as leverage in the larger society, itself an important political strategy.[18] Organizations to help women better realize this purpose came close behind.

The belief in women's innate and superior morality was ingrained long before the end of the nineteenth century, a characteristic of particular importance in the West with its limited social institutions and transient population.[19] Women who were power-

less and voiceless before the law and in politics found power in
the implicit assumptions about domestic values and women's elevated status within the family. The domestic ideal also helped redefine acceptable masculine behavior and values outside as well
as inside the family.[20] "Village improvement," benevolent work,
and self-improvement through study clubs were juxtaposed against
a culture that seemed to tolerate or foster drinking, gambling, violence, and prostitution as perhaps unavoidable and often profitable endeavors, especially in western towns.

Women's activism not only offered a critique of a more masculine culture and behavior, but also protected the interests of
women and children in conflicts, especially in the West. From
1850 to 1890 the West had the highest divorce rate, with the
states of Idaho, Oregon, and Washington among the top ten states.
Women brought almost 70 percent of the suits under more liberal
judicial interpretations of matrimonial cruelty than existed elsewhere in the country, where old and intractable codified legal
practices made such actions difficult or unacceptable.[21] Women
in the West were also the first to be given full voting rights, for
reasons discussed later.

Women's assumed moral superiority contained within it the
dormant roots of radical moral reform through direct social action. But it required building a bridge from the private world of
home and family to the public sphere of policy and politics.
Women, positioned to deal with the negative side effects of industrialization and urbanization, also began to work on bureau-
cratizing benevolence into institutions, one of the most significant legacies of women's clubwork.[22]

From the ranks of mobilized women came those who would
later fill Protestant churches, women's clubs, and reform campaigns for causes such as the WCTU. Those steeped in this tradition in turn became leaders of programs and institutions capable
of imposing their values and norms upon other classes and ethnic
groups.[23] Ideals of citizenship, mastery of passions, and sharply
drawn roles for women were values in ascendance. They were ex-
pounded in popular literature, advice books, sermons, and elsewhere. Women's roles—rearing and guiding children, saving men
from dissipation, sanctifying the home, and so on—were deemed
vital to home and community and thus to national health and
prosperity, especially in the face of fast social, economic, and technological change. A conservative force used in progressive ways,

the domestic ideology valued duty, service, education, and citizenship. Voluntarism and philanthropy were parts of that whole.

Most women clung to pervasive nineteenth-century ideals of culture and gentility, even those working for wages to support their families or those who of necessity worked the fields alongside their husbands. They returned to their domestic duties and lives as soon as they could. In the West, as in the East, "women of the 'better sort' defined respectability, fettering one another with social restraints."[24] Seeking an outlet for sharing their vision of this better world, such women came together in organizations. There were so many organizations and members that it is difficult to tell which came first in each place. In Washington, certainly, "first" status belonged to the Columbia Maternal Association.

THE HONOR OF BEING FIRST

As with most searches for famous "firsts," there turn out to be many antecedents. Benevolent societies and reading circles gave rise to other clubs in other forms. The women's study club movement is generally said to have begun in New England, with the founding of both the Sorosis Club in New York and the New England Woman's Club in Boston in 1868, the same year the Fourteenth Amendment gave all U.S. citizens—except women and Native Americans—the right to vote. Other writers claim that the first woman's literary society appeared earlier, in 1852, founded by Lucinda Stone in Kalamazoo, Michigan, as the Ladies' Literary Association.[25]

Others award "first" status to the Hearth Stone Literary Society of 1852–58, which counted as members Sorosis Club founders Alice Cary, Kate Field, and Mary E. Booth.[26] Transcendentalist and writer Margaret Fuller met with other women for intellectual study and "Conversations" beginning in 1839, a year after the Columbia Maternal Association began, although one of her contemporaries called the conversations "more of excellent lecturing on her part than of conversation on the part of her class."[27] The meetings continued for five winter seasons. African-American clubwomen can find early club roots in the Female Benevolent Firm organized in 1848 in Boston to provide shoes and clothing for women and children who had traveled the Underground Railroad.[28]

Others go further back in time, to 1790. Thirty-eight women members of the Congregational Church in Chelsea, Connecticut, agreed to meet weekly for reading, conversation and prayer. They created a Ladies' Literary Society in 1800. The minutes reflected a growing awareness of women's potential, spurred by topics of discussion at each meeting. In 1802 the group voted to provide four children with books and funds to enter school.[29] In 1803, as Lewis and Clark charted lands in the Northwest, the Chelsea group voted to use its funds to improve women's access to education. The money went "to give better schooling to the misses, near relatives of the first members," the minutes said. The following year the women continued their study of history and other topics and talked frequently about woman's nature. No records of meetings beyond 1805 were found, but the group supposedly dissolved about 1820, to be superseded by a reading society in 1825.[30]

Early benevolent societies also included study, but it was study of religion rather than culture or "self-development," mixed with fundraising to distribute Bibles and tracts or send missionaries to convert the "heathen" at home and in distant parts of the world. Church mission boards educated poor youth and Protestant clergymen, then sent them and their families to remote posts, as happened with the Whitmans. The link between Protestantism and voluntarism in the new American republic was forged in the rise of voluntary associations.[31] The idea of action through organizations, male or female, captured the heirs of Calvinism in hundreds of voluntary associations. In these groups women often had leadership roles, particularly as they began to dominate church membership.[32]

The Columbia Maternal Association, however, came from another category of clubs called maternal associations. In New England and a few other places in the 1820s and 1830s, concerns about childcare led women to meet informally in these associations. After meeting to discuss mutual problems of rearing children, women began to meet to discuss other facets of their lives (or ideas quite outside their immediate lives). Tracing the development of a variety of women's organizations in New England, beginning with the 1805 Female Religious and Cent Society of Jericho Center, Vermont, historian Nancy Cott found maternal associations in a half-dozen cities.

These early alliances gave women not only association but also skills at making decisions and raising money to address social problems they chose to solve.[33] Such groups often invited speakers and discussed the literature on child-rearing, domesticity, and

Christian motherhood. They offered publishers a ready market among the increasing number of women who were literate. Books remained a luxury item, but many maternal associations established libraries that made books available to members, giving them access to at least a handful of works.[34]

THE COLUMBIA MATERNAL ASSOCIATION

The Marcus and Narcissa Whitman mission in southeastern Washington on the Walla Walla River (then part of the Oregon Territory) was one of the first mission outposts to see a family. There Narcissa Whitman and the wives of other missionaries founded their own maternal association in 1838. Although removed from all that they previously knew, they remembered the maternal associations in New York. Later recognized as the oldest women's club west of the Mississippi, the Columbia Maternal Association met at the Whitmans' Waiilatpu Mission, eight miles from what is now Walla Walla, Washington, or at separate sites as necessity dictated. Mary Walker described the group in her diary entry for September 3, 1838: "We formed a Maternal Association . . . to meet on the second and last Wednesday of each month. I am appointed vice president. We are to hold meetings at each station and report to the recording secretary as often as practicable."[35]

Narcissa Whitman (profiled in this chapter) was educated at the noted Emma Willard's Female Seminary in Troy, New York, and the Franklin Institute. She had arrived at Waiilatpu in March 1836 with her husband Marcus and high hopes for useful service. Eliza Spalding, another missionary wife, ended up at Lapwai some 120 miles away in November 1836, three years after her marriage to Henry Spalding. Lapwai, located in what became Idaho, was a few miles south of Lewiston at the confluence of the Snake and Clearwater Rivers. Other missionaries and families followed them.[36]

Despite the distances separating them, the women resolved to sustain their Maternal Association. Although able to see each other only occasionally as a group, they decided to observe the same time each day in meditation and prayer, spinning an invisible but powerful thread of connection pulled taut at nine each morning. The Spaldings and their baby visited the Whitmans, and the group later welcomed the Grays and six others. These missionaries had found another site on the trail between Fort Walla Walla (established first in 1818 as Fort Nez Perce) and Fort Colville northwest of Spokane, which became the Tshimakain

Mission,[37] but wintered over with the Whitmans in their crowded quarters.

The missionaries held a formal meeting in 1838. While the seven men of the mission held a business meeting on Monday, September 3, the six women of the mission formally organized the Columbia Maternal Association. Narcissa Whitman was named the group's secretary-treasurer. A year later members held their annual meeting on Tuesday, September 3, 1839, in conjunction with the mission meeting at Lapwai. The women able to attend this meeting included Spalding, Whitman, Gray, and Smith. Subsequent diaries show that the women of the missions who could held the scheduled meetings on the second and last Wednesdays of each month, for years, until the untimely deaths of the Whitmans and a dozen others in 1847 at the hands of a few disease-plagued and vengeful Cayuse Indians.[38] However, the association did not die with Whitman. It was carried on by the women in other places, and at least partial records of the group were maintained through 1850.[39] Besides Spalding, Walker, and Gray, other early members included Mary Augusta Dix, Mrs. Cushing Eells, and Sarah (Mrs. A. B.) Smith. Eells and Walker went to Tshimakain near Kettle Falls in northeast Washington, while the Smiths from 1839 to 1841 ran a mission among the Knee (Nez) Perce at Kamiah on Idaho's Clearwater River. The women of the Protestant outposts also regularly circulated and read *Mother's Magazine,* a popular publication of the Utica, New York, Maternal Association. At their meetings they typically discussed child-rearing and current events, meditated, and prayed.

Initially only two of the members of the Columbia Maternal Association were actually mothers, suggesting that the women gained more than advice on child-rearing from meeting and reading papers. Although the group gradually grew to a dozen or so women who could only rarely meet, they did what later study clubs did: they circulated papers to one another on current issues. The group's constitution stated that the meeting time "shall be spent in reading such works as relate to the great object for which we associate, in conversation & in prayer for divine assistance & a blessing on our efforts for the immediate conversion of our children, also that he would glorify himself by rendering them eminently useful in the church."[40] It also stated each member will "qualify herself by prayer, by readings & by all appropriate means, for performing the arduous duties of a Christian mother,

& suggest to her sister members such hints as her own experience may furnish or circumstances render necessary."[41] The papers the members wrote and circulated generally concerned cultural and spiritual subjects.

Walker and the other women who formed the Columbia Maternal Association knew they were in some peril. They agreed to look after one another's children in case something happened to one of them, as indeed it did. After Walker left the area, she formed another maternal association in 1849 at Forest Grove in Oregon. It too was organized by women "for the purpose of prayer and mutual counsel" upon maternal duties, and they also pledged to one another to take in a mother's children if she died.[42]

PROFILE: NARCISSA PRENTISS WHITMAN

Daughter of a judge and trained as a teacher, Narcissa Prentiss found her calling early. At a church service she heard the Reverend Samuel Parker tell of four Native Americans who had traveled all the way to St. Louis in search of "blackrobe" missionaries and the power of their Bible. Narcissa and other Presbyterians were greatly influenced by stories of this event, taking it as a sign that missionary work was needed in the West and would be welcome. Narcissa, a graduate of the progressive seminary run by Emma Willard, wanted to help.

Narcissa was so impressed that she applied to the Board of Foreign Missions for a position teaching the Indians, but her application was refused in part because she was an unmarried female. She resumed her teaching position at a school near Prattsburg, New York, where she had been born in 1808. She met Dr. Marcus Whitman in 1835 and was drawn by his own desire to travel West to minister to the Native Americans. He made an exploratory trip, and they were quickly married on his return. They left Missouri in 1836, along with William Gray and Henry and Eliza Spalding, who later took over the Lapwai Mission in Idaho. Traveling overland in an arduous but exciting trip, they were accompanied by Hudson Bay fur traders. They arrived at Fort Walla Walla, a fur trade outpost built in 1818, five months later. After a two-month sojourn at Fort Vancouver farther down the Columbia, where they were given seeds and plants, the women returned to a primitive mission that gradually grew into several buildings and a small farm.

Narcissa, twenty-eight, established a school to teach Christianity, English, writing, and music. Initially content, she soon became frustrated. She was often unnerved by the actions of nearby Native Americans, such as the Cayuse men who walked in and out of her kitchen, waiting for food. The Whitmans built a second adobe house away from the lowlands of the river, and in March 1837 Narcissa's daughter Alice Clarissa was born. Joy turned to tragedy, however, the year after the Columbia Maternal Association was founded. The baby, then about two years old, made her way to the river one day with her drinking cup, where she drowned. This event, combined with the difficult and not very successful work of educating and converting, made Narcissa begin to question her purpose in this isolated place. Nevertheless, she and her husband persevered. In addition to the school and house, they eventually built a small hospital and grist mill, raised livestock, and grew rye, oats, and barley over the intervening five years.

In 1844 a message came ahead from one of the wagon trains asking them if they would take in the orphaned children of the Sager family, whose mother died of disease after their father died in an accident. The seven children ranged in age from fourteen down to a malnourished infant. There were already four children at the mission from previous misfortunes on the trek to Oregon, but they found room for seven more. One of the Sager children later recalled that the dark-haired Narcissa was of necessity and perhaps by nature a hard taskmaster. Others found her patient and kind, but a disciplinarian.

As a founding member and an officer in the Columbia Maternal Association, she maintained a network with other missionary wives. An annual report noted that Spalding and Whitman constituted a committee to select what each member of the group wrote upon during the year. Topics covered issues that related to gender roles as well as maternity, such as "hindrances to maternal associations," duty of "inculcating the spirit of benevolence in our children and what will best promote it," "the importance of the aid and cooperation of our husbands in training our children," "the influence we exert over our domestic [sphere]," and "the influence of domestics on the minds and morals of our children."[43]

More wagon trains trailed past the mission, but a shortcut bypassing it reduced some of the traffic. Unfortunately, those who were ill or in desperate straits were most likely to make the detour to the Whitmans' mission doorstep. Some brought measles or other diseases that cruelly killed many Native Americans who had developed little resistance to the strange pathogens. Reportedly, half of the local Cayuse tribe, the original occupants of the Blue Mountain region at the corner of Oregon and Washington, died. Angry tribal members noticed that those at the mission lived while Indians who used Whitman's medicine to fight disease continued to die.[44]

Over that final winter seventy people were crowded into the mission, divided between an "immigrant house" and the mission house itself. At the end of November 1847 two members of the tribe came to the house demanding medicine. One of them killed Marcus Whitman with a hatchet. One of the Sager children came to his aid, but was shot, and the shot signaled an attack. Narcissa was shot in the chest when she moved past a window. She and a dozen others died of their wounds. She was thirty-nine years old.

Those still at the mission—thirty-three women and children— were herded into the four rooms of the immigrant house and held captive for a month. They were ransomed through the negotiations of Peter Skene Ogden, a noted explorer and local manager for the Hudson Bay Company. The survivors were brought to Fort Walla Walla downriver then transported to Fort Vancouver, Portland, and the Willamette Valley, where some of the children were farmed out to other missionaries.

The incident touched off an outraged and vengeful response and transformed the Whitmans into martyrs. This symbolic culmination of settler conflicts with the native population became the Cayuse War. Five men supposedly guilty of the massacre were hunted down and hanged after hasty trials. Although the Whitman Mission closed, its tragedy added to the mystique of the West, eclipsing the mission's importance to the settlement of the region and Narcissa's creation of the Columbia Maternal Association. The group continued as other members carried it with them to Oregon.

THE MATERNAL ASSOCIATION

Maternal associations began early in the nation's history and grew rapidly. According to historian Clifford Drury, as early as 1815 Portland, Maine, had a Maternal Association, which claimed to the first in the United States.[45] Groups typically elected officers, adopted a constitution, and met regularly to discuss the religious, educational, physical, and moral education of children. The size of the movement, because of inadequate records, is frequently underestimated. For instance, two rural New Hampshire counties alone in 1836 reportedly contained thirty-eight maternal associations representing one thousand women. Unlike most reform movements after the Civil War, maternal associations seemed to receive much of their support from the lower middle class, researcher Richard Meckel found.[46]

By 1824 a maternal association existed in Utica, New York, near Narcissa Whitman's home. Drury also found that mission women in the Hawaiian Islands in 1832 had a maternal association, as did Chicago in 1834. About 1832 the Utica group decided to publish the influential monthly *Mother's Magazine,* which continued until 1888. Its faithful subscribers included Narcissa Whitman and the Columbia Maternal Association. The $1 a year magazine quickly became popular, inspiring new maternal associations and competing publications. It contained articles on obedience and discipline, prayer, Bible study, and family worship. Religion and death figured prominently in the contents.[47] Death was well known to its readers. Many children died before the age of five (49 percent of all deaths in New York City in 1853),[48] while tuberculosis and disease epidemics also killed many adults.

Although the magazine was largely silent on politics or topics like infant care and prenatal care, it did touch some early women's rights issues. It disapproved of the custom of "tight lacing" of corsets and advocated exercise and education for women. Another historian looking at the material found the content evangelical, but surprisingly eclectic. Issues included essays on child education and republicanism by philosophers such as John Locke and Jean-Jacques Rousseau and on the importance of maternal education by writers such as Hannah Moore and Daniel Webster, along with the pieces on religious training and moral reform. The magazine spurred the creation of two other magazines, also sold for $1 a year.[49]

Mother's Magazine also carried a few reform-oriented articles, such as a review of a book by one of the Beecher sisters, titled *The Evils Suffered by American Women and American Children.* Citing one of the earliest surveys ever conducted on a social welfare issue, the publication recounted the poor conditions of elementary schoolhouses, noting that the survey found 3,319 of them unfit for children, 7,000 with no playgrounds, 6,000 without seats, desks, or toilet facilities, and 8,000 without proper ventilation. The data came from an 1844 report by the New York superintendent of schools.[50] Use of the survey as documentation of social problems became part of the women's club arsenal several decades later.

The Columbia Maternal Association is interesting in several respects beyond its early timing. As it grew, some new members not only came from outside the missionary structure, but also were not white women. The *metis* wives of Hudson Bay officials joined the group. They included Jane McDonald, who joined in 1839, during the time she and her husband Archibald lived at Fort Colville, where he was commander. Another was the wife of Archibald McKinlay, who was in charge of Fort Walla Walla from 1841 to 1846. She joined in 1842.[51]

The constitution of the Columbia Maternal Association, recorded by Mary Gray in the original record book, recommended that the day of the annual meeting and the anniversary of the birth of each child be noted by members through a day of fasting and prayer. It ended with a prayer of hope that resonates with the later *Club Collect*. "May He who giveth liberally & upbraideth not ever preside at our meeting & grant to each of us a teachable, affectionate & humble temper that no root of bitterness spring up to prevent our improvement or interrupt our devotions."[52] Along with devotions, self-improvement was at the heart of this club, as it was for the hundreds of secular study clubs founded later.

The women in their 1839 annual report lauded the birth of four children to members but lamented the death of Whitman's daughter at the age of "two years, three months, and nine days." Parallel meetings were held at Wieletpoo (Waiilatpu). "The removal of Mrs. Smith to the upper Knee Persis country & Mrs. Walker & Eelles to the Spokan have scattered our number so that there has been one Sister at Waiilapu & one at Kamia but not withstanding we are thus separated I trust our hearts are united in this great work & that no one has at the hour for United Maternal prayer forgotten to present her petition before the mercy seat," Gray wrote.[53]

Eighteen months before her death, Whitman wrote *Mother's Magazine*, enclosing $18 for multiple subscriptions. Her published letter noted that of the six who then formed the association Gray had left for Willamette, Smith for the Sandwich Islands, and McDonald for Canada, while others had moved to "the Lower Country" and formed a separate society. In the letter she called the Columbia group the Oregon Mission Maternal Association, adding that its members claimed forty-six children, but six of them had died over the intervening ten years from drowning, croup, and scarlet fever. She noted that after the death of her own daughter she and her husband had adopted eleven children and three

"half-breed" natives, later adding a thirteen-year-old nephew.
She referred to the addition of the children orphaned by the
deaths of Henry and Naomi Sager on their way from Ohio to Oregon, he from a buffalo stampede while turning the wagon to avoid
it, and she from "camp fever" following childbirth on the trail less
than a month later. The Whitmans later became their legal
guardians.[54]

The Flow of the Pioneers

Within a dozen years after the Whitmans came west, large numbers of settlers began moving into Oregon Territory. Ultimately
over 50,000 traveled by wagon into the Northwest. Most of the initial pioneers settled in the fertile Willamette Valley of Oregon, inland and parallel to the coast along the Willamette River flowing
into the Columbia near Portland. Cities near its banks included
Albany, Corvallis, Eugene, Salem, and Portland. In 1843 the first
large group of people started the 2,000-mile Oregon Trail trek
from starting points in Missouri.[55] Between 1840 and 1860 the
thousands of families who came represented a broad cross-sec-
tion of economic, social, and ethnic groups.[56]

What they found in the Northwest discouraged many, especially
the women who came. Commercial, educational, and social services were nonexistent, underdeveloped, or in transition. Lack of
consumer goods and transportation networks made vast distances
and isolation even worse. Women, mindful of the existing boundaries between men's and women's work, had to work in the West
alongside the men, doing whatever needed to be done, whether
that meant driving teams, herding cattle, building fences, or keeping the books. However, most of the work for women on the trail
and off was domestic, in a partnership that made development
possible. It is true that some had to help in "men's work," but they
did not like it. They found it not liberating, but simply hard work
and a reflection of how difficult conditions were, although some
took pride in having done it well. Others found it a source of
shame. They resumed traditional women's roles as soon as they
could.

Later, pioneer status, like being descended from "Puritan stock"
or the rebels who fought in the Revolutionary War, conferred social status. Even Boise had a Society of Mayflower Descendants in
Idaho. As with the Mayflower pioneers, tracing genealogy to the
original Oregon Trail pioneers became something of a fetish, as if

those who came later and built communities did not count as real pioneers. Rail access along the route did not come until 1884 with the completion of the Oregon Short Line through southern Idaho. Those who came by wagons generally walked the long route. Roughly one in ten of them died along the trail, most from cholera, although typhus, scurvy, dysentery, and other dangers such as lightning, rattlesnakes, and starvation killed many (Indians killed only a few hundred). Cholera from contaminated water was particularly virulent, killing some victims in as little as twenty-four hours. The typical pioneer was not poor, although many families sacrificed all they had to put together the $400 or more needed to come west.

CREATING TOWNS, CITIES, STATES

The missionaries came to chase souls; a few decades later many others came to chase dreams of gold and the grand wealth it brought a privileged few. There was also wealth in supplying the men headed for the mining camps in Idaho, Oregon, Canada, and even Alaska. They provided a ready market for the businesses that arose to meet needs of both miners and farmers, supporting settlements. The ultimate mark of recognition sought by residents—statehood—came to Oregon in 1859, Washington in 1889, and Idaho in 1890. Other landmarks in the region's development were technological, such as cross-country telegraph connections in 1864 and regular steamship service connecting Seattle and San Francisco in 1875. In 1870 Seattle elected its first mayor; by 1880 the city had 3,533 people (just slightly fewer than Walla Walla), along with gas lights, boardwalks, and theaters.[57]

Thirty years before, when settlers petitioned Congress in 1852 to carve Washington out of the huge Oregon Territory, the entire white population of what was to become Washington Territory was less than 2,000, compared to a native population estimated at more than 20,000 and Oregon's population of 13,000. Within eight years the white population of both ballooned to 65,000.[58] The rapid growth was spurred by more than gold and nationalism. The Donation Land Claim Act, which for a while gave women the rare right to acquire public land in their own names, allowed a couple to claim 640 acres of prime Oregon land. Although the allotments were eventually reduced to 120 acres and the wife's share eliminated altogether, the lure of land for every settler in Oregon drew thousands. It also drew land speculators and conflicts with tribes when settlers reached their destination. The traffic was so heavy that the ruts in the trail cut by thousands of wagon wheels can still be found in the deserts of south Idaho and eastern Oregon.

Women who came first found conditions hardest. Oregon's Catherine Wails Alexander recalled some of the isolation and dreariness that made clubs and associations so welcome.[59] She was born in Oregon in 1856 five years after her family had claimed land east of Salem on Howell Prairie. "We were taught to be housekeepers and homemakers. There were not many shows or entertainments, and if there had been we didn't have the money to patronize them," she said. Social highlights included occasional barn raisings, quilting bees, and annual Fourth of July celebrations, which people planned for months.[60] Entertainment consisted of potluck parties, dances, speeches, touring musical groups, debates—and reading clubs.

Education, poorly funded because of the rapid growth and sparse tax base, was a perennial poor cousin in local budgets. Short school terms, long distances, school closures when money ran out, and inadequate facilities and teachers were common, especially outside the small cities. Settlers provided schools through their subscriptions. Subscription schools, run by women, were common. Teachers signed up enough pupils at a monthly fee to open a small school and boarded with area families.

The reason public health programs and sanitation later became an issue for women's clubs in the Northwest is symbolized by what happened in one Oregon town. It is difficult for us to imagine the devastations from disease in small settlements and their impact. Martha Jane Allen, born in Salem in 1855, said her two youngest brothers died in 1877 of diphtheria, called "putrid sore throat" back then, when a "severe scourge" of the disease plagued Umatilla County in north-central Oregon.[61] Residents did not realize how contagious it was, and women's attempts to help one another's families had fatal side effects.

"The neighbor women would visit back and forth and when one of the children died they would all go to the funeral," Allen recalled. They spread both solace and sickness. Her brothers had been in the same class at school, which was dismissed when the outbreak began. "When school reassembled the teacher called the roll of their class, and of the eighteen children that had belonged to it, only two answered the roll call. The other sixteen had died of diphtheria,"[62] she wrote matter-of-factly.

Another early immigrant described the privations women endured that made association and material prosperity for communities seem both so important and so distant. Martha Ann Minto came to Oregon by ocean in 1844 at age thirteen. By fifteen she was married and was living in Willamette Valley.[63] She made do with one stew kettle, three butcher knives, two sheets, and a small feather mattress. When her husband joined the Cayuse War following the raid on the Whitman Mission, she cut up the sheets to make shirts for him and ended up sleeping on a pile of straw.

She explained why women used to having much more stayed in the Northwest and were so anxious for schools, stores, and clubs. "People say they would not have stayed, they would go right back. I would like to know how we could go back. It took nearly a year to get here by a vessel; and we had no horses, nor cattle, nor anything to haul us across the plains; we had no provisions; we could not start out naked and destitute in every way. There were no shoes nor stockings to buy, and if there were we did not have the money to pay for them." She eventually got two large flowered earthen plates from someone who came from the Sandwich Islands, then several years later added a few tin dishes. "The first year we were married we had just 75 cents worth of sugar. We never had a bit of tea or coffee; the coffee made was pea coffee."

What stock Minto and her husband accumulated was stolen or destroyed by Indians, poisonous snakes or plants, or packs of wolves. "The wolves also destroyed our hogs, notwithstanding our screams and shouts." Indians frequently came around and unnerved her, but did her no harm even when her husband left his sixteen-year-old wife for the Cayuse War.

She and the other children who settled in Oregon "did not go to school more than three months—some before and some after I came here—and that was just the way with the rest of the children here at that time. I think that was one of the greatest misfortunes we had to grow up under. We could outlive our destitution, and everything else of the kind, but we could not get an education so easily." The simple words of this passage show why clubs centered on education, including efforts to establish compulsory school attendance laws and literacy campaigns.

It is not surprising that schools and libraries—both windows upon the world—were among the first institutions women supported in the Pacific Northwest once they found a collective voice. Nor is it surprising that social events—dances, extended visits, parties—took on great importance as women (and men) tried to establish a culture and get human contact. Even berry and fishing expeditions became communal activities. Social events were generally planned and organized by the women.[64]

SETTLING IN

Bunch grass and sage gradually gave way to crops, and promoters' promises to real prosperity. In 1882 *Harper's Magazine* informed its readers that "wheat of the best quality" could be easily grown in eastern Oregon and Washington, and the bunch grass, "unlike the prairie-grass of the Western States, forms no sod or turf, does not need breaking, and the first ploughing will produce a crop."[65] Farmers, able to clear only a dozen or so acres a year, might have disputed this. Nevertheless, the patchwork of productive farms led to further development and fed the small but growing cities of the Northwest.[66]

In the interior, which railroad promotions dubbed Washington's Inland Empire, Walla Walla became the primary city, flanked by Dayton and Colfax. By 1879 the Northern Pacific had finished its survey of the route through the interior and construction began. Before railroads, freighting patterns followed the settlements. In the 1860s there was much freighting between points on the Columbia River and the mines of Idaho and eastern Oregon, primarily from Umatilla or Wallula backward over the Oregon Trail into Idaho. Towns like Lewiston, Spokane, and Boise owed their growth, if not their existence, to supplying the thousands who poured into mining camps and towns.

As settlers followed miners or farmers, bankers and merchants came too, the "progressive" men every community sought. They brought their own clubs with them, as did their wives. Within a few decades Spokane dominated the inland region. In the south, rich farms came out of federal land policies or the Northern Pacific's land grant offices. Migration from Oregon east along the Columbia, with a left turn at The Dalles, led to settlement of Yakima and the Kittitas Valley after the Walla Walla area and the Palouse began to fill.

The land drew eastern investors too with their own big dreams about the mythical Oregon Country. The Moxee Farm six miles from North Yakima with 6,400 acres of experimental crops and rangeland was owned by National Geographic Society founder Gardiner G. Hubbard and his son-in-law, Alexander Graham

Bell. They even tried to raise tobacco at the site, but, like other land speculators, lost their farm in the panic of 1893. Marshall Field, the Chicago merchandiser, bought 15,000 acres in Whitman and Spokane counties.[67] Other easterners were approached to invest in mines, or huge irrigation projects, enhancing the region's development and eastern claims to it, gradually making the region a kind of colonial outpost economically, culturally, even politically.

From Tents to Stores

It was the discovery of gold—first at the center of the state in 1862 and elsewhere in the state shortly after—that led to Idaho's settlement. Miners and their suppliers, and soon farmers and ranchers and their suppliers, spread the length of the state over the next few decades. Many came from California and Oregon.[68] Between 1880 and 1890 farm acreage in all three territories of the Northwest went from almost 6 million to 12.4 million acres.[69] Farmers formed a much more permanent group of settlers than did the miners, although miners became a good share of the market for farmers' crops of oats, barley, wheat, or fruits and vegetables. Sheep and cattle ranchers also came to exploit the rangeland, and stockmen gradually emerged as an economic force, especially in south Idaho and east Oregon. By 1890 the railroads had created new markets and heightened the pace of development. The free open range finally ended in 1905, replaced by a permitting system on federal lands. Eventually the federal government exercised ownership rights to over half the territory, much of it deemed worthless land at the time.

In the Northwest, the island communities typically consisted first of tents, then of small log cabins, even lean-tos. Places like Lewiston, Idaho, were dubbed "ragtown." A mark of a town's status was the construction of buildings from boards, some even two stories high. False fronts common in the West suggested downtown permanence and prosperity. Brick buildings said even more about a town's progress. Supplies—food, clothing, building materials—came dearly, if they were available at all, especially before the railroad web. Women, as always, made do with what they had. If economic development is measured in material goods, it came to the West through increased choices in clothing, furnishings, food, and social institutions. Canned goods and velvet ribbons supplemented the necessities of flour, fuel, and salt.[70] Well before the turn of the century the Northwest had become "urbanized," with its island communities sitting in a sea of often undeveloped, inaccessible, or federally owned land.

LODGES, LYCEUMS, LIBRARIES

Like the women who brought ideas of maternal associations or mite societies, some of the men who came brought their clubs and lodges with them. As communities—whether mining-based or agricultural-based—grew and conditions improved, residents looked for social and intellectual stimulation. They created debating societies and organized lectures. Beginning in the 1830s, the lyceum movement became important to the women's club movement and its leadership. The lyceum movement, a series of lectures and forums designed for public consumption, helped women like Catharine Beecher and Frances Willard spread their ideas.

Willard described the hard early years of the paid lecturer with a cause as contrasted with the power and support of a female setting in a club or association. In 1878, the year before she was elected national president of the WCTU and three years before coming to the Northwest, she worked freelance for the WCTU, going "on a bureau" (i.e., a Lyceum Lecture Bureau tour). It turned out badly, in her view. "To go from the genial, breezy, outdoorsy temperance meeting, the warm, tender, exalted gospel meeting, the homelike, sisterly, inspiring Woman's Christian Temperance Union Convention, into a human snow-bank of folks who have 'paid to get in' and are reckoning quietly, as one proceeds, whether or not they are really going 'to get their money's worth,' is an experience not to be endured with equanimity by anybody who can slip his head out of its noose," she later wrote.

"To have a solemn 'Lyceum Committee' of men meet you at the train, take you to a hotel of funereal dreariness and cooked over cuisine; to march upon a realistic stage that no woman's hand has beautified or brightened; to have no heartsome music or winsome prayer preceding you and tuning your weary spirit to the high ministry for which you came; . . . all this is 'nerve-wear' to no purpose." The fee of $25 did not compensate for this "nerve-wear" or the uncomfortable travel it required, she wrote.[71] The movement, with its lecture series format and focus on ideas, influenced later women's study clubs and women's sense of self when a few bold women dared become lyceum lecturers and thus models.[72]

What happened at Oregon City at mid-century shows the im-

portance placed on lectures and literacy. Oregon City, founded at
the falls of the Willamette a few miles upriver from Portland, was
Oregon's largest settlement in 1850, with 933 residents.[73] Water
powered two flour mills, five sawmills, and prosperity there, although the town was eclipsed by Portland and its port. As early as
1842—as the Columbia Maternal Association was meeting—-it
had its own Pioneer Lyceum and Literary Club. The town also
had a library assembled in 1844, with settlers sharing what reading material they had. The Pioneer Club, also called the Oregon
Lyceum, met regularly during the winters of 1842–46, discussing
issues of a cultural nature and adding political topics such as the
advisability of establishing an independent government in the
new country.

One participant said later that the group began as the Falls Debating Society, but by 1844 it was known as the Falls Association
then the Pioneer Lyceum and Literary Club.[74] Beginning in 1844,
the Falls Literary Association produced its own handwritten community newspaper, called *Like It or Lump It*.[75] In 1845 the tiny library was incorporated by the provisional legislature; 100 shares
sold at $5 each for purchase of more books, creating a collection
of 300 volumes. It faded about 1850 following creation of a territorial library at Oregon City, moved in 1852 to the capital, Salem.

The Peoria Lyceum, largely a debating club, emerged in 1860
in Peoria, Linn County, Oregon. It brought lectures, and members
paid dues of 25 cents. Members debated far-ranging historical or
philosophical issues, such as "which has caused the most misery
to mankind, intemperance or war," "are the African race equal in
intellectual powers and genius to the Europeans," and "does geol-
ogy correspond with divine history and revelation."[76]

Lecturers and theatrical troupes came to many towns in the
Northwest, even talks illustrated with slides.[77] This cultural activity made the crude conditions and hardships more bearable
and gave a new dimension to raw communities. Groups, often exclusively female, also sponsored social activities and fundraising
campaigns for community benefit, such as raffling quilts to meet
school or church needs.

Oregon's First? The 1863 McMinnville
Ladies' Sanitary Aid Society

Organized female activism has often responded to the stresses of
war. Even during the Revolutionary War, women joined forces to

produce goods such as shirts for soldiers or to raise money to help
in the war effort. Historian Lori Ginsberg found in her study of
women and benevolence that the Civil War consolidated an entire
generation's conception of benevolence and social change. It became for many women as well as combatants the central experience of their lives, leading many of them to seek access to the
public, even political world. It also introduced them to the fundamental tools of activism—fundraising, lobbying, lecturing, organizing. Prior to that time the rhetoric of female benevolence
separated morality and politics, which also led some women to
question the morality of women who supported radical political
causes like suffrage. Women had to choose between purity and
politics, but in the 1850s and especially after the Civil War some
began to see that public influence, if not direct political involvement, was a better path than benevolence or "moral suasion" to
address problems.[78]

By the time of the Civil War, benevolence and activism melded
into women's efforts to support troops engaged in the war. Their
activism after the war continued in many places, including Oregon. Oregon had one of the earliest independent women's clubs in
the Northwest, the McMinnville Ladies' Sanitary Aid Society. It
was founded in 1863 in a Willamette Valley town about 30 miles
southeast of Portland. In tiny McMinnville, sixteen women met on
May 25, 1863, to do their part in the war effort. "We, the ladies of
McMinnville and vicinity, do hereby form ourselves into a society
for the purpose of rendering such assistance as may be in our
power to the U.S. Sanitary Commission, or to the U.S. Christian
Commission."[79] They adopted a constitution and a 50-cent membership fee. They worked at projects while one member read to
them from letters and articles received from the East, such as
news of similar work begun by other women or accounts such as
descriptions of conditions at Andersonville prison.

Members talked a lot about how to raise funds. Monthly contributions made by members through pledges were 25 or 50 cents
each, tapering off some as the war wore on. "Work was plenty and
the members industrious," wrote the secretary in the August 10,
1864, minutes. Oregon was too far away to send supplies, so the
women focused on money. They knitted socks, selling them for 50
cents a pair, and made quilt tops for $2.50. They dunned resi-
dents for contributions and organized fundraising dinners and
events.

In the minutes for May 25, 1864, Mrs. D. J. Yeargain, secretary, described what motivated them. "Lady, have you a husband, a brother, a parent, now struggling on either side, in this dreadful conflict, and are you still unmoved by the suffering your hand might relieve? Mother, have you a son, one who still lingers around your fireside, a solace and a comfort in your old age," destined for the battlefield? "And will you yet refuse to assist in relieving his distresses? And should he linger out a miserable existence in some unfriendly hospital, his memory will be to you a perpetual reproach, and ever sting your conscience with the fact that he perished of your neglect."[80]

Donating to the cause from the Northwest was not easy. First gold and silver had to be changed to paper money to send to Portland. Unfortunately, paper money was worth half the value of the gold and silver, requiring separate account balances and double bookkeeping. Correspondence in club records noted that in June 1864 the group initially forwarded $120 in U.S. currency to the U.S. Christian Commission in Portland. That was followed by $134 in October 1964, $505 in January 1965, another $120 in April 1865, and $116 in September, all forwarded to the U.S. Sanitary Commission to support Union efforts. The letter they received from P. C. Schuyler, Jr., for the Oregon Branch of the Sanitary Commission thanked them "on behalf of our sick and wounded soldiers for this additional testimonial of sympathy which the ladies of your town feel in their behalf." Even the children of McMinnville were thanked for the $21 they provided the Sanitary Commission.[81] Their record of contributions, raised in a poor and only recently settled area by women of little means, was remarkable.

However, from the beginning, some regarded the club as both unwomanly and unorthodox. The club's experiences were recorded in two slim notebooks, by secretary (Mrs. D. J.) Yeargain and treasurer (Mrs. H. V. V.) Johnson. The women faced criticism and vocal opposition, but also found considerable support, as the club's success demonstrates. The membership crossed social and church lines, which were less distinct in the Northwest than in other regions. The president, Mrs. G. C. Chandler, was wife of the head of McMinnville College, and club members included a number of pioneer names. Even suffrage leader Abigail Scott Duniway, then a resident of nearby Lafayette, paid a membership fee to the organization, one of her many organizational involvements.[82] In addition to cash, the women collected donations in the form of wool, cloth for quilting, and food.

Ultimately forty-three women of the small community were members at some point. However, not all members could or would do the group's work, not an uncommon complaint throughout the history of voluntary associations. "The whole number of membership during the year is 43, many of whom however do not cooperate with us, being non-residents, and some residing near us being very seldom in our circle," wrote the treasurer in her 1865 annual report. The members who did most of the work knew the need was great.

"We were few in number, weak in faith, but our hearts were moved to sympathy; and animated to exertion, by the tales which reached us of their great sufferings and uncomplaining endurance of sickness, privation and death, to preserve for us, as well as themselves the blessings of Liberty," the treasurer wrote in their last annual report. "We had too the example of many noble women, who were laboring with their hands and giving up even their heart's dearest treasures in the great conflict. Why should we sit still? We organized, and addressed ourselves to our work, and as we went forward discouragements were not lacking, and many were the criticisms of those who 'went not with us.'"[83]

WOMEN'S ORGANIZATIONS AND THE CIVIL WAR

The civilian and military managers of the Civil War armies had prepared for armed confrontations, but not very well for the difficult problems of feeding, clothing, and housing soldiers or caring for the wounded or ill, especially after the first few disastrous battles. Yet as historian Robert Bremner details in writing about philanthropy during the Civil War, leaders were suspicious at worst and ill prepared at best to handle civilian enterprises aimed at assisting in the war effort. Ultimately Lincoln authorized the U.S. Sanitary Commission, initially to help with the treatment of the sick. Thousands of women across the country, even in Oregon, mobilized to respond.

The McMinnville meeting records show that while only a few came to meetings consistently, the pledges and work continued unabated. In addition to fundraising, the women furnished soldiers with copies of the New Testament.[84] The sprawling Military District of Oregon, made up of the state of Oregon and all of Washington Territory (which included Idaho and parts of Montana and

Wyoming as well until Idaho Territory was created in 1863), was firmly in the Union fold, although some supported the Confederacy, especially those who came from the western counties of Missouri. Oregon raised six companies to form the First Oregon Volunteer Cavalry in 1862, followed by another cavalry company in 1864–65, affecting women in the remote territory very directly. Companies of Oregon volunteers based at Fort Walla Walla were ordered to patrol Oregon's link with the East, the Oregon Trail, which had become particularly hazardous in the stretch across southern Idaho as the migrations continued despite the war. They explored and mapped much of the area, built roads and military outposts, located springs and other sources of water, and improved access and thus the expansion of whites and their traffic into the Northwest, historian Alvin Josephy found.[85]

In all, the McMinville group held twenty-five regular and three special meetings, "generally characterized by amity of feeling and harmony of deliberation." These women—as women elsewhere— discovered the rewards of working with other women toward a common cause. They also sowed the study club idea soon harvested. "After the transaction of business our time has been occupied by readings of instructive and profitable matter, bearing upon the object for which we were laboring."[86]

After Success, What Next?

The McMinnville club, like other clubs in other times, celebrated once it reached its goal then wondered what to do with itself. The amount raised by the women "exceeds the most sanguine expectation that any one of us indulged a year ago. In every effort we have made the result has been more than equal to our brightest anticipations, and though we would not indulge in too much self-gratulation yet we may take encouragement feeling that our work has not been in vain."[87]

Finally, at the 1865 annual meeting, the group recognized the fighting was over, but there was much to be done for widows and orphans. "And there is also a great field of Christian labor among not the slaves but the *American citizens of African decent* [sic], and it is our privilege to have a part in this great work." Men also came to this meeting, but left when officers were elected. The women decided to carry on and meet once a month. But by August the group came to grips with the loss of its galvanizing focus, as later groups galvanized by suffrage had to change or perish

when women got the vote. It decided to disband, sending its re-
maining $8 to the American Tract Society.[88]

In a rare record of personal reflection for club records, the treasurer mulled over what the women did and where they might go
from there:

> Having finished our retrospect let us turn and cast an inquiry at
> the future. What has it in store for us? Is our work finished? Shall
> we now fold our hands and let our energies sleep? Or shall we rather
> feel that they have been awakened only to find more active exercise
> and wider and still increasing scope in the field of our great Master
> who has said "The poor ye have always with you."
>
> Perchance the channel through which we direct our little rills of
> benevolence must needs be changed. If God shall bless us with a re-
> turn of peace so that the weapons of war shall no more do their de-
> structive work and the suffering body no longer claim our atten-
> tion—still the war against sin and eternal death is going on and
> comfort for the soul, and food for the mind, are just as much needed
> as ever. Let us not tire then, or be weary in well doing, but labor on
> in the best light.[89]

This group of industrious women apparently could not agree on
which light to follow in the coming decade. The record ends.

IDAHO'S 1864 LADIES' MITE ASSOCIATION

One kind of women's benevolent association and activism came
in the form of church-related mite societies. Although they were
not the independent women's groups that are the primary focus
here, these groups helped women find a voice and others who
were like-minded. *Mite* referred to a small value or contribution
and reflected the practice of collecting coins at meetings (and
perhaps women's limited view of their own ability to contribute to
church efforts). An early example of the mite society, and one of
the earliest women's clubs founded in Idaho, was the 1864 Ladies'
Mite Association located in the mining boomtown later called
Idaho City, northeast of what became Boise. Mite societies typically met weekly for Bible readings, often collecting and contributing pennies for a fund later used to buy religious study materials, support domestic missions, or help the poor. From this the
groups typically moved to more participatory roles, such as running Sunday schools or campaigns, gaining organizational skills
and competence along the way.

At the time Idaho City (also called Bannack) eclipsed the nearby
village of Boise, fueled by the discovery of gold nearby in 1862. In

fact, the population of Idaho shifted from the north to the south with the discovery of gold in Boise Basin in 1862 and the Owyhee Mountains in 1863. Thousands of hopeful prospectors had arrived in Idaho City by the end of 1862, and the profitable pursuit of placer mining and quartz ground meant that suppliers, professionals, and artisans soon followed, headed south from Lewiston by land and water. By September the population of Idaho City had swelled to 6,267, surpassing Portland to become the largest city in the Northwest for a while, with something like half its population consisting of miners and the rest "support staff."[90]

The Ladies' Mite Association, according to its secretary, had as its purpose "to procure means to pay the debt of the First Baptist Church of Idaho City."[91] Officers included women identified as Mrs. Kelly, president; Mrs. Pinney, vice-president; Mrs. Goodell, treasurer; and J. B. Knight, secretary. Pinney's husband James chased gold in the West, then opened a store in the Boise Basin in Bannack City (renamed Idaho City). His wife Mary died at twenty-five in 1869, and he went on to Boise, where he became a theater owner and mayor. Mrs. Kelly may have been Lois Kelly, wife of Milton Kelly. He later owned and edited the *Idaho Statesman* in Boise and became a territorial Supreme Court justice. They already had four children when they came to Boise Basin in 1862.

The Reverend H. Hamilton described the immense problem facing this small group—namely, a debt of about $3,000. He had purchased the church and parsonage for the use of the Baptist Home Mission Society for worship. The group was informed that a newspaper could be printed and sold to benefit the society, at a cost of one hundred copies for $20. The women did publish the *Ladies Mite*—at least a few weekly issues—in 1864. Printed by the *Boise News,* it consisted of four pages edited by Isabelle Butler and Mrs. Rees. Other fundraising ideas noted in minutes included holding concerts, selling books and merchandise, arranging tableaux, or running an express office for the town. In August the group decided on a familiar course for female fundraising—the preparation and sale of food—deciding that "eatables [would] be sold by the plate, $1.50 for plate and coffee, also that there be extra tables for cakes, ice cream, etc."[92] The industrious women also found and signed up subscribers to the Baptist Church, for $5 to $25 each, and managed to get the goods and labor donated for the restaurant they planned to run during a fair. The group's records show the women raised $1,079.75. Their record ends with that achievement.

Another early example of an active mite society was the Ladies' Mite Society of Trinity Episcopal Church, one of Seattle's earliest churches, founded in 1865. Established by 1870, its mite society also engaged in major fundraising. Members organized bazaars and charity balls to meet church and community needs.[93] Occasionally, the mite or church societies, especially later in the century, broke away from the church to form secular study clubs, as happened with the African-American Evergreen Society in Seattle.

Almost as soon as they became towns, the towns of the Northwest brought lecturers. With the traffic in speakers came new ideas, even the radical idea of suffrage for women. The Idaho legislature in the 1860s had considered a bill to give women voting rights, and a number of women in the Northwest tried to vote following the Civil War and the passage of the Fourteenth Amendment in 1868. The optimism that came with claiming the West carried with it a paradox. It meant a certain openness to new configurations in communities and new social arrangements. Yet its very emptiness often led community leaders in conservative directions, hoping to recreate the kind of communities and culture they left behind. These tensions, and the potential for significant change in the Northwest that might provide a beacon for the rest of the nation, also brought leaders of social movements, including advocates for women's rights.

Susan B. Anthony Comes West

Several national women's rights leaders made important lecture tours of the Pacific Northwest well before 1900, including Frances Willard, Carrie Chapman Catt (who lived in Seattle for a time), and Susan B. Anthony. They saw opportunities to steer development of the West in their direction before constitutions and customs made the region rigid. Anything seemed possible under the starry optimism of clear western skies, even the right for half the population to vote in this democracy. During the sixth session of the Idaho Territorial Legislature a Welsh physician named Joseph William Morgan (D–Oneida County) introduced the idea, arguing in part that Idaho women ought to have the vote because women in neighboring Utah and Wyoming had it. His opponents countered with the Blackstonian argument that man and wife were one unit and to give women their own vote would play havoc with family integrity. Morgan's bill failed, and legislators henceforth made him chairman of all activities relating to women, including "ladies day" at the legislature. His bill to give the ladies the vote died on a tie vote.[94] Word of it spread.

In 1871, well before the WCTU emerged as a force in the Pacific Northwest when Frances Willard came through a decade later, Susan B. Anthony and Elizabeth Cady Stanton took their cause to the West. They met in Chicago then traveled to Denver. While in what was then Laramie City in Wyoming, the first territory to validate women's right to vote, Anthony wrote in a letter of finally "moving over the soil that is really the land of the free and the home of the brave—Wyoming, the Territory in which women are the recognized political equals of men."[95] However, the press was decidedly cool to the suffrage leader. It concluded she was out of her "proper sphere," a scold, a masculine woman, "a monstrosity in petticoats."[96]

Those who filled the halls to overflowing to hear her came not out of commitment, but with a great curiosity to hear the woman lecture. For women to speak from platform and podium to mixed "promiscuous" audiences was more than a novelty—it was to some a gross distortion of what a woman should be or do, as many women besides Anthony were reminded. It is hard to imagine how difficult it was for women to step forward to take up causes or speak publicly on issues, whether it was to present papers, lobby legislators, or campaign for ideals such as women's civil rights. One reason for the club movement's success was that clubs offered safe settings, not only a haven for women to study and deliberate issues of public importance, but also a safe "platform" from which to speak to an understanding and supportive audience.

After they reached California, the two women parted. Anthony headed north "to accept the numerous calls to go up into Oregon and Washington Territory." In August she took the ship *Idaho* for the passage to Portland. The voyage of seven days through rough seas sickened her. At Portland she met first with Abigail Scott Duniway, editor of the *New Northwest* and herself a founder of women's clubs. (Duniway, an important leader for decades in the Pacific Northwest, is profiled in chapter 8.) Anthony's lectures in the Pacific Northwest were designed to raise funds for the cause of suffrage (and Anthony's debts), and Duniway told Anthony she had two months' worth of engagements lined up in Oregon and Washington Territory. Anthony herself had her doubts about staging successful lectures in the sparsely populated area.[97] Nevertheless she persevered, in hopes of adding to the $350 in profits she had deposited in San Francisco, where her defense of a woman jailed for killing her abusive husband caused even more commotion and outcries against her than her lectures. She and Duniway agreed to split the proceeds from the Northwest tour.

Anthony's first Oregon lecture at Portland, like her others, received a lukewarm if polite reception and a generally favorable if noncommittal response from the local newspapers. However, the *Bulletin* in Portland printed a lengthy attack in verse on the suffrage campaign—and women who gave public speeches—that began with these lines: "Along the city's thoroughfare, / A grim Old Gal with manly air, / Strode amidst the noisy crowd, / Tooting her horn both shrill and loud."[98] Elsewhere the paper actually praised Anthony's speechmaking abilities, but said what she proposed would create anarchy in homes and chaos in society. After Portland, Anthony met with women and lectured at Salem, Oregon City, The Dalles, and Walla Walla. At Walla Walla the church doors were closed to her, so she spoke in the schoolhouse instead. Although she had "good houses" everywhere, money—always in short supply—was hard to get.[99]

Anthony continued her journey in October to Olympia in Washington Territory, which required some dedication. She traveled 100 miles via the Columbia to the mouth of the Cowlitz, followed by 90 miles of grueling stage ride, 60 of them "over the roughest kind of corduroy." She arrived at a stage stop called Pumphrey's Hotel at 6 P.M., only to be awakened at 2 A.M. to travel another 14 miles by coach lanterns until breakfast, another 18 miles to dinner, then 30 miles of "splendid road" to finally reach the territorial capital of Olympia, south of Seattle. By November 4 she was in Seattle, full of praise for the evergreen beauty of the sound.[100] She was back in Olympia for the Territorial Convention a few days later, meeting with Duniway and Mrs. A. H. Stuart. Wherever she traveled in the Northwest, she often spawned small suffrage clubs.

THE NORTHWEST'S FIRST SUFFRAGE CLUBS

Stuart, spurred by Anthony's words and presence, started a suffrage society and other women's clubs. Duniway later called Anthony's appearance before the legislature significant, as "the first hearing on record before a legislative assembly at which women were invited, without expressed desire on their part, to address such an assembly."[101] During her trip through Oregon she also lectured in Oregon City, Eugene, and Roseburg, where she inspired yet another woman who became a notable early leader in the Pacific Northwest, Bethenia Owens Adair (profiled in chapter 4). At Jacksonville she had the unpleasant experience of being pelted with eggs, but most appearances were less painful, at least physically.

Her appearance at Roseburg in Southwest Oregon was organized by Owens Adair, herself later a lecturer and WCTU leader, who in a speech to the Portland Woman's Congress later described a situation and sequence of events not unknown to Anthony. She told the women she got a telegram from Anthony directing her to secure a place for a lecture. She arranged for a church, but the proprietor of one of the largest saloons in town said he would give a free supper and dance at the hotel to keep people from attending her lecture. Anthony's supporters ran a countercampaign, soliciting the men's wives to come to the lecture while the husbands were at the saloon. At the time Roseburg had 500 people and sixteen saloons, according to Owens Adair. Despite the anti-Anthony supper and dance, the curiosity about Anthony and her message and the publicity filled the church.[102]

Back in Portland before returning to the East, Anthony met with a Mrs. Eliot, wife of the Unitarian minister, who came with temperance worker Harriet W. Williams, a woman who used to entertain Anthony in New York. They too formed a local suffrage society the week she returned. Buoyed by that news, Anthony was soon saddened by an Associated Press report that while in the West she was visiting saloons and associating with low characters, based in part on the fact that she of necessity spoke at a saloon at one of her stops.[103] Attacks on her character, while common, were always disquieting to Anthony, as they were to any woman who valued her reputation. What later became known in politics as character assassination and denigration by ridicule often swirled around the women and clubs who engaged in cultural politics and activism.

Anthony and Duniway in their tour of Washington and Oregon had inspired more than the 1871 formation of the first Women's Suffrage Organization in Washington Territory. They also had a small measure of success. In November the Washington Territorial Legislature gave women the right to vote at least in school elections, as did the Idaho Territorial Legislature. Although Anthony's lectures did not sway community leaders to endorse her view of women's rights, her lectures did expose men and women to two significant points. The first was the idea of women's rights, in voting, legal equity, equal pay, and employment opportunities. The second was the vision of women speaking out publicly on political issues. In all, with Duniway organizing her appearances, Anthony in two months delivered sixty speeches in churches, courthouses, and schoolhouses throughout the Northwest. She had traveled a remarkable and difficult 1,800 miles in fifty-six days, speaking for forty-two nights and on many days, "and I am tired, tired," she wrote. "Lots of good missionary work, but not a great deal of money."[104] At the time there were roughly 91,000 residents in Oregon Territory and 24,000 in Washington Territory. Most of them were more interested in railroads and immigration policies than in women's rights, but many came out to hear Anthony argue the cause anyway.[105]

New roles for women were gaining momentum in the Northwest, and their first widespread organizational vehicle was the WCTU. In 1882 a speech reprinted in the *New Northwest* delivered by J. T. Long in Astoria, Oregon, distilled attitudes toward women's role in reform. Long said the "Coming Woman" would not only be a voter but also would astonish man with her talents, inventions, and energy. "She can and will banish the evils of intemperance, licentiousness and tyranny from its [home's] precincts." He painted a utopian vision of cooperative culinary and other shared skills and manufacturing, freeing women from drudgery and isolation. Woman will be "man's truest friend, safest counselor, strongest advocate and best adjutant."[106] Anthony, Duniway, Owens Adair, and others, by speaking out, offered examples of women moving into public affairs, with or without the vote. Women's collective regionwide involvement in the Pacific Northwest first took form in the Women's Christian Temperance Union. As the first statewide women's organization in Washington, Oregon, and Idaho, it backed a wide array of causes that amplified women's voice in public affairs and cultural politics in dozens of local communities.

The Coming of the WCTU

The WCTU legacy, in issues, leaders, and organizational framework, did much to channel women's future activism. The network of interconnected unions in each state faded almost as rapidly as it arose as other club alternatives and causes presented themselves to women of the Northwest. Just as Anthony's tour of the Northwest spurred creation of women's organizations, Frances

Willard's tour of the Northwest roughly a decade later did the same, but on a wider scale. Women, some of whom had already been involved in temperance work, were more eager to sign on to the broad agenda of the WCTU in larger numbers than to the more controversial cause of suffrage.

Few independent women's organizations existed in the 1870s and 1880s in many locales in the Northwest; suddenly with the WCTU women found an opportunity to work collectively toward a vision of the common good and counter what they perceived as the most negative forces in their communities. During its heyday, the WCTU in the Pacific Northwest flourished, bringing together many women, some of whom then used WCTU leadership as a springboard to other groups and offices. They founded and led subsequent organizations in the region into other kinds of activism, but the rituals, formats, and even the causes of those groups owed much to the WCTU.

"OUR LITTLE BANDS"

The WCTU in the Pacific Northwest, 1880–1900

Drinking, that male prerogative, had long ago been deemed dangerous for women because of the way it tended to reduce their inhibitions. Dangers for men were less apparent (or more acceptable). For more than a century in the United States, the tavern or saloon was an important gathering place—for men only. The saloon gave men a means of solidifying their own relationships through the rituals of buying and sharing drink without the constraints women either faced or imposed. It reduced the distance between classes and gave men a site where they could develop social relations and make connections, especially in places that lacked other institutions as did the Northwest. The saloon also supported major economic forces, from barkeeps to whole industries. Going to the bar was a precious right, a right—because they had it—that made men superior and conferred status because they had the money to spend in this fashion and such places to visit.[1]

However, the custom also led to the abuse of alcohol, the psychological abandonment of the family, loss of financial and emotional support for women and children, and sometimes the victimization and abuse excessive drinking has always caused. Saloons became a natural site for female activism. The abuse of drink and its link to the abuse of family galvanized WCTU activism, especially in the face of a system that failed to protect families legally or financially. The appeal of the WCTU movement as holding out hope for victimized women and children was typified by the experience of one member of the Oregon WCTU, Mrs. Lucy Whiteaker, first president of the Polk County union and superintendent of the LTL (Loyal Temperance League) in 1885.

In Indiana, her father decided to chase the gold of California in 1849. She was fatherless at age six. Her mother later married an old soldier and schoolteacher "of fine face and figure." But he "struck terror to their hearts" by his drunken habits, threatening to kill them all. The mother repeatedly forgave his "terrible actions," only to end the marriage in separation "as fear of her life and exhausted patience was all that was left." Said Whiteaker: "Seeing these sights when a child made a deep impression on my mind of the awful sin of intemperance, and I have joined every temperance society that came along my way, and have done all I could to encourage the work of temperance." She became known in the Oregon group as "one of our Old Reliables."[2]

In 1874 the national WCTU emerged. Soon after Anthony returned to New York, the national temperance crusade of 1873–74 led to the spectacle of some outspoken women organizing prayer sessions on saloon steps or seeking signatures on abstinence pledges, although this highly visible crusade was not the first one. The Daughters of Temperance had emerged in Indiana in 1849. Indeed, many of the women who were leaders of the WCTU in the Northwest came from Indiana or the Midwest. It sponsored a hatchet crusade in 1854, destroying several saloons in Winchester, Indiana. Other localized efforts emerged, especially in the Midwest, but with limited purpose and little coordination. Coordination came with the Women's Christian Temperance Union, formed in Fort Wayne two decades later in 1874, which soon had 250 women representing twenty-two counties in Indiana.

This crusade, as it captured followers, marked a transition from a focus on the home to a focus on the public realm in the name of the home, for a larger number of women than ever before. It pulled women into the cause of temperance first and soon other causes as well, especially under the leadership of Frances Willard, who linked those causes to the umbrella concept of protection of the home.[3] There was little in American culture or politics that was sacrosanct under the WCTU's increasingly broad application of the "do everything" concept.

Just as the cause of antislavery galvanized the moral fervor of another group of women and through it or later Civil War activism they learned organizing, fundraising, lobbying, demonstrating, petitioning, and speaking out (they called it "agitating"), workers in the cause of temperance gained the same important skills. By creating a personal network they empowered themselves and created a context for activism that incorporated other goals such as suffrage. It gave them a sense of fellowship and identity as unions bridged the personal and political and the local and national. Unions also brought attention to community and social welfare issues in a way that later shaped study club organization and activism as women sought new cultural norms.

In the Northwest, the WCTU had particular importance for women. They found in the WCTU a means to influence their environment and a place where women were in control. Although generally unsuccessful with legislative proposals and often ridiculed, the WCTU movement and its timing were critical in giving women a collective voice in the Northwest. Leaders like Oregon's Eva Emery Dye and Abigail Scott Duniway, Idaho's Gertrude Hays and Emma Drake, and Washington's Emma Ray and Bethenia Owens Adair began their public work and honed leadership and organizational skills in the WCTU unions of the Northwest before moving on to other women's organizations.

The WCTU's success can be measured in two significant ways. Besides limits on alcohol sale and consumption, it brought issues such as suffrage and property rights for women to the attention of legislators and the public, including other women, and gave women a public voice, a vehicle to make the transition from private to public. The WCTU made it possible and permissible for women to reach beyond themselves and their homes to challenge cultural and governmental priorities, a vital first step to reordering those priorities. In short, the WCTU gave women power to capitalize on the domestic ideology and a practical pattern of organization to do it.

Frances Willard Comes West Too

After the Civil War, reform ideas pulled female adherents into organizations that promoted causes ranging from women's rights to temperance to world peace. The 1874 Women's Christian Temperance Union linked moral fervor to political action, the private domain of home to the public domain, and the power of organized womanhood to the causes the women valued. The movement spread like a flood, swelling activist passions and channeling activism. Frances E. Willard—teacher, college dean, and president as well as world lecturer and savvy leader—expanded and energized the union, moving it beyond its Protestant, small town roots. She served as its president for nearly twenty years, taking that office in 1879 after resolution of a controversy over whether the WCTU approach would be narrow and single issue or broad.[4] Broad-based home protection won, and Willard took over, exercising skillful and artful political leadership.[5]

She recognized that making temperance a norm was like rolling a barrel up a steep hill against the weight of a culture of male drinking and entrenched economic interests. The country had 750 breweries with investments in and income from alcohol production and distribution, a powerful alliance that separated itself from the social issues connected to drinking. However, it met a worthy foe in Frances Willard and the WCTU forces in the Northwest. In the Northwest, the women along with groups like the Anti-Saloon League succeeded in getting prohibition measures passed well before the national Volstead amendment passed.

Willard displayed charisma as a speaker and skill as a leader. She was no stranger to organized womanhood. Her own club involvements included membership in a Shakespeare Club at Pittsburgh Female College where she taught and being secretary of the American Methodist Ladies' Centenary Association. As an admirer of Margaret Fuller she decided to use Fuller's "Conversation Classes" for women as a model for her own teaching and in college was in a Minerva Society that sponsored debates, essays, and literary papers. This club activity preceded her temperance work.[6] When she became national speaker for the WCTU, everywhere she appeared she found three or four organizers lined up to help in her work, including the Northwest.[7] Willard, along with a few others like Jane Addams, came to the conclusion that contrary to prevailing thought men did not necessarily become poor because they drank, but the reverse. Therefore she believed the government needed to establish welfare programs and restructure its economy as it enacted restrictive drinking laws.

In her lectures Willard called alcohol a stimulant that excited men to strike down women and children "for whom when sober they would die."[8] Key to the success of the temperance crusade over "demon rum" was the image, all too often accurate, of decent men who were drunk striking their wives and small children or leaving them destitute. It was that image that gave weight to the cause of temperance and national prohibition in 1920. Cities, counties, and states gradually divided into camps of "wets" and "drys" and the laws followed, one by one. Washington went dry in 1914, and the other states in the Northwest followed. Ultimately coalitions of midwestern and rural interests were responsible for passage of the prohibition amendment, interests Willard courted in her lecture tours and through statewide organizations in the Northwest and other regions.

national speaker /

In 1883 Willard came to organize and energize the movement in Oregon, Washington, Idaho, and California, only four years after her election to the WCTU presidency. It was part of a campaign to make the WCTU a powerful national organization with broad-based regional representation. At the time she took no salary from the organization but had backers for her trip. Her lifelong ally Anna Gordon came with her, and they visited towns in California, went to Oregon by steamer, worked the Puget Sound area, visited British Columbia, and traveled via the Columbia and Snake Rivers to Lewiston, "the only town ever quarantined against us, so far as I remember," she wrote.[9]

Her visit to Lewiston, at the request of a brand new union organized there, was not welcomed by all. Lewiston commerce supplied miners and settlers as they moved inland. At the time, municipal authorities had announced that no public meeting could be held in Lewiston because of the danger from "diphtheritic contagion." The Lewiston union had earlier persuaded her to detour to the town to create a territorial convention. Coming from Walla Walla toward Lewiston by steamer, Willard received a telegram that said the mayor had closed the town to assemblies of people due to an outbreak of diphtheria.

She was not deterred. "We had traveled thirty-six hours by river steamer for the express purpose of meeting the good women at this head of navigation on the Snake River and did not propose to be defeated," Willard wrote later. She suspected a liquor traffic ruse, so came anyway. She found that it was no ruse, although the outbreak had weakened considerably by that time. The union gained permission from the local Board of Health to hold a private meeting in a friend's parlor on July 19, 1883. There they formed the Territorial Convention of the North Idaho WCTU, with Francena Buck, president.[10] Buck was the wife of an Idaho federal judge. Another officer, Kate Thatcher, was the wife of C. A. Thatcher, a merchant who sold pianos, organs, and dry goods. The group later secured a room in the downtown Benson building, and Lewiston women donated tables and reading material, including magazines, newspapers, books, and religious tracts, to create a library of sorts, something the WCTU did all over the Northwest.

The Membership and the Plan of Work

The methods of the WCTU changed as its goals changed. The WCTU established the idea of a "plan of work" through a series of

departments working toward specific goals, headed by superintendents, a methodology other clubs later adopted. There were
other important aspects. It was the WCTU that from its earliest
days (at least in the West) used women's given names in its publications, regardless of their marital status. It was the WCTU that
heightened a recognition that women—in the name of the home
and home values—could take action outside the home sphere.[11]
And the WCTU played an important role in creating a distinctly
female consciousness and cohesion, a sisterhood that supported
collective action on what we would label feminist causes, such as
equity in women's legal, political, and educational status. The
breadth of the organization and its causes, which had as many as
forty-five departments at a time, was great, as was the range of reforms proposed. However, local organizations had considerable
autonomy to set their own goals and strategies to meet local conditions. In the West, the compression of time and maturity of the
WCTU by 1885 led to more immediate action on political issues,
such as suffrage and property rights, than happened elsewhere.

Although the WCTU avowed itself open to all women without
restriction, the organization drew most of its membership from
women who were middle-class, middle-aged Anglo-Saxon Protes-
tants who lived in towns and cities, many of them from midwestern states.[12] Nationally, as in the Pacific Northwest, WCTU activism included holding mass meetings, drafting and circulating
petitions and literature, and organizing social groups and services
to offer alternatives to drinking. The WCTU also fostered in members a certain clear-eyed realism about issues of public concern,
rather than the sentiment women were expected to follow, with
its "moral suasion" techniques.

The WCTU's Agenda for Reform

"Protection of the home" as a guiding principle led to other forms
of cultural politics to reorder governmental priorities. These included universal access to education and changing women's status
and communities through property and voting rights. Members
also concerned themselves with labor reform, school programs,
prison conditions, prostitution and pornography, and the radical
issue of birth control. Their belief in the power of education to
save society and the need for community alternatives to counter
the social benefits of saloons as well as control behavior led them
to establish reading rooms.

The WCTU members, not unlike women in the study clubs that followed, focused on education both for its intrinsic benefits and as a site of reform and social change. As an organization, it pushed the idea of kindergartens, for children of the poor in particular, as a means of offering them a better environment, free of privation and degeneration. The WCTU also promoted teaching "scientific" truths about the effects of alcohol and tobacco in an era when patent medicines often included alcohol or narcotics and alcohol was still viewed as a "tonic." It also sought better and brighter public school programs "so that they [the children] shall from the first have placed before them images of the highest beauty and grace," in a time when discipline and rote recitation dominated school curricula.[13]

The WCTU's institutional agenda included reforming prisons, creating juvenile justice systems, redeeming instead of punishing "fallen women," and other reforms, not unlike reforms sought by later Progressive era women's clubs. It also supported using the ballot as a means of accomplishing the organization's disparate goals through government and capitalized on the concepts of virtuous womanhood and motherhood to argue for the reforms.[14]

The issue of suffrage itself was initially divisive within the WCTU in the closing decade of the century, as it would be within the General Federation of Women's Clubs after the turn of the century. Nevertheless, the WCTU gained a large, powerful membership, much larger than other national organizations. It claimed 500,000 members in 1890, while the new General Federation of Women's Clubs had perhaps 40,000 members and the National American Woman Suffrage Association (NAWSA) had even fewer.[15]

In the Pacific Northwest, the WCTU tried to influence the configuration of its new communities while shaping a small group of female leaders who soon moved into then out of the WCTU ranks to found other organizations. Later club members and leaders tended to shun the WCTU. They avoided the WCTU's moralistic and sometimes religious fervor and its vision of the future in favor of choosing from a more sophisticated and less fervent array of clubs and programs. Less millennial in outlook and oriented more to personal development than selfless service in the cause of temperance, later clubwomen seemed to abandon the WCTU as it lost its luster and perhaps its focus, especially after Willard's death. After explosive growth in what became each state of the Northwest, the organization went into decline before the end of the first

decade of the nineteenth century, superseded by women's organizations that were more varied, more "modern," less rigid, less
mission-oriented, and more local.

In many places in the Northwest and in many ways, the WCTU
bridged Civil War activism and the advent of the woman's study
club movement. By 1883, the year Buffalo Bill Cody began his
Wild West shows and the railroads gave the country four time
zones, Willard had visited Portland, Lewiston, and Seattle. By 1885
chapters (called unions) of the national organization dotted the
Pacific Northwest. By 1895 the WCTU forces had pushed through
the legislatures a few successful proposals, such as a police matron bill in Washington to keep women and children from being
placed with male criminals or processed by male guards or a law
requiring schools to teach scientific temperance as in Idaho.

What was perhaps most significant about the WCTU in the Pacific Northwest was the cross-fertilization of ideas and methods
combined with its ability to find and grow leaders in the relatively
sparse population of women. Or perhaps the leaders found the
WCTU. In several places the local membership rolls of the WCTU
carried the names of women who later founded study clubs or led
suffrage campaigns or both. Nationally, the WCTU represented an
early wave of women's activism whose initial leaders were more
often connected to early churches than to later women's clubs.
That was less the case in the Pacific Northwest than in areas with
longer histories.[16] In all places, however, the union was un-
abashedly political from its inception, and through it many
women learned practical methods of lobbying, public speaking,
voter education, the value of sisterhood, and the power of organized action. According to Anne Firor Scott, the WCTU probably
contained more suffragists than did the two national suffrage organizations combined.[17] The organization was also unique in the
circle of women it embraced, crossing class, ethnic, and even
racial boundaries, although its membership remained moralistic
and mostly white and Protestant.

However, in city after city in the Northwest, the powerful WCTU
began to wane at the turn of the century after Willard's death.
New activists founded their own clubs then chose to ally nationally through the new General Federation of Women's Clubs. Unlike the leaders of the 1880s, the activists in the later women's
club movement seemed not to be struck from the same mold as
the early WCTU activists. Some women saw their moral zeal and

political agenda as at worst repellent, at best unsophisticated and antithetical to their own ideas of self-improvement and genteel culture, with its quieter political activism. This was the case particularly in Washington, less so in Oregon and Idaho. However, these women who moved beyond it owed more to the WCTU than many realized then or now.

For instance, in many locales in the Northwest the very first reading rooms, those nascent city libraries, were founded and staffed not by members of study clubs, but by the WCTU first, as an alternative to saloons. Members believed such rooms could improve the lot and behavior of local citizens by making reading material beyond tracts and newspapers available. For instance, in Boise the influential Columbian Club, rightfully proud of its efforts to establish public libraries throughout Idaho, began in 1895 with a reading room established there by the WCTU in 1889.

The WCTU recognized the need for alternatives to the friendly saloons that emerged in new, remote towns of the Northwest like watering holes in the desert, where options for social contact were more limited than elsewhere in the country. "Most of the Unions propose establishing libraries and reading rooms. This work is very much needed," wrote Mary McGee, a WCTU officer, in 1887 from the railroad siding town of Nampa, Idaho, connected by a short line to Boise 20 miles away. "In many of our towns there is no place open to young men during the long winter evenings but the barroom and saloon." Libraries were more than a distraction, however. They were sites for struggles over behavior. "Having reading rooms, making them homelike and attractive, will save many from sin," wrote McGee.[18] Her husband was president of the Nampa Land and Improvement Company.[19]

Further, the WCTU recognized it had a hard-nosed, sober reputation and needed to counter that impression in its social work, especially with young people. "Under the social element comes the department of young women's work and parlor meetings," said the 1888 Idaho WCTU report. "In the parlor meetings we are able to interest and gain the influence of some who would never enter our ranks through regular or public meetings. The afternoon or evening meetings of the drawing room can be made so pleasant that the butterfly of society and the lover of the wine cup will not realize they are among radical temperance people. We need not lower our colors, nor be false to our principles because we try to influence for right by social pleasures."[20]

The WCTU in Oregon

In Oregon, the WCTU began officially in 1880, before Willard came, with the appointment at the national level of Elizabeth A. P. White as vice-president for the state organization. Related temperance activity had been going on for most of a decade before that, especially in the Portland area. Her mother, Rebecca Clawson, had organized the first local WCTU group in 1881, in Portland.

The temperance movement came to the Northwest about the same time the WCTU was founded in the Midwest. The Oregon State Temperance Alliance created in Portland in 1871 campaigned in nearby Oregon City in 1879, establishing a series of lectures there and at The Dalles. Portland began in the 1840s as a small trading center with valuable ocean access down the Willamette River via the Columbia. Within a few decades it had become a leading city in the Northwest, especially as gold mining and agriculture in the West expanded. The city prospered from supplying those markets. In 1870 its population was 8,293. By 1890 it had increased more than fivefold, to 46,385.[21]

As happened to temperance worker Susan B. Anthony on the other side of the country (she worked for temperance before turning to suffrage), men tried to dominate the movement and the meetings, much to the irritation of Oregon's Abigail Scott Duniway and other women. Portland in 1874 had a Woman's Temperance Prayer League. Such irritation spurred interest in the WCTU. The Oregon Temperance Alliance met again in Eugene in 1880 and proposed a state amendment to "prohibit manufacture, sale, or gift of intoxicants as a beverage." In 1882 it petitioned the legislature for liquor control, collecting 9,522 signatures, about the time the WCTU began to spread into the Northwest.[22]

The pledge documents from the Portland Woman's Temperance Prayer League of 1874 contained 2,120 names gathered from April 10 to July 7. Members said there was one saloon in Portland for every forty residents, and a band of twenty brave women began visiting Portland's saloons to do their work, not far behind the marches and sit-ins women conducted in the Midwest that gave birth to the WCTU. It was not easy work for the Multnomah County women. They were vilified with satire, attacked by drinkers, and even had firecrackers tossed at them.[23] But they were committed to the cause.

The Portland temperance movement attracted and gave voice to a woman who told one of its stories and later became one of the chroniclers of the history of the Pacific Northwest, Frances Fuller Victor. Married to a naval engineer ordered to California during the Civil War, she became a widely published writer, from poetry to novels to journalism to history.[24] After she came to Oregon in 1865 she wrote a popular pamphlet titled "Woman's War with Whisky," the legendary story of two temperance workers who sought abstinence signatures in Portland's Webfoot Saloon. The proprietor threw them out, calling them whores, the ultimate insult to womanhood. The bar then became the special cause of relentless temperance workers. They showed up every day and demanded entrance or sang hymns and prayers outside, chasing away customers until the proprietor closed the place in 1874, just as the crusades that resulted in the WCTU gained steam. It was one of the Oregon movement's success stories, and Victor's work popularized it.

Like Victor, leaders of the Oregon WCTU came from the Midwest, often from Illinois. Clawson, founder of the Portland WCTU in 1881, was succeeded by White, her daughter, who became the first Oregon Territory WCTU officer. Born in Indiana, she had been educated in the Friends Boarding School, which later became Earlham College.[25] The second state president, who had to step down for health reasons, was Elizabeth (Mrs. H. K.) Hines. It was Hines who spread unions across the state. They became a functioning Oregon State WCTU in Portland in 1883, when Frances Willard and Anna Gordon came and issued the call for a state union.[26] The first meeting was attended by sixty women who adopted sixteen departments of work. The Oregon WCTU had thirty-two local unions by 1886. Oregon's specific plan of work included socials for sailors, policing tobacco sellers and sales to minors, reform schools, prison work, and kindergartens. The organization grew fast. Oregon unions went from the thirty-two in 1886 to eighty-three in 1891, with almost 2,000 members.[27] But by 1900 its influence had begun to wane.

Oregon WCTU leader Hines was an Oregon pioneer with religious connections, like many women who took up WCTU work. Elizabeth Jane Graves Hines was born in Covington, New York, in 1828. Educated at Genessee Wesleyan Seminary at Lima, New York, she and her minister husband H. K. Hines were sent to Oregon Country in 1852, the year before Washington Territory was carved from Oregon Territory. They began work in Portland's Taylor Street ME Church. She also worked for the WCTU in

Washington and Idaho and "did the first hard pioneer work for the WCTU of Oregon."[28] She died in 1890.

One of those involved in early WCTU efforts in Oregon described the time in her 1885 diary.[29] Catherine Julia Adams of Hillsboro, near Portland, wrote that she attended WCTU meetings there, but the turnout was frequently low. She was appointed a delegate to the convention in East Portland and decided to go. She and four other women traveled to Portland on June 24 for the meeting at the Ladies Hall. "We were ferried across the river and after a long and dusty walk of about a mile we arrived at the hall where we were kindly received," she wrote in her diary. She described the meetings as including much singing and prayer, scripture reading, and many reports.

The fear women had of public speaking and the role of leadership was described rather matter of factly in her entry for the events of June 26. "Mrs. Riggs was elected to president's chair instead of Mrs. Hines but was so shocked she could not collect her thoughts so as to refuse before she was duly elected. She said she did not want the office but would serve through the morning. Mrs. Hines seemed so tired and feeble she needed rest." A later vote put Riggs permanently into the chair. After reports of committees, discussion of future work, and other activities, the meeting ended. "Got home from convention. Had splendid time," Adams wrote; she began her part in the cause. She circulated pledge cards to get signatures to promises of temperance, which she and others described as a not always pleasant activity. Besides getting members to carry pledge cards, the Oregon WCTU had organized its own lecture bureau by 1887, despite women's fears of public speaking.[30]

Anna Riggs, the reluctant new president described in Adams' diary, also brought her WCTU background from the Midwest, to Oregon from Illinois. She had won many honors in WCTU work at Bloomington before coming to Portland, including work on the board of managers for the *Union Signal,* the WCTU's official publication. Anna Rankin Riggs was the eldest child in a large family. In Oregon she was remembered as a founder of the Refuge Home established by the Oregon State WCTU in 1883. She became president of the state organization in 1885, when poor health forced Mrs. Hines to step down.[31] Riggs later edited a monthly publication dating from 1903 called the *Woman's Federation.* This temperance-oriented publication included much information on women's club activities and features on pioneer women.[32]

SOMETIMES "TIRESOME WORK"

Adams' diary also offered insights into the daily lives of many of the women in the Pacific Northwest near the end of the nineteenth century, and what life was like for those women who carried this cause into the community. In her entry for July 3, 1885, Adams described going in groups of four "to visit the drinking men" and invite them to the temperance meeting. "We are laughed at, talked about, called weak-minded men and women, but as long as we are in a good cause we don't mind it much. The weather is very hot and the roads quite dusty. It is very tiresome work circulating the pledge. The thermometer is at 106 in the sun and 102 in the shade. There are over 300 names."[33]

The spell of hot weather also put harvest ahead a month, and WCTU activities were lost in the accounts of her responsibilities for processing and putting up food and feeding big harvesting crews. On July 17: "Made kettle of soap yesterday. Our folks are nearly through haying. Threatens rain. Nice cool weather. . . . There is to be an ice cream festival tonight after the Temperance meeting." On July 24 Adams canned plums all morning, went to a carpet bee in the afternoon making rugs from rags, then went to a temperance meeting at night. The meeting included speeches, music, "speaking pieces," and socializing until 10 p.m. The WCTU had six chapters in the Portland area alone.

Near Portland, the Beaverton WCTU Band of Hope began in 1882 (a Sons of Temperance chapter existed as early as 1856 in Multnomah County). In 1885 the Beaverton WCTU heard Bethenia Owens Adair speak. (Owens Adair, a physician and one of the more intriguing women in Pacific Northwest history, is profiled in chapter 4.) The Beaverton group, like others, elected a series of department heads or superintendents whose department titles reflect the methods of early WCTU activism in the Northwest, including what social and political issues were on the minds of its members: Heredity and Hygiene, Evangelistic Work, Conferences with Influential Bodies, Unfermented Wine, Young Women's Work, Fairs and Public Gatherings, Work among Foreigners, Union Signal, Juvenile Work, Tobacco Habit, Temperance Literature, Sabbath Desecration, and Flower Missions.[34] The group's members referred to one another as "sister," and by 1886 meetings included literary exercises. Besides getting signatures members also boldly paid visits on men who "broke the pledge" prohibiting drinking, tobacco use, and profanity.

As with later organizations, lectures and socials were WCTU tools for outreach. Ada Weed, another physician important in Oregon and Washington history, used the WCTU and women's rights as a platform. She combined her limited professional training and the podium to engage in cultural politics by bringing attention and her expertise to women's rights issues, such as women's need for more education and professional opportunities and less restrictive clothing, besides the issues of temperance and suffrage.

PROFILE: DR. ADA M. WEED

Drs. Ada M. and Gideon Weed initially were trained in the practice of hydropathic medicine, with its holistic medical therapies that included the popular "water cure" used by many people in the East about mid-century, including Susan B. Anthony. Seeking opportunity, the Weeds brought their services to Oregon's newly settled Willamette Valley, to Salem in 1858. Not yet thirty, Ada began a series of lectures about the need to improve the lot of frontier women, to a mixed reception at best.

The sight and sound of a female lecturing in the years around 1860 was a novelty to some and a revolting spectacle to others. Weed's ideas—radical at the time—were that women needed better education, more opportunities, and enhanced rights in both dress and marriage. She also championed health reform and temperance a decade later as a WCTU leader in Seattle. One of the tenets of hydropathy was its rejection of the use of drugs of all kinds, including alcohol, in favor of healthful habits.

Born in Illinois in 1837, Ada Weed at nineteen had moved to New York City to enroll in 1856 in Dr. Russell T. Trall's Hygeio-Therapeutic College, one of the few medical training programs then open to women. Trall shared many of the views of women's rights leaders and advocated professional training for women. Ada married a classmate in the school's lecture hall, and early in 1858 they sailed for San Francisco. From there they traveled to Oregon, where they found a need for care and no competition for their services. She was apparently the first woman practicing in Oregon with a medical degree, such as it was, according to historian G. Thomas Edwards.[35]

Salem at the time had grown to 1,500 residents, making it the second largest city in Oregon. The Weeds' facility included baths, a gym, and rooms for patients. She also advertised her obstetrics services. As Edwards notes in his detailed history of the Weeds, frontier women were used to doctoring one another and their families and there was at the time a bitter national debate beginning over professionalized medical care, a debate quickly localized as other physicians moved into town. The Weeds apparently became controversial, and Ada became the special target for criticism from Asahel Bush, the cantankerous editor of the *Oregon Statesman*. He denounced reformers in general and Ada Weed in particular.

"The true sphere of woman is in the domestic circle," he wrote. "There the true woman finds abundant scope for the exercise of the highest and best faculties with which God has endowed her; there she is the chief ornament and attraction, and there she excites the holiest and purest emotions of which the heart of man is capable," he added. "Those women who, from misfortune, are compelled to seek employment in other directions, invariably call forth our pity and sympathy; but when a woman voluntarily leaves the domestic walks of life, and embarks in those pursuits which properly belong to the ruder sex, our pity gives way to quite a different emotion."[36]

Bush's criticism of this western professional woman reflected the mood of the eastern cartoons satirizing women who pursued legal or legislative power as they carried babies in their arms. As for women practicing the professions of medicine or law: "Imagine, for instance Madame the Doctress, making her usual morning round of visits, with a pair of pillbags upon one arm, and a squalling babe of six months on the other; or Madame the lawyer, in an 'interesting situation,' arguing a case of crim. con. before a judge who divided her attention alternately between the suit in progress, and the suckling of a pair of twins."[37]

Weed did not take the criticism in a ladylike fashion. She fought back, and Bush opened the paper's pages to debate her and decry the pressures for change in women's status that she represented. The two exchanged attacks and counterattacks in subsequent issues of the paper. Weed continued her lectures, branching out to other locales in Willamette Valley between The Dalles and Eugene. She and her husband also practiced medicine for several days in each locale. They both frequently lectured in churches or courtrooms, he on hydropathy, she on women's issues, sometimes to women-only audiences.

Despite their highly visible efforts (or perhaps because of them), the Weeds were unable to make a financial success of either their practice or their lectures and left for California in 1860. They followed the silver strike to Nevada a year later, returning to California in 1868. By 1870 they had landed in Seattle, where she eventually began clubwork and he, with benefit of eighteen weeks of additional training at Chicago's Rush Medical College, advertised himself as a physician and surgeon.

His medical practice and their investments in real estate made them both financially successful and able to continue their reform efforts. They established the Seattle Hospital in 1874. According to historian Edwards, Gideon Weed also helped organize both the Territorial Medical Society and the King County Medical Society and played a key role in getting legislation passed to create a state medical board. He served as a regent of the University of Washington 1879 to 1888 and pushed for the medical school there. His career and reputation flourished. He was even elected mayor in 1876 and instituted municipal reforms. He was also the town's health officer. The Weeds built an elaborate combined house and office in the city.[38]

Ada meantime continued work on her causes. She became a director of the Library Association, was twice elected secretary of the Woman's Board of Missions in the Congregational Church, and served as president of the Seattle WCTU. She even entered local politics, running against three men for Seattle school director in 1883, but apparently got only one of the 154 votes cast. She remained a worker for temperance and later began also to lecture and publish statements on women's suffrage, declaring her support in 1887. Like other WCTU leaders, she advocated it as a means to temperance, bringing the criticism of Oregon club leader and suffrage worker Abigail Scott Duniway, who fought to keep suffrage and temperance separate issues in voters' minds. The act granting suffrage to women in Washington Territory was overturned by the territorial Supreme Court. Weed then helped organize a campaign to fight the court's decision, to no avail.

The Weeds in 1890 moved to Berkeley, where their children attended the University of California. She continued to speak out on reform until she died of cancer in 1910 at the age of seventy-three, the same year women finally earned the right to vote in Washington State. Her daughter Mabel carried on her parents' reform traditions, ultimately becoming assistant director of the California Department of Social Welfare.

The importance the WCTU attached to reading (including tracts) and literacy as a means of redemption, as a leveler, and as entertainment is evident in the proliferation of reading rooms supported and staffed by members. The first building in Oregon erected and owned by the WCTU was said to have been located at Corvallis in 1884, in the rich farmland of the Willamette Valley. Money for the WCTU building was raised by subscription. Members paid off the debt by 1890, despite a purported attempt by a saloon owner to buy the mortgage. The building was a substantial 30 feet by 60 feet and two stories high. WCTU-owned buildings in Oregon's New Era, Albany, and Sunnyside followed. By 1884 reading rooms were also open in Portland and Salem, closing only for a smallpox epidemic.[39] The WCTU gradually established reading rooms throughout most of Oregon.[40]

The president of the Multnomah County WCTU published the Oregon WCTU's official history, written by Elizabeth Faxon Additon. A midwesterner named Frances Eleanor Gotshall ran the print shop. The official history called her the only woman in Oregon to head a successful printing company. It added that she "has fully demonstrated that a woman can be a part of the great business world and not lose any of her sweet womanliness."[41] She also became the first financial manager and associate editor of the Oregon *White Ribboner*. In 1891 the Oregon WCTU organization had started what became the *Northwest White Ribboner*, soon adopted by Washington, Idaho, and Montana as well as Oregon as the official WCTU publication.[42] Organization publications like this one gave women who produced them an outlet for writing while enhancing organizational communications.

WCTU SERVICES IN OREGON

Northwest WCTU unions also rescued women and children in times of need through their services. The lack of a social welfare "safety net" marked deficiencies in the structure of the new, fast-growing cities of the Northwest, which did not have the institutions of older cities. In 1888 the East Portland WCTU established its Baby Home, beginning with only $7 and a little secondhand furniture. Yet this meager facility cared for 132 children in one year, according to the WCTU history.[43] Founding and managing humanitarian projects like this was a role that fell to women's groups in the absence of benevolent or governmental help. The women later used their organizational clout and the documented need to force cities and states to turn them into government services.

In the 1880s the Central Portland Union started a Woman's Exchange. Through the sale of goods made by women the organization hoped to help women support themselves and their families. It also founded an Industrial Home for women and girls, with its own kindergarten, day nursery, and sewing school. This project became part of the state WCTU's Refuge Home for Women, because members felt the need of the hour was for a refuge for "unfortunate" women and girls rejected elsewhere. Located at two sites, it finally moved to Thirty-first and Glisan on land donated by a wealthy benefactor, Mrs. William Ladd, wife of an entrepreneur with banking and real estate interests there. This institution had Anna Riggs, the WCTU state president and one of its founders, as the head of its board of managers for years.[44]

The Refuge Home later became a Florence Crittenton Home. In 1899 New York evangelist and philanthropist Charles Crittenton, friend of Frances Willard, came to the Northwest. In fact, he came several times. Crittenton in 1883 had begun founding homes for unwed mothers and their babies, in memory of the four-year-old daughter he lost.[45] From WCTU foundations, similar homes emerged in Portland, Seattle, and Spokane, managed by local boards. The homes often became the literal and spiritual salvation of those stigmatized "wayward" girls and women who resided there. Also, Florence Crittenton Purity Circles existed in Dayton, Walla Walla, and Colfax in Washington, in Pendleton, Grants Pass, Eugene, Roseburg, The Dalles, Oregon City, and McMinnville in Oregon, and in Wallace, Idaho. The circles and the WCTU unions helped support and furnish the homes, organized mothers' meetings, and distributed cautionary literature to girls.[46]

The WCTU homes certainly filled a community need, but they also stigmatized occupants. The *Oregonian* in 1892 called the Refuge Home a "refuge for the lost and fallen among women and girls," whose "work for the reformation of lost womanhood" included attempts to "guide and control young girls early abandoned to the chance companionship of the street; it does care for the necessities of maternity and helpless infancy born to an inheritance of sin and shame." It said the home's residents came from various places, "variety theatre, the brothel, the jail, the Boys' and Girls' Aid Society, and from domestic service; from city, street, and rural district, but all alike needing the protection and discipline of such an institution." The men who left them in this condition apparently did not need or were not available for such "discipline."

The article conceded, however, that the victims were not entirely at fault. Many of the girls were left motherless in childhood or abandoned by brutal parents. "Some have mothers living, and have been ungrateful and disobedient, and some poor girls have not had good homes or careful mothers."[47] By 1889 the Oregon WCTU's president's "untiring efforts" at the legislature secured an appropriation of $5,000 for the Refuge Home at Portland, fitting the pattern of cultural politics repeated through the Northwest of creating an institution to meet a community need, pressuring government to fund it and eventually assume its management as a legitimate state activity.

Attacking the problem of unmarried mothers and "sexual ruin" from a behavioral standpoint led WCTU leaders to look to the state to curtail male exploitation. The WCTU got a bill introduced to raise the age of consent for sexual activity from fourteen years to eighteen, with Dr. Bethenia Owens Adair and Anna Riggs pooling their efforts in the legislature. However, Adair and Riggs "obtained the promise of support from many members of the legislature, only to have the bill 'snowed under' through the opposition of the chairman of the committee to which it was referred," writes the WCTU historian.[48] In 1890 the WCTU also laid the groundwork for a reform school for boys to be established near the state capital of Salem, to keep "incorrigible" boys from being sent to jail "to be shut up with old hardened offenders."[49]

SOCIAL JUSTICE AND REFORM

An important goal for the WCTU and later women's clubs was reform of the justice system, especially for women and children. In the nineteenth century, especially with overcrowding, it was common practice in local jails throughout the country to hold together convicted criminals, those awaiting trial in either civil or criminal cases, drunks, vagrants, people detained as witnesses, and frequently the mentally ill—people of all ages, often in terrible conditions where the weaker were easily victimized.[50] Women directed efforts at this problem in the Northwest, especially where it affected women and children. In 1891 the Portland WCTU began hosting Pacific Coast WCTU conferences, and the Oregon WCTU began a campaign to get a police matron into local jails. The efforts of the WCTU and other women's groups led to the employment a few years later of Lola Greene Baldwin, the famed Portland police matron and protector of young women.

The Oregon WCTU also began working with Native Americans,

establishing unions on Oregon's Indian reservations beginning in 1891 at the Umatilla reservation. The reservations contained the remnants of various tribes in the Northwest. The Umatilla reservation in the northeast corner, established by 1855, combined the Wallawalla, Cayuse, Nez Perce, and Umatilla tribes. In 1895 the state organization met in Roseburg. At the meeting, members heard the words of a letter from Lizzie Kants, herself a Native American. It stemmed from union activities on the Warm Springs Indian reservation in north-central Oregon south of The Dalles. Through an 1855 treaty, tribes had ceded 10 million acres for 464,000 acres of reservation land and promises of government payments and hunting and fishing rights, a deal precipitated by settlers moving in. The area tribes, later called the Warm Springs Confederated Tribes, consisted of 1,355 people in 1855.[51] They and remnants of other tribes throughout the Northwest endured various attempts over the years, accelerating in the 1870s, to "civilize" them, end their traditional native practices, or ameliorate the worst effects of contact, including alcoholism and disease. Part of that came with WCTU contact in the 1880s, and subsequent clubwomen's initiatives relating to health and education issues, especially in the 1920s.

Reprinted in the WCTU history, Kants' letter described more than a WCTU event; it symbolized cultural exchange and adaptation and prevailing attitudes about both race and gender.

> There is a great difference between a white woman and an Indian woman, unless they are both drunk, and then they are both on the same level. Drink will carry a woman farther down than it will a man. Oh, I cannot use strong words enough to tell you how I hate the whisky. It has ruined my people. . . . This society is working for the good of our people; nearly all of the trouble that comes to us now is because of whisky. It is a shameful thing for my race to drink. . . . They tell us that we are a dying race, but whisky will kill us faster than anything else.[52]

Accompanying the letter was an artifact presented to members that they interpreted according to their own lights. It was an 18-by-27-inch banner on tanned hide, bordered with soft fur and embroidered with Indian symbols. The symbols included a white star at the center, termed the Indian symbol for light, with a peace pipe at the bottom. Around it was a serpent symbolizing intoxicating drink. "Above the pipe of peace is a tomahawk, the Indian symbol of war; but around the handle of this tomahawk is tied a beautiful bow of white ribbon to show that the only war they are now engaged in is a battle against King Alcohol," said the report of the meeting.[53] The WCTU showed some ethnic sensitivity; it held a temperance convention on the reservation, "for Indians by Indians and with none present but Indians."[54]

Although a small part of Oregon's population, African Americans also were touched by the WCTU. For them, the course of the WCTU was uneven in Oregon. There the first organized work began in 1899. Lucy Thurman, identified by the Oregon WCTU history as "national leader of the colored forces," had agreed to speak before the WCTU at its state meeting in Ashland, as the "leading feature of their program, the drawing card," but "unforeseen circumstances" had prevented her from reaching the city.[55] However, she came through Oregon a decade later, attending receptions in members' homes.[56] This time, black women in Portland organized a new temperance union and named it for her. At the 1911 meeting Mrs. W. W. Mathews, wife of the pastor of the AME Zion Church, read a paper entitled "Secret Sins." The paper was so well received that the women attending wanted to give it more exposure and decided to read it again at a second and larger meeting held at the church.

The Lucy Thurman Union sent invitations to all African-American women in Portland to come to a joint meeting early in 1912, and the union served tea. After hearing the paper, a number of women decided to form an organization that would "stand for and work for higher ideals, progressive ideas and a pure home life," but it was not the WCTU. Some felt they could not take or demand from others the total abstinence pledge. Nevertheless, the resulting organization became the base for an important group for Oregon's African-American women. Called the Colored Women's Council, in 1914 it joined the National Association of Colored Women.

THE LEGACY OF THE OREGON WCTU

Another group the WCTU sought to protect was the female traveler. The Multnomah County WCTU unions led the way in several innovations adopted by subsequent women's clubs. For instance, WCTU concerns about women coming by train into Portland being victimized led the county WCTU to hire Mrs. M. E. Miles in 1896 as a Travelers' Aid matron who met "unprotected girls" at the union depot. Later placed on the railroad company payroll, Miles was treasurer of the county group at the time.

Travelers' Aid societies to steer women traveling alone to respectable boardinghouses and employment agencies run by legitimate groups were a common program of women's clubs. They were designed to intercept women in city danger zones (or perhaps keep "dangerous" women from setting up shop). Ideas of protection also fueled the WCTU push for institutions for female juveniles and adult women, part of a strategy to protect women from male victimization and foster sexual purity. The ideology was evident in phrases like "fallen woman."[57]

The Portland unions also created a "noon rest" for working women in downtown Portland at county headquarters. It doubled as a classroom center and employment bureau, despite perennial funding problems. Establishing a haven or safe harbor for working women, for rural women and children coming into town, for pregnant, unmarried women, for jobless, harried women, or even for themselves was the way women responded to the prevailing culture and women's needs.

A speaker at the dedication of the WCTU noon rest site in Portland described the cultural politics these women—and later clubwomen—played with such facilities. "It is the desire to make this room an understood and recognized headquarters for women, that here they might find comfort, rest and good reading matter," she said during ceremonies. "Our country friends, coming in to shop, will find here a most convenient resting place. To the large number of saleswomen who so graciously wait on us at the stores, we ask the privilege of being also gracious to them, by supplying them with a comfortable, convenient place to rest during their noon hour."[58] Eventually the WCTU building became the site of a Working Women's Club. It was no longer a WCTU enterprise by 1892, the same year the WCTU affiliation with the Refuge Home also ended, early in the decade that began to see a decline in WCTU devotion and membership.[59] By the end of the decade, in Oregon as in Idaho, the WCTU began to wane as the primary voice of organized womanhood.

The WCTU In Idaho

The WCTU came to Idaho soil at Lewiston in 1882, only a year after it came to Oregon. Its leaders, like Oregon's, were comparatively well educated. The WCTU arrived with a Civil War nurse and graduate of Lawrence University named Francena Kellogg Buck from Illinois. In fact, Buck had direct links to the national offices. She had worked in Chicago for Willard and the WCTU. She too had worked as a professional, employed as the first female bookkeeper in the Potter Palmer firm in Chicago.[60] Bertha (Mrs. Potter) Palmer gained national fame as manager of the women's activities at Chicago's Columbian Exposition of 1893, the world's fair that spurred formation of Boise's Columbian Club and others as well.[61]

Some of Lewiston's churches had temperance societies before 1882, which were mobilized with Buck's arrival into a union of the WCTU, the first local union organized in Idaho Territory. It was Buck who induced Willard to come up the river and stop at remote Lewiston during her tour of the Northwest.

Lewiston itself began with gold-seekers coming by steamboat up the Columbia and Snake Rivers in the 1860s. At Lewiston they obtained supplies and pack animals for the search for gold in the heart of Nez Perce country.[62] Provisioned, they headed for mining boomtowns like Pierce, Warren, Oro Fino, Elk City, or further north. Many of them had come east from Oregon's Willamette Valley farms. Others used the Columbia to get to gold fields in the southwest part of Idaho at Silver City or to towns in the Boise Basin in the 1860s. By the 1870s much of the wealth from that initial boom had left the state, precipitating dramatic economic decline. But in the 1880s new gold finds in the Coeur d'Alene mountains of the north, and Wood River valley in the south, set off another explosion of economic activity.[63]

A mark of a city's maturity and permanence was its cultural sites, and Lewiston, formerly "ragtown," had its own. Two years before Willard's visit, the Grostein and Binnard Opera House opened and became the site of many cultural events, including locally produced dramas. The first brick building in Lewiston was the California Brewery, built by the Weisgerber brothers in 1878.[64] By 1880 Lewiston also had that other mark of civilization, public schools.[65]

Women who organized WCTU unions in Idaho, as elsewhere, often founded other clubs too. After Buck organized the WCTU, she also organized an important women's study club called the Tsceminicum Club, which with the WCTU founded a free library in Lewiston. The Tsceminicum Club began meeting in 1898, the same year the first class of mostly women graduated from Lewiston State Normal School, to become sorely needed teachers after only six weeks of schooling. The club had forty members, many of them early women's rights advocates. In fact in 1896 Lewiston had been the site of a July 4 parade for women's right to vote as part of the successful statewide campaign for women's suffrage.[66]

THE IDAHO WCTU READING ROOMS

The WCTU also surfaced in Boise the same year Willard visited the Northwest, and the local newspapers ridiculed it. The Boise WCTU chapter of 1883 had forty members and established its own reading room. The Idaho WCTU report for 1890 described their efforts to keep the library of Boise City afloat. Some musicians gave a benefit concert, and a series of book and ice cream socials helped gather subscriptions, resulting in fifty new volumes and $120.[67]

The contents of this small library kept users in touch with outside events. The reading room received six daily newspapers plus several papers printed less frequently. The Boise union also brought in lecturers and paid their expenses "without trouble and are very positive the temperance sentiment is gaining ground, though the saloons are multiplying. Twenty-five public lectures have been given," said the report. The Boise union, south Idaho's mother union, had seventy-six members by 1890.

Near Boise the Caldwell WCTU began in 1887, only four years after a land improvement company headed by Kansas senator C. A. Caldwell platted the site. A detailed account describing the union's efforts to establish a small public library there demonstrated the problems women often faced in their efforts to carve a place in the community structure for reading in place of drinking. The first president was a Mrs. Lee, a doctor's wife, who raised $75 through a series of ice cream socials. A local jeweler then gave the women permission to keep the books in the back of his store, and the women staffed it. The tiny library moved to a photography gallery then finally to the new Presbyterian-related College of Idaho campus in 1892. In 1899 a committee of the WCTU, Mrs. Gipson, Mrs. Foote, and Mrs. Stevenson, reopened the reading room to give men an alternative to the local saloons. Then located in what was described as a little shack reading room on Arthur Street, it survived on donations, ice cream socials, and home talent entertainments, according to Lalla Bedford, later librarian.

Efforts to get city fathers to establish a permanent city library with standing in city priorities were discouraging. "We knew the men as a whole were not in sympathy with the idea, and it was not exactly exhilarating to know that people would like to run when they saw you coming, and considered you and your reading room project a nuisance," wrote Lina M. Gipson, club member. "But some of the gentlemen were very kind, and we have always had a warm place in our hearts for those men who were nice to us, as we used to put it." The reading room had many community friends, as organizers found out "when we would give, once a year, a dinner, or some entertainment, to help along our expense fund and enable us to send for a new order of books."[68]

Voters finally approved a library tax in 1903. Even then, city officials balked at levying it. Gipson's notes indicated that the women's elation over the election turned to frustration. "You can perhaps imagine our elation, after the hard struggle we had. But when the new council made its appropriations for the coming year there was no mention of anything for library support." When they objected they were told, "not too politely," that the city already had more ways to spend money than there was money to spend "and that there was nothing for the library." That attitude persisted in Caldwell until 1906.

Other WCTU leaders in Idaho made a career for themselves out of WCTU priorities and the confidence membership gave them. One of them was Dr. Emma Drake, a WCTU leader who gained fame as a writer and also became an Idaho legislator.

PROFILE: DR. EMMA F. ANGELL DRAKE

Emma F. Angell Drake, who gained national influence as a popular writer of medical advice, was elected president of the Idaho State WCTU and to the Idaho legislature. Born in New York in 1849, Drake lived in Massachusetts, Kansas, and Colorado before moving to Idaho. She attended Northfield College in Massachusetts and practiced in both Denver and New Plymouth. She practiced medicine for twenty-five years, but gained her fame as a writer of medical books and advice pamphlets. She also lectured on temperance and social reform. She settled at New Plymouth, a planned community built around irrigation not far from Boise. The turn-of-the-century community had as a covenant in its deeds that no alcohol could be sold there.[69]

Drake published widely about taboo topics and thus may have had more cultural influence than most local or regional leaders of social movements. Most of her work appeared in the Self and Sex Series, dubbed the "Ought to Know Books," printed in multiple editions by the Vir Publishing Company of Philadelphia. She with Mary

Wood-Allen, also a physician, published four books for women, while Sylvanus Stall wrote similar books for men.

The women's books included *What a Young Boy Ought to Know, What a Young Woman Ought to Know, What a Young Wife Ought to Know,* and *What a Woman of Forty-five Ought to Know.* The books were published from 1899 through 1928. The publisher touted "the plain language—readily understood by everybody." A page of printed endorsements included leaders of the women's movement and Progressive era campaigns such as Judge Ben Lindsey, Josiah Strong, Mary Livermore, May Wright Sewall, Charles M. Sheldon, and many others. Even Frances Willard and Grace Dodge praised the series.

These early self-help guides mixed scientific information with moral principles. Drake's book aimed at older women discussed the little discussed and often misunderstood problems of menopause, leading one newspaper reviewer to call it "full of most admirable practical advice, and it is written in a sympathetic manner which is the outcome of oneness of sex between the author and those whom she addresses."[70]

The books were probably enlightening and useful in the context of the time. But Drake's published advice, while providing useful information to women on formerly taboo topics, also spread misinformation of the sort that was popular at the time. For instance, her *What a Woman of Forty-five Ought to Know* described the changes of menopause. Published in 1902, it warned women that the effects they suffered during the natural process of menopause were directly related to their behavior during puberty. In *What a Young Wife Ought to Know* (1908), Drake, a minister's wife, advocated infrequent intercourse in marriage as a mark of civilization, in the hope that such attitudes would decrease the power of sexuality and free women to wear less restrictive clothing without fear of arousing men.[71]

A *Washington Post* article of 1908 quoted her as claiming presciently that men's smoking damaged the health of both women and fetuses, and she proposed the rather severe remedy of separate bedrooms. She held that deformities in babies were also caused by various headache powers, anticonstipation teas, and alcohol consumption.

Drake was elected to the Idaho legislature in 1918. In office she worked for women's causes in particular, according to writer Gladys Rae Swank. She introduced House Bill 82 for an eight-hour workday for women, which passed the House but died in the Senate. She and Representative Carrie White sponsored a bill for segregation of the sexes at Idaho Industrial Training School, but it too met that fate, as did their measure requiring the wife's signature on contracts.[72] However, most of her measures eventually passed.

In Idaho, Drake was remembered for her work in the WCTU and as a refined, independent, and competent professional woman. She and her minister husband had three children. She also wrote books on baby and child care and may have been the first woman to give a talk on sex in the schools. Later she too mounted the platform, giving Chautauqua lectures before returning to New Plymouth to live.

WCTU leadership also began taking on the community infrastructure as well as lobbying for legal changes and speaking out. For example, in the southeast Idaho town of Eagle Rock (now Idaho Falls) lived a widow with two children. Rebecca Mitchell had come to Idaho in 1882 and worked initially as a Baptist missionary and teacher. Within a few years she had become an organizer and officer for the WCTU. Mitchell, from Illinois like many other WCTU leaders, organized a school when she discovered there was none.[73] She is also credited with starting the first reading room in Eagle Rock in the winter of 1884–85 at the Baptist Church, with herself as librarian. Besides the local WCTU, she helped organize a Village Improvement Society and a beautification program for the city.

By 1891 many of the original books in the library were lost or worn out and few had been added, so the library was dormant for four years. In 1896 the WCTU took charge, and again the library was patronized by young people. It remained open until 1901, when the Round Table Club, a local study club, began agitating for a city library. Mitchell also helped build the statewide WCTU organization at the same time that the national WCTU became the largest women's organization in the country.[74] Mitchell, with her delicate features and frilly hats, was highly visible statewide. She worked hard for women's right to vote, first as paid WCTU organizer then as part of the Idaho Equal Suffrage Association, going statewide for that cause.[75] She was even named chaplain for the Idaho legislature, said to be the first woman in the United States to have such an appointment. In later years she published an autobiography.

The Idaho Territorial WCTU

By 1887 Idaho had a Territorial WCTU. It held its second meeting in 1888 in Shoshone, a south-central town on the high desert plain founded in 1882. As a railroad center, Shoshone was a magnet for the surrounding area and soon had a reputation for bars and brothels. The WCTU meeting brought a different kind of attention. The Idaho organization's ambitious departments, each headed by a superintendent, included Children's Work, Scientific Temperance Instruction, Press Work, Temperance Literature, Young Woman's Work, Parlor Meetings, Hygiene and Heredity, Legislative Work, Prison and Jail Work, Flower Mission, Railroad Work, Evangelistic Work, Mothers' Meetings, Social Purity, and Suppression of Impure Literature. However, one officer of the club was still dissatisfied with the level of activity. She noted that the National Union had forty-eight departments, while only a few of those were undertaken in Idaho.

Dues were $1 a year, 20 cents of which went to the territorial WCTU and 5 cents to the national organization. Officers included Henrietta Skelton, president (referred to in the meeting report as "the mother of the WCTU of Idaho"); Mrs. Lee of Caldwell, vice-president; Mary E. (Mrs. J. A.) McGee, Nampa, corresponding secretary; Eva (Mrs. J. H.) Barton, Boise, wife of a Presbyterian missionary, recording secretary; and Mrs. J. V. Wallace, Boise, treasurer. Most of these names and names of other members appear elsewhere in later study club rolls. WCTU members often became officers in those groups as well.

One example was Alice (Mrs. J. C.) Straughn, treasurer of the Idaho WCTU in 1889, who became a leader of Boise's Columbian Club and of the Idaho Federation of Women's Clubs.[76] Other examples included Gertrude Lindsey Hays, the Boise WCTU union's corresponding secretary in 1890, and Laura Moore Cunningham, treasurer of the Boise City and later the state WCTU.[77] They too became leaders of the Columbian Club and associated with dozens of other community causes and clubs within a few years. The WCTU in Idaho, as in Washington and Oregon, provided leadership training and inspiration to several women who later took important positions in Idaho clubwork and community campaigns. Or perhaps potential leaders found the WCTU and took charge.

Laura Moore, who with her father frequently entertained Boise's elite social circles, first lived in a mansion on Grove Street where a reception, called by the *Statesman* "a social event," was held for the WCTU.[78] She was born in 1869 in Boise. Her father Christopher, who came to find gold, found more money in business than mining and founded what became the First National Bank of Idaho. She married in 1898. Her husband J. W. Cunningham, with W. H. Ridenbaugh, founded the city's first electric light company in 1887. Cunningham was also vice-president of his father-in-law's bank and treasurer of the school board. Ridenbaugh's wife was the tenacious and gifted Idaho leader Mary Black Ridenbaugh (profiled in chapter 6), who created clubs, university curricula, and institutions. The connections within the small cities of the territories were close, with those active in one enterprise—male or female—becoming active in others as well. In fact, Laura Moore Cunningham, who later lived in a Warm Springs mansion, also held a seat on the board of the Children's Home Society for over thirty years. When she died, she was characterized as "a truly great lady-she lived for others."[79]

The report of the 1888 WCTU meeting in Shoshone indicated that since the first annual meeting in Boise four new unions had been established in the state. Mary McGee noted that although Idaho had much potential for growth, its small population (and great distances) hindered it. "It is no child's play becoming a member of the WCTU. Few women wish to be drones among these busy workers," McGee wrote.[80] Receipts from individual unions ranged from $2 from Nampa to $64.50 from Boise City. Blackfoot, Caldwell, and Eagle Rock also now had unions.

By 1889, only one year later, the WCTU had truly become a territorial organization for women in Idaho, in a state that stretched nearly 500 miles top to bottom and 300 miles side to side, split by nearly impassable geography into north and south. There were twenty-three local unions north to south.[81] The report from the mining town of Quartzburg boasted that, with only four exceptions, every woman in the town—a total of twenty-two—had signed up for WCTU membership. A handful of the local unions reported having established reading rooms in their towns.

The WCTU from its inception in Idaho and the Northwest had an active if seldom successful legislative agenda, at least the first time around. The reform agenda and civic activism of the Idaho WCTU took the women boldly into territorial politics, where they were avoided or tolerated, sometimes ridiculed, occasionally heeded. President Henrietta Skelton in her report under Franchise Department said the group had learned a lesson when it presented a petition at the 1889 Constitutional Convention "to give women the power to protect themselves," with mixed results, including an attack by Abigail Scott Duniway on the WCTU forces. Skelton called for agitation to rouse the conscience of the men to action despite women's reluctance to speak out. "Wrong always seeks a conspiracy of silence, for it cannot bear investigation. So let not one of us stifle agitation just because we don't like it. Self must ever be put out of sight in our work." She recommended adding suffrage as a department to the organization.[82]

Idaho WCTU leader Skelton had asked the territorial legislators for help "to build a wall around this state—put out strong drink." She spoke on behalf of morality and motherhood and concluded by presenting a bouquet to the delegates and inviting them to an ice cream social to be held in their new WCTU reading room in Boise. "I appeal to you and to all Idaho. There was a mother once who held you at her knee. There was a mother once who placed into your life all that which is noble and good," she said, making her emotional appeal both for women's suffrage and for prohibition.[83] Although unsuccessful in meeting her goal, she brought both issues into public discussion before those who had the power to decide them.

Corresponding secretary Mary McGee wrote that no active work was done during the 1889 legislative session because the WCTU could not get its petitions on two issues introduced as bills. One was for a local option vote on alcohol, and another would have raised the age of consent to sexual activity.[84] However, the WCTU president and forty women of the Boise City Union presented two additional petitions to the Constitutional Convention meeting in July 1889, "praying that they would put a clause in the new Constitution, prohibiting the manufacture and sale of alcoholic liquors as a beverage, and also one for the suffrage of women; as a majority of the delegates were controlled by the saloon element, both the petitions were rejected." She noted that two Idaho cities had given women, if property-holders, the right to vote on school questions.[85]

Petitions, the recourse of the powerless, were where most women's organizations, like the WCTU, started when they tried to change the legal and political order. In Idaho in the late 1880s the WCTU's individual unions initiated and circulated petitions for various causes, including the right of school election suffrage (Bellevue) and a local option vote on alcohol and raising the age of consent (Nampa). The report from the Coeur d'Alene union distilled the opposition the WCTU often faced. "Please do all you can to help and hold this Union, they have a town of 300 people, and ten saloons."[86] Many noted WCTU's success in getting scientific temperance taught in schools, which was by now Idaho Territorial law.[87] Membership in 1889 totaled 508 women in 25 unions throughout Idaho, which then had a population of about 80,000.[88]

As other kinds of women's clubs began to emerge, however, the Idaho WCTU's annual report reflected some of the signs of decline for the most powerful women's force in Idaho, as happened in Oregon. The 1890 report from Montpelier in southeast Idaho was grim. "I wish I could give you something in glowing colors that would be pleasing to hear and helpful to others to know. Our Union has a little grace, not much gumption and not a mite of grit," wrote the beleaguered secretary. "We can wear our badges if we can do nothing else, and that brings down on our heads the jeers and ridicule of the popular side of town. If we ever do get the horns in our grip we shall have the grip to hold on, we hope."[89] Nevertheless, local unions reported fundraising and other successes, occasionally through new departments. For instance, Shoshone reported it served an oyster dinner during court week, clearing $100, which kept the reading room running during the winter. Further, a generous Mr. Allen had given the group 150 books as a beginning for its library.

The Fourth Annual Convention of the WCTU held at Blackfoot in 1890 noted that Rebecca Mitchell of Eagle Rock (Idaho Falls) was allotted expenses and $300 a year as superintendent of the franchise department.[90] She held suffrage meetings in Idaho Falls and Blackfoot, but found that getting a suffrage amendment passed would be difficult.[91] However, Eagle Rock reported that women had gained the right to vote in school elections; through successful fundraising efforts the WCTU was able to donate $25 worth of domestic goods "to a poor family during sickness last winter."

By 1900 the decline was apparent. There were fewer club reports. The names in the reports and leadership coincided less with later women's club leadership or memberships, and the annual report detailing the year's activities was only thirteen pages long compared to forty pages in the early years. By 1902 records show there were only 248 members in eleven unions, less than half the earlier total despite Idaho's population growth. By 1905 the annual reports of the state conventions were even smaller, the list of local unions shorter, the state budgets smaller, and WCTU goals less lofty. The WCTU by then seemed more and more taken up with contests, literature, and lectures, in a pattern that was repeated a few decades hence as the women's study club movement and its federations declined after a surge of power.

THE WCTU IN WASHINGTON

The WCTU came to Washington in 1883, only a year or two after it arrived in Idaho and Oregon. Twenty members signed up after Willard and her successor, Anna Gordon, came to Seattle. It too grew fast. The Washington WCTU counted 629 members in King County alone the following year, more than in either Idaho or Oregon and reflecting the larger population base.[92] The WCTU also expanded rapidly in Seattle, with six unions in the city by 1891, the year the Populist Party was founded.

As happened in Portland, the women organized institution-based programs and services to meet pressing urban social needs women faced. They included a children's day nursery and an orphan's home, supporting them through baseball benefits, suppers, and luncheons, even selling drinking water from a booth in Pioneer Square.[93] In 1893 it and other unions got the legislature to pass a Police Matron Bill, although it was not consistently followed. Also as happened in Portland, the WCTU in 1889 funded and opened a White Shield Home for "fallen women" and unwed mothers and their infant children in Tacoma, the port town on Puget Sound south of Seattle. There the Western Washington WCTU supported Maude Turrell's proposal to create the home. Fundraising efforts and business community support put the home into its own handsome brick building overlooking Puget Sound in 1892.[94] This home also became a Crittenton home before the turn of the century.

By 1890 the WCTU claimed 885 members in Washington. As in Oregon and Idaho, members opened and staffed reading rooms. Here the pattern of decline occurred again—by 1898 the WCTU membership in Washington State had dropped to 574 as women found other groups. However, the WCTU's national meeting was held in Seattle in 1899, perhaps the first large national organization to meet in what was then still a small and remote city, convening there after Willard died in 1898. By 1900 twelve unions reported 390 members. A push to make Washington State dry led to a boost in membership with claims of over 2,000 members in 1905, but by 1915 the number statewide was half that and falling, as county after county then the state went dry in 1916.[95]

The pattern of leadership training via the WCTU also occurred in Washington, especially for the early club leaders. Several women in the Pacific Northwest went from WCTU leadership to assume powerful positions in the state federations, trained, tested, and emboldened by their WCTU experience.[96] Also, the WCTU, as a truly national and statewide organization in scope, offered these leaders a unique perspective on organized womanhood that transcended local and sometimes parochial club boundaries.

For instance, one of the leaders in the important Tacoma WCTU was Amy Stacy, who in turn became one of the founding presidents of the Washington Federation of Women's Clubs. Born in 1839, the daughter of a Presbyterian minister in Maine, she came to Washington in 1886 after becoming a teacher of "high mathematics" in New York. She later became known as the mother of the Washington Federation for her leadership in creating it and ensuring that it was nonsectarian and open to all. She also advocated traveling libraries and conservation issues. Well-educated and engaged in professional work like several other Northwest leaders, Stacy later became a professor at Whitworth College, then located in Tacoma.

One of the boundaries facing the WCTU was the boundary of race. In Washington that intersection took some interesting twists. The Northwest had a small population of African Americans concentrated in its largest cities, although it was less than 1 percent of the population in any of the three Northwest states until well into the twentieth century. However, like Portland, Seattle also had an African-American WCTU union. One of its founders, Emma Ray, also became an important leader in the region for many causes before she left.

Seattle's influential African-American AME church had its own Widow's Mite Missionary Society, which gathered small contributions to help support widows and orphans. As part of a nexus of early female activists, many of its members also were members of the Frances Harper Union of the WCTU. Harper, its namesake, was the first published African-American novelist and an abolitionist. The women founded the union in Seattle in 1891, with Emma Ray (profiled here) elected president of the group of about fifteen women.

PROFILE: EMMA RAY

Ray was born a slave in Springfield, Missouri, in 1859. She married her husband Lloyd in Kansas in 1887, and they moved to Seattle in 1889, one of the first black families in the city. They were part of a small but steady flow of African Americans into Seattle and Portland. They sought economic opportunity in the West, like many others, but also came to escape the repressive post–Civil War South. The Puget Sound was about as far away from it as they could get. It was not necessarily hospitable, however. "There were but few of our own people in Seattle when we came in 1889 and at times I got very lonely," Ray later wrote of those early years.[97]

By 1900 there were about 300 African Americans in their small community, and they began establishing institutions and organizations for mutual support, including two black churches. In 1891 Ray organized fifteen women of the Jones Street AME Church into the Frances Ellen Harper Union. The union took its role seriously. The women began helping both the black and white poor housed in the King County Jail and inhabiting the red-light district below Yesler Way, the avenue that belted the waist of the city.

The WCTU union provided services to an outcast group further isolated and disadvantaged by their race. Members took care of people who were ill, sitting with them and cleaning their homes and clothes. The women also visited jails and held prayer meetings as part of their outreach efforts. Historian Quintard Taylor found that the union's highly visible work with criminals, addicts, and prostitutes garnered praise from fellow activists, but opprobrium from the Reverend J. Allen Viney, their pastor.[98]

Viney disapproved of their good works and the attention it took from the church. He felt the union, whatever its name, was doing a form of "church work," and he was displeased with the classes of people who were the focus of the union's efforts. Those people who lived below the belt of Yesler Way in Seattle were often part of the network of widespread prostitution, drinking, and gambling there, typical of port cities. According to historian Taylor, the pastor's attitude reflected a deep division in the African-American community itself, which saw itself as an aspiring, permanent, middle-class group. They resented the lower-class transients who gave their race a bad name.

Members of the WCTU union became discouraged and disbanded the union after the church withdrew its sponsorship. They were fearful of damaging the church's future and hindered in their work by the loss of support. Emma Ray refused to give in, however. She joined one of the white WCTU unions and continued her rescue work.[99] Feeling alienated from the African Methodists, the Rays became Free Methodists in 1899. Under that church's sponsorship, she and her husband Lloyd became leaders of the Olive Branch Mission services in Pioneer Square.[100]

At the national convention of the WCTU in Seattle in 1899 African-American WCTU activist Lucy Thurman came to address the attendees and was entertained at home by the Rays among others. As WCTU "Superintendent of Temperance Work among Colored People" Thurman urged reorganization and revitalization of the union, as she did in Portland at appearances there a dozen years later. Former and new members created a new union, recognizing Ray's work by electing her as president. Ray continued with her WCTU work only until 1900, when she and her husband left to return to Kansas to take up mission work there. By then she had also been named King County superintendent of jail and prison work for the WCTU.[101] She later wrote an autobiography about her work among the fallen and downtrodden, titled *Twice Sold, Twice Ransomed*. It was published in 1926.

Although the WCTU prided itself as an organization open to women of all races, backgrounds, and beliefs, the unions were not exactly integrated. Frances Harper herself criticized the leadership of the national WCTU because no black women had been admitted to its southern organizations.[102] Nevertheless, the organization recognized women of color engaged in WCTU work and offered support and encouragement to them. For instance, in King County, the WCTU in 1911 extended a special invitation to an African-American union called Rebecca to join it.

There were connections that crossed racial lines, but many criticized the WCTU efforts, like later club efforts, to include black women as too little and too late. Willard herself was naive at best and somewhat racist at worst when it came to matters of race relations, as her remarks over the years indicated. However, African-American women capitalized on the WCTU and women's study clubs for the same reasons their white sisters did—education, social justice, services, mutual support, and, in their case, "racial uplift" in the face of a system and culture prejudiced against them.

The Impact of the WCTU in the Northwest

The rise of the WCTU and the issues members pursued in the Northwest were connected to the conditions and nature of the region in the closing two decades of the century. Temperance was an important issue because of the cultural politics in many of its towns and cities. Transient yet fast-growing mining, logging, and agricultural developments often trailed with them saloons and prostitutes but few services or amenities. Communities—let alone community institutions—lagged behind growth and commercial development. Violence and privation dogged many towns and many families. The transience and initial disproportionate numbers of men created an environment not exactly hospitable to women and children in many places. Women through the WCTU and later groups tried to create a sense of community and order by advocating controls on behavior, fostering the benefits of literacy and reading, and seeking political power as part of a moral imperative. The unions concurrently worked to strengthen women's legal status and political standing, with some success, by connecting them to domesticity rather than equity, as women's realm. "Protection of the home" as a guiding principle led to other WCTU goals to benefit women, from suffrage to labor reform to property and education rights.

The presence, boldness, and diversity of the WCTU in the Northwest connected women in the region to others outside the region as well as inside. It also paved the way for the hundreds of women's study clubs that followed, some coming right on the heels of the WCTU activism and following a plan of work along the same lines in their local communities. The work that the WCTU did in establishing reading rooms, in lobbying for better legal treatment of women and children, and in empowering women to speak and act in concert tunneled an opening in the wall excluding women from public affairs. Its light pulled the women who came after toward it, in the same general direction but without the intrusive moral or religious fervor the WCTU sometimes imposed. The organization left more of an institutional legacy in the cities of the Northwest, but it was perhaps more important in the smaller and more remote communities, places where women had less contact with urban trends or the club movement that was growing elsewhere in the country.

The lasting impact of the WCTU in the Northwest is difficult to determine, except where the organization established institutions such as reading rooms or refuge homes that later became accepted public institutions sustained with public funds. The WCTU began to fade as a power within a couple of decades after its founding in the Northwest. However, its impact on the process of settlement and several social movements is clear. Many of the women who were WCTU leaders early in the movement became founders and leaders of several influential women's organizations that followed, including suffrage organizations, particularly in Idaho and Oregon. And the clubs they founded borrowed a practical organizational pattern, plan of work, and supportive culture familiar to the WCTU. That perhaps was its most significant legacy for women in the Northwest.

"ORGANIZED WOMANHOOD"

The National Movement Comes Northwest, 1885–1905

Boise, like growing cities everywhere in the United States, was full of clubs for both men and women before the century ended. Historian Arthur Hart lists some of the clubs for men and women of varying classes and ethnicity that existed in Boise. Besides the WCTU and the churches and their circles there were fraternal organizations and women's auxiliaries. Boise's clubs included lodges such as the Masons, Odd Fellows, and Knights of Pythias and patriotic groups such as the Grand Army of the Republic and the Daughters of the American Revolution. There were also the cause-oriented Boise Prohibition Club, Salvation Army, and Jesuit-sponsored Pioneer Educational Society, and, in response to the former, a Liquor Dealers Protective Association. Professionals already had their societies, and the city had industry-connected groups including a lumber dealers' organization with a wonderful name, the Concatination of Hoo-hoos. In addition, the city had an Irish Fenian Brotherhood, a Scottish Caledonian Club, a German Harmonie Society, and a New England Society. It had athletic groups such as the Jockey Club, Gentlemen's Driving Club, Boise Athletic Club, German-American Athletic Association, Polo Club, Rod and Gun Club, and Pastime Club. For cultural interests, besides the women's Columbian Club, residents could join the Dickens Club, Holland Literary Circle, Bonne Heure Society, or Philharmonic, among others.[1]

The Boise example demonstrates one of the aspects of U.S. society and culture that most impressed observer Alexis de Tocqueville in the nineteenth century—the American propensity to carve its populace into groups, where clubs and fluid affiliations pulled members together in new arrays of social configurations. From men's private clubs and secret brotherhoods came ideas for women's social clubs, but with many differences. Issues of class, race, and place played out differently in sites like Boise, Seattle, and Portland, reflecting their community aspirations, their stage of development, and the needs of new residents, including women, who brought a female perspective to community and civic priorities. Even the distinction of rural versus urban came into question, as rural towns took on an urban state of mind. Clubs became both a testing and proving ground in cultural politics, offering paths to community action, networks of personal and professional support, and enhanced republican ideals. They also offered newfound status.

THE POWER OF ASSOCIATION

Women's clubs had already begun to proliferate, and observers of the national scene recognized the need for and latent power of association. Among them was Civil War leader and writer Mary Livermore. In 1893 she contemplated the future of women's clubs, calling this craze for organizing the result of coming to regard humanity not as a collection of individuals but as a solidarity. "We reach out our hands to one another, and multiply associations for common work and common purposes." It was not, therefore, "a mere blind craze that is sweeping women into clubs and leagues, fraternities and orders, unions, granges, and other societies. It is the trend of the age; an unconscious protest against the isolation in which women have dwelt in the past; a reaching out after a larger and fuller life; a desire to keep in touch with other women who are thinking and acting independently; it is a necessary step in the evolution of women." Further, women were now conscious that something "is lacking in their lives that is conspicuous in the lives of others who are busy in many useful activities, which they long to share."[2] Livermore herself was one of the preeminent organizers of what were largely women's campaigns to raise money and relief for the Union in the Civil War.[3]

Tocqueville, reflecting on the trials of democracy, described the phenomenon in class terms, but also recognized the power of association to effect social, political, and cultural change. He concluded that voluntary organizations in the United States served as a substitute for the stable societies and class relationships of Europe. "Americans of all ages, all stations in life, and all types of disposition are forever forming associations. There are not only commercial and industrial associations in which all take part, but others of a thousand different types—religious, moral, serious, futile, very general and very limited, immensely large and very minute." Americans meet "to give fetes, found seminaries, build churches, distribute books, and send missionaries to the antipodes. Hospitals, prisons, and schools take shape in that way," he wrote. Further, "if they [Americans] want to proclaim a truth or propagate some feeling by the encouragement of a great example, they form an association. In every case, at the head of any new undertaking, where in France you would find the government or in England some territorial magnate, in the United States you are sure to find an association."[4]

The negative side of this tendency, Tocqueville and others noted, was to enforce rather than dispose of hierarchy in a democratic society through formation of small, private coteries that then imposed arbitrary and artificial distinctions to separate the group from the egalitarian crowd—the mob, as others might say. Clubs for men and women could and did create hierarchies and artificial distinctions, using ritual to enforce attitudes of solidarity and exclusion. However, clubs also served as a democratizing and leveling force where members were excited by issues and goals, empowered by the organization itself to take action.

WOMEN EVERYWHERE ORGANIZE

The dimensions of the women's club movement nationally by the turn of the century were phenomenal. One magazine of the time offered a rough guide through the topology:

> Besides every possible variety of literary club, from Shakespeare to the faddists', there are art and mystic clubs, ethical societies, kindergarten associations and mother's congresses, and historical institutions (Daughters of the Revolution, Colonial Dames, Daughters of the Confederacy); there are women's village improvement societies, street-cleaning bands, civic clubs, woman suffrage societies, and associations of collegiate alumnae. Then there are the infinite philanthropic enterprises, whose missions are as varied as are the requirements of the submerged classes.

An important regional example of the philanthropic, single-purpose clubs were the hundreds of guilds established in Washington State over the years to support the Children's Orthopedic Hospital in Seattle.

But there were more:

> There are study clubs in parliamentary law, in economic and social conditions, in penology, charities and corrections; also in industrial conditions and home and foreign missionary work in connection with every religious denomination. There are secret lodges

and fraternities, insurance corporations (such as the Ladies of the Maccabees); temperance and social purity unions; likewise a women's relief corps, a universal peace society, a national body of Jewish women and of colored women, a federation of American business women, a national association of nurses and many political organizations.[5]

And, as the writer noted, every well-organized club of any size had its own club departments of finance, education, literature, reforms, civics, arts, and sciences, as well as its committees to investigate state institutions, industrial conditions, and laws affecting women and children. Clubs variously concentrated their efforts on practical reforms and humane measures, such as getting women placed on school boards and library committees or police matrons in jails where women and children were confined and female physicians in institutions where women were treated.[6]

By 1900 Idaho, with its small population of 123,000 and recent statehood, had New Century, Woman's Century, Twentieth Century, and Current Event clubs scattered in towns over the state. Clubs with names like these gave a new dimension to clubwork, because they stressed combining study with action, according to one club historian.[7] Earlier clubs had also woven study and action together to benefit their communities, but now activism had a harder edge to it, a collective can-do spirit in a dynamic age at the dawn of the new century. The growing faith in science and reason, in efficiency, expertise, and progress as pathways to prosperity, combined with women's newfound confidence in themselves and in the power of collective action. This led some groups to new levels of boldness in addressing social problems and community culture. Members felt less hampered by strictures of gender and emboldened by success.

Once the General Federation of Women's Clubs (GFWC) came into being, its membership went from 40,000 in 1890 to 100,000 in 1896 to 800,000 by 1910, passing the million mark by 1920, yet it did not represent even the majority of the women's clubs in the United States.[8] One estimate holds that fewer than half of the existing women's clubs chose to affiliate with the GFWC, although the contention is difficult to prove. Constituted primarily (but not exclusively) of middle-class women (or women who shared what we now label middle-class values), the clubs heightened women's sense of civic consciousness and leanings toward reform, even within more conservative groups.

Women who were active in one club often were pulled into others. The clubs themselves invited visitors from sister clubs in the city and in the region. National officers frequented the Northwest. The national federation priorities became local and regional club agendas and vice versa. In individual cities clubs and women from diverse backgrounds found they could agree on a plan of action to meet some civic need, regardless of personal differences. They learned the practical process of creating consensus and developing a plan of work. They also found they could exercise collective muscle to influence political structures even where they were closed to them. Club membership became more than a sideline. It became nearly a full-time professional commitment for some women in the Pacific Northwest as elsewhere.

The Dalles—A Case Study in Oregon

What happened in one comparatively small settlement along the Oregon side of the Columbia River where the Oregon Trail travelers crossed from Washington, known as The Dalles, offers an example of how quickly clubs developed in Northwest towns. Established in 1850, The Dalles was a prosperous small town that supplied Oregon Trail travelers on the final leg of their long journey. It soon became a prominent port for steamboats on the Columbia.

An 1898 issue of a newspaper titled *The Dalles Times-Mountaineer,* published by the Ladies of The Dalles Public Library, listed the women's clubs found in this one town. In an article entitled "Women's Societies," the dates these women's groups were founded also demonstrated the breadth of the club movement even in the Northwest before the turn of the century. The list included many clubs that never joined either the state or national federations. Most such clubs have now been lost to history except for scattered references such as this one.

What happened at The Dalles also suggests a rough chronology for women's activism and diverging interests, going from church aid societies to the WCTU to benevolent organizations to lodge auxiliaries to patriotic groups and women's study clubs. The long list for The Dalles with its population of 3,029 in 1900 included, in rough chronological order, over twenty organizations: Congregational Church Ladies' Aid Society, founded in 1863; the Good Intent Ladies' Aid Society of Methodist Church, 1879; The Dalles WCTU, 1881; St. Vincent's Charitable Society, 1885; the King's Daughters (who made clothing for the poor, primarily children), no date; the Woman's Relief Corps (auxiliary to the Grand Army of the Republic), 1889; German Ladies' Aid Society, 1893; the Taine Class, 1893; St. Paul's Guild, no date; Ladies' Aid Society of the First Christian Church of The Dalles, 1892; Willing Workers Society of Calvary Baptist Church, 1894; Degree of Honor, Auxiliary to OUW, 1894; Order of Eastern Star (Masons), 1895; the Lutheran Ladies, 1896; the Women's Mission Circle of the Calvary Baptist Church, 1896; Pacific Circle Women of Woodcraft, auxiliary to Woodmen of the World, 1896; Harmony Temple No. 12, Rathbone Sisters, 1896; and Rebekah Lodge, auxiliary of Independent Order of Odd Fellows, 1898.[9] These clubs were followed by the Sorosis Club, founded in 1902, and The Dalles Woman's Club, founded in 1911, listed in later federation publications.

This expansion of women's clubs reflected a large national cultural and social movement. By the 1880s, historian Glenda Riley writes about the Great Plains, there were so many clubs available that women frequently belonged to as many as fifteen to twenty clubs at a time, secular clubs of enormous range.[10] Women's clubs in the Pacific Northwest swelled with the commerce and immigration that came with the railroad connections. In Washington, that happened in Tacoma when the transcontinental railroad, extended by Northern Pacific, reached its city limits first in 1883, much to Seattle's irritation. Seattle did not get its own railroad line node in the Northwest web until later, when the Great Northern Railway extended its line. The web increased the number of clubs along with the population as women with club experience elsewhere in the country moved to town. Between 1880 and 1890 Seattle's population alone grew more than tenfold in ten years, from 3,553 to 42,837 people.

The long-awaited railroad web finally connecting towns and cities throughout the Pacific Northwest in the 1880s and 1890s offered more than immigration, commerce, and access to markets. It also put those towns on the lecture circuit and made travel to state and national meetings more feasible. Clubs sponsored speakers who addressed controversial issues, from "race suicide" to women's rights. They brought concerts, plays, and opera. And railroad transportation, with its cheaper and quicker access to goods, also brought the books and magazines clubwomen valued as the tangible embodiment of civilization, education, refinement, and improvement. Men's clubs also proliferated, sometimes spurring women to found their own.

MEN'S CLUB CONNECTIONS

Understanding of the women's club movement is enhanced by looking at how men's clubs influenced it, an intersection often overlooked. This helps clarify the distinction between benevolent organizations and social clubs, a line that women's clubs some-times blurred in their zeal for community betterment and self-im-provement. It also illuminates the prevailing organizational cul-ture to which women reacted, sometimes attracted, sometimes repulsed, but influenced nonetheless.

One category of men's association was the fraternal order, which held an important place in American social structure in the second half of the nineteenth century. W. S. Harwood in the *North American Review* in 1897 calculated that fraternal orders had 5.5 million members out of a total adult male population of about 19 million. The number is probably inflated, but the orders had a significant membership. These voluntary nonprofit associations were patterned after European benevolent secret societies, them-selves modeled on the Freemasons. The Independent Order of Odd Fellows, an important fraternal association in the West, was introduced into the United States in 1819. The fraternal orders had a tradition of the lodge system of organization, democratic self-government, confidential meetings, and rituals combined with social activity and member services such as paying death benefits. The first American fraternal order was the 1833 Improved Order of Red Men, which included ritualized Native American customs. Even trade unions adopted the lodge form of organization.

Historian Mary Ann Clawson found that the rise of fraternal or-ders offered insights into issues of class, race, and gender and their intersections with capitalism. If women through their organiza-tions reacted to the isolation and restrictions of gendered domes-tic life, then that same cultural framework also isolated men from domestic life. Fraternal orders reflected in part men's efforts to recreate a kind of "domestic" sanctuary safe from the feminization of the domestic sphere, particularly during a time of economic in-stability, increasing mobility, urban facelessness, and aggressive individualism linked to social Darwinism, all characteristics of the late nineteenth century.

The fraternal order movement, like the later women's club movement, also grew fast. After the Civil War, one chronicler counted 300 different lodges and fraternal orders before the end of the nineteenth century.[11] What defined fraternalism as a social

form in the late nineteenth century, Clawson concludes, was re-
liance on four common elements—corporatism, ritual, masculinity, and proprietorship, in a model of solidarity.[12] Fraternal lodges
and clubs became a middle-class men's haven, one that former
members tried to recreate in the Pacific Northwest in the early
years of settlement.

Lodges in a few places in the Northwest also served as seats of
vigilante law enforcement, in other places as vehicles for civil government and civic betterment, and in others (perhaps all) as
closed, masculine preserves. Where women were included they
were segregated in auxiliaries whose support roles reinforced existing gender roles, yet fostered the same class-related exclusionary status. The importance of the orders to the men who had been
members is reflected in the fact that as the emigrants on the Oregon Trail carried with them their worldly goods, a few of them also
carried treasured dispensations for new charters, beginning in
1846 with authority from the Grand Sires of the Odd Fellows
Lodges in St. Louis, Missouri, and Washington, D.C.[13]

Groups were established in Salem in 1852 and in both Oregon
City and Portland in 1853, only a few years after the cities themselves were founded.[14] The Portland group formed a woman's
auxiliary group, the Rebekah Lodge, in 1855.[15] A lodge was also
instituted at The Dalles in 1856. The Odd Fellows, like other fraternal orders, were hierarchical, with members sorted into as-
cending degrees or ranks.

The first lodge group in Washington Territory was founded in
Olympia in 1855. The territory at that time included north Idaho
and north Montana. Olympia, the site of the first session of the
Territorial Legislature in 1854, became the capital and the site of
much club activity. In 1862 the Washington Odd Fellows united
with the Grand Lodge of Oregon, but gold strikes on the Fraser
River in Canada and at Oro Fino in Idaho led to such an exodus
from Olympia that the lodge was suspended by December.[16] Other
lodges appeared in Walla Walla in 1863, Vancouver in 1866, Seattle in 1870, and even remote Waitsburg in 1871, with its population of 109 in 1870.

The community stability that lodges and women's clubs sought
to foster was hard to come by in some places in the West. For instance, the existence of the Walla Walla lodge was also threatened
by gold, the gold of the Bannack (Idaho City), Boise, and Placerville mines in Idaho, causing the membership to drop precipi-

tously as it had at Olympia.[17] The Olympia lodge was resuscitated by the end of the decade, but this remark from a 1913 history of the lodge distills the nature of early settlement in these territories: "Lodges had been established in the only towns of promise in the Territory—Olympia, Walla Walla and Vancouver, and with the exception of Seattle there were no other centers that gave hope of anything but transient settlement."[18] The Odd Fellows Lodge came into Seattle in 1870, along with secret fraternal societies such as the Good Templars and Knights of Pythias.[19]

Women's auxiliaries followed many lodges, but most women were left out of this exclusionary and ritualistic movement. Those in the auxiliaries generally served in a support and service role, never a central role in men's lodge activities, although some lodges tried to give women more of a role later. Women missed out on the formal fellowship and sense of belonging such lodges offered members. Another kind of organization stressing men's fellowship also influenced women's groups, especially in urban areas. This was a different kind of men's group, the urban, urbane, and very private social club. According to an 1873 club historian, New York City then had 100 such clubs with 50,000 members, three-fourths of them married. Half of the members were "bankers and heavy businessmen, men of extensive financial transactions and responsibilities." Others were professional men, "literary lions," and those who aspired to club ranks. Only London had more clubs, he wrote proudly.[20]

THE EXALTED MEN'S CLUBS OF NEW YORK CITY

The men's private social clubs differed from the fraternal organizations, but they too had an impact on the women's club movement and what some women's clubs aspired to (or consciously avoided), even to the point of fearing connotations of the word *club*. The New York clubs began with three organizations in 1838, at roughly the same time that maternal associations began to grow among women of a different class elsewhere in New York State. Very much an elite movement at first, the Americanized men's social clubs tended to be less political than their English counterparts, with their labor "less mental; their admission to the sanctum less socially authoritative, and their material less homogeneous."[21] Their historian, Francis Fairfield, described one club in nearby Middletown, Connecticut, as being a conversational club composed of professors, lawyers, doctors, clergymen, and professionals, a kind of forerunner of the study club. However, New York had "as yet nothing of the sort, unless the Woman's Club may be regarded as holding that position."[22] He referred to the educational and intellectual focus of Sorosis, founded only five years before his history was published.

Unlike the women's clubs, the men's clubs were expensive enterprises, typically costing members $40 to $60 in initiation fees and steep monthly dues. They carried names like City Club, Beethoven Club, Andrew Jackson Club, Gotham Club, and Liberal Club. Fairfield compared the clubs to cafes, which gave a man a place to eat, drink, smoke, and read the papers, a home "where he sees friends, writes his letters, dines, and spends the greater part of the day."[23] The writer did not include in his list of benefits clubs as places where professional and personal networking took place. That was assumed. Fairfield said gambling was generally forbidden and behavior decorous. He asked, why should women be concerned?

Men's clubs offered several advantages and their own rituals of behavior: an "admirable" table prepared for members; a library with "a splendid collection of rare and interesting books" and magazines from the circulating library; a writing room with little tables and supplies; and a ventilated smoking room "with its after-dinner stories and cigars of the finest brands." They also offered these men of leisure large morning rooms with "all the leading papers, aired, cut and temptingly laid out for perusal," in addition to dressing rooms and bathrooms, all that "luxurious tastes can demand," except bedrooms.[24] Except perhaps for the smoking room, women too would very much have enjoyed the considerable personal, cultural, and social benefits of such clubs. Women who knew about them or about lodge quarters recognized what women without club resources missed. Some women's clubs avidly pursued building their own clubhouses, such as the influential Century Club of Seattle founded in 1896. However, most women rejected the closed, self-aggrandizing, class-driven model of the men's social clubs, certainly in the Pacific Northwest, although elite social clubs were founded for business and professional leaders in the Northwest soon after the major cities reached a certain point in their economic development.

Like the women's clubs, the men's social clubs and fraternal orders declined in membership and importance in the decades after World War I. Their decline was due in part to the success of groups previously excluded. Women, blacks, the working class, and immigrants all gained political and social power, and many entered the public arena of American life. Changing customs, a growing middle class, and greater acceptance of women in various social and professional settings weakened the appeal of all-male, class-oriented institutions. Their formation in reaction to nineteenth-century urbanization and industrialization no longer served the purpose it formerly did, and such groups diminished in influence.

Women's study clubs contained elements of some types of men's clubs, particularly those organized to recognize and support the arts. For instance, the Century Club, founded in New York in 1847 just as the first pioneers took to the Oregon Trail, boasted of Washington Irving and William Cullen Bryant as members. Its goal was "the cultivation of a taste for letters and the arts and social enjoyment." Members included artists, writers, lawyers, judges, and "commercial men," and later publishers and professional men "of all sorts." The club, as an outlet for its members, established *Century* magazine, which became an important cultural and literary magazine.[25] Women's clubs also frequently published magazines and newsletters or sponsored exhibits. This Century Club, however, required a pricey $100 initiation fee and monthly dues of $36 for a clubhouse near Union Square. In comparison, the priciest women's clubs in the Northwest charged $10 a month in dues. Most charged $1 or $2 in monthly dues when they were founded.

The men's Century Club, which had grown to 600 members by 1873, shut out potential members who received two or more "black ball" no votes on their candidacy, a process adopted by some women's clubs who wanted to limit size and/or exclusivity. Members saw as their purpose, as did later women's study clubs, promoting art and literature by establishing and maintaining a library, a reading room, and a gallery of art, at least for a few.[26]

MEN'S SOCIAL CLUBS IN THE NORTHWEST

Exclusive men's social clubs existed in the Pacific Northwest as well, founded not all that many years behind the New York clubs, with the same networking, dealmaking, privilege, and privacy. One example of such a club for business and community leaders was Portland's elite Arlington Club, incorporated in 1881. The club actually dated from 1867, when thirty-five business and professional men gathered informally to organize a "Social Club."

They saw themselves as a "company of men" who "cherish the opportunity to fraternize for mutual enjoyment and relaxation, and to discuss destiny pertinent to them and the city," according to a club history cited by historian E. K. MacColl. The members rarely separated the public interest—what was good for the city—from their private interests—what was good for them in their model of civic and political culture. The club's roster included the city's wealthiest men.[27] Banks, utilities, railroad companies, and Oregon's senators were well represented in club rosters.

Elsewhere, Boise had its Arid Club, founded in 1890, and Seattle its Rainier Club, founded in 1888. The wives of these men often belonged to their own elite social clubs, planning elaborate society events, but seldom did their names appear on the rosters of the typical women's club. Sometimes these wealthy women organized important philanthropic efforts to found an opera house, a children's hospital, or other community services, but rarely did they seem concerned with or focused upon either self-improvement or restructuring the cultural, social, legal, or political environments of their communities, as were the women's study clubs.

WOMEN IN NEW YORK CREATE A CLUB THAT SPEARHEADS A MOVEMENT

The advantages men had in their social clubs (at least those few who could afford membership) spurred a few women to consider creating their own clubs. That happened with the Sorosis Club in 1868, the year generally claimed as the founding moment of the national women's club movement. In fact, Sorosis was created specifically in response to being shut out of a men's club activity, in this case, the Press Club of New York and its dinner for Charles Dickens.

In March 1868 this professional and social club for reporters and editors invited Dickens to dine with members at Delmonico's at the end of his U.S. tour. D. G. Croly, managing editor of the *New York World,* bought $15-a-plate tickets for himself and Jane Cunningham Croly, his journalist wife who wrote under the name Jennie June.[28] Soon other men were trying to buy tickets for their wives, irritating some club members, which in turn irritated Jane Croly and other working journalists who happened to be female.

From their conversations with one another and with other women emerged the idea of creating a setting of their own—a "woman's club." Five women subsequently met at Croly's home to establish a club to "supply the want of unity and secular organization among women." Croly said she and other women "were hungry for the society of women . . . interested in the thought and progress of the age, and in what other women were thinking and doing."[29] They had no plan of work then, nor any plan other than to be egalitarian and support one another in personal and professional endeavors. This differentiated them from earlier women's organizations.

These women were also somewhat sensitive to issues of class that often divided women. "The first club, it was felt, must be homogeneous, hospitable to women of different minds, degrees, and habits of work and thought—it must be representative of the whole woman, not of any special class of women, for the idea of clubs for women was too new to admit of a system of exclusion and division; besides which, it was opposed to the spirit of club life."[30] Clearly members rejected many of the tenets of male club life. The club contained, however, the rather atypical grouping of many of the leading female writers of the area.

They met a week later and selected as the club's object "to promote agreeable and useful relations among women of literary and artistic tastes," independent "of sectionalism, or partisanship." The document called upon the imagery of male fraternity. Furthermore, the club "aims to establish a kind of freemasonry among women of similar pursuits, to render them helpful to each other, and bridge over the barrier which custom and social etiquette place in the way of friendly intercourse."[31]

The club filled a niche and continued to grow. Its initiation fee, in contrast to the high costs of the men's social clubs, was $5. The members met monthly, for lunch and conversation, sharing expenses. The problem of finding an appropriate name persisted. Croly said members found Bee images unacceptable, *Woman's League* sounded too political and belligerent, *Sphinx* hinted mystery and concealment, *Columbia* was hackneyed; after going through dictionaries, the group decided on *Sorosis* as a novel and graceful name. Croly became vice-president, and poet Alice Cary president. By June 1868 the club had fifty members, up substantially from the fourteen who first attended.[32] By contrast, the more reform-oriented and better-organized New England Woman's Club drew 135 to its first meeting in Boston, also held in 1868.

At one point the New York Press Club, the impetus for Sorosis, invited club members to breakfast, but the men did all the talking. The women's club decided to respond in kind, inviting members to tea and denying them the opportunity to speak. The groups later got together annually for dinners at Delmonico's, without restriction on speaking.[33] Including men in a few annual events controlled by club members became a tradition for many women's clubs.

Women in the more politically active women's clubs recognized that they had to work through men to accomplish their goals (and allay men's suspicions). Members also recognized that their clubs were potential targets. To justify their organizations to men, and to themselves, they developed a tradition of calling upon female exceptionalism and connecting it to female activism. Men should be included in club activities, said Portland Woman's Club president Mrs. J. C. Card in her 1897 presidential address. "Let us often invite men to our meetings, and having them here, let us so hospitably entreat them that they will go away knowing the Woman's Club as it is, not as a hostile war party of irreconcilable 'new women,' but as a gathering of high-minded ladies, who are earnest to know and to do."

But at the same time these were women who "have not sunk the love of beauty in the acquisition of knowledge, nor the charm of life in pursuit of their rights; in whose lives bloom the sweet and gentle virtues which have been the peculiar possession of womankind since the world began, along with the fuller knowledge, the wider intelligence which unobstructed study, fearless thinking and unhampered opportunity bring."[34] Men frequently were invited to some club activities at least on an annual basis, although they were generally social affairs rather than work sessions.

LOOKING FOR A VOICE

The Sorosis and the New England Woman's Club of 1868 laid down diverging tracks for later women's study clubs. Sorosis membership included a number of professional women caught up in careers made difficult by the restrictions on gender. The members of the New England Club, which the stalwart Julia Ward Howe led as president from 1871 until 1910, consisted mostly of women who did not work for wages but made reform their careers.[35] Initially the pursuit of careers or jobs, in the classic sense, seemed far too selfish to them, despite the potential for reform such women could carry into professional lives.

The fluid cross-fertilization of East and West was evident even in the New England Woman's Club, founded by Caroline Severance in Boston in 1868. Severance, the first woman to lecture in Boston before a lyceum association, in 1855, was a tireless worker for temperance, abolition, and reform, later founding the Friday Morning Club in 1891 in Los Angeles after she moved to California. It became the largest women's club in the country, with 300 members by 1897 and 1,000 by 1909. She also worked for women's suffrage there.[36]

The success and growing visibility of the Sorosis and New England Woman's Club spurred the formation of other widespread organizations, alliances, and even experiments, like the short-lived Woman's Parliament in 1869, the 1873 Association for the Advancement of Women, the 1888 National Council of Women, and the General Federation of Women's Clubs in 1890. Croly had hoped the Woman's Parliament would become a permanent body, a kind of shadow government representing women on subjects of vital interest to themselves and their children, such as sanitary reforms or female labor. In this parliament, women would have the privilege of voting and debating public affairs. Her idea lost by a vote in Sorosis, however, because many members wanted the club to remain more social and less political in nature, an issue that came to divide many clubs.

Those who wanted to pursue it adopted a resolution creating the Women's Council of New York City. The resolution's statement on philanthropy expressed a prevailing belief about assistance and the worthy poor and the promise new methods held. "Resolved, That charities, however extensive, are only palliatives, not cures, of social disease, and that having learned how to work in the 'small things' of their own churches and communities, women must now turn to the 'greater things' of the world itself, and bring their experience and their energies to the task of a thorough social regeneration."[37]

The idea of concerted national action resurfaced in the Association for Advancement of Women, which held annual conferences known as the Congress of Women. Consisting of an elite body of a few hundred women, meeting mostly in the Northeast for the presentation of papers and discussion, the group had modest goals in comparison to more radical suffrage organizations. At the conferences, members focused on education, social welfare, and women's unique role as moral guardians. The last congress was held in 1897, eclipsed by both the rise of women's clubs throughout the country and the creation in 1888 of the National Council of Women, which united representatives of dozens of national suffrage, temperance, and other organizations, and then the General Federation of Women's Clubs, founded in 1890.

The women's club movement was not a tidal wave flowing west as it is sometimes conceived. Local club histories show the movement to be more like a rising tide, a welling up, but it resulted in a flood nonetheless. Names and programs were replicated in many places. In 1902 women in The Dalles had a Sorosis Club, as did the women of Spokane. The names *Fortnightly, Sorosis,* and *Century* were used in many places by many groups. Pullman, Washington, and Eugene, Oregon, two university towns, both saw a Fortnightly Club established in 1893, each founded by the wife of the new university president there. Perhaps the original Fortnightly Club was established in Chicago in 1873, with Jane Addams, Bertha Palmer, and Ellen Henrotin counted among its early members. Nearly all the presidents of the huge and influential Chicago Woman's Club received "their first club training" in the Fortnightly.[38] Club leaders of small groups often became leaders of large clubs focused on civic activism in the Northwest too. One type became a training ground for the other type.

Ideas and methods spread. The fluid women's club movement took diverse forms, creating a new taxonomy of women's organizations. The study clubs, the primary focus of this book, constituted one of those forms, but as club minutes demonstrate, there was considerable overlap with other forms. Study clubs tended to focus on self-improvement, culture, and social problems. The society clubs staged social events; moral reform societies, related to the early-nineteenth-century examples of women's organized activism, continued campaigns; charitable societies supported particular causes or populations, such as hospitals or orphanages.

The social heritage clubs took on civic improvement projects from time to time, groups such as the Colonial Dames, the Daughters of the American Revolution, the PEO, and the Eastern Star; the auxiliaries to men's organizations grew; church groups, with long histories of activism as female mite societies, cent societies, prayer societies, missionary societies, and sewing circles, continued; community improvement clubs, often with both male and female members, took up practical projects in their towns or neighborhoods. Study clubs occasionally had male and female members. In those organizations that included both men and women, men tended to fill the leadership positions, or the women were consigned to auxiliary or support groups.[39] All the categories, however, were permeable. Club projects crossed categories, and sometimes clubs themselves changed from one to another.

Later, partly as an outgrowth of club activity and access to professional training early in the twentieth century, women began to form their own professional associations, taking up causes and concerns related to the profession. Teachers, nurses, writers, and other professionals created their own organizations for support, validation, education, and networking, spurred by the fact that men's professional groups were often closed to them. New groups such as the Business and Professional Women also reflected the rise in women's outside employment.

Sometimes the clubs became schizophrenic about their purpose. For instance, the original Sorosis Club claimed not to be a philanthropic or charitable organization; "in fact, it persistently disclaims any benevolent object in its existence, except the general one of collective elevation and advancement," founder Croly wrote. Yet the original Sorosis—although unique in declaring itself a self-improvement and study club from the start—soon found itself unavoidably engaged in social activism. Shortly after its founding it named a committee to investigate the foundling asylums in New York and the high infant mortality in them. Croly, Mrs. Horace Greeley, Mary Owen, Anna French Dinsmore, and others collected "an astonishing array of facts, which were presented to the Club, and published in the *World* newspaper, June, 1869." Once the press took up the subject, a new Protestant foundling asylum was founded, followed by a Catholic one.[40]

The club soon named a philanthropic committee for inquiry and investigation into causes and conditions "with a view to individual enlightenment, into methods best suited to reduce the amount of evil and suffering, and advance the sum total of right-doing and happiness."[41] In this way, social activism for Sorosis and hundreds of other clubs was bound up with self-improvement and enmeshed with concepts of progress and modernism. A department set up for philanthropic or welfare work became the focus for the club, or new concepts studied under social welfare were tested in village improvement.

The Sorosis Club exemplified the trend. Gifts and grants from Sorosis over ten years' time included clothing and passage to Europe for a consumptive woman and her infant, $50 to yellow fever victims at Memphis, flowers to the West Point Soldiers' Burial Ground, clothing to survivors of a fire in Milton, Pennsylvania, $50 to the Working Women's Protective Union, $281 "to needy persons," and a $100 Christmas gift to Children's Aid and another charity, plus $100 loaned to a widow. It was quite an effort and outlay for women of limited means who defined themselves as not engaged in benevolent or philanthropic work. They raised money for these causes through "entertainments" (such as an illustrated lecture on Japan), donations, and benefits.

Club members then as now used considerable creativity to raise funds for their projects. In addition to lectures, bazaars, plays, tableaux, and other staged events, some clubs, especially in remote areas, produced newspapers to meet a community need, boost literacy, and raise money.

Club Newspapers in Pacific Northwest Towns

Women were often anxious to undertake new challenges that gave them not only new skills but also greater visibility while meeting community needs and raising money. Although frontier editors were usually men, clubwomen, recognizing the need for a community newspaper, in a few places started their own. Such papers ran on a shoestring and often were produced without benefit of modern printing technology, a stopgap until a publisher set up shop. Later in a community's history a group of women might take over an existing paper—with the owner's support—to produce single editions they could sell to raise money while they explored controversial issues like suffrage.

An example of the former occurred in Idaho mining town of Soldier on the Camas Prairie. There women in 1893 formed the Soldier Literary Society. Their project for civic improvement was to start a newspaper. They began publishing their own handwritten newspaper. The *Soldier Weekly News* came into being on January 13, 1893. "We make our editorial bow on the sea of journalism, with some misgivings as to our untried ability to please all, but with the aid of the members of this Society and an earnest effort on our part, we hope to issue a weekly, a journal which may interest and amuse each and every member of this Society."

The editor added that the paper would be "strictly independent" on politics and solicited contributions. It was also to be a high-toned effort. "Any article calculated to injure the feelings of any member of our Society or any citizen of our place will not be accepted. As many of the 'home staff' possess decided talent in the journalistic line, we may expect newsy and interesting contributions." The paper had lined up a number of correspondents and promised legislative coverage as well as news of events of interest in the area.[42]

A few club leaders ended up in journalism. In the mining town of Salmon, Idaho, a club leader undertook publishing the newspaper there. Ada Chase Merritt, who ran the weekly for years, was vice-president of the Salmon Chautauqua Literary and Scientific Circle. She was an officer in the Woman's Relief Corps and Order of the Eastern Star. In 1900 she ran for treasurer of Lemhi County and won and in 1893 had been the only female delegate to the state's silver convention, according to historian Leonard Arrington. She and her husband Henry Clay Merritt had moved from Nevada to Salmon in 1883. She initially taught school and in 1888 bought an interest in the local paper, which she ran until 1906. Besides the paper, she ran a job-printing shop and a storefront. A Democrat who became a Populist, she was not afraid to engage in the kind of political criticism her male colleagues used.[43]

A number of years earlier, beginning in 1879, women were listed as editors of the *Advocate* in Idaho City, northeast of Boise. The paper, with student correspondents, also covered nearby towns. The Idaho City staff for the handwritten newspaper included as a young student reporter Permeal French, who later held positions as an officer in several women's clubs and won fame as Idaho's elected superintendent of public instruction. She embodied for many what women could do, given education, civic involvement, and the right to vote.

PROFILE: PERMEAL JANE FRENCH

Permeal Jane French was born in 1868 in Idaho City. Her father was a miner, and her mother often took in sewing to supplement the family income. Academically gifted, she was fortunate when Oxford-educated Gilbert Butler came to find gold but ended up teaching, according to biographer Richard d'Easum. French excelled in her academic work and went to school at Notre Dame Academy in San Francisco, graduating in 1885.

Her father died in 1884, and Permeal came back to help with a boarding house her mother had started in another central Idaho mining town, Bellevue, not far from what became Sun Valley. She worked at the boarding house for a few years but had dreams of better jobs. French gained some local fame for her roles in regional social and cultural events such as plays. With the help of a local legislator she was nominated for the position of journal clerk of the Idaho Senate for the second session of the state legislature and won, 12–6. Paid a substantial $5 a day, she kept the proceeding records while gaining political understanding and connections.

She became a teacher at nearby Hailey in 1895, where she was also a member of the Hailey Literary Society. The next year she taught at Silver City, a mining boomtown in the huge county covering the southeast corner of the state. There she assisted the man who had been state superintendent in 1892, leading to her own decision to pursue the office herself a few years later. While in Owyhee County she made several influential friends, including Belgian-born mining magnate J. R. DeLamar. Historian Arthur Hart says that oral tradition claimed that DeLamar bought the Moore Mansion in Boise from banker Christopher W. Moore as a home for the future Mrs. DeLamar. Supposedly the object of his affection was Permeal French, but she turned him down.[44] She never married.

In Silver City French was involved in many Catholic Church and community events. She gave elocution lessons in her spare time and showed up as a speaker on Fourth of July programs. Suffrage came to Idaho women in 1896, and she decided to run for state superintendent in 1898, capitalizing on suffrage—and a split in the Republican Party. In 1893 the legislature had set up elected county school superintendents and also set the salary of the office of state superintendent at $3,000 a year, no small sum then.

She won easily. With the help of women's clubs and others, while in office she got bills passed that gave her power over the county superintendents and strengthened the state's public schools. The bills included provisions that strengthened teachers' rights and required them to pass exams in order to teach. They also set responsibilities and limitations on trustees. As the chair of the educational committee of Boise's Columbian Club, she was in a good position to support their proposals and federation proposals such as bills supporting property rights for women and the right of married women to sue. Elected state superintendent twice, French was defeated in 1902 in a Republican tide. She returned to Hailey and the Bellevue boarding house nearby (her mother had since died), rejoining the Hailey Literary Society.

When agricultural land opened up in a new development in southeastern Idaho near what became Richfield, she entered the drawing through a friend, and her number won the right to buy. The land sold for 50 cents an acre plus $35 an acre to buy permanent water rights from the new irrigation company. To the surprise of many, she kept the land and even worked it before finally selling it, spending summers there from time to time. In 1908 her old friends on the University of Idaho board of regents, which by then included Columbian Club and WCTU leader Gertrude Hays, remembered her. They decided French would be the perfect woman to serve as the new dean of women for the university. French had worked in the capitol building alongside S. L. Hays, Gertrude's husband and state attorney general, when she was state superintendent. She also spoke at the 1902 ceremony dedicating the new dormitory at the University of Idaho to Mary Black Ridenbaugh, also a Columbian Club leader, who fought for the university and programs for women while she was regent.

At the University of Idaho French had a long and illustrious career. Over the decades she instructed hundreds of young women in manners and morals while she enforced strict disciplinary codes. She entertained visiting dignitaries frequently and was heavily involved in all the university's affairs. Thousands of students over the years, male and female, came away from the University of Idaho with personal Dean French anecdotes, stories that reflected both her sternness and kindness.

She took a leave of absence in 1921 to do academic work at George Washington University and gained an honorary degree. She also received two degrees from the University of Idaho. She became, quite literally, an institution at the university before she retired in 1936.[45]

Editors of the 1879 newspaper included Emma Bright, Nellie Davis, and other women, and perhaps some other students like the eleven-year-old French. Boise City editors included sisters Carrie and Ella Cartee, working for editor and manager Thomas Haney. The paper also covered the mining towns of Placerville and Granite Creek.[46]

The surviving issue contains a desultory report on local school conditions:

> It [the school house] has three windows and thirteen desks, and three slabs without any desks. There are thirty-nine scholars going to school now but there are some more scholars to come yet. This school house is very old and all the things which are in it. This

school house is a very dirty one. The more you scrub it, the dirtier it looks. It has been scrubbed very many times but still it looks dirty. The stove which we have is a very old one, it has been here ever since the first time of school. I would rather go to school than to stay home.

The passage also shows why women in clubs often tried to brighten schoolrooms as more than a matter of aesthetics.

Hungry for news, local residents made these homegrown enterprises successful in the years before a "real newspaper" with press and editor came to town. The papers helped create a sense of community as they informed readers. Such handwritten papers, often produced with use of crude copying techniques, provide insights. The February 10, 1893, issue of *Soldier Weekly News* noted that its circulation was increasing rapidly, as was its advertising.[47]

From Church Societies to Study Clubs to Causes

Women long had been the mainstay of churches, especially Protestant congregations. Church societies frequently began as sewing circles that combined handwork with discussion of religious works. As early as the 1830s in urban areas many members had moved beyond church-centered groups to secular temperance campaigns such as the WCTU, to missionary support, or to rescue work out in the field, albeit frequently under the direction of ministers. However, toward the end of the century some church-related women's groups remade themselves into study clubs. An example was found in the Mt. Zion Baptist Church, an African-American congregation in Seattle, itself founded in 1894.

The church soon had an active Ladies' Aid Society that staged most of the church's benefits and fundraising projects. In July 1901 the members established what they called a literary society to reach beyond the church. The resulting Evergreen Literary Society became a popular organization, bringing dozens of lectures, dramas, and concerts to the African-American community.[48] For African-American women, excluded from most of the mainstream social institutions, belonging to these organizations was doubly important. In such organizations they found empowerment, a sense of belonging, and control over their own affairs. Club activities and events enriched their lives and fostered the shape of their self-improvement efforts, which they called "uplift." They also used them as vehicles to provide community services and meet needs in the African-American community not likely to be met elsewhere or to establish stable social and class status. And through them women accrued affirmations of self-worth as well as the important network other women found in organizations.

An Oregon example of the transition from religious to study club programs was the Women's Missionary Society of the Congregational Church in Albany. The women organized in June 1889 to cultivate "a missionary spirit among its members." By December 1890 they had decided to focus on a single subject for each meeting and have all members speak on it. Society dues were 5 cents a month, and the women decided to open the group to men as honorary members—if they paid $1 a year. By 1891 the women had decided to begin social welfare work "by assisting some needy society." They sent clothes and other aid to Hood River, Oregon, and Yaquina, Washington, to assist women and families poorer than themselves. For self-improvement and education they also began to study missions in exotic places, which became an avenue for the study of cultures of distant lands.[49]

An Idaho example is found in the Amphictyonic Council, begun in Parma, an agricultural development outside Boise. The club was founded in 1897 as a church support group. Its formal transition to study began with what members called an "experiment." Members selected articles to read at a meeting then discussed them. By 1901 the minutes show members began presenting papers and working on a public library for Parma. Besides offering a social center for women, the club helped get the first church built at Parma then tackled civic improvement through city beautification and trash cleanup. It raised $54 through an oyster feed and bought a church organ used in the school until the church was built.

The club later established a membership fee dedicated to the library fund and eventually joined the Idaho Federation of Women's Clubs. By 1910 club records show more direct activism. It lobbied the city council for enforcement of ordinances and garbage collection. It successfully established and staffed the city library. The Amphictyonic Council had by then grown large enough to divide into departments to match member interests and time commitments. They included historical, educational, household economics, legislative, civic, and arts and crafts committees and one for general federation projects.[50]

The emboldened women of the Amphictyonic Council were not above using confrontation to enforce social morality in their town, according to a local history. They once held an unscheduled

emergency meeting to deal with some "suspicious-looking females who had showed up and pitched their tents right in town."
The clubwomen supposedly delivered a note reading "your business is known and you better move on," signing it the Amphictyonic Council. The unwanted women left.[51]

Women sometimes fell away from other groups to create new
clubs to respond to particular needs or interests in a city. The department of one large club might become an independent organization. This was a dynamic system where a perceived need was
followed by an organizational response. Such was the case in
Spokane, when several organizations flowed out of one, and again
a physician, Dr. Mary Latham, emerged as a key leader.

PROFILE: DR. MARY LATHAM

The Ladies' Benevolent Society of Spokane, founded in 1889 as
the city's first independent women's organization, materialized to
handle community welfare needs. Members also began agitating
for formation of a humane society after a man brutally beat a horse
to death on a Spokane street. In the rough streets of the new city
stray dogs were frequently picked up by city police and clubbed to
death, a practice criticized by the local newspaper as well as by the
women.[52] One of the outraged women became secretary-treasurer
of the resulting Humane Society, which also took on children's
needs. She was Dr. Mary Latham, a physician who had settled in
Spokane in 1887.

Mary Archard Latham was perhaps Washington's first female
physician with what others viewed as standard medical training
and practice. Born in Ohio in 1844, she graduated from Claremont
Academy and married Dr. E. H. Latham in 1870 at age twenty-five.
They had three sons, and it was not until the 1880s that she herself pursued medical training, graduating from the Cincinnati College of Medicine and Surgery in 1884. Latham felt privileged to be
part of the first class of women to be admitted to the clinical wards
of Cincinnati General Hospital as full-fledged students. She began
practicing in Cincinnati, but moved to Spokane in search of a health-
ier climate. When her husband subsequently moved to the Okanogan
Reservation to continue his practice there, she stayed in Spokane.

Latham claimed a specialty, women's and children's diseases. In
a move that validated her training and expertise by the standards
of the time, the directors of Spokane's Bio-Chemic College elected
her to the professorship of obstetrics. As a physician she also

chaired the Washington Branch of the Queen Isabelle Association (medical department) of the Columbian Exposition.[53]

Active in community causes as well as medical circles, she along with other women walked Spokane's streets canvassing house to house to collect books or donations for the city's library. This effort consolidated WCTU reading rooms into a public library for Spokane, established in 1894. Latham remained a director of the Humane Society and also took over management of the Spokane Children's Home, a Ladies' Benevolent Society project. It grew from a plan to establish a home for the indigent. As Spokane's first charity, the campaign gained considerable public support, and a ball in the Van Dorn Opera House contributed needed funds.

At first the home housed both the elderly and children, but in later years became the Spokane Children's Home. The group established a Women's Exchange for the sale of homemade items to provide poor women a means of income.[54] It also allowed members who made goods to sell their products and retain some of the proceeds. Later Latham realized a dream, to open and run a hospital for women on the North Hill. Like Idaho's Emma Drake, she also wrote about her views on medical issues and cultural politics for area newspapers and magazines.[55] She was remembered for them and for the humanitarian projects and programs she created.

Sometimes women's clubs grew out of a hunger for networking and action, with little idea of what programs or causes the group might pursue. For instance, several women in Idaho's Mountain Home met in 1903 "by invitation for the purpose of organizing a club."[56] According to club minutes, the group initially called itself the Matrons Club. Two months later, one of the members reported that "she had learned that one club was studying music and another art education. She was in favor of taking up the work of the old masters in art if agreeable to the club."[57] However, in the tradition of form before substance, the women spent time selecting the club flower and colors before determining what they would study.

Finally the group chose the name *Sub Rosa* and decided to create village improvement and educational committees. It had also established parliamentary drill and book reviews as regular features. By April the group had opted to study Henry Wadsworth Longfellow and James Russell Lowell and presented papers on village improvement. By the end of the year Sub Rosa members—as happened in other study clubs—began answering roll call with something from current events or a favorite quotation. The women had also settled on some practical projects for community improvement, such as graveling the school grounds and raising money for furnishing a gymnasium.[58]

By 1908–9, only five years after the club was founded, the club's elected president was Mrs. L. B. Green, who went on to lead the state federation through passage of an extensive legislative agenda. Village improvement now included politics. In June the group's program was "The Immigration Problem" (a growing concern nationally) and "What Should We Tell the Child." In September the women studied the relationship between psychology and physiology and the fresh air movement.[59]

These brief examples show organizations in flux in the Northwest and responsive to personal as well as civic concerns. They justified their activism as church-related, then home-related, then as community-minded and personally broadening. In the Pacific Northwest, where many areas were not even settled until 1900 or even later, the organizational flux and rapid change from one level of activism to another were compressed in time and of necessity perhaps more localized in outlook than elsewhere in the country. This organizational development also coincided with a major cultural and political shift in the United States, the rise of professionalization with its companions efficiency and expertise. It also reached club ranks. The trend made them better organized, more effective, and even more efficient, reflecting the guiding principles of the Progressive movement and faith in the future of organized womanhood.

The Professionalization of the Club Movement

Caroline French Benton was one of those who had professional advice for women's clubs. Benton, who wrote a series of consumer-oriented books from *Woman's Clubwork and Programs* to *Living on a Little*, wrote *The Complete Club Book for Women* in 1915. In it she noted that there was no difficulty in starting a club. The question was what should members study? Here she said club members divided into three distinct classes.

The first, she said, consisted of women absorbed for years in domestic duties, to whom the world of books had been practically closed. The club they needed offered self-development and the study of art, music, and literature, "where their hungry minds will be fed." The second type reflected a new generation of women, who were less acquiescent to traditional values and purposes of women's clubs. They were young women, often college graduates, who felt they had already had enough of books. Instead they wanted a club whose energies were devoted to the good of the community. "Who can stop to write dull papers on Italian Art in this day of efficiency?" she said they typically asked. Between those two groups she said there was a third, made up of women who had kept up their reading "in spite of family cares, and who also believe in the practical work outside the home." But these women lacked self-confidence, and speaking in public was impossible. "Even to lift a voice in a club discussion is a serious matter."[60]

The perfect club would provide opportunities for all three types, including helping women to find their voice. It would offer training "to the timid woman who fears to hear her own voice. At first she may merely read a club paper, but little by little she learns to give a quotation, to put forth a motion or offer a suggestion; and finally she finds she can speak without notes, or take her part in a debate and hold her own with self-possession and dignity." For the more action-oriented, there was no limit to community work, such as "questions of hygiene, tenement house wrongs and immigrants' problems." Such women would make the woman's club a center of social service, she said. She recommended against choosing a miscellaneous program for a year's work. "Too often such a choice means a grotesque range from Life in Early Egypt to the Waverley Novels, and from the Panama Canal to Spring Flowers."[61] This seemed to happen more than occasionally in the Northwest, probably due in part to developing programs that reflected individual members' interests and/or expertise in the spirit of consensus. She advised clubs to be egalitarian, to establish a spirit of comradeship, and to open their doors to broader membership.

In her practical how-to guide for municipal housekeeping for clubs, Benton advised enlisting all the clubs in town to work toward some particular collective end if possible—the key issue was "teamwork." To find causes, she recommended taking an inventory of town features and services, checking the condition of roads, yards, water and sewer systems, parks and playgrounds, railroad stations, schools, and tenements. She advocated reading books on town betterment before attacking reforms and researching what cities and clubs elsewhere were doing or hearing from experts on topics like pure milk.[62] Other profitable programs Benton described included a series on systematic housekeeping with papers taking a scientific approach to issues such as laundry and cooking.

Benton included a separate chapter on using woman's problems as a special club focus. She suggested women's employment and working conditions or women struggling with life in a tenement. In discussing the "sick poor, in country and city," Benton proposed a paper on how to help them without injuring their pride and "how relief can be given without pauperization."[63] The chapter on woman's problems ended with an important topic, the relation of women to the state, embodied in issues such as property laws, divorce, the legislative process, and suffrage. The book also included bibliographies on study topics and a model club constitution. Benton's book reinforced what thousands of women felt they were doing or could do together.

As we look back at these clubs they seem homogeneous—white, rather traditional and middle-class in values if not economic status, and generally Protestant, which of course they were. The members themselves, however, recognized that these rather large categorizations covered many differences and variations. They saw the process of club growth and involvement not as homogeneous and status-oriented, but as quite the opposite. They believed they were creating significant new social arrangements and enhancing education and status through a fundamentally democratic social movement and changing the prevailing culture even as they reinforced some aspects of it.

For instance, an Oregon club newspaper of 1898 reprinted a "platform" adopted by the Woman's Club of Lincoln, Nebraska. "Since its object is to help and be helped the following women are invited to become members." The article listed twelve categories of women who were welcome:

> 1) The university graduate; 2) The woman of common school education; 3) The self-educated woman; 4) The woman who belongs to other clubs; 5) The non-club woman; 6) The woman who does not believe in clubs; 7) The woman who does not wish to join a club; 8) The woman who wants to be a member for the name of it; 9) The woman who wants to attend the club meetings but twice a year; 10) The tired woman, full of domestic responsibilities, who wants to be a sponge, fold her hands, take in what the bright, free woman who needs an audience has learned, and then go home refreshed, to her treadmill; 11) The woman without companionship; 12) The young woman and the young-old woman.[64]

Another writer of the time saw greater religious tolerance developing through the club movement. "Every observer recognizes the growing tolerance among all classes of differences in religious belief. Perhaps no one has measured the share that the woman's club has had in the nurture of this tolerance." She credited the very nature of study programs themselves as fostering the tolerance.[65] She noted this particularly in regard to myriad Protestant sects—and it was requisite "that the Hebrew and the Romanist be brought into our club membership," which happened more readily in the Pacific Northwest than in many places with more entrenched social and neighborhood lines and larger populations.

The clubwomen also saw themselves as very different from what they called "society women" and we would call upper-class or elite. One club leader remarked that "even society women are beginning to turn to it [the club idea] as a form of social life which also includes mental stimulus and true recreation." She added that the qualifications for membership were great levelers. They included "real worth, mental and moral endowments, and not the extraneous circumstances of wealth or supposed status. . . . rich and poor alike stand upon a perfect equality there."[66]

Within clubs women found a sense of companionship, self-confidence, and a focus their past activities often lacked, relieving their physical and psychological isolation. Those who had long been members remembered later the camaraderie of the club and a sense of delight in all the papers and discussions "on science, art, literature, education, philanthropy, drama or domestic affairs," as one described it.[67] Another, speaking at the National Council of Women meeting in 1891, said that before the clubs women "in countless homes dwelt in isolation and with no more cohesion or unity of purpose than sands on the shore." Their lives were "pinched and narrow, . . . poor and dumb, yet they aspired for something larger than they had ever known."[68]

Not surprisingly, club members in their zeal to "do everything" sometimes got caught up in causes that were not well considered. One writer described such an experience in one of her own clubs. The club began a campaign to prevent further destruction of songbirds, taking the cause to the public schools, arguing with sportsmen, and writing columns in the local paper about the issue. The group succeeded in arousing public sympathy. However, at one meeting where women sported new spring millinery, somebody counted fifty aigrettes adorning bonnets, leading the writer to propose to the president that she should perhaps do some missionary work in the club itself on behalf of birds.[69]

THE HOUSEWIFE'S UNIVERSITY

In addition to community betterment, the clubs vigorously pursued educational development both for self-improvement and for cultural politics. Women's clubs offered women great opportunity to learn more about a wide range of topics and issues, giving them a window on the world. At the time the movement began, women were by and large excluded from higher education. Oberlin College in Ohio was the first coeducational institution, open to women in 1833 (although it like later institutions pushed female students into a nondegree track). That school caused considerable controversy with its decision to admit both white women and African Americans, but it kept the doors open, making it especially important to black women.[70] Institutions did not freely open their doors to female students at all until much later.

Women seldom had access to more than a basic education. The early club leaders in the Northwest who were college educated were unusual. Although the need for literacy for women as well as men was broadly recognized by the middle of the nineteenth century, few women went beyond basic skills, despite the growing clamor for educating women as republican mothers raising citizens.[71] Daughters of comparatively wealthy families who extended their formal educations attended various "finishing schools" offering limited and gender-bound curricula, such as needlework, French, art, and music. In the middle of the century female seminaries (especially Emma Willard's Troy Female Seminary, first open in 1821) offered more extensive but still gender-bound educational opportunities. It was not until after the Civil War that colleges and universities began allowing women to enter their programs. Excluding technical and women's schools, 31 percent of the institutions admitted women by 1870 and 65 percent by 1880. By 1890 almost 72 percent admitted women.[72] Indeed, early efforts by women's clubs often included petitions supporting women's admission and fundraising for scholarships enabling them to attend.

But for the vast majority of women who did not or could not go to college, or even high school, clubs were like classrooms. Clubs offered a substitute for the intellectually hungry woman or a kind of continuing education for those who had some higher education. Some study clubs were continuations of the intellectual stimulation and contacts women found in college groups. Study clubs did not offer equivalent classwork, but were similar in exposing their "students" to the world of ideas and requiring papers, analysis, research, discussion, and even organized plans of action.

Ella Dietz Clymer, representing the Sorosis Club at the 1891 National Council of Women, remarked on this benefit clubwomen enjoyed:

> Club life supplies in some degree the place of higher education to those women who have been deprived of the advantages of a college course. What college life is to the young woman, club life is to the woman of riper years, who, amidst the responsibilities and cares of home-life still wishes to keep abreast of the times, still longs for the companionship of those who, like herself, do not wish to cease to be students because they have left school.[73]

She also noted that clubs offered a model for teaching governance and practical training for using the vote wisely, once women got it. And there was always the personal enrichment education brings. "The club idea represents woman's craving *to be* rather than to do."[74]

Some doors that remained shut in the East and Midwest began to open for women in the West. One western state after another gave women the right to vote and even elected a few to office, a fact that was not lost on eastern suffrage leaders. In fact, women in the Northwest in some ways enjoyed greater freedom than women in either the East or South, where traditions were more entrenched and gender demarcations more confining and less permeable. The newness reflected in the term *West* also reflected new roles and radical possibilities for women.

One of those important freedoms was greater access to higher education, long a professed goal of many women's clubs. In 1891, the year Stanford University and the land-grant universities in Washington and Idaho opened, a professor at Vassar and Wellesley spoke about coeducation in the West before the National Council of Women meeting in Washington, D.C. She praised the West for being more progressive in educating women on an equal footing with men. "In the West especially has the higher education of women been well supported by the government of the separate States and by institutions that have been founded under the auspices of private individuals." The speaker said that in the West 165 of the 212 institutions were coeducational, and some of those were even founded by women.[75] The new land-grant colleges established through the 1862 Morrill Act offered unprecedented educational opportunity to both men and women (although some schools, like the University of Wisconsin, continued to put women into separate curricula once they came to school).[76]

As the club movement picked up momentum, it changed, just as it changed the women who participated. Clubs used the powers of information and ritual to create a different sense of place in their world. No longer were churches and homes and home values their only reference point in the quest for control of resources and cultural landscapes. Ideas of self mixed with ideas of service, and new political alignments as well as fostering the arts and social justice became part of their new mission. Both education and political enfranchisement were needed to acquire the improvements they wanted. Clubs sought both. Programs, rituals, practices, ideals, and mutual support in new configurations and models were fundamental to the progress of the new century and women's role in it.

"MAKING OURSELVES ANEW"

Life in the Club, 1890–1910

Many of the small settlements in the inland Northwest floated like islands in a sea of sagebrush, the tough, fragrant, silvery green shrub that came to symbolize the West. It also became a symbol to the Columbian Club of Boise, founded in 1892. The women felt it important to choose a club flower and chose *Artemisia,* the sagebrush genus, for the club and its sage green and gold for club colors. Soon they adopted another ritual, one used in club after club. Members were expected to broaden one another's horizons by answering roll call with a favored quotation or some bit of information about current events, as a way to share news about the world and themselves. Clubs made differing choices in their club colors, flowers, mottos, and procedures, but all used the power of ritual to bind members together as they strove to meet common goals and a larger purpose.

Women banding together in the Northwest created space and identities for themselves through new customs, new ways of accomplishing goals, new relationships, and new and improved selves. That included the development of rituals as part of a new way of life in their clubs. Ritual, as a kind of repeated performance, bonds a group together and links its past, present, and future to its members.

Using a particular ritual in a particular time and place calls attention to itself and to the group, diverting attention from other settings as it creates a certain way of seeing the group and society. Rituals offer a satisfying consistency in their patterns, an emotional attraction, and aesthetic values. They have a power to define or mediate reality, as the club (or fraternal order) has power to define perspectives or a "style of feeling."[1] Just as rites reinforce ideas of passage, rituals reinforce a sense of fraternity and cohesiveness. They create a club identity that transcends yet contains and validates the individuals who are part of it. They become a tangible enactment of an ineffable social ideal.

Virtually all of the women's study clubs engaged in some form of ritual, from set patterns for presenting papers to answering roll calls in a certain way. Out of an aesthetic sense women's clubs also found it important to choose unique club colors and club flowers, team colors of a sort, which were then used in the trappings of meetings and programs such as table decorations and banners. Most chose a club motto as well, some witty phrase or general statement about service, culture, or education that served as a common guidepost or reflected shared values. Some added an "object," a generalized goal statement for the group. For instance, the motto of the Portland Woman's Club, which chose the local low-growing shrub with purple berries called Oregon grape as its flower and colors of green and white, was "In great things Unity; in small things Liberty; in all things, Charity." The club's object was "to foster friendly relations and secure concert of action in intellectual, philanthropic and social activities."[2]

Clubs developed other rituals as well, often connected to the arts and putting themselves at center stage. Members frequently wrote and staged elaborate skits and plays each year, satirizing themselves and others. Some put on stage performances of works by local playwrights as fundraising activities, often in the form of humorous melodramas popular at the time. Some staged tableaux (static, costumed symbolic representations of ideas and events) and charged money for seeing what poses had been constructed behind the curtain. Other rituals involved individual participation and competition, as in answering roll call with current events or quotations.

Of course, ritual had always been a critical part of the male fraternal order. Initiation rites, secret greetings, complex ceremonies, and titled ranks of order to which members aspired were customs held in common in such groups, often shrouded in secrecy. Men through rites symbolically connected to baptism and birth regenerated themselves in their exclusive organizations, creating a new kind of family in this band of brothers, made equal partners within the organization. It was no accident that WCTU unions and later study clubs freely used the terms sister and *womanhood*.

Rituals within clubs also reinforced unity and exclusivity in

class, gender, and race and created alliances in the face of change
and all the new opportunities for diversions and consumption.
The doors of clubs could be closed against new immigrants, blacks
migrating to the cities of the North and Midwest after the Civil
War, or a new working class. For men, they also could be closed
against women who were challenging existing social, economic,
and political structures from the security of their sanctified home
realm. For some men, saloons served some of the same purposes
fraternal orders and clubs did for other men and women. For
women, their clubs fostered a female space, private and protected
from the male gaze, where women could test new roles and develop new insights and capabilities.

Rituals, to be complete, called upon symbols. Club colors, mottos, papers, and roll calls all carried symbolic importance. Some
clubs fashioned another ritual out of attempts at self-improvement. They designated someone to serve in the role of critic to advance proper behavior and speech. Critics pointed out foibles in
manners, or pronunciation, or papers, or the conduct of the meeting. In fact, the Sorosis Club itself considered having a committee
of three at each meeting report "upon all violations of business,
order, incorrect speech, faulty manners, and whatever would be
improved by faithful, intelligent and benevolent criticism."[3] This
particular proposal was rejected, but the idea and the spirit behind it remained in many clubs.

The names clubs took for themselves were also symbolic. Clubs
were named for the heroines of antiquity, literary celebrities, or
Greek words. Sometimes clubs took the names of exotic flowers
or the more utilitarian route of the time that meetings were held,
such as Thursday P.M. or Fortnightly. Sometimes names expressed
the place, such as the Portland Woman's Club, or the era, such as
the Twentieth Century. Sometimes they changed what they
called themselves midstream to fit the dynamic nature of club activism. Regardless of the name, motto, or colors, many of them
also adopted a formalized ritual of method that governed their
meetings and their relations—the elaborate code of parliamentary procedure.

THE RITUALS OF PARLIAMENTARY PROCEDURE

In reading club minutes I was struck by the emphasis placed in
most of the clubs upon parliamentary procedure. For instance, the
founders of the influential Olympia Woman's Club, which elected

suffrage leader Abigail Stuart its first president, felt it necessary to copy fifteen pages on parliamentary procedure—by hand—from the *Encyclopaedia Britannica* to use for guidance before it could proceed. Many clubs designated an official parliamentarian to consult as a procedural expert, and some had parliamentary drill as a regular feature at each of their meetings. Clubs regularly appointed parliamentary critics to keep the rules straight.

One reason for the perceived importance of parliamentary procedure may be one of the widely held perceptions about women in the nineteenth century. One of the earliest criticisms of women, especially of women collected into organizations, was that they were incapable of working together toward common goals. Their meetings would degenerate into gossip, chaos, or argument. Women, emotional and knowing nothing of parliamentary law, would not be able to govern themselves or accomplish anything worthwhile, critics said, often sarcastically.[4]

The attention to parliamentary procedure—with its focus on governance, consensus, and the democratic process—gave the women more than a ritual. It offered a powerful tool to use not only to counter the prevailing viewpoint about women, but also to take members through the thickets of relationships when women of differing backgrounds, ideas, and visions tried to work together. Parliamentary procedure as an operating system protected the expression of differing views, yet forced organizations to move forward in making decisions and resolving differences in a rational, equitable fashion that protected debate.

The ritual study of parliamentary procedure was important to women who had no direct political power or standing, whose public pronouncements were embarrassing and suspect even to themselves. It was also important to women who saw parliamentary procedure as the language of democracy and power, but one spoken exclusively by men. Further, if understood and used properly, the rituals and complex rules carried their own code of authority. And, as happens in organizations, expertise in the process could become a surrogate for the lack of power itself.

One Oregon club president saw that danger. Near the turn of the century she criticized the club fixation on parliamentary procedure. "The reference to parliamentary law leads to the suggestion that there is always danger in a deliberative body of making parliamentary rules into a sort of fetish," the president of the Portland Woman's Club said in 1897. "Lawyers are not the only people who lose sight of the merits of a cause in the technicalities of its management. Witness the way in which 'the rules' have tied half the business of our Congress hand and foot."[5]

Nevertheless, parliamentary procedure, and the practice of it, gave these women confidence in their ability to consider larger issues and see them through to their completion in an equitable manner. As a form of democratic exercise that evolved out of male-dominated decisionmaking traditions, it carried status. It also enabled women to flex the muscles of democracy and develop skills in the reliable if cumbersome methods used in "real" governance, an area that excluded them.

A brief look at the evolution of parliamentary procedure and its use in voluntary organizations demonstrates its value to clubwomen. *Robert's Rules of Order,* first published in 1876 and revised in 1893, 1904, and 1915, was derived from the rules of the U.S. House of Representatives. The increasing number of voluntary societies led Henry Robert, a major of Army Engineers assigned to San Francisco, to develop a pocket manual that "ordinary societies" might use. The resulting book—*Pocket Manual of Rules of Order for Deliberative Assemblies*—and its revisions gained such rapid and widespread acceptance that *Robert's Rules* came to be identified with parliamentary procedure itself.

Any person who has felt energies dissipate in a meeting and time fly by as discussion wanders into side issues, or who has quietly bemoaned the failure of a leader to gain closure on any of the issues at hand or, worse, watched a leader impose personal decisions on the group or cut speakers off, understands the appeal of parliamentary procedure to groups of women meeting regularly on virtually unlimited topics and projects. It is not surprising then that study of parliamentary procedure and parliamentary drill were incorporated into many clubs. Use of parliamentary procedure was particularly common in study clubs involved in community activism.

The business of debate, motions, voting, committees and boards, nominations and elections, officers, quorum, orders of business, and so on, was a new and unwieldy concept to the women who began using it. As with any language code, expertise also served to exclude the less knowledgeable and admitted its practitioners to a special club. However, its use also helped ensure preservation of order and civility. Differences and disagreements could be handled dispassionately without the meeting disintegrating into chaos or personal attacks and the will of the group could be expressed rather than the will of one individual.

Yet even the writer of the rules recognized they could be abused. "While it is important to every person in a free country to know something of parliamentary law, this knowledge should be used only to help, not to hinder business," Robert wrote. "One who is constantly raising points of order and insisting upon a strict observance of every rule in a peaceable assembly in which most of the members are [unfamiliar with] these rules and customs, makes himself a nuisance, hinders business, and prejudices people against parliamentary law."[6]

CLUB EVOLUTION

Women's clubs varied one from the other and with the passage of time. It is perilous to talk of what was typical. However, there were certain similarities in design, function, and evolution, particularly for the study clubs in the Northwest getting underway later than many counterparts elsewhere in the country. The Northwest clubs shared a pattern. What began as a simple, largely social club, with accessories of tea and poetry as one writer put it, gave way to the department club. The initial club study departments typically included literature, art, music, education, finance, current topics, philanthropy or social welfare, household or domestic economics, and broad issues lumped under the term *social economics*. The departments held separate meetings, sometimes weekly, and at times developed completely different programs of work from the umbrella club. Some women worked in only one department; others joined several departments or several different clubs. The umbrella organization called all the women together in less frequent sessions to handle general club business meetings or social affairs, often monthly.

Special speakers or courses of work were engaged for the separate departments, based usually upon the direction of a standing committee. By the turn of the century more than one critic was concerned about the departments and personal causes supplanting the interests of the club itself. "We are one club, not as many different clubs as we have departments, and if we would escape faction and dissension, every member must constantly feel that her allegiance is due first to the whole club," said the president of the Portland Woman's Club in 1897. Departments should not act independently without the club's sanction and needed to recognize that the department was subsidiary to the club and its aims. She added, "There is enough and too much in the world now of the fierce struggle for rights, of harsh self-assertion, of bickerings and strife; it should be ours to add to friendliness and gentleness and peace."[7] Department activism sometimes led to conflict and controversy in club ranks, as her remarks indicated.

The pattern followed by the Portland Woman's Club, founded in 1895 a few months after Congress passed the Carey Act opening up new lands in the West, was typical of one type. The group, open to all women, decided any five members could form a club department, selecting their own line of study and leadership. Select they did. By 1900 its 129 members could choose from German, Oregon history, parliamentary law, Shakespeare, the home, French, ancient and modern pottery, Browning, philanthropic, musicale, and library departments. It had begun with departments of study limited to American literature, music, German, French, art, and Shakespeare.[8] This club had Oregon suffrage leader Abigail Scott Duniway (profiled in chapter 8) as its president in 1902–3. Any woman could join, if she had the membership fee of $2.50 and the endorsement of two members. Quarterly dues were 75 cents. Sarah Evans, later the legislative chair and president of the Oregon Federation of Women's Clubs, followed Duniway. (Evans, who became a nationally recognized leader, is profiled in chapter 9.)

Other Portland Woman's Club presidents included the sharp-tongued Mrs. J. C. Card, Mrs. Levi Young, Mrs. Cleveland Rockwell, Julia Comstock, and Grace Watt Ross, women whose names often appeared as the forces behind many community efforts and later professional achievements. For instance, Young, who came to Oregon from New England, attended the federation biennial at Denver and later was hired by the University of Idaho regents as preceptress (a kind of combined dean of women and housemother) for the new women's hall (itself named after another club leader, Mary Ridenbaugh). There she also chaired the Domestic Science department and sat on the Board of Discipline, in charge of the home life (and a good share of the education) of girls at the institution. As an example of the exchange among the clubs of the Northwest, she also appeared as lecturer to Boise's Columbian Club.[9]

Some study clubs focused on the arts, the role of the arts in society, and how the arts could be used to improve the culture. Sometimes the study of individual writers was used as a vehicle to discuss social issues. An example is evident in the development of the Fortnightly Club of Eugene, Oregon, one of several Fortnightly clubs in the Northwest. Organized in 1893, it joined the state federation in 1904 and the general federation in 1910. The club defined its object thus: "To bring together women interested in artistic, economic, philanthropic, literary, scientific and social pursuits with a view of rendering them helpful to each other and useful to society."[10] Its study of literature was typical in its subjects and methods and reinforced an American canon.

In 1898 February included roll call responses about "the material progress" of the century and one-minute talks by members. Two weeks later the topic was Nathaniel Hawthorne as a literary artist, with discussion of "Is Hawthorne's psychology morbid?" On March 16 the topic was Longfellow and Oliver Wendell Holmes; on April 6 John Greenleaf Whittier and Lowell as poets of antislavery and literary activity in the South since the Civil War. By April 20 the club had moved to "great American historians," including a review of *McLoughlin and Old Oregon* written by club leader Eva Emery Dye (profiled in chapter 5). On May 4 the women took up evolution of the American magazine and its place in the library, on May 18 American humor and humorists, and on June 1 American essayists and Walt Whitman, who was rare in study programs. All these topics were researched and presented by individual club members.[11]

Within a decade, however, literary study gave way to more immediate issues. By 1902 this club too had established a free library, "of itself sufficient reason for the existence of our club life."[12] In 1907–8 the club had, in addition to ongoing study programs, a Room Committee, Investment Committee, Floral Committee, Civics Committee, and Program Committee, with over fifty active members. By 1911–12 the club had added Emergency, Press, Hygiene, Music, Suffrage, and Oregon Literature and Folklore committees to its program. Partly as the result of the work of Oregon's Bethenia Owens Adair (profiled here), the topic for study for the year was eugenics, including the subtopics "race-regeneration through selection, education for parenthood, and physical race improvement."

Adair, the Oregon woman who spurred club and political interest in the idea of eugenics, was one of the more intriguing early leaders to emerge in the Northwest. Her life also speaks to the dangers of success in realizing what others later viewed as the worst aspects of Progressive era reform and social engineering.

PROFILE: BETHENIA OWENS ADAIR

Bethenia Angela Owens Adair became a physician, writer, WCTU leader, and lecturer on women's rights. She also became a tireless and effective proponent of eugenics, on the winning side of some of the worst abuses of state power and control. She went from being an illiterate homesteader's daughter, married at fourteen and divorced at eighteen, to entrepreneur, practicing professional, and civic leader in the Northwest. She did it alone, on the force of her personality and determination to overcome all the obstacles in her way.

She was born in Missouri in 1840, the daughter of Kentucky-born parents who were in one of the earliest wagon trains to Oregon, arriving in 1843 with capital of 50 cents. Bethenia was one of nine children. Through hard work and some luck her father became successful at several ventures, including building a crude schooner with some friends in 1848 to use to get to the California gold fields, leaving his family behind for a time as many gold-seekers did.[13]

Bethenia was married at fourteen to a neighboring farmer, Legrand Hill. By the time she was eighteen her ne'er-do-well husband was abusing their sickly son. She left him and returned to her parents' farm at Clatsop, with their two-year-old son in tow. "And now, at eighteen years of age, I found myself, broken in spirit and health, again in my father's house, from which, only four short years before, I had gone with such a happy heart, and such bright hopes for the future," she wrote in her 1906 autobiography.[14]

With her father's help, she launched divorce and custody proceedings. That was rare among farm women before the Civil War, but Bethenia Owens was a rare person. Her divorce case, heard at Roseburg, was contested because of the child; she said that her widowed mother-in-law was anxious to have the boy. But her father had hired Stephen F. Chadwick, a local lawyer and postmaster. It was a good choice. He later became legislator, judge, and then governor of Oregon in 1877. She won her suit, eventually gaining both custody of her son and restoration of her maiden name.

She decided to make a better life for herself and her son through educating herself. She was proud when she finished the third grade reader in her first four-month term, as she helped her family with milking, housework, washing, and ironing. Her younger brothers and sisters helped take care of her son. Later, on her own at Oysterville near the mouth of the Columbia, she took in washing and sewing, picked berries, and studied from 9 P.M. to midnight. She said she paid for her son's keep by being up at 4 A.M. to milk cows at the place where she stayed and washing after school and evenings.[15] She continued her education and got dispensation from area school officials to teach.

She created her own subscription school, not an uncommon method of putting together a school in rural areas, by signing up sixteen pupils for $2 each for the three-month term. She held school in an old Presbyterian church. She managed to save $25, adding to it the 50 cents a gallon she got for picking blackberries.[16] After a year she applied to take the certification exam for teachers and landed a teaching job at $11 a month first at Bruceport then at Oysterville near Astoria. Eventually she saved enough money to buy a half lot in Astoria and contracted with a carpenter to build a small home. "I was as proud as a queen of my pretty little home, which was the first I had ever really owned; and the fact that I had earned it all myself made it doubly prized."

From Astoria she and her son moved to Roseburg in southwest Oregon, where she, like Abigail Scott Duniway, survived and even prospered by starting a millinery and dressmaking store. She taught herself the trade by copying others. After twelve months of hard work, she was earning a remarkable $1,500 a year, enabling her to buy a home and send her son to college in 1870, to the University of California at Berkeley. Having longed for further education herself, and feeling she had a talent for nursing, she decided to go to college too. Supposedly, when she announced that she planned to study medicine she became a social outcast in Roseburg; her friends felt she had by this disgraced herself, she wrote, adding that only two men—Oregon pioneer and friend Jesse Applegate and attorney Chadwick—encouraged her to study medicine. She said the others called it "a wild goosechase," demeaning for a woman to pursue.[17]

Owens arranged with suffrage leader Abigail Scott Duniway to employ her son on her paper before she left for medical school and he for college. A contact in Portland suggested she study at Philadelphia. She spent a year at Philadelphia's Eclectic School of Medicine after being rejected by more mainstream medical schools. Although the school was not first rate—specializing in hydropathy—it did admit women, although some time after she graduated its reputation slipped further when a dean was convicted of selling fraudulent degrees. She felt she overcame its shortcomings by hiring a private tutor and attending the same lectures and clinics in Blockly Hospital that all medical students in the city attended.

She landed in Portland and opened a practice in, among other procedures, electrical and medicated baths. In the meantime she sent a younger sister through Mills College and her son to medical college. Her son, then nineteen, entered the medical department of Willamette University and made her proud when he graduated. She later bought a drugstore for him, after selling her property in Roseburg for $8,000, and decided to further her own medical education by getting more training and touring Europe. In 1878 she ended up at the University of Michigan, receiving her degree in 1880 and priding herself on missing only one class lecture. She went with one of her classmates to Chicago for hospital and clinical work, joined by her son, now Dr. Hill. After six months, she, her son, and two other female physicians traveled Europe's great cities and medical centers.

"Then I felt I was in a position to meet any male physician on a par so far as medical education went, and so I returned to Oregon and began practicing in Portland," she wrote. But her work in hospitals and her own experiences had led her to the conclusion that women in particular suffered from bad laws, and she decided to "dedicate my life to the securing of better laws and the creation of a sentiment against the double standard of morals." She began working in the WCTU and giving lectures.

In Oregon, she got reacquainted with Col. John Adair. She married him in 1884 at age forty-four. At age forty-seven she gave birth to another child, a daughter, who lived only three days. Depressed, she spent the next several years in a rural practice based at their farm near Seaside. After a postgraduate clinical course one hot summer in Chicago, she and her husband moved to Yakima in south-central Washington, hoping that a drier climate would help her rheumatism. She redoubled her efforts on behalf of women, speaking out boldly for temperance, for suffrage, for less restrictive clothing for women, and even for dropping the awkward custom of riding sidesaddle.[18]

In 1891 she and her husband adopted a son, and in 1905 she began to think of retirement but found new causes instead. Frances Willard had appointed her the state superintendent of heredity and hygiene for the Oregon WCTU, and she began concentrating funds and time in that effort. She came to believe that eugenics—including forced sterilization—was the answer to social evils and a better future. For whom was less clear. She wrote in a letter that the idea first came to her in 1883 in conversation with the physician in charge of the Oregon Insane Asylum. She began writing in earnest about the idea over twenty years later in 1904.[19]

"The greatest curse of the race comes through our vicious criminal and insane classes," she said in a speech. "To my mind this is the element that should be dealt with, not by chloroform or strangulation, but by the science of surgery, for if their power to reproduce themselves were rendered null, a tremendous important step in advance would have been taken, not only without injury to life, but often with positive benefits to the victims themselves," she wrote. "I believe it would be more effectual than the penitentiary door, the hangman's rope or the torches of the South. It is a well known fact, that any animal when rendered sterile, loses much of its vicious and ungovernable nature and soon becomes docile, useful and contented."[20]

The only objections, she added, would be first sentiment and second "what I would term false ideas of personal rights." She had also worked with WCTU president Anna Riggs earlier on legislative proposals.[21] That experience gave her insights into the political process. She called her bill "the most radical preventive legislation ever considered in the west." It was indeed radical. "It provides for sterilization of all those convicted of statutory crimes, of criminal degenerates, of incurably insane and similar cases."[22] A bill to do this was introduced in both the Washington and Oregon legislatures in 1907, titled "An act providing for the sterilization of feeble-minded, epileptic and insane persons, and prisoners in the penitentiary."

Her bill was defeated initially, passed but was vetoed two years later, lost again in 1911, but made the ballot as a referendum in 1913 and passed. She continued what became a long-term public campaign to get public acceptance for her ideas about eugenics, despite opposition. "I am so accustomed to being abused and called a pest and a crank that I was not discouraged, but went to work once more to educate the public as to what the bill was and the good it would accomplish."[23]

In 1917 Oregon put it into effect—one of the few states with the questionable record of establishing a large-scale program of sterilizing criminals and others, although comparatively few actually suffered the surgery because the eligible candidates were more narrowly defined as criminally insane men convicted of assaults and confirmed criminals, what we today call repeat offenders, with a case by case review. Other states copied the plan she initiated.

Owens Adair spent large sums of money and most of her later life promoting her idea, convinced that "in days to come the public will realize that what I have done has been of vast benefit to the state and to humanity."

In the 1920s she lobbied for a bill requiring examinations of those who apply to be married "as to their health and mental fitness." It became law in 1922. She felt it was unfair to coming generations to pass on "handicaps of subnormal mentality or bodily ills of their parents." In a statement chilling for its potential applications, she said, "The day has come when we should have better babies as well as better calves and pigs. The farmer insists on having the best possible sire for his livestock and we should see that our babies are guaranteed health and happiness by insuring that they do not have degraded or degenerate parents." She was not alone in her views. Eugenics gained national popularity.

Shortly before her eighty-fifth birthday, Owens Adair wrote to Fred Lockley, the popular journalist and columnist who had written about her remarkable life earlier.[24] She said she was in good health, except for a lame hip that needed use of a crutch. "Most people rust out," she noted. Owens Adair continued her campaign even after death. She provided in her will for a Eugenics Institute that would bear her name to be built on twenty acres she owned. She had been advised not to build it there, but on the University of Oregon campus. Someone had also gently suggested that if she wanted a memorial building a library for boys would be appropriate, but she said, "It didn't appeal to me."[25]

Some of the dangers and reforms clubs talked about reflected fears of immigrants. For instance, the concept of "racial poisons" included afflictions such as alcoholism, lead poisoning, drugs, and inherited tendencies to disease. Also, at the end of the nineteenth century reformers, politicians, ministers, physicians—and many women—were worried about the declining birthrate of white Anglo-Saxon families, which dropped by more than 50 percent in 100 years, from 278 live births per 1,000 women aged fifteen to forty-four in 1800 to 125 births in 1900. Average family size went from 5 children in 1800 to 3.42 children in 1910,[26] spurring talk about "race suicide," a topic that found its way onto club programs, although the birthrate in the Northwest far exceeded the national rate.

Besides libraries, the form of activism all clubs could support with minimal controversy was "village improvement." Women who looked around them found dozens of practical ways they could make life better right outside their own doors, especially in the Pacific Northwest. The Columbian Club of Boise in 1900–1901, like hundreds of clubs, had what it called a Town and Village Improvement Department. Its agenda was typical: it pursued enforcement of the ordinance prohibiting the disease-spreading and distasteful habit of expectorating on city sidewalks, persuaded the city council to prohibit the destruction or mutilation of the city's shade trees to erect telephone and electric light wires, planted trees around the courthouse, and got trash cans placed on the streets. The club's Building Department secured and "made a success" of the Rest Room in the City Hall, specifically designed for the use of women who came into the town from outside the city.

"They can hardly believe that all the comforts afforded them are free of charge. It was said that this was the first united effort that had ever been made to relieve the burdens of a day in town," wrote Columbian Club president Mary Black Ridenbaugh in her report.[27] Women's clubs in towns in agricultural areas, such as Twin Falls, Idaho, frequently established this amenity for rural women, while clubs in larger cities such as Seattle and Portland established retreats and rest rooms for working women. Creating spaces for women was the overall goal.

RURAL CLUBS EMERGE

Women settled in the growing villages, towns, and cities of the Pacific Northwest found it comparatively easy to make contact with other women there and join the women's club movement. Women in isolated homesteads, tracts, and farms had the same needs, but more difficulty making and continuing contact. One aspect of the larger women's club movement that has not received much attention is the rural clubs, particularly important in the West and a direct outgrowth of the women's club movement. Founded late in the period under study and generally connected to large-scale farming developments and irrigation projects in the interior Northwest, the rural clubs provided vital contact and support for women who were isolated not only from one another, but also from many of the amenities women in other cities found themselves establishing.

A description of the arid places that later opened for irrigated farming demonstrates the importance of the rural club contacts to the women who settled these areas, where distances between spreads and towns were great. This description of Idaho's Cassia County on the Snake River plain came from one of Idaho's territorial governors, Mason Brayman.[28] He wrote of suffocating heat and trails with "deep furrows of alkali dust filling the roads and even the plains, ready to rise into the air like light snow. . . . It drifts into the house, covering beds, tables, etc., and, with the thick swarms of flies, makes quiet or comfort or cleanliness impossible." He described its effects on the local residents. "I am beginning to find excuses for the men being filthy and coarse, and for the poor mothers for ceasing to wash the faces and clothes of the children. The women here, much to their praise, do contrive to keep tidy."

In the sagebrush-covered desert divided by the Snake River one settler described the beauty of a million stars glinting at night and the wild winds raging for days at a time, moving fields from one place to another. "On everything within the house lay a thick gray powder. . . . skin thickly coated, eyes red and smarting, teeth gritty," wrote homesteader Annie Pike Greenwood.[29] Survival was hard-contact and clubs were part of some other world cut off by dust and hard work.

Before the turn of the century pamphlets bragged about the advantages of Washington farming communities like Walla Walla, Sunnyside, Yakima, Kennewick, and Pullman, which competed for immigrants and investments. That quadrant of Washington also competed as a region with the irrigated developments in south Idaho. The brochures boosting the arid places touted the agricultural production possible with irrigation, but were woefully short on information about irrigation methods and water sources, to the detriment of hundreds of settlers who ultimately gave up.[30]

In south Idaho, northeast Oregon, and southeast Washington, the bounteous Snake and Columbia Rivers promised to turn the choking dust into productive loam and crops if settlers could only get their water to the land. The Carey Act of 1894 gave each state in the West a million acres of land if entrepreneurs could find a way to irrigate them with private or public capital. They did, using elaborate pipe and canal systems filled with water from diversion dams. By 1900 Idaho ranked first in irrigated land in the Pacific Northwest, and its projects such as the irrigated Twin Falls tract south of the Snake became a national showcase.[31] Just as they came to Oregon for the land a half-century earlier, they came for the land again, struggling to keep up with their debts. Sagebrush was hard to clear, and packrats, woodticks, bedbugs, and fogs of flies plagued households, as did hot summers and cold winters spent by some in tarpaper shacks. But within a few years crops from cabbages to barley to beans, along with wheat and potatoes, began growing fast and full in the volcanic soil, once water touched it.

Women engaged in sidelines to make additional income. For example, they developed home industries like selling eggs or raising poultry, which was, like other work close to the home site, the woman's responsibility. By 1910 poultry raising, especially of turkeys, had become an industry in and of itself.[32] The flocks grazed on the hillsides like the sheep and cattle, fattened in feed lots on wheat and corn, then were shipped to markets in the East. The isolation and hard work for the women whose husbands worked the land in these immense irrigation projects in Idaho, Washington, and Oregon were extreme. Sometimes the women and children worked the initial homestead claim while the men worked more distant acreage in order to claim and plant more land.

Many women moved to the area near the turn of the century well aware of the women's club movement from their prior locales. That loss, along with the lack of home technology or even adequate supplies, exacerbated their loneliness and privation. Greenwood, a pioneer on Idaho's Minidoka tract, commented on the fate of such women.[33] "The sanest women I know live on farms. But the life, in the end, gets a good many of them—that terrible forced labor, too much to do, and too little time to do it in, and no rest, and no money. So long as a woman can work, no matter how her mind may fail, she is still kept on the farm, a cog in the machine, growing crazier and crazier, until she dies of it, or until she suddenly kills her children and herself."[34]

Some broke or felt their lives fade away. Others gradually mastered their claims, built homes, and prospered, aided by agricultural and home technology. Conditions eased, but the isolation remained for many. They formed what alliances they could, through churches, family networks, neighbors, or rural clubs. As areas became more stable and settled, farmers survived and prospered, and clubs in the country proliferated too. Those who lived outside towns lived different lives in different social and communal groupings than did those who lived off the commerce or services in towns. Isolation, seasonal changes in work patterns, the growing awareness of social and technological developments, and the club movement created a strong appeal for rural clubs. Greenwood, a teacher at several rural schools, was a member of the Greenwood Friendship Club and Hazelton Civic Club.[35]

Rural Clubs in the Northwest

In the early winter of 1911 two women spoke to one another in a department store in Twin Falls and to their amazement discovered they were country neighbors. Here almost everybody was a newcomer. The two women decided to organize a social circle, calling it the Unity Club. Later, with six other such clubs, the Unity Club joined a rural clubs federation.[36] A few miles away, the Filer Woman's Club was organized in 1910 by a group of nine homesick women. They voted to study Italian art the first year "and have since wondered why we pioneer women thought that subject was important to us at that time," said one of the members. This club, like others, became a meeting place for both town and country women and a place to address mutual problems.[37]

One of the first rural clubs in Idaho was the 1899 Four Leaf Clover Club of Albion, organized for civic improvement and service. Another early club was the Culture Club of Rupert, organized when the tract opened for settlement in 1905. The Rupert club began when a group of seven farmers' wives met with Mrs. A. C. DeMary. The club even sent delegates to the state federation meeting in 1906. The Rupert club's territory was huge, with members from an area covering over sixty square miles of the Minidoka tract. Like many clubs, it disbanded during World War I.[38]

Like their city counterparts, the rural clubs accomplished much for their communities. In Kimberly, south of Twin Falls, the Ladies' Pioneer Club, consisting of ten women in 1906, had as its goals civic improvement and the promotion of friendship among the women of the community. Its first project was acquiring land for a city park, landscaping it, and giving it to the town of Kimberly. For years it also furnished books for the grade school, hot lunches for 250 students (many free), cod liver oil to delight needy children, and instruments for the school band. It also formed a Parent-Teacher Association, sponsored a preschool clinic for years, and, like clubs everywhere, did Red Cross work during World War I.[39] In Emmett, an agricultural area outside Boise, the 1909 Crescent Improvement Club was created by rural women for civic and self-improvement as well as sociability and relaxation. First called the Helping Hand Club, it helped needy families, raised money to help build roads, paid one girl's way through high school, and helped students finance college.[40]

As happened in cities, clubs organized not for benevolence but for study found themselves the likely or only vehicle to care for women or families in dire straits. Such was the case with several women in what Greenwood in her autobiography dubbed the Ladies' Fancywork Improvement Club. A woman Greenwood described as beautiful, with dark eyes, rosy cheeks, and chestnut hair, came from Galesburg, Illinois, to a tarpaper–covered shack on the Minidoka tract and watched her family steadily degenerate. To compound her problems, her husband was sometimes abusive to the family of five. Finally she took to her bed—permanently ill.

A committee from the first women's club in the tract, including Greenwood, went to call on the woman. They found her lying amid bedbugs and excrement. The women bathed her, killed the bugs, and fed her food they had brought. Her family, ordered away by the unfortunate woman, had apparently ignored her plight. The next role of the club was to get her admitted to a sanitarium, where her children visited her until she died. "She had reached the bottom from which there is no climbing up. She died as the result of the births she had accomplished; she died because of what her children had been compelled to endure and because of what they had become by reason of it," Greenwood wrote.[41] Any community-building cultural politics came much too late for this woman, as it did for many others in the West.

For most, however, prospects were much less grim, and some homesteads became prosperous farms. Gradually the rural developments grew cities, and city-type clubs, but the rural clubs remained important in many places in Idaho and the Northwest for decades. The rural clubs were generally untouched by state and national federations, one of the reasons their names have been lost, but they too felt the need for area allies to work on larger projects. In 1915 rural clubs and farm women in south Idaho created their own network, the Twin Falls Rural Federation. Beginning with seven clubs, it ultimately included twenty-five clubs throughout the sparsely populated area. The Twin Falls group operated a restroom in town and a women's exchange for five years.

During the war the women turned the facility into a work room to benefit refugees. Its accomplishments included formalizing

woman's place in modern agriculture by setting up a home economics demonstrator as part of the Farm Bureau. It started hot
lunches in many rural schools and addressed health concerns and
facilities in rural communities. The rural federation, like its city
cousins, also took up politics. It took credit for getting Carrie
Harper White elected to the 1919 legislature to work for a tuberculosis hospital for Idaho, eventually established at Gooding.[42]

In Washington, rural clubs proliferated in the central and southeastern parts of the state at about the same time that irrigated developments brought them to Idaho. They carried names like
Sagebrush Sisters and Handy Hands. Claimed to be the first rural
women's club in Washington was the Orchard Ridges Club of
1907.[43] Another source claims "first" status for the 1903 River-
side Woman's Club, which carried the motto "Gleaners in the field
of knowledge." It joined the federation in 1904.[44] In 1912 the
Home Interest Club also joined the federation. Another very early
group was the Union Flats Women's Club near Pullman. Other
early rural clubs were situated around towns like Sunnyside and
Yakima, towns built by irrigation.

There were many such clubs in the agricultural areas of the
eastern part of the state in or near tiny settlements, most unfortunately now forgotten. Historian Alex McGregor identifies in the
Palouse area of southeastern Washington alone a handful of such
clubs attached to small settlements in large areas. Mockonema
had the Don't Worry Club, Clinton the Stitch and Chatter Club,
Hooper the Get-Together Club and the later Community Cheer
Club (CCC Club). The Get-Together Club had a noble purpose:
"To promote community spirit by seeing, talking, and doing good,
and overcoming evil with good."[45]

In Washington, as in Idaho, the rural clubs also began holding
their own collective meetings, first convening in 1914. A project
of the collective group was the beautification of Blaine Park in
Grandview. Other early member groups included the 1910 Neighbor Club, the 1911 Bethany Mothers' Club, the 1911 Green Valley
Progressive Club, and the 1912 Jolly Ranchers, organized to promote "neighborliness," as, apparently, was the East Mabton Get-
Acquainted Club started in 1917. Another group was the 1912
North Country Club, which made quilts for the Red Cross and the
needy and sewed for Selah Hospital.[46] Projects undertaken by
these clubs also included local philanthropic efforts. For instance,
the Euclid Homemakers Club, founded in 1913, bought a piano

for the Euclid School, sponsored educational loans for girls, and supported a boy and girl residing at Lakeland Village, a state institution.

CLUB METHODS

Rural clubs, as an offshoot of the women's club movement, eventually merited professionalization too, an issue addressed by club expert Caroline Benton. She included a chapter on rural women in her reference work on designing women's clubs programs. A bit condescendingly, she emphasized the importance of such clubs to women "on farms and ranches and in little villages, whose lives are monotonous, who have no lectures or concerts to attend and few magazines or new books to read. They, above all the rest of us, need intellectual stimulus."[47] To start a club, she suggested a few women get together initially on a regular basis, perhaps reading something aloud, until members' confidence grew. As a practical matter, she recommended dividing the small club into committees of two, each pair being given one book to read and "master." Meanwhile, the president might study the life of the author, perhaps by writing the state librarian and securing a traveling library case or ordering a book or two if no encyclopedia or other resources were available.

After presentations, there should be discussion encouraged at each meeting, with members telling what characters they admired or disliked and what great moral lessons the book contained. Finally, aside from working on self-development in this way, she said the rural club could undertake work for the community of immense value. She suggested using the growing body of material about better farming, better sanitation, and other topics. Subsequent efforts beyond education might include improving the public schools and improving the community's cultural life by arranging lectures or concerts at the schoolhouse "with stereopticon shows, dances, tableaux, and whatever will make the community happier and better."[48] Again, women were encouraged toward the common purpose, rural or urban, of civic improvement through access to books and other media.

Awareness and ambition often were hooked to one another. Women in many clubs, rural or urban, wanted action beyond study. For some women, it was not a matter of progressing from study to activism, or rural to urban, but of finding a channel for their activism. The clubs merely provided the means. However, other women took a slower route. From the study of literature or arts, many clubs moved to study of social problems and from that to a city council or legislative agenda. From study of social problems, the clubs quite naturally moved to action on social problems.

For many study clubs, including many in the Northwest surrounded by community needs, the shift happened within a season; for some, it never happened at all. A few clubs stayed with the study of art and literature throughout their existence, while others moved into addressing social problems and moved back to the safer havens of study after a few years. Sometimes the same club housed women who from the beginning pushed for civic reform and others who sought only study and self-improvement. The departments often managed to keep both kinds of members in the club. The federation motto—"Unity in Diversity"—recognized and accepted the variations. Almost all of the study clubs, however, had some component of philanthropy or civic activism built into their programs of work.

Club activity empowered women in a distinct pattern. Women met and began to study literature and one another. They became confident and adept critics as they analyzed works and artists. They grew in confidence through the presentation and discussion of papers and issues. Some never moved beyond this edifying process, although topics changed annually. Some began to study how great works and writers related to current events and to their own situations and began to examine current problems in that historical, cultural, or political context. Another common progression in programs of study was to look at the women of the past, which led to study of women of the present. As clubs studied women's roles they usually moved to study then action on social, political, and legal problems of the day affecting women.

In clubs, as in other organizations, it was useful to retain a sense of humor. For instance, the Monroe, Washington, Research Club, organized in 1911, had developed a set of three club commandments by the 1920s, published in club literature: "1. Remember thy club engagements; 2. Thou shalt be prepared for roll call; 3. Thou shalt not at the 11th hour begin to hunt material for thy paper."[49]

From Clubs to Actual Schools

Some study clubs, especially in larger towns in the Northwest, found themselves creating classes and even schools to meet their goals. Portland's clubs offer an example. By 1901 the Portland Woman's Club, the Portland Woman's Union, and the Young Women's Christian Association formed an alliance to initiate what began as a school of domestic science in Portland, supervised by a board of directors. Its program included Tuesday evening cooking demonstrations for working girls over twenty, with an admission fee of 10 cents. Wednesday afternoon demonstrations for housekeepers cost 25 cents, and Friday evening demonstrations for girls under twenty were free. In addition, the school offered a set of daily classes morning and evening. The list of offerings focused on practical skills—young ladies' classes, matrons' classes, waitress classes, a class for nurses from St. Vincent's Hospital, and a language class for Japanese women. All were well attended, according to sponsors.

Every station in life was represented, organizer Edith Niles boasted in a club magazine. "The two most enthusiastic classes were the nurses and the Japanese. The former quickly appreciated the value of a knowledge of invalid cookery. . . . The Japanese were eager to learn, and their interest and progress was marked." Besides classes, Niles said, there would be a housekeepers' conference "designed to reach and bring together women of all classes for a general discussion of domestic problems and perplexities, a sort of clearing house for domestic ideas." Further, the women hoped through contributions of "endowed desks" to offer free instruction to a class of girls from the public schools, with participation to be granted as a reward for excellence in studies.[50]

Clubs, in whatever programs they sponsored, confronted perpetual funding needs. By 1912–13 the Portland Woman's Club had more than departments organized to meet these needs. It had established the Philanthropic Committee Fund, the Tubercular Fund, and the Building Fund, with $4,000 sitting in the bank. Committees by then included Department, Press, Calendar, Membership, Social, Visiting, Publicity, Resolutions, Philanthropic, Educational, Civic, Public Health, Hall, Chautauqua, and Public Market, with a special committee named Suffrage Campaign, which Sarah Evans chaired. By this time committees did specific programmatic work and the departments and classes had coalesced around general topics that sounded much like a curriculum: literature, current literature, dramatic art and expression, biology, social science, and home economics, all meeting twice a month.[51]

Unlike the large and active groups such as the Portland Woman's

Club, some groups stayed small and narrowly focused. Some clubs also kept an exclusive approach to membership (in part to continue to hold meetings in one another's homes). In fact, almost all clubs across the country eventually had to begin limiting the number of members out of practical consideration, according to club historian Theodora Penny Martin, as some clubs counted hundreds of members. That was less true in the Northwest than elsewhere. Clubs with large memberships, mostly in cities, were traditionally department clubs.[52]

An example of the small traditional study club was the Twentieth Century Club in Portland, begun in 1893 by Jennie E. Wright, who had lived in New York and Chicago before coming to Portland. The membership of the group, which was strictly a study club, was limited to ten women who were bound by rule to attend every meeting and perform the work assigned except in case of severe illness.[53] Once in a while, study clubs were mixed, with both men and women as participating members, as happened with the Monmouth Literary Association in Oregon's Willamette Valley, organized in October 1898, and the Delphian Club of Pendleton, organized in 1913.[54]

THE PRIMACY OF LIBRARIES

Regardless of the origins of the club and attitudes toward activism, virtually every club agreed on one goal—the importance of reading to its vision of culture and community. To win at cultural politics required not only reading and studying for self-improvement, but also making such reading available to every citizen in every community to change their lives too. Women's clubs considered themselves both forward-thinking and the conservators of culture. In the West, where women's interests competed with saloons, men's secret lodges, a transient and sometimes violent population, a dearth of community institutions, and few social support networks, women turned to libraries as both a resource and a gift of permanent opportunity and enrichment to their communities. Through reading rooms and libraries they engaged in a quiet power struggle over the future direction of their settlements and cities, the ultimate village improvement.

5

LITERATURE AND LIBRARIES

Culture and Citizenship, 1900–1915

In 1898 the Ladies of The Dalles (Oregon) Public Library explained why they adopted libraries as a cause. They spoke for hundreds of clubs engaged in cultural politics over the culture of reading: "It is a fact where library movements have originated in these towns, women have been the promulgators. In the mad rush and search for material wealth, which characterizes the century, the majority of men are not finding the time to devote to library pursuits," and it falls to women. However, women's exceptionality made this acceptable, the women believed. "This is a division of labor which does not seem unfair, since woman's greater refinement and innate love of the good, the true and the beautiful must forever claim her interest in that which tends to the development of the highest culture. In response to the growing need women's educational clubs are spread broadcast through the land."[1]

This "development of the highest culture" was bound up with education, and education itself instilled character in their thought. Reading and libraries were conduits for education and self-improvement and thus improved character and citizenship. This line of thought intersected with the rise of both professionalization and bureaucratization, making libraries sources of information, expertise, and cultural transmission in a Progressive age. And they were the most efficient means of distributing that collective wisdom equitably to those otherwise denied access to it. Clubwomen throughout the Northwest committed themselves to creating libraries.

In a study club, the ritual of study and analysis itself was as important as the content of a year's programs, rituals of reading, of research through reading to present and discuss ideas, politics, or the arts. Women were essential to the elevation of the culture of reading in the late nineteenth and early twentieth centuries. The genesis of public libraries in women's clubs manifests the role the clubs played in spreading the culture of reading and giving it special value. In city after city and town after town throughout the Northwest, the public library began as a women's club reading room or a women's club project. Their seeds sprouted in small WCTU reading rooms offering an alternative to the fellowship of the saloon in a setting where women and children were also welcome. Early libraries in the Northwest also took the form of heavy wooden boxes placed on end on tables, with their doors propped open to reveal the titles inside to the public. Clubs established an extensive network of traveling libraries to bring the benefits of literacy and reading directly to the many remote parts of their huge states.

CONSERVATORS OF CULTURE

Within their own circles, members of traditional study clubs felt themselves conservators and purveyors of culture. They valued the opportunity to learn about writers, artists, and the new ideas of the age, in a quest for self-improvement and enlightenment in a time of social upheaval. Such study offered them a way to incorporate art into their daily lives and connect it to a kind of civic activism. They used it to justify the directions their civic activism took, through beautification and conservation campaigns. They called on the philosophy of romantic individualists such as essayist and poet Ralph Waldo Emerson to legitimate their ventures into the cultural realm. Emerson's emphasis on beauty and the arts, on individual action, and on transcendence of the spiritual over the material held special appeal for study clubs, where he frequently became the focus of programs.

Reading itself is cultural behavior in issues of style, such as manner, time, and place of the act, apart from the issue of content. Women's study clubs formed their own interpretive community and brought certain expectations to the act of reading, studying, and discussing literary works.[2] Reader response theory shows how important it is to recreate how and for what purpose these women used the texts they studied and promoted, rather than assuming some universal meaning for "classic" literature. They saw their rituals of researching topics, writing papers, and presenting and discussing findings as a way to elevate and broaden the level of the culture surrounding them. They felt the same way about libraries, viewing them as democratizing and liberating institutions, but also institutions that encouraged participants to step toward liberation and education along certain cultural paths.

What happened at Nampa, a railroad town in southwest Idaho incorporated in 1890, demonstrated the passion and commitment to libraries. That year Elizabeth McRobbie Karcher founded the Woman's Century Club. The women held out as their foremost goal getting a library for the town. The twenty-seven members gathered reference books, purchased books, and donated others to the cause. They also took turns as staff librarians, putting the collection in accessible downtown business locations. The club then asked the Carnegie Library Foundation for support and in 1906 submitted plans for what was to become Nampa's Carnegie Library. This small club donated its own collection of books and $265 toward furnishings, plus money toward the painting of the rooms after the library was built.[3]

Books were and are material cultural artifacts, objects of production as well as aesthetic objects. The "best" books represented a particular tradition and worldview and exposed readers to realms of history, biography, and current affairs. Books were also important measures of aspirations and connected to class. For women, books were "markers of taste" and thus of status. The level of a family's intellectual aspirations was more significant than its economic stature in encouraging ambition and class mobility. Using several generations of an influential Indiana family of women as her "interpretive community," historian Barbara Sicherman found that books and the act of reading, and communicating about what was read, gave them a "common language and a medium of intellectual and social exchange that helped the women define themselves and formulate responses to the larger world." The same words apply to the women's study clubs.[4]

An added tension emerged for this interpretive community over defining the West, particularly the West of the imagination, and whose image of it prevailed. Women had their own imagined West, reflected in their narratives, their club programs, their goals. Theirs was a West where spaces in this land of economic opportunity were home-centered, safe, cultured, even refined. Myths, our prevailing cultural narratives and stereotypes, inform the actions that shape history. The stories of cowboys and Indians left women out, as did tales of explorers and economic conquest popular in the East as its understanding of the West. This view of the "Wild West" also spread through new media forms such as the dime novel, where women usually were relegated to saloons or victimhood.

Jane Tompkins in writing about the power and influence of Westerns as a genre and the rise of the mythology of the old West argues that the Western owes its nature and popularity in part to a reaction against the growing dominance of a women's culture in the last half of the nineteenth century and women's "invasion" of the public sphere after 1880. Men gravitated to a "womanless milieu" and a set of violent rituals (i.e., gunfights) in a world of minimal use of words.[5] Women perhaps were becoming more successful than they realized at cultural politics, at least in bringing attention to the culture of reading by imposing the idealism of the home.

One writer bridged the chasm between male and female versions of the West of the imagination with graceful and accurate depictions of life there for men and women. She also bridged East and West and linked the British literary tradition to an emerging American one. She wrote primarily for eastern readers, using the exoticism of western locales as many other writers did. While in Idaho, she helped found one of Boise's principal clubs before she left for California. However, her ambiguity about eastern culture and the western landscape dovetailed with women's experience of the West and the conflicts over culture. She became nationally famous for her writing and illustrations and was well known even before moving to Boise in 1884.

A remarkable and talented woman, Mary Hallock Foote lived almost a decade in Boise or the hills above it. Her work both countered and reinforced prevailing views about the West of the imagination, but she offered a female perspective as someone who had actually spent many years in the West's landscape and developed an appreciation both for it and for what its new residents tried to impose on it.

PROFILE: MARY HALLOCK FOOTE

Mary Anna Hallock by 1876 was already a successful illustrator in New York. Her work had appeared in *Century, Scribner's,* and *Harper's* magazines. She later became famous for her dispatches from western outposts where she and her husband lived, including Boise.

Born in 1847 into a Quaker family in the Hudson River valley, she was remembered as small and delicate but greatly determined, leaving to study art on her own in New York City in 1864. By the 1870s she was doing magazine and book illustrations for writers with major reputations, including Longfellow and Whittier.[6] In 1876, at age twenty-nine, she married the young civil engineer Arthur Foote in New York, who took her with him to seek his fortune in the West. They left for California, and a letter to a friend and editor of *Scribner's* describing her new home led him to encourage her to write more of her vivid accounts of her experiences in the West for publication.

Her marriage to the dreamer from Connecticut took her to remote western sites—a mine south of San Francisco, Santa Cruz, Colorado's 10,000-foot-high Leadville, Idaho's capital, and back to California. Mary Foote soon began selling articles, short stories, and illustrations about the West to various publications. After they moved to the mining town of Leadville, her writing began to gain her considerable fame as an "authentic" writer of the West. Her novel *Led-Horse Claim* used Leadville as a backdrop.

A few years later the Footes moved to Idaho, where her husband attempted a visionary if impractical irrigation scheme near Boise. He envisioned a huge canal to collect water from the Boise River where it comes out of the foothills toward the city to irrigate thousands of acres in the valley, turning miles of sagebrush desert into cropland. The young engineer became a stock character in Foote's fiction, and much of what she wrote later was autobiographical, based on places and events she had seen. In her work, she reflected the sense of adventure and optimism and loss that pervaded the West of the imagination.

Her husband did the initial work on the project that later became the New York Canal, although for the Footes it was a failure despite years of hard work and sacrifice. The huge project exceeded his grasp and available capital. During their years in Idaho she used her impressions of it, including its irrigation schemes and orchards, as settings in her essays and novels. Her work added to the mystique about the West and also gained praise for its attention to accuracy in details and graceful writing from a female vantage point. In all, she wrote a dozen novels between 1883 and 1919, published mostly by Houghton Mifflin.

Her books described life in mining camps, on irrigation projects, and in small, raw towns of the Northwest with stories different from the usual western adventure stories carried in some of the same magazines. Her stories of the south Idaho being created by irrigation began appearing in *Century* in 1889 just as the women's club movement began spreading through the region, Her personal life, with its sharp contrasts between rugged and undeveloped frontier settings and the genteel life she knew in her Northeast publishing circles, became the inspiration for the Pulitzer Prize–winning novel *Angle of Repose* by Wallace Stegner, who used many of her own words in the work.

When she moved to Boise in 1884 it had about 2,000 inhabitants and none of the amenities this well-educated easterner missed. She found herself alternatively irritated, excited, and isolated. In private letters to a friend in the East she complained about the high prices for inferior goods and all the social calls and pretensions of the Boise women, who were fascinated by her presence among them. Facing economic hardship and long separations from her husband, she finally moved away from the city and nearer where her husband worked on the dam above Boise.[7] They lived above the Boise River in an unusual lava rock house with two-foot-thick walls circled by a shady porch. It was about ten miles east of Boise, not far from where Lucky Peak Dam is now located. Later she exalted what the settlers had accomplished in the arid valley in the space of thirty years, but her years in Idaho were hard. Thirty-seven years old when she arrived, she suffered "heartbreak, failure and discouragement," as she and her husband worked on his irrigation project.[8] Sometimes she was the family's primary financial support.

Her life in the river canyon appeared in a series of drawings, "Pictures of the Far West," published in *Century* from 1888 to 1890.[9] Her decade in Boise became the subject of *The Chosen Valley,* published in 1892, the year the Columbian Club began meeting. The plot added a scheming and unethical promoter as a complication for a young engineer's dream. When the real irrigation scheme failed, the family moved into Boise, living in her sister's boarding house, where she did much of her writing and worked in the Columbian Club before moving to California. Although her husband could not finish the canal, he was on hand when others completed his project in 1909, giving him credit for his vision if nothing else. In Boise, she frequently attended social functions, and as a charter member and officer of the Columbian Club she was part of the fundraising committee to furnish the Idaho Building at the Columbian Exposition. She designed some of the furniture and supported the club in several ways before she left.

She wrote a friend of her years in Idaho: "Dreamers we are, dreamers we always will be, and what is folly and vain imaginings to some people is the stuff our daily lives are made of. And there are thousands like us! If there never had been, there would be no great West."[10] She died in 1938.

LITERACY AND CITIZENSHIP

Concepts of literacy and citizenship were inextricably linked in the nineteenth century. The result of linking literacy to education and citizenship was a new stratification of class, a stratification with moral rather than economic connections and imperatives.[11] Mass education, valued as a democratizing force, had an unintended consequence, like many social programs. It served to magnify differences in education level and ability, with resulting differentiations in status, which were also emphasized in women's clubs. Class terms, as opposed to concepts of higher and lower orders, were a nineteenth-century development. They took over what was traditionally described in other hierarchical words such as *rank, order, degree,* or *estate.*[12] Class terms connote class consciousness, even when they are denied, including terms like *literate* or *educated.*

Ideas about literacy and class control subsequently infused concepts of culture, whether called high or low, classic or popular, transcendent or vulgar. A sense of culture, like most human relations, exists in a force field of relations of cultural power and domination, as cultural historian Michel Foucault describes. With it comes a tendency of the dominant culture to critique and reorganize popular culture, often by excluding, confining, or co-opting its forms. The controversy over dime novels and working-class reading demonstrates the process, even now, and is an issue frequently ignored in discussions of culture and library collections. One kind of narrative that co-opted the simple appeal of the dime novel was what critic Michael Denning terms genteel, moralistic narratives cast in the dime novel format, such as the stories of Horatio Alger, which he says constituted a middle-class moralizing about and to the lower classes.[13] The so-called sentimental novels women wrote in the nineteenth century offer another example of the moralistic narrative, where character rather than economic class was paramount.

Despite changes in printing technology and bookbinding, books remained largely out of the grasp of working-class populations, especially at points more distant from the manufacturing and publishing centers of the East. Free public libraries were scarce, not just in the Northwest, but throughout the country, even into the

1870s. A Bureau of Education survey in 1875 found more than 3,600 subscription, society, college, institutional, and professional libraries, but fewer than 350 libraries nationwide open to the general public without charge. Most of those were in New England and the older parts of the Midwest.[14] If women's clubs were "the woman's university," then public libraries were "the people's colleges," conferring on the many the opportunities for learning and improvement previously enjoyed by the few and offering "uplift" as a by-product. In addition, access to libraries, for those who used them, fostered independence through self-education, self-development, and self-help, regardless of individual economic or social standing.

The relationship between literacy, libraries, and education—and the lack thereof—was painfully obvious to clubwomen in the West, if the class issues were not. They knew their communities lacked the resources to offer residents even ordinary access to basic information and knowledge. The women were particularly sensitized to issues of education and access since they generally were excluded from it, at least at higher levels. The underlying motivation was something more—to offer a societal good that also elevated the values missing from a commerce-centered vision of community with a political culture that supported it and excluded services and programs the female perspective gauged as important.

The physical construct of a public library, with its open-ended access to what was believed to be the best the western tradition had to offer in a setting of order, was the ultimate self-improvement opportunity. And, for those who valued measures like opera stages and statehood, a good library was the standard-bearer in community validation. It was also a tangible and permanent end product for the hard work of clubwomen, who not only scratched together books and dollars for their reading rooms but also organized major fundraising campaigns or lobbied city councils for support of public libraries through taxes. Many even initiated negotiations directly with the all-important Andrew Carnegie Foundation for the construction of libraries throughout the Pacific Northwest and bullied city councils into passing the library tax required before the foundation would lend its financial support.

Steel magnate and philanthropist Andrew Carnegie in 1879 gave his first library funding to the town in Scotland where he was born. He was there when the first cornerstone was laid in 1881, when he was nearing eighty years of age. In a staggering achieve-ment, over the next twenty-five years Carnegie's foundation gave $56 million to build 2,500 libraries in the United States and world-wide. It based the size of the gift on the size of the community, usually $2 per capita, and required the city to commit to main-taining the library and buying books and employing staff for it.[15] In town after town, women's clubs built the bridges that induced cities to make the commitment that made the Carnegie libraries possible, after demonstrating the need for a public library facility through reading rooms often shuttled all over town in makeshift quarters.[16]

A CLUB'S LIBRARY BECOMES THE STATE'S LIBRARY
The record of the Columbian Club in Boise demonstrated how clubs directed their library efforts. The Columbian Club in 1893 expanded a WCTU collection into what became Boise's reading room in the City Hall. The Columbians later donated the ground on which the Boise public library was built and were instrumental in securing the grant for the building from the Carnegie Founda-tion. Ultimately, the Columbian Club also built a State Traveling Library, made possible through legislation sponsored by the club. Ten cases of books the club collected began rotating among Idaho communities that had no library facilities.[17] Ten cases grew to a remarkable two hundred eventually, continuously circling Idaho and in the custody of local women's clubs at each stop. Club lead-ers begged and bullied freight lines and railroads into moving the boxes for free, leveraging those who said yes against the others.

A memorandum bill dated June 16, 1899, to Boise Travelling Libraries from A. C. McClurg and Co., Booksellers, Chicago, pro-vides insights into orders and costs. The club got a bill for $9.58, which included a 30 percent discount, for one each of these books: Shorthouse, *John Inglesant;* Clemens, *Tom Sawyer;* Wilson, *George Washington;* Tarbell, *Early Life of Lincoln;* Gaurier, *Win-ter in Russia;* Ellis, *Great Cattle Trail;* Lanier, *English Novel;* Stevenson, *Across the Plains;* and several other books. A month earlier, the women had spent $108 on books and freight, for the latest fiction and nonfiction. Club officers sought discounts from all major publishers, and most complied.[18]

Later president Gertrude Hays described the process the em-boldened women used. "We watched the register of the old Over-land Hotel, and when anyone of prominence arrived, Mrs. Beatty, our chairman, and I would put on our best bib and tucker and proceed to interview him, usually with satisfactory results."[19] The brash strategy worked. The initial ten cases containing 592 books were put on display at a public reception in the hall of the capitol building before being sent out in June 1899. By the next time the legislature met, the club had thirteen cases in the field, traveling free or at discounted rates (typically freight bills were $4.10 each) after members also buttonholed railroad officials.[20]

To information-starved and isolated rural communities, the traveling bookcases must have seemed like Christmas in July. The bookcases also offered the organizers opportunities to define in the most basic ways what literature and culture were. The women of the club devoted considerable time, energy, and money to the development and management of this resource, which expanded rapidly. By 1900 the new library stations included other women's clubs that had agreed to participate, such as the Outlook Club in Weiser, the Woman's Literary Club in Mountain Home, the Albion Improvement Society in Albion, and the Century Club in Nampa, which required a staffing commitment from each club.

The first cases went to Nampa, Weiser, Silver City, Warren, Blackfoot, and a few other places. By 1900 stations were designated at Nampa, Blackfoot, Payette, Emmett, Albion, Middleton, Delamar, Star, Hailey, Weiser, Warren, Trade Dollar (Silver City), and Mountain Home. Meridian had discontinued for lack of a librarian, and other cities had applications on file. On the legislative front, in 1901 the club secured passage of a law creating a Free Traveling Library Commission, with funds to enlarge and keep the library cases moving. The club donated its thirteen cases to the state in this early private/public partnership, the model of cooperation clubs sought on other projects.

Physically the traveling libraries consisted of heavy boxes made of strong wood. Each had double doors, a lock and key, and an inside shelf. Club documents indicate dimensions of 20 inches high, 10 inches deep, and 34 inches wide, with double doors opening up to a space divided into four cubicles containing the books. The box was to be placed on a sturdy table so browsers could examine the contents. Each case held fifty to sixty books and included juvenile selections, fifteen works of fiction, and twenty miscellaneous books. Cases were lodged in private homes or club-staffed reading rooms.

Columbian Club president Gertrude Hays described how they

were used. "The books are divided into late fiction, juvenile, history and classics. They are free to any one in the community in which they are placed, to take home and read providing they comply with ordinary rules such as returning them within a certain time and taking care of them." She said cases stayed in each place three months "and are then sent on to another station and another case takes its place."[21]

However, women in clubs, like women (and librarians) elsewhere, found controversy in trying to choose what books constituted the "the good, the true, and the beautiful," worthy of making available to all. At The Dalles in 1898 the library was barely a year old, having been organized by a few women who met "and armed ourselves" to find "victims to the smiles of the soliciting committee," as they put it. Yet the women had to deal with complaints about books purchased by the buying committee. They had purchased or acquired 230 volumes as of 1898, with fiction predominantly represented. But tastes differ, club leaders said with tact, noting that some called the offerings trash. "What is a buying committee to do?" asked the women's edition newspaper editor.[22]

Although it has long been recognized that clubwomen commonly worked for libraries in their communities, few actually surveyed the cities to measure their contribution. A library survey conducted by Idaho state librarian Henry T. Drennan documented the club role in developing most of the public libraries throughout that state. He found that Idaho by 1910 had five Carnegie Libraries—in Boise, Pocatello, Nampa, Moscow, and Lewiston.[23] It also had thirteen public libraries and reading rooms, all fostered and supported by women's clubs. His list also included no fewer than 158 library stations in the state, which received collections from the Traveling Library.[24]

PIES AND BOOKS

Bringing reading to their communities and getting residents, especially male residents, to change customs and partake required some ingenuity in what today would be called marketing. One example, at the new irrigation development at American Falls, Idaho, occurred when eight members of the Syringa Club gathered 100 books from members in 1907. The club then started a library housed in two small rooms in the back of a drugstore, with shelves made from apple crates. The women kept it open two afternoons and two evenings each week. To interest young boys in reading the books there they advertised that each boy using the room the following Saturday could have all the pie he could eat. Girls seemed to need no such inducement. Funding for the library was provided through "home talent" plays, dances, and candy and lemonade sales. A druggist donated the proceeds of his soda fountain one day a month to the cause.

A newspaper's description of the reading room established in Boise reveals the operation of the larger reading rooms that soon became official libraries.[25] The club had ordered $150 in books at the same time the WCTU donated 500 volumes from its own earlier reading room. In 1896 the Free Reading Room and Circulating Library, now a project of the Columbian Club, housed two tables where readers found the latest magazines and periodicals, from *Scientific American* to *Harper's Weekly* to *Puck*. Readers also had access to the latest government reports, such as geological surveys and mineralogical reports. The larger of two rooms was set apart for readers, and the chairs were usually filled, because it averaged forty-five visitors a day. The room at the head of the stairs, "whose open door gives a cordial invitation to enter, is the book room. It has 180 feet of shelf room, filled with books, over 1,200 volumes in all, classified and arranged in such a way that one may easily find what is wanted, though the efficient librarian will gladly get it if asked."

The Columbian Club had donated the books and furniture to the city and pressured the city to take over management and funding of the operation. The money for operating expenses of $33 a month came from the entertainment committee of the Columbian Club, private donation, subscription fees and fines, and the sale of old papers. The paper noted that all the money taken in by the club since 1894 had been expended on the library, an indication of its priority. In a region that was information poor, the idea of having an array of useful and ennobling material at any reader's fingertips was heady. It was both a useful service and a powerful metaphor for the city's progress and intellectual wealth.

Embracing Aesthetic Ideals

Women in study clubs had from "experts" and their own reading relatively clear-cut ideas of what was the highest and best in American culture. Tastes in the Pacific Northwest clubs, as in the East, leaned heavily to England's and New England's poets and playwrights. In most cases interests and thus programs broadened over time to include regional literature, local history, and civic or social issues as well. The transcendental writers—Hawthorne, Emerson (but seldom Thoreau, Melville, or Whitman)—appeared regularly on study club programs. Occasionally European writers, usually playwrights such as Henrik Ibsen, were subjects. Shakespeare was always a study club favorite. The Brownings, Whittier, Lowell, and Longfellow were among other cultural icons whose names appeared frequently in the yearbooks.

Emerson, with his spiritual insights about art and beauty and his call for an end to the distinction between the fine and useful arts, appealed particularly to those women who aspired to entering higher and better cultural realms. His background as a philosopher and appreciation for art history typified the club approach to the arts, which explored historical connections and developments in art. Emerson also carried forward a message that indicted existing American culture, with its look back to the courtly muses of Europe and focus on elitism and the material realm. Instead he envisioned a new egalitarian American culture, with America in all its variety and natural wildness as the proper focus for art. Emerson's art was therefore democratic and accessible to thoughtful people—like women—and not just an intellectual elite. As a romantic individualist, he also glorified the position of the artist, thinker, or poet as valuable and necessary to the national community, a thought women in study clubs cherished in the face of social and economic change.

Emerson's self-reliance connected to their ideas of self-improvement and their felt need to change America's climate. "The Americans have little faith. They rely on the power of a dollar; they are deaf to a sentiment. They think you may talk the north wind down as easily as raise society," he wrote in "Man the Reformer" (1841). The women hoped to prove him wrong. "The poet is the sayer, the namer, and represents beauty. He is a sovereign, and stands on the centre," he said in "The Poet" (1844).[26] Here the women hoped to prove him right and elevate the position of art in an increasingly materialistic and mechanistic age. Other writers making frequent appearances in annual study club programs in the Northwest were the English Romantic poets—William Wordsworth, Alfred Tennyson, less frequently Percy Bysshe Shelley, John Keats, and Lord Byron—and the American William Cullen Bryant, all of whom emphasized the relationship with nature and ideas of sublime and noble art.

Although appearing less frequently than Emerson, the name of John Ruskin also frequently showed up on programs in the Northwest. The English critic's rejection of the European masters and look toward modernism in aesthetic thought influenced ideas of culture and art in the United States. Ruskin also developed a moral justification for art, connecting it to spirituality and putting it on a high plane, an idea that resonated with clubwomen. To women who held strong ideals about morality and virtue and the sublime power of the arts, his sense of the aesthetic held high appeal. "How to give all access to the masterpieces of art and nature is the problem of civilization," wrote Emerson in "The Conduct of Life," arguing for public rather than private ownership of art. It was a charge many clubwomen took seriously. Some brought books to their towns; others brought music or art.

In 1912 art that was not copied from old masters came to Idaho through the efforts of a Pocatello clubwoman and the Idaho Federation of Women's Clubs. An exhibit of oil paintings from the Chicago Society of Artists plus a second exhibit of watercolors and etchings by the Chicago Water Color Society came through Idaho. Through federation efforts, particularly of Dr. Minnie Howard of Pocatello as head of the art committee, the art circulated through thirty Idaho towns. The federation at the time had twenty-eight club towns in the state, and the exhibits played to standing-room only crowds. In 1913 an exhibit of fifty-four paintings from the Society of Women Painters of New York made the same circuit. To the federation's delight, the attendance in some communities exceeded the town's population as neighboring community residents traveled to see the paintings.[27] Dr. Howard and her club cohorts were proud of the results.

PROFILE: DR. MINNIE HOWARD

"Dr. Minnie" was born Minnie Frances Hayden in Missouri in 1872. She began teaching at age seventeen, without having attended high school, by studying nights to pass the state teacher exams.[28] After marrying W. Forrest Howard in 1894 at age twenty-two, she attended two normal colleges in Kansas and Illinois. She went on to Kansas University Women's Medical School, graduating with a degree in 1899. She taught intermittently to support herself as she worked toward the medical degree.

She and her husband practiced medicine together in Kansas, and she was one of the founders of the Larned, Kansas, library. They soon moved to Pocatello, at the eastern end of the Snake River plain in south Idaho. They continued to practice together for eight years after coming to Pocatello.[29] After the birth of her second son, Richard, Dr. Minnie gave up the practice of medicine. Two other sons followed. As their children were growing up, she worked in the leadership of both the WCTU and the Congregational Church. She also developed a fascination with local history.

More politically partisan than many clubwomen, she called herself a Populist, but later worked for Idaho's Republican Party and the national Prohibition Party. According to her biographer Mary Kennedy, Pocatello residents saw her as forceful, talkative, and perpetually surrounded by interesting clutter. The whole family reportedly was fond of cross-country excursions in pursuit of points of interest in local history, sometimes cutting across the sagebrush and even fording shallow rivers in their quests. She eventually became president of the Southern Idaho Historical Society and director of the Oregon Trail Memorial Association.

Howard also headed the drive to get a Carnegie Foundation grant for the Pocatello Library, which was erected next to the family home on South Garfield in 1908. Two years later the whole family trekked to Vienna and spent a year there as their son Forrest studied medicine. In fact, all four Howard sons completed medical school.

Ezra Meeker, who had crossed the Oregon Trail by ox team in 1852, visited Pocatello in 1907. He spoke to the Women's Study League while she was its secretary. His remarks spurred her interest in local history to even greater heights, which were fully realized a decade later. Meeker came back to Pocatello in 1916. The Howards, Meeker, and an Indian guide named Joe Rainey managed to locate the original site of Fort Hall on the Snake River Bottoms. Fort Hall had been an important point for thousands of emigrants coming west, but its exact site had been lost. The study league supported Meeker's efforts to gain recognition of the entire Oregon Trail by getting the trail marked and memorialized.

Howard helped create the Southern Idaho Historical Society in 1922, serving as its first president, and embarked on a new career writing about local history. Meeker, now in his nineties, was invited back, and work began to memorialize Fort Hall, which was about to be covered by American Falls Reservoir. At the urging of the Historical Society, Howard, the Daughters of the American Revolution chapter, and others, Congress ultimately approved special coinage for the Oregon Trail. Meeker got the first coin to be minted; Howard got the second. The profits from the sale of the coins built memorials and monuments all along the trail.[30]

During World War I, Howard became president of the local Red Cross. In that capacity she organized war work for six women's organizations in the Pocatello Federation of Women's Clubs: the Women's Civic Club, Art Club, Thursday Music Club, Study League, DAR, and WCTU. The clubs threw themselves into fundraising work through women's usual methods, such as bazaars, sewing, and knitting, having been generally excluded from the leadership of the men's fundraising efforts. In fact, by November 1917 the women had donated 280 pairs of pajamas, 241 surgical gowns, 223 bedshirts, 144 ice-bag covers, 100 bathrobes, 84 hot water bag covers, 80 pairs of bedsocks and 80 operating helmets, 60 operating caps, and 2 boxes of surgical dressings.[31]

Howard was a national committeewoman from Idaho to the National Prohibition Party in 1912 and was involved in the peace movement, attending the second Conference on the Causes and Cure of War in 1926. She also continued her interest in temperance. The deterioration of Native American society as a result of alcohol abuse on a nearby reservation and elsewhere led to her work with the Indian Welfare Department of the General Federation. She wrote letters and delivered radio addresses on the topic in the 1930s.

The GFWC response to her public entreaties in 1939, however, was to tell her to direct her remarks about liquor to the Indian Office only as a member of the WCTU, not to represent the federation in her campaign. Howard was also a member of the American Medical Association, American Association of University Women, Civic Club, Art and Travel Club, Study Club, and DAR.[32]

The study of whatever writer was on the club agenda was often intense and meetings long. For example, the small Entre Nous Club of Mountain Home, the southwest Idaho desert waystation between Twin Falls and Boise, was led by Mrs. Samuel Gray Rhoads, who had worked in Denver clubs before coming to Idaho. Programs at each meeting followed a typical pattern: readings from the biography of the author in question, with roll call answered by quotations from that author. Then a magazine article of interest with original comments was read to the group and discussed, followed by paper(s) presented on the artist under study, then a piece of classical music, and last the study of parliamentary rules and debate. Such meetings frequently took the better part of a day. Yet this club also found time to rent a room on Main Street for a free reading room to house newspapers, magazines, and the traveling library cases. Club members, twenty in all, proudly noted that the club began working for a free library for others before starting a library for its own use.[33]

Others, heady with the newfound power of collectivism, grew irritated with clubwomen who remained so fixed on study when so much action was needed. The connections between art and activism were distilled in a committee report to the 1906 meeting of the General Federation. Kate Cassatt MacKnight described the typical club view combining literature and activism. Clubs spent months "studying the idealism of Tennyson, or the scathing arraignment of all that is sordid" found in Browning, or read Thomas Carlyle, "becoming imbued with his scorn of the pettiness of the pretentious world." Then they came at last to John Ruskin, "with his appeal for more simple and spiritual living, for more beautiful surroundings, and less destruction of all that is fine and noble in ourselves, and in our surroundings." After all this, "one naturally begins to open one's eyes, to look about, and to inquire if we have any right to continue to live amid hideous surroundings; or to permit the children of our 'land of the free' to be destroyed by drudgery, or vicious environment; or to stand idly by while the grandest, most beautiful, and picturesque scenery in our country is destroyed by the blind greed of grasping commercialism!"[34]

Strictly literary study clubs still had an important role in civic work, according to MacKnight. She added that consideration of "the great civic questions of the day" led literary clubs to a "deepening of character, and in growing that genuine respect in which the club will be held by the community in which it is placed." She suggested club civic work be divided along three lines—municipal sanitation, municipal cleanliness, and "the city beautiful."[35]

Clubwomen often found connections others missed between art or history and present-day problems in the name of culture and environment, sometimes using them to counter the ideas of rugged individualism, commercialization, and virility fostered by men fearful of the "feminization" of culture. Sometimes they found new heroes for women, as an Oregon writer did. Eva Emery Dye wrote historical novels about the region, like Mary Hallock Foote, putting women in the forefront of the imagined West. She also made Sacajawea, the Lewis and Clark expedition guide, an icon for women's role in the West and recognition in the Northwest.

PROFILE: EVA EMERY DYE

In her long career Eva Emery Dye played many roles. She was a WCTU worker, women's club founder, suffrage leader, and published novelist. She also helped establish the Willamette Valley Chautauqua, one of the largest and most successful in the country.

Like other Northwest leaders, Dye began her career of service in Oregon writing for the WCTU. In 1890 at Oregon City she wrote an ode to the WCTU that was adopted by the Oregon WCTU and printed in its official history. The work compared the band of volunteers to crusaders, the vanguard of a new world. "Though we seem but a handful we hear the firm tread / Of the army of Progress, aye marching ahead, / And our feet fly to join them, we fling away fears, / Not drafted we go, but as bold volunteers."[36]

Dye was born in Illinois in 1855. She and her husband Charles, a lawyer, both graduated from Oberlin College in 1882. To get through college she taught school and saved, working at Oberlin as a librarian.[37] They married the year they graduated and came to Oregon City in 1890, where she engaged in WCTU work. She also became chair of the Oregon Equal Suffrage Association in Clackamas County. In 1902 she wrote a historical novel, *The Conquest: The True Story of Lewis and Clark,* which brought her and its heroine considerable fame. Although later historians questioned some of Dye's conclusions, the book identified Sacajawea as a major contributor to the success of the Lewis and Clark expedition through the Northwest and thus the westward exploration, lionizing the Shoshone Indian woman. It was printed in at least four editions and widely read at the time, often showing up in club book discussions.

In fact, it was Dye's work, according to Ronald Taber, that linked the mythology of Sacajawea to the very real political cause of women's rights. She fostered a view of Sacajawea as evidence of women's heroism and rightful role in the development of the Pacific Northwest, thus furthering the cause of women's suffrage. Indeed, the guide's role leading the white men through the area and interceding with tribes along the way had been minimized or ignored in previous accounts of the journey.[38] Soon after her book was published, the Portland Woman's Club created the Sacajawea Statue Association with Dye as its president, with the goal of building a monument to the new hero to match all the existing monuments to great men in U.S. history. Dye had actually called for this in her book.

"Sacajawea, modest princess of the Shoshones, heroine of the great expedition, stood with her babe in arms and smiled upon them from the shore. So had she stood in the Rocky Mountains pointing out the gates. So had she followed the great rivers, navigating the continent," Dye wrote in *The Conquest.* "Some day upon the Bozeman Pass, Sacajawea's statue will stand beside that of Clark. Some day, where the rivers part, her laurels will vie with those of Lewis. Across North America a Shoshone Indian Princess touched hands with Jefferson, opening her country."[39]

Dye also had long wanted to start a program to benefit a wide range and number of people. She realized it by organizing the Gladstone Chautauqua of Willamette Valley, the most successful such enterprise west of the Rocky Mountains. It was Dye who hired the speakers and nurtured the organization until she died.[40] Chautauquas, before the rise of modern media, combined speakers, entertainment, and fairs, even band concerts and baseball tournaments during long summer meetings.

The Gladstone Chautauqua's humble beginning was as a cultural education class in Dye's home, attended by over sixty people. She persuaded Judge Harvey Cross, an Oregon native, to donate 78 acres of land for a special Chautauqua park. Two years later it was the site of a huge wooden structure dubbed the "beehive." It had a capacity of 5,000 people.[41] It was funded by local businessmen from Oregon City who contributed $5 each for a share of stock. It also offered display booths for the WCTU, the Grange, and other organizations, all for a $1.50 season ticket for a week's entertainment. The Gladstone Chautauqua pulled in audiences primarily from Portland and Oregon City. From Portland, some eight miles away, 25 cents took patrons to the site by either electric railway or steamboat. Meals cost a quarter, and lodging in a tent $2 a week.

Typically, a day's program at Chautauqua began at 11 A.M. with a lecture, usually aimed at women. After lunch came other lectures on political or literary topics, followed by a band concert at 2 P.M. Baseball games—a popular attraction—were then held at 3:30 every day, with teams from all over the Pacific Northwest entering the Chautauqua league. Following supper came another concert at 7:30 and a literary reading at 8, followed by a main attraction lecturer at 8:15. Speakers varied widely, and the Chautauqua gave a forum to African-American leaders, political candidates, and even tribal representatives as well as religious leaders.[42] Sometimes national speakers such as William Jennings Bryan spoke there to overflow audiences.

The Chautauqua movement helped spur the founding of university extension programs and summer schools. Like club programs of work, the Chautauqua programs and university extension provided opportunities for adult or continuing education to those who otherwise would have been denied them, including thousands of women like Dye. She said her Gladstone Chautauqua offered "intellectual privileges" to "college men and women, worn out farmers' wives, teachers, preachers and working men . . . the greatest purely intellectual gathering west of the Rocky Mountains."[43] The Chautauqua movement touched several places in the Northwest. There was a small Chautauqua in Puget Sound and a popular Chautauqua series that pulled people from northern Idaho and eastern Washington every summer to Spirit Lake in Idaho. Even the small Idaho town of Kendrick had its own Chautauqua in 1892, with five women and a local minister organizing it.[44]

Sympathetic to regional cultural efforts and history, Dye long argued for support for female writers like herself and for cultural recognition of Oregon and the Northwest during a time when the Northeast seemed to dominate publishing. For instance, Dye's review of a book written by another Oregon woman appeared in the *Oregon Historical Quarterly* in 1906. The book she reviewed was *Letters from an Oregon Ranch* by Katherine McClurg. "If the East knows little of Oregon and cares less, if Oregon herself ignores her artists with pen and brush, where then shall come our place on the literary map of the nation?"[45] Dye herself wrote a series of novels about the pioneers, including *McLoughlin and Old Oregon,* published in 1900. Other published works included *McDonald of Oregon: A Tale of Two Shores* (1906), *The Soul of America: An Oregon Iliad,* and *Stories of Oregon* (1916).

As leader of the Sacajawea Statue Association, the project of the ambitious Portland Woman's Club, Dye and the association managed to raise $7,000 between 1902 and 1905 to commission a female sculptor, Denver's Alice Cooper, to create the bronze statue of the Indian guide. The women had raised the money through a national campaign, even selling Sacajawea spoons and buttons. The statue itself was unveiled in ceremonies at the Lewis and Clark Centennial Exposition in Portland in 1905, a symbol of women's importance to the continued development of the West.[46] As happened in Washington State, the NAWSA held its convention at the Lewis and Clark Centennial Exposition to gain attention for suffrage and push the state toward approval.

Dye formally presented the statue at the exposition. In 1906 she became chair of the suffrage campaign committee. Despite the campaign, the statue, the speeches, and the exposition, voters rejected the proposal in 1906 and again in 1908 and 1910, a source of pain and humiliation to the Oregon leaders, especially after Washington and California gave women the right to vote in 1910 and 1911, respectively. Oregon women finally succeeded in 1912. Dye died in 1947 at the age of ninety-two.

In a 1904 address to the Oregon Federation of Women's Clubs another leader decried endless study with no clear purpose. "Our work is practical, inasmuch as there are now not so many and long encyclopedic papers on subjects the writers know nothing about, but there is an earnest study into matters concerning which we need wisdom and knowledge, and as intelligent citizens of human beings we intend to learn about," Adelia Wade of Pendleton told delegates from thirty-six member clubs representing 1,454 Oregon women.

"We are striving to learn how we may make our homes better; how we may form public opinion on abuses that exist in laws that affect our homes and families; we are interested in public school laws, in our state institutions for the unfortunate, the delinquent and the criminal. We want to know how we can help in that most practical work that helps the children, the young people, that preventive work that is so vastly better than reform work." She repeated one of the criticisms of women's clubs' work, that it was scattered and shallow and thus ineffective. "We cannot do well if there are 'too many irons in the fire,' but the elevation of our homes, our communities and the public sentiment of our whole state, educational and civic betterment, all this is our legitimate field of labor."[47]

MIDDLE-CLASS AND MIDDLEBROW?

Later critics drew a distinction between their own ideas of an elite cultural aesthetics and the kind of broad-based arts culture clubwomen like these promoted, situated as it was between the aesthetic sense of a small, elite culture and a mass culture. Deeming their culture "middlebrow" (i.e., conservative and unsophisticated), popular, and pretentious, some critics denigrated it on the basis of the traditional aesthetic and social values it promoted. Such criticism, like using the term *middle-class* as a pejorative, often missed the point. The clubs' focus on the arts and activism provided a sense of stability and continuity as well as opportunity for education and experimentation. Its focus was on what was ennobling, aesthetic, and accessible in an uneasy time of shifting standards and concern about new mass entertainments amid fears that American culture was losing ground to "race suicide" and immigration. As with the creation of the canon, standards of quality seemed to be male-oriented, male-dominated, and exclusive, despite women's extensive participation as both writers and readers. Central to the clubs' idea of culture were literacy, literature, and reverence for the book and the commitment to promote aesthetic standards reflecting the "highest and best." This was also perceived as women's unique role.[48]

Ideas of "highest and best" led inexorably to hierarchies in taste and stratification of cultural productions, with those in positions of power defining the standards in the cultural wars. Art, music, theater—and books—became increasingly stratified in the nineteenth century in a tension between widely shared ideas of culture and the exclusivity of elite cultural forms. Clubwomen, in the middle of the tension, sought simultaneously to reinforce ideas of "highest and best" while spreading those ideas and opportunities to ever larger circles. It was hard to have it both ways, but many clubwomen tried, especially to counteract what they viewed as the negative effects of a rising tide of mass popular culture.

Although the forms of media changed, the debate about their effects on behavior raged then and throughout the twentieth century, with intermittent attempts to control the "worst" of the content. The "highest and best" competed with the "vast wasteland" for control of the popular consciousness, but images of elitism remained firmly attached to the arts, despite the clubs' proselytizing and idealism. Even libraries, the legacy of women's clubs, as they professionalized became more concerned with information access than with social control through limits on content. Community clubwomen were no longer involved in the selection of materials.

FROM LITERATURE TO LOBBYING

City Case Studies, 1885–1915

As clubs moved outside their own circles and into the larger community, women found themselves confronting other cultures and arcane systems, especially in the larger cities. It happened in Spokane in the 1890s, when a woman's club tried to intervene to protect a Chinese child. There reform-minded women had established a Humane Society, precipitated by the beating deaths of animals in the city. They also wanted to protect children, including a local Chinese girl. She was caught in the debilitating cultural practice of binding the feet of upper-class female children, keeping them tiny and fragile, sometimes with crippling results. The women directed their attention to the proprietor of a fancy goods store in Spokane named Ah Yen. Angry over what he was doing to his eldest girl's feet (and perhaps some of the larger issues the cultural practice represented), they visited the parents. They found the father less than receptive to their interference. The women thought the police should be called in.

A newspaper account of a subsequent reporter's visit to the house draws in a few words the cultural differences that clubwomen and reformers encountered in attempts to "Americanize" immigrants and the nativist attitudes that sometimes colored their work. The reporter found a house with quaint "Mongolian" furnishings and representatives of a culture where "women [have] no petticoats, where the laborers have no Sabbath . . . where to take off your hat is an insolent gesture; where writing runs from right to left, . . . and where the feet of the female children of aristocratic birth are bandaged from infancy until they stop growing."

He saw the girl with the bound feet and found a mother who could not speak English, "but her husband can talk 'Melican' like an auctioneer." He told both the reporter and the clubwomen that the feet of the females of common Chinese could grow, "but his family was descended from the Wei dynasty, and he defied anybody to compel him to let his daughter's feet grow as large as the feet of American girls." The very thought made him angry.[1] The cultural and sexist practice left the clubwomen in a quandary. After discussion, the women finally decided that there was no other compelling evidence of cruelty to the child and that she was not suffering greatly, so they dropped the matter in favor of more pressing community issues.

There was much to be done to shape their fast-growing towns. This chapter reviews club undertakings affecting life in the major cities of the Northwest—Portland, Boise, Seattle-Tacoma, and to a lesser extent Spokane—as case studies of the impact of club activism. It also recounts the Northwest's history of ethnic and racial diversity and how groups such as African Americans responded to the club movement. What happened in these cities also evidences the shift of private philanthropy and institutions to public support and the changes in legal political status the women sought.

Until the closing years of the nineteenth century, the social welfare of citizens was generally perceived as the responsibility not of government, but of private charity and benevolence, with only a few exceptions. Further, the regulation of commerce and merchants was a function of the market, without government interference in what were historically private transactions between sellers and buyers. However, many clubwomen wanted to change that. Women pursued a set of priorities that expanded club concerns and countered the prevailing culture, with its tendency to social Darwinism and tacit support of laissez-faire capitalism. Because women in the Pacific Northwest came late to the club movement, many brought with them ideas of reform that filled the air with debate about the nature of government and government's relationship to citizens, in an era of reforms now labeled Progressive.

As used here, *politics* is not confined to legislating, administering, and policymaking, what political historian Philip Ethington calls the "output" of politics, but includes policy "inputs," where discourse, culture, and culturally created institutions affect state action and political institutions, bending them to the will of those controlling the "inputs." Ethington, in writing about gender and the public sphere in the 1800s in San Francisco, argues that women challenged men's domination of the political public sphere "by entering it and transforming it" through their voluntary associations.

Further, women from the 1880s forward laid siege to the liberal theory framework exalting individual freedom, attempting to re-define "the 'base' on which the state rested, that is, to redefine authority, sovereignty, freedom, justice, and the public sphere itself." Ethington adds that this also brought the women into conflict rather than alliances with male Progressives and their ideas of reform. Women's social welfare rhetoric, he notes, was different. It was about social needs rather than rights, sheltered under the spreading umbrella of maternalism as an ideology.[2]

New Methods for a New Era

The fluidity of the Northwest's communities, changes in technology, and ideas of progress fermented with the yeast of the new social sciences and powerful economic forces. The women's club movement mixed its own priorities into this batter. The rise of the social sciences such as sociology and psychology brought with them new "scientific" methods and an awareness of a larger world, which clubwomen adapted to their own uses. They used surveys and paid more attention to the psychological needs of the objects of their attention, such as new ideas about child development, and forged ahead.

Clubwomen expanded the traditional idea of sisterhood and applied it to the growing population of working women sometimes exploited in the cities of the Northwest, establishing schools and residences for them. Some sought legal protection for them. Successes in passing Oregon labor laws protecting women led to a landmark U.S. Supreme Court decision upholding states' rights to pass protective labor laws a few years later. The case itself was built not on argument and precedent alone but on social science methods and findings.

The Pacific Northwest saw many different clubs working on issues of social welfare, beginning with the WCTU in the 1880s. In the Northwest, the exponential growth of settlements and cities far outpaced anyone's ability to provide services, even in the context of limited turn-of-the-century services. Providing aid, where it existed, became the role of private groups and charity, rather than a role for taxpayers and public authorities, especially where they had little tax base to use. Women's clubs filled in with needed services, then wanted government to assume responsibility and offer more protection for citizens, particularly the powerless citizens they dubbed "the worthy poor." Their female gaze placed high value in particular on protection for women, children, and families. The larger cities of the Northwest, which had some of the worst social problems, offered a proving ground for what they and their clubs could and could not do to change the existing culture.

Charting the most influential of the range of clubs in the major cities of the Northwest outlines what was happening, to greater and lesser degrees, in virtually every town under the rubric of village improvement. The deeds and very existence of many clubs, some of them of great importance to their communities at the time they were organized, have now been lost to history, especially those that were not affiliated with the federation or careful to deposit their records with archives.

Several patterns emerge from club minutes. Clearly, initial club leadership consisted disproportionately of a few well-educated professional women and wives of various businessmen, although few of them were wealthy, at least at first. Many of these women made clubwork their professional careers. The pattern also shows that the clubs melded self-improvement and community improvement and sought a changed role for women. The clubs wanted more political power and influence for women, often justified with a conservative stance toward women's exceptionality rather than using the more radical equal rights arguments. They had a pattern of extending ideas of culture and beauty tangibly, through community projects from art exhibits to city parks. They also sought controls on behavior through regulation, from inspection of public markets to ordinances against spitting on sidewalks. They created institutions such as alternative schools, then pressured communities and states to make them a public responsibility. That progressive outlook in this new age, however, could not see across certain boundaries. While religion, economic class, and ethnicity were permeable in the Northwest, race was much less so.

ISSUES OF RACE, CLASS, AND STATUS

Unfortunately, the GFWC motto "Unity in Diversity" did not mean racial diversity. The education, support, and expansion of class contact many women found in their clubs did not generally extend to women of color, whether Native American or African American, unless they founded their own clubs. The attitude that many pioneers (and some of their historians) brought with them into Oregon Country and the Pacific Northwest held that it was the Anglo-Saxon destiny to carry the highest and best in western civ-

ilization across the land. This sense of the Great Northwest and
manifest destiny led them to a land conceptualized as empty, as
something to tame and claim, and a view of themselves (and their
systems) as superior.

Americans in the West often felt ambivalent about groups who
were not as "American" as they or who were perceived as economic threats. Some immigrants felt ambivalent about other
groups of immigrants, however, on the same basis. Distribution of
ethnic and racial groups varied in the Pacific Northwest, but immigration was heavy throughout its development, especially to the
West Coast. The Puget Sound area of Washington had significant
Scandinavian immigration, as did parts of north Idaho. Both Portland and Boise saw German and Jewish immigration. Seattle and
Portland had significant Chinese immigration, as did the mining
towns of Idaho, and later Japanese populations grew on the West
Coast. Portland in 1890 had 4,740 Chinese, 519 African Americans, and 20 Japanese residents.[3]

Immigrant groups had varying experiences. Some sought quick
assimilation, while others maintained distinct cultural differences
and neighborhoods or even whole towns. Some, like the Chinese,
faced violence and legal exclusion. Much of the railroad building
in eastern Washington and Idaho was the hard work of Chinese laborers—over 7,000 Chinese graded the roadbed along the Snake
River, along with 1,000 whites.[4] The Japanese moved into Idaho's
agricultural areas around the turn of the century. They also were
found in the agricultural developments of central Washington.
The rich farmland of the Palouse region on the border of Washington and Idaho attracted a significant Russian population called
Volga Germans.

Other ethnic groups included Basques, primarily sheepherders,
who migrated into southern Idaho communities and settled
around Boise. Greeks emigrated to Pocatello as railroad employees, Swedes came to Idaho's panhandle for the logging and agriculture, and Irish moved into a number of cities in the Northwest.
Early in the twentieth century transient Hispanic agricultural
workers moved into southern Idaho and south-central Washington, starting a pattern of itinerant farm work. Although African
Americans moved into the cities of the Northwest, their number
was small, consistently totaling 1 percent or less of the population. However, they left their mark on the region in many ways.
Over the decades groups came to the Northwest at different times

for different reasons, sometimes from western sites such as Nebraska, the Dakotas, or California, sometimes from homelands overseas.

Among the foreign-born, the most immigrants came to the Pacific Northwest from Scandinavia, Great Britain, Canada, and Germany, with those from southern and eastern Europe not arriving in significant numbers until the first decade of the next century.[5] The Northwest felt greater pressures from immigration than the rest of the country, with a higher percentage of foreign-born residents. It reached a high of 22 percent in 1900 in Washington, compared to a national average of 14 percent. Idaho had 15 percent and Oregon 16 percent. Ethnic clubs, sometimes in the form of neighborhood clubs in ethnic areas, eased the transition for immigrants. For instance, ethnic clubs for women in Washington included the National Council of Jewish Women, the Daughters of Norway, the Fidelia Club for Italian Women, the Vasa Lodge, the Japanese Methodist Girls' Club, and the Slavonian Women's Lodge.[6] Concerns about immigration and race frequently surfaced in club programs, especially after the turn of the century, tacitly linked to (or occasionally countering) fears of radicalism and talk of race suicide.

One historian estimated that over the decades perhaps 10,000 African Americans participated in the migration of nearly two million people to the Pacific Northwest (including Montana), settling more consistently in cities than did the other immigrants.[7] As the cities grew, African Americans organized neighborhoods and community institutions that paralleled the institutions from which they were excluded, institutions that gave them a sense of support and permanence, such as churches and women's clubs.

AFRICAN-AMERICAN WOMEN'S CLUBS AND RACE PREJUDICE
Although white women's clubs in the Northwest frequently supported black women's clubs and their clubs were eventually included as full members of the General Federation, clubs and members of the two races did not often intermingle. Sarah Evans, who became president of the Oregon Federation of Women's Clubs, assisted in the formation of the Federation of Colored Women's Clubs in Oregon. She said that thirteen clubs were represented at the initial meeting and noted that five of the delegates were college graduates. "Their efficient manner of conducting their meetings and the manner in which they reported amazed me. They are

taking up the study of the lives of great people of their race and have done much charitable work." She urged the Oregon federation to assist the new organization.[8]

The women's club movement flourished in the Northwest's urban African-American populations and added substantial benefits to their neighborhoods. The African-American women's clubs in many ways matched the idealism and cultural reordering sought by the women's club movement as a whole, while providing more services and social welfare than many white women's clubs. Given the greater educational, economic, and social limitations on black women, their clubs were perhaps even more important to them than to other women, particularly for those who aspired to "belong" and adopt cultural standards reflected in the club movement as a whole.

Historian Frances Jones Sneed, in looking at the African-American women's clubs in Spokane, disagrees with the prevalent idea that ascribes club membership to an effort to gain a middle-class image and status more acceptable to whites. Instead of this white-oriented perspective she uses the perspective of the African-American women themselves, finding them much more concerned about mutual support and social welfare than about white acceptance and status. Also, while white women's clubs worked against nineteenth-century perceptions that women could not work together, black women faced that problem plus the problems of racism and far less leisure time than their counterparts. Sneed also concludes that any class privileges African Americans enjoyed in Spokane and elsewhere were most often due to education, since other avenues were closed to them.

Women's clubs in the African-American communities showed rich variations. In Spokane there was a small black community by 1880, which had grown to 723 by 1910. It included fewer professional women, and most of those who worked for wages worked as domestics. In 1890 two black churches were founded, and a key event was the formation of the Phyllis Wheatley Club for Girls, which came out of church membership. Women's clubs there included the Booklovers Club, to encourage reading of the classics, the Spokane Negro Dramatic Club, and the Merry Matrons Club, which catered dinners to raise money. The oldest was the Dunbar Literary Club for study of poetry, with emphasis on African-American writers. There was also a Grandmothers Club and Ashanti Club and the Spokane Colored Republicans Club, which had male and female members and sometimes elected women as officers. The Spokane City federation of African-American women's clubs predated the state federation.

These clubs often had a focus on art and culture, but also raised money for social causes, especially those that promoted children and family interests and opportunities for blacks. Eva Smith, an 1899 University of Idaho graduate, was one of the more active club members and a role model in Spokane, an example of the "racial uplift" clubwomen sought. Sneed found that Spokane had both middle-class and working-class clubs for African-American women, and occasionally both groups were represented in one club. Clubs were an important institution for African-American women, providing self-definition, friendship, and support while strengthening the family and making members feel important.[9]

In the Pacific Northwest, as nationally, more African-American women than white women worked outside the home as the primary support for themselves or their families. Between 1890 and 1920, 40 to 50 percent of these women worked as "breadwinners" compared to 12 to 25 percent of white females and 15 to 16 percent of Native American and Asian women. According to census figures, of the 800,000 women living west of the Mississippi in 1900, about 370 were Japanese, 4,500 were Chinese, 6,000 were Native Americans, and 12,000 were African Americans (both the Chinese and Native American populations were probably undercounted).[10] Although African-American women and men supported the domestic ideal of the female as homemaker and mother, male unemployment, low wages, and restricted opportunities made it a necessity for their wives to work. Women were generally concentrated in the lowest-paid occupations, most often domestic work.[11] Those who were economically successful engaged in managing hotels, running boarding houses, operating hair parlors, or investing in real estate.

Frequently, African Americans in the Pacific Northwest protected their political or civil rights through temporary, single-purpose organizations, ad hoc groups without formal structure. For instance, the Portland African-American community mobilized in 1876 when the city prohibited black children from attending public schools. They hired a white lawyer to sue the school system and dropped the suit when the board agreed to set up a city-supported segregated school. However, parents continued to protest about the school, using an economic argument about the cost of keeping a separate system, and in 1880 the board relented and merged the separate program.[12]

Race as a Study Club Issue

Race, which had a much different and broader connotation at the turn of the century, defined as relating to one's own cultural group, appeared as a topic on study club programs. Racism did not, except in rare circumstances. The 1880s—just as the WCTU began spreading through the Northwest—was a period of particular antipathy toward the Chinese in the West. Congress passed the Chinese Exclusion Act in 1882, and unemployment and a severely depressed economy led to anti-Chinese crusades and riots in Washington and Oregon in 1886. In 1888 white residents of Tekoa, Washington, ordered all Chinese to leave town.[13] Sylvester Pennoyer ran for governor in Oregon on an anti-Chinese plank and won.[14] The Chinese were generally ignored by women's clubs in the region, except for occasional English classes or reform efforts to take Chinese "sex slaves" out of brothels, notably in San Francisco.

While women's club programs covered a plethora of civic issues and social problems, treatment of the Chinese or other populations who were targets of racism seldom surfaced there, other than as study of China as an exotic place and culture or of immigration policy as a national issue. However, many study club programs addressed African Americans in cultural, historical, or political contexts in laudatory—if sometimes patronizing—tones. Achievements, talents, history, or needs of "the African race" were often topics of study.

Women's clubs in the Northwest did, from time to time, especially in the 1920s, also turn to nearby Native American populations. Like their missionary and WCTU predecessors, their efforts often yielded poor results despite good intentions. The attitude clubwomen held toward the Native American population reflected the attitude many in the country held about the process of cultural conflict: that assimilation and the destruction of traditional native practices were in Native Americans' best interests, despite an incompatible national idealism about the noble Native American in the West of the imagination.

For instance, Mrs. John N. Alley, Lewiston, chaired the Indian Affairs department for the Idaho Federation of Women's Clubs. Her 1922 study found that Idaho had a population of 4,017 individuals on tribal lands, 1,039 of them school-aged children, many

of whom attended school irregularly or suffered from the scourges
of tuberculosis and trachoma. Indians in the northern part of the
state were more prosperous, she found, with their own homes and
skills at raising crops, than were the Native Americans around
Fort Hall in the southeast part of the state.[15] Her survey resulted
in some lofty federation goals and a program of action, but not
much seemed to come of it. The clubs of the Northwest frequently
tried, at least on a limited basis, to meet some of the basic survival
needs of nearby Native American populations. Their programs
consisted of practical attempts to clothe, feed, educate, and med-
icate them, especially the children, hoping ultimately for assimilation as their route to happiness.

THE CLUBS AND THE IMMIGRANTS

Historian Mary Ritter Beard in her survey of women's organizations discussed clubwork with immigrant populations. She found
that many of them studied "the needs, customs and labor of foreigners first as well as they could." Study was followed by survey
and then by English language classes where needed in a drive toward literacy, with other training classes offered as well. One survey report distilled the attitude of many clubwomen toward the
immigrant "problem." "It has been abundantly shown that the
bulk of the immigrant's own burden and our burden because of
him are due not to viciousness or abnormality of any sort, but to
sheer helplessness," said the report.

"He is exploitable raw material, and he is exploited, and held,
until he can push out of it, at a low grade of living detrimental to
him and to the community. And the one effective measure to help
the helpless is to bring them to a condition in which they can protect themselves." That included learning to read and write, learning job and life skills, and learning English.[16] In many places, settlement houses became the site of that kind of activity and social
science experimentation. In other places, as in the Northwest,
women's clubs assumed much of that responsibility. Some places—
like Seattle—had both. Settlement houses and sometimes clubhouses became sites for meetings, nurseries, kindergartens, and
classes—and also fostered reform and reformers.

Women set up study programs and civic projects for immigrant
populations in the Northwest's larger cities. Some offered classes
in English and other topics. Some ran medical clinics. Some set
up meetings and cultural events for them or helped find employ-

ment. Eventually most were abandoned when sponsors were overwhelmed by the needs or members' dedication flagged. In the interim a few programs gained governmental support and many individuals who needed help got at least some attention.

URBAN CASE STUDIES IN CLUB ACTIVISM

The major cities of the Northwest with their growth, immigration, and up and down economic cycles lagged in other forms of development. On the coast especially, the cities had large transient populations who followed the seasonal industries. Although census data clearly defines *city* versus *rural* in terms of population, terms like *rural* or *urban* reflect more than numbers; they reflect attitudes as a matter of self-definition and aspiration as much as totals. Indeed, the distances in the Northwest made towns of small regional sites and cities of towns that drew customers from a large surrounding area, offering what residents associated with cities. The social and economic configurations of these places felt the impact of women's club activism. The port towns of the Northwest had all kinds of amenities, including large red-light districts, and the men in them outnumbered women in the early decades.

After the turn of the century, commercial and industrial growth in the region meant that more and more women began entering the work force, further changing the social patterns and relationships. Economic growth and industrialization brought expanding employment and also worker exploitation. Activist clubs in the major cities of the Northwest addressed work issues by monitoring abuses and supporting legislation for protection of working women, on the one hand, and offering services for them, on the other. At the same time, with consumerism and unregulated businesses came concerns about consumer protections and public health as well. From consumer protection to mothers' pensions, the clubwomen of these cities expanded expectations about government's role on behalf of citizens. Each city's experience also shows how clubs changed their own priorities and methods to meet social and cultural shifts, leaving the heated rhetoric of motherhood behind in a shift to the rhetoric of efficiency, social science, suffrage, and progress.

WOMEN'S CLUBS IN PORTLAND

Portland, at the commercially important confluence of the Columbia and Willamette Rivers as they move toward the Pacific

Ocean, was a village of only 900 residents in 1851, the year the Oregon Territorial Legislature incorporated it. Portland's history was a story of migration and movement. By 1860 African-American artisans and unskilled laborers began drifting in. In 1862 they founded the People's Church, an interdenominational congregation, and created the Portland Colored Immigration Society to bring other blacks into the city.[17] By 1870, 30 percent of the city's population was foreign-born, when the state's foreign-born population was just under 13 percent. By 1890, 59 percent of the population or 27,000 people were either foreign-born or had at least one foreign-born parent, a higher percentage than in any cities in the West outside of San Francisco.[18] By 1890 Chinese residents outnumbered blacks nine to one, at 4,790.[19] As of 1890 sizable migrations from Scandinavia and southern and central Europe came to Portland as well, behind the German and Irish waves. All this made Portland the most diverse and heterogeneous community in the state, with considerable effect on the nature of the city and its clubs. Oregon's state population in the meantime exploded, from 13,300 in 1850 to 413,500 in 1900.

Organizations created to address some of Portland's growing community needs often overlapped. They included in 1873 the Oregon Society for Prevention of Cruelty to Animals, about the same time that women began temperance work there, followed in 1880 by the Oregon Humane Society to prevent cruelty to human beings as well as animals. In 1885 community leaders established the Boys and Girls Aid Society of Oregon to improve the lot of homeless, neglected, or abused children. By 1889 the Refuge Home for Women had been established through the WCTU "to rescue fallen women and girls who desire to escape from a life of shame."[20] Also in 1889 the Patton Home for the Friendless came into being to provide assistance, food, clothing, fuel, and necessities to "the afflicted and friendless," an institution run by women. These community welfare organizations were followed by others of a different sort: the Portland Chamber of Commerce (with a hefty $300,000 in capital) in 1890 when Portland's population reached 62,000, the Portland Art Association in 1892, and the Oregon Yacht Club in 1903, demonstrating the diversity of community organizations.[21]

Portland, perhaps more than other cities in the Northwest, was soon stratified by an economic elite engaged in commercial activity, interconnected through family, economic, political, and social control.[22] However, few of the women who were part of this elite group ever appear in the rosters of club leadership. The two exceptions from a list of twenty-one wealthy founding families were Georgiana (Mrs. Henry L.) Pittock, the newspaper publisher's wife who helped found the Portland Women's Club, and Mary (Mrs. William S.) Ladd, wife of a merchant and banker, who was involved in several philanthropic projects and donated land for the Florence Crittenton home there. Georgiana Pittock, resident of Oregon by 1852, married printer and paper manufacturer Pittock in 1860. That was the same year he propitiously gained ownership of the *Oregonian* in settlement of back wages for his printing work on the paper.

THE 1887 PORTLAND WOMEN'S UNION

In 1887, as the slow ferries across the Willamette gave way to Morrison Street Bridge and gas and oil lamps gave way to electric and incandescent lamps, a group of women began meeting in Portland. They decided they wanted to operate a boarding residence for young, self-supporting women, especially those in Portland for the first time. Founders of the Portland Women's Union that year were Mary Hodgdon, Rosa F. Burrell, and Mrs. T. E. Clapp.

Hodgdon reflected the professional education, activism, and prior experience common to club leaders in the Pacific Northwest. Born in Massachusetts, she graduated from Ipswitch Seminary. At the suggestion of the Reverend S. H. Marsh, then president of Pacific University in nearby Forest Grove, she came to Portland in 1861. She taught at the university a year, then opened a private school at Portland in the basement of the First Congregational Church. In 1867 she went to Walla Walla and taught at what was then Whitman Seminary, returning to Portland in 1871, where she remained involved in the public schools and sixteen years later began the Portland club.[23]

The cross-class and interdenominational nature of this women's club (and community sensitivity to class issues) was described by the *Oregonian:* "The Portland union was the first one in the U.S. to place itself upon the broad basis of woman for womankind, irrespective of class or creed. It dispenses benevolence, not charity; safety, not reformation." But as a result of rumors president Rosa Burrell felt the home had to explain itself. Some members of the community were suspicious of this new "boarding house" for young women when "female boarding house" was a common euphemism for brothels.[24]

The home needed larger quarters and made a series of moves, culminating in a four-story home constructed in 1917 and named after Martha Washington. The first home, a house on Flanders Street, was named Anna Lewis Hall after one of the club's founders. It housed twenty young women. The problem of decent housing was a difficult one for "respectable" and naive young women, especially prior to 1900. "The girls came in from the country towns to work in stores or do sewing, the only fields open to them in those days," later recalled president Mrs. Roger S. Tracy.

The home the Portland Union ran for working women had many restrictions. It required admission applications, adherence to strict rules, and testimonials of character. It closed at ten, and lights were out at eleven. The working women who lived there paid rent in proportion to their wages. The larger home the club built was located at 18102 Southwest Tenth Avenue, a stolid structure fashioned of dark brick with a huge columned portico and a formal fountain out back. It included a library, a drawing room, a recreation room in the basement, a writing lobby across from a bank of windows, and an outdoor garden court. Portland State University eventually acquired the building, and yet another location was found for the club home.

The existence of the home itself demonstrated the lack of social services in Portland when it became the target of applications for admission from older women who found themselves destitute, creating a problem for the club. The 1891 report from the head of the Household Committee described the club's solution. "Perhaps I may once more say here that our class of guests is restricted to young women—at least we cannot admit as permanent boarders aged women, . . . although we turn away no woman without providing for her as well as we find it possible to do," physician Emma Welty wrote. "We send them to their homes in the East, or to their friends, if such can be found; to the Hospital if that is needed, and keep a care over them while there; or to charitable or reformatory institutions, as they variously belong. Not a few women come under our care who do not properly belong to us. To all such we give the best attention possible."[25] The house income, mostly from board and room charges, was $25,562 that year—a huge sum for a group of women to manage—and they spent all but $702 of it on the house, lunchroom, and other activities connected to the enterprise.

However, by 1896, despite their efforts, the house was not full of the women for whom it was intended, and president Mary Jones had her own answer as to why. "A scarescrow [*sic*] has been erected over us as a weathervane, and its name is charity." She said residence at the home should not be considered charity, but support, like a scholarship. "We need to take a step upward, until the bare mention of the word 'institution' does not give us nervous prostration for fear someone has heard us call this boarding-house an institution," said Jones.[26] The issue was more than charity, however; it included reactions to the elements of social control reflected in the rules of the institution, part of a patroniz-ing (or matronizing) morality that interfered and irritated even as it protected.

The 1895 Portland Woman's Club

Another Portland club particularly interested in improving the lot of working women was the Portland Woman's Club. The tireless club worker from Olympia Mrs. A. H. Stuart inspired a group of Portland women to form a club that had a charter membership of seventy-eight. Founded in 1895 at the home of Mrs. W. W. Spald-ing, its first officers included Mrs. J. C. Card (who also became an officer in the Federation, the Consumers' League, and other clubs), Caroline Dunlap, Julia Comstock, Frances Harvey, and Mrs. N. B. Cox. In 1896 it sent president Card as its delegate to the federation meeting in Louisville. Founder Caroline Cock Dunlap was Oregon's first kindergarten organizer and teacher (in 1882), coming to Oregon in 1853 with her parents and settling near Olympia.[27]

By the time of its first annual report in 1897 the Portland Woman's Club had grown to 116 members and had an average at-tendance of 70. Meetings included recitations, music, and no fewer than fifty-five papers and addresses during the year, forty-three of them presented by its own members.[28] Some members wanted to start a philanthropic department, for which the inci-sive president had a warning that clubwomen everywhere would have done well to heed, especially with regard to efforts to correct the behavior of working women, immigrants, and other groups. "Far be it from me to repress any noble enthusiasm for doing good; I only wish to point out that nothing so makes the judicious grieve, and the wicked rejoice, as hasty and ill-considered at-tempts to right some wrong or suppress some evil, ending, as hasty attempts of the kind are pretty sure to do, in the confusion of the assail and the escape of the assailed," said Card. "For us, unarmed and unprepared, to attack the mighty hosts of evil, may be heroic, but it is futile."[29]

Many clubs took the heroic route nevertheless, including the Portland Woman's Club, which piled up a distinguished record on social welfare issues, including wage and hour laws, child welfare, and public health. The Public Welfare Department of the Portland Women's Club worked for and helped pass both child labor laws and laws regulating newsboys' work in Oregon. By 1903 Oregon had a child labor law prohibiting children under fourteen from being employed in factories, mines, workshops, and telegraph, telephone, or messenger offices. It also investigated working conditions for women and conditions in the city jail, bringing remedial public attention to both. In 1904, following a survey of Oregon school laws, it launched a campaign to increase teachers' salaries. Teachers then as now were mostly women and were paid much less than male counterparts. In 1913 it was instrumental in finally gaining passage of a mothers' pension bill.

The club also worked with a dozen state agencies to improve conditions and policies affecting children and young people. It provided $500 for a woman's clubroom on the Lewis and Clark Exposition Fairgrounds and worked with the Travelers' Aid Society to place women at railway stations to meet young women and prevent them from being victimized. It also made dozens of ongoing contributions to social welfare programs, from the Women's Convalescent Home to the Florence Crittenton Home in Portland. Its Public Health Department, under Dr. Esther Pohl Lovejoy, led a campaign against the disease-spreading public drinking cup and old-fashioned roller towel. It helped make consumer advocate Sarah Evans the market inspector to monitor compliance with pure food and sanitation ordinances it helped get passed. With the Legislative Committee and the Oregon Federation of Women's Clubs, it won the fight for the first Pure Food Law enacted in Oregon.

Besides establishing a library, it supported a curfew ordinance in 1899; in 1900 it supported an ordinance to force Portland retail stores to close at 6 P.M. to protect working women. It sponsored the first cooking school in the city, using a club member as instructor, and members began presiding as hostesses at summer Chautauquas. In 1901 the club sponsored what its historian called a cultural success but a financial failure in a series of lectures. In 1902 members won their fight to preserve trees in the plaza downtown, working through the city council. In 1904 the club worked for a city plan to provide sandboxes and play facilities for children in the park blocks. In 1905 it fostered special activities connected to the Centennial held in Portland. It established a scholarship and in 1910 raised $1,200 for endowment of a free bed in the Open Air Sanitarium, which over the years "cured many tubercular women."[30]

From 1900 on this club took up civic issues of wide variety, from regulating cuts of meat to industrial school lectures to demonstrations from working women. In 1901 its home department established a farmer's market downtown, where "dealers and farmers may meet and exchange produce and find shelter for themselves and teams."[31] The women from this club, the Portland Woman's Union, and the YWCA met together that year to discuss uniting efforts to create a School of Domestic Science. On November 12, 1901, the group forwarded a petition to the city council supporting formation of a Consumers' League and also heard a lesson on the "Physiology of Digestion."

THE PORTLAND CONSUMERS' LEAGUE

Later that month the Home Department of the club actually created a Consumers' League and called its first meeting in 1901. Members were asked to take a pledge "that I will not make purchases after five o'clock on any day, not after twelve o'clock on Saturdays, and that if a package cannot be delivered before six o'clock on any day it is to be delivered the following morning."

Dr. Mary Anna Cooke Thompson, one of the signatories, became a suffrage leader. Born in New York City, she studied medicine with two La Salle, Illinois, physicians after moving to Chicago and began a practice for women in the Midwest. She married Reuben Thompson, and they had six children. She came to Portland in 1867, where she practiced for twenty years, primarily in obstetrics. In the 1880s, like other professional women in the Northwest, she took a leadership role in campaigns for suffrage and other human rights issues.[32] The Portland Woman's Club later honored her as an outstanding member, calling her an ardent feminist who saw her dream realized when she herself voted in Portland in 1913, the oldest member of the club at that time.[33]

The Consumers' League of Portland under the Portland Woman's Club sponsorship became an influential and important organization. About the same time the club created the Consumers' League, the educational department endorsed Mrs. C. E. Sitton, one of their charter members, as the first woman candidate for the school board. She won and served on the board from 1901 to 1911. It also helped establish kindergartens in schools, worked for free textbooks in public schools, and fought for women's suffrage.[34] The Portland clubs through advocacy and the powers of education, government regulation, and public spending altered the attitudes toward social welfare issues at the city and state levels. The clubs provided a vehicle for rallying women not only to act on perceived community problems, but to enact their vision of the ideal city.

THE AFRICAN-AMERICAN CLUBS OF PORTLAND

Club activism came later to African-American women in the city. The Women's Co-op (later called the Multnomah Women's Club) was organized in 1914 by Ruth Flowers, who became its first president. The Colored Women's Council was formed by Portland clubwomen, and Lillian Allen, wife of W. D. Allen, owner of the Golden West Hotel, was its first president. Years later the council's member clubs included the Altruistic, the Literary Research, the Fleur de Lis, and the Harriet Tubman Club, in addition to the Multnomah Women's Club.[35] The Colored Women's Republican Club and the Rose Bud Study Club were organized and added to the national council lists in 1915.[36]

In 1917 nine Portland clubs went beyond city limits to organize their own Oregon Federation of Colored Women's Clubs, which soon grew to seventeen member clubs.[37] The African-American women's clubs stressed community service, fundraising for scholarships for girls, education, the arts, and various social and political activities, such as the Literary Research Club's study of the laws of Oregon relating to minorities.[38]

In Oregon, the white clubwomen eventually voted to exclude black women from the clubs, despite the efforts of some advocates to get them included. The issue of admission of black women into the women's clubs was pushed forward by some members in the clubs of the West, as in New England, with mixed results. Washington, among a few other states, passed a resolution in 1902 opposing any restriction of the right of African-American women to enter the General Federation. So did the Portland Women's

Club.[39] The General Federation sidestepped the controversial issue while lending rhetorical support to clubs for African-American women who formed their own national alliances.

Women's Clubs in Boise

Some early clubs coalesced to answer a national call for state or territorial representation in a major event, as happened in Boise when women responded to the call for Idaho to be represented at the important Columbian Exposition in Chicago in 1893. However, the resulting 1892 Columbian Club was not the oldest study club in the state. It was preceded in 1888 by the Shakespeare Club of Idaho Springs, formed by Cora Bullis, and the Treble Clef Club in Coeur d'Alene. Neither group joined the federation.[40]

The Board of Lady Managers for the Columbian Exposition had representation from Idaho in the form of Alice Ramsey Straughn, WCTU leader and wife of the surveyor general of Idaho. She became the official Idaho hostess at the exposition. She and Carrie Logan (wife of Thomas Logan, Boise's first postmaster and a four-time mayor) called a "women's mass meeting" in what was then the capitol building on May 2, 1892.[41] Thirty-five Boise City women showed up, twenty-eight of whom signed on as members (six of them single women), "to secure full representation of the industries and interests of the women of this vicinity at the Columbian Exposition."[42] The governor allowed the women to continue meeting in the capitol building. They elected Victoria Louise (Mrs. Alfred) Eoff, president; writer Mary (Mrs. Arthur D.) Hallock Foote and Fanny L. Cobb, wife of newspaper publisher Calvin Cobb, both vice-presidents; and Frances C. (Mrs. J. W.) Huston, treasurer.

These and the Woman's Columbian Club leaders who followed were relatively prominent women in the small city of Boise, and several of them had been active in the Idaho WCTU during the 1880s. Eoff was married to a banker. Hays was married to a prominent attorney who later became mayor of Boise and state attorney general. Other leaders included Mrs. A. L. Richardson, wife of the clerk of federal court, and Mrs. James H. Hawley, whose husband became prosecutor, mayor, and eventually governor.

The women quickly began raising money. They even asked the schoolchildren of each county to donate a few cents for the benefit of the Children's Building at the fair. The meetings of the group rotated among the various offices in the capitol until Elizabeth Hallock Sherman offered her dining room and a small reception room for meetings. The members divided into groups of eight, with each expected to raise no less than $25, creating both competition and some creative ideas for raising money. One member made and sold cottage cheese to meet her share. President Eoff decided to hold a promenade concert on the capitol grounds. The committee had the gates in the iron fence around the capitol block chained, with the gatekeeper instructed to collect 25 cents from each person entering. The sale of ice cream and cake raised more.[43]

The club took on the task of furnishing and maintaining the reception room of the Idaho Building at the fair and lobbied the legislature of the new state to appropriate the $50,000 needed for construction of the Idaho building. Eoff and a committee of Cobb, Straughn, Ridenbaugh, Foote, Logan, Mary Pinkham, and Richardson—mostly wives of early entrepreneurs and territorial officials—managed the whole enterprise. Pinkham, county president at the 1889 WCTU meeting in Boise, was wife of a deputy U.S. marshal who became treasurer for a railroad.[44]

Eoff was called by later historians the leader of Boise's club and social life during her forty-seven years there.[45] She and her banker husband Alfred built an expensive residence at Second and Main. Eoff, with her wideset eyes and penetrating gaze, did not miss many opportunities to be of service to Boise and to master the game of cultural politics. Born Victoria Marsh in Ontario, Canada, in 1859, she ended up in San Francisco with a married sister after her parents died. There she married a man who worked his way up from bookkeeper to cashier in the Wells Fargo Bank, coming to Boise in 1886, where he founded the Boise City National Bank. Besides the Columbian Club, Victoria Eoff also founded the Idaho Children's Home and St. Luke's Hospital. She and her husband received many guests in their "at homes," through whist parties and formal dinners. "An invitation to the Eoffs' splendid residence at 120 Main was cherished by all who had social ambitions," historian Arthur Hart writes, adding that their house was described by the *Statesman* as palatial. It became home to Governor James H. Brady in 1908. Eoff continued her career of community activism and social prominence until her death in 1933.[46]

Artist Foote loaned some of her artwork for the exhibit and even designed furniture for the Idaho building, including an oak settee, table, and chairs that eventually came back to the club as furnishings for the clubroom. Pillow covers and linen were embroidered with syringa, the fragrant, white-petaled state flower. Noted singer Clara Louise Kellogg (later Mrs. Stackrosh) gave china for service, and a woman was hired at $40 a month to serve tea to visitors at the fair and care for the room. The women's speeches delivered at Chicago, the Woman's Building with its displays of women's achievements, and women's involvement in creating the state buildings all provided an important opportunity to showcase women's accomplishment—and women's potential—at the Chicago exposition.

The exposition became a watershed of sorts for women. Over 300 papers and lectures were presented at the fair, on dozens of topics important to women.[47] Unfortunately, the African-American women who sought representation were excluded, and the Native Americans who were included were there more as objects than as participants. However, women's role in the fair on the eve of the woman's century was a national story with symbolic importance, as was the fair itself.

The following year, the women of Boise decided to continue their club and to start a circulating library for the city's benefit. The mayor and city council granted them a room over the mayor's office. The club took over the small WCTU book collection and opened for business, furnishing the room with some of the furniture made to order for the Idaho Building at the fair. In 1895 the group managed to hire a librarian and found it had to set some rules regarding delinquent books and library conduct. Minutes showed the posted Reading Room rules as follows: "1. no smoking allowed, 2. noise and loud talking prohibited in the halls and reading rooms, 3. no books taken from or returned to shelves except through librarian, 4. remove overshoes in the hall."[48] That same year the club decided to open the library Monday evenings to accommodate work schedules, and it soon opened other evenings too.

A book committee began to buy additional books and magazines, and for years a congressman sent it all government reports. For seventeen years a club friend gave it *Century Magazine*, the magazine begun by the New York men's club described earlier that printed many of Foote's stories and illustrations. Many townspeople donated material from their private libraries. The free library expanded to four rooms within a few years. Gradually the city assumed some of the expenses, but subscriptions (at $2 a year, waived for high school students), donations, and fundraising organized by the club remained its mainstay. The library charged $2 a year, or 25 cents a month, to use books outside the reading rooms.[49]

In 1895 Ella Cartee Reed, earlier one of the editors of the Idaho City *Advocate,* was made the first librarian. By then it offered citizens their choice from a collection of 832 books. She was paid $20 a month and held the job for nine years until city officials took over the project. In 1898 a trained librarian from Indiana was hired to come to Boise to catalog what was now 2,000 books in the collection and to teach library methods, staying in homes of club members for three months.[50]

The club added a literary department to its structure with the idea of members presenting papers for discussion. The very first paper read to the group was on woman suffrage, and the second was on laws of Idaho relating to women, both of which became club targets.[51] The Columbian Club's organization was unusual in one respect. It decided to establish an advisory board of five men, elected by the board of directors. The move to an advisory board was shrewd on the part of club founders, who recognized that the men's presence improved the chances for favorable reception of their community projects.

The initial group included five of the most powerful men in the city, men who could help the club accomplish whatever it wanted to do. However, by design they had little direct role in the operation of the club. In 1900 the advisory board included Judge James H. Beatty (whose wife Mary chaired the educational committee about 1900), banker Christopher W. Moore (whose daughter was a social and club leader), Walter E. Pierce, publisher Calvin Cobb, and James H. Richards (whose wives were officers).[52] Beatty, a proper, nondrinking attorney, Civil War veteran, and delegate to the constitutional convention, became a U.S. district judge.[53] Pierce owned a real estate and insurance firm; Cobb published a newspaper and was president of the Statesman Printing Company; and Richards, a lawyer, was elected mayor of Boise.[54]

The Columbian Club's objects were first to establish and maintain a "Circulating Library and Free Reading Room" and second "to take up any other line of work which shall be designed to promote the highest interests of the city." Meetings were held the first Saturday of each month (unusual in that such timing accommodated working women), and its standing committees were membership, book, library, entertainment, literary, and "town and village improvement." The largest committee at that point was composed of ten members. In the winter of 1896 the women took to the stage to raise funds, something large clubs sometimes tried. They produced a play called *The Mock Trial,* with most of the lawyers in town taking part in this mock breach of promise suit done up as drama. Also notable was writing, producing, and selling "The Woman's Edition of the *Statesman,*" the local newspaper, with the women pocketing half of the proceeds, a not inconsequential $395.[55]

In January 1897 the women sponsored a grand ball held at the Natatorium, an elaborate Moorish-styled multistory social center with a dance floor and swimming pool warmed by hot springs. It was dressed up in red and white for this event, one of many fundraisers for the library. Such events evoked memories of corseted matrons brought by carriages and hansoms to the end of Warm Springs Avenue, where ladies "wafted their fans to dispel the omnipresent rotten-egg smell from the sulphurous natural hot water."[56]

A few months before, in 1896, after the ambitious women of the club had added their town and village improvement department, they immediately began taking small steps that regulated behavior, such as getting a sidewalk expectoration ordinance passed, posting "do and don't" placards in public schools, and campaigning for a City Park. In 1898 they got a curfew ordinance passed and began mothers' meetings for child study, adding an educational committee under Gertrude Hays, then club president.

Hays had been in Idaho since 1886, when she arrived in Soda Springs as an eighteen-year-old teacher, according to biographer Betty Penson-Ward. There she married attorney Samuel Hays, and they left for Boise. He later became Boise's mayor and Idaho's attorney general. Mother of five children, Gertrude Hays was not only an officer in the Boise WCTU but moved through leadership roles in other clubs in the city as well before taking the helm of the Columbian Club and later the state federation. Her capacity for leadership also took her into the realm of politics. She was a member of the nominating convention of the Democratic Party in 1905 and in 1906 was named to the board of regents for the University of Idaho, where a dormitory was named for her as it had been for club cohort and regent Ridenbaugh, another Columbian Club president.[57]

Mary Black Ridenbaugh was a lifelong cultural and political leader in Boise, whose activism spread all the way to Moscow as a university regent, an advocate for domestic science, and a founder of many programs and institutions.

PROFILE—MARY BLACK RIDENBAUGH

Known as one of the five beautiful Black sisters (they also had six brothers), Mary Black was born in 1857 in Missouri to Charles M. and Annis M. Black. Her family was part of a train of one hundred wagons headed for Oregon when she was a child. When their oxen began to die, thirty of the families stopped along the way to establish Dixie, near what became known as Caldwell, Idaho, in 1864, then moved to a ranch and stage station fifteen miles east of Boise. They lived at what became Black's Creek, a stage stop between Boise and Mountain Home.[58]

Her father, a Confederate colonel, later moved the family to the Wood River area below what is now Sun Valley, where the family ran a profitable stage line carrying gold from the productive Golden Chariot and War Eagle gold mines. The girls went to boarding schools, and Mary Elizabeth became a teacher. She had attended St. Michael's parish school in Boise and later St. Vincent's Academy in Walla Walla. She taught school for two years at Dry Creek in Ada County. In 1878 she married Boise lumberman William Ridenbaugh, who became one of the city's wealthier businessmen. He was twenty-four, and she was twenty-one. He had come to Idaho in 1872 to work for his uncle Morris, who was also superintendent of the Northwest Stage Company. His uncle's sudden death left Ridenbaugh in charge of the family lumberyard the same year he married Mary. He completed an important irrigation canal begun by his uncle that, like a Boise street, still bears his name and developed houses using geothermal heat and the first electric company. In the meantime she became a leader in educational and cultural affairs in Boise.

They first lived on fashionable Grove Street, then lined with maple trees, moving later to a showplace called "The Mills." A founder of the Columbian Club, she was also Ada County delegate to the state suffrage organization during the successful 1896 campaign. Later, as president of the Columbian Club in 1900–1901 and chair of its building committee, she made it her personal goal to establish a women's dormitory at the university at Moscow. She had been named to the board of regents for the school partly as a result of her interest in education and women's access to it.

When she came to campus for the dedication, she asked what the building was to be called, but no one could tell her. She also noticed an odd gap in the brickwork. It was filled with a plaque revealed only at the ceremony. The building was named Ridenbaugh Hall in her honor in 1902, only the third building constructed on campus, thanks to a $25,000 legislative appropriation for a women's dorm she and the Columbian Club sought.

"I thought at first it was my epitaph," she joked. "But I am proud and happy over the compliment and I shall devote all my energies to the work of building up the institution." She later described the new hall for fifty women. "The hall is simply beautiful and will make an ideal home for young women. Dining rooms in most similar places are cold and cheerless. It is not so at the new hall. The ceiling is low and the color tints are harmonious and artistic." In her remarks at the dedication she said it was the special desire of the women of the state that a home should be supplied to young women who might attend the university.[59] She worked toward establishing domestic science as an academic program at the university and complained about political influence over the institution, a common complaint from women about institutions and politics in general.

She also pursued a public library for Boise. In her report, she described the effort. "We have no salaried officers, we have no money compensations. We have no permanent abiding place, we are free to embrace any work which will meet the needs of the times, and the aspirations of the future," she wrote. "No one can accuse us of any possible selfishness. The honor of being an officer is offset by the hard work the office entails."[60] She was instrumental in getting a Carnegie-funded public library building and served on the library board of trustees. With Gertrude Hays and Eva Dockery she also organized the Idaho Congress of Mothers in Idaho, a forerunner of the Parent-Teacher Association (PTA). She was also active in the women's guild of St. Michael's Cathedral and chaired the committee that built the 1925 Columbian Club clubhouse.

Described as "elegant and willowy," Ridenbaugh traveled widely, entertained grandly, and founded several cultural and social welfare groups to improve life in Boise.[61] However, as biographer Betty Penson-Ward notes, "a lot of hard-working steel lurked underneath her fashionable cool."[62] She acquired the background, political acumen, and reputation to be named to the University of Idaho board of regents, an unusual role for a woman of that era. In fact, she served on the board of regents under three governors, from 1901 to 1907.

An advocate for women's space at the university and in education, she also personally helped plan the new women's dorm and a curriculum in the new "science" of home economics.[63] She was pressed to run for various elected offices, an honor she declined, but during her lifetime she served on dozens of boards and pursued many causes.

In 1891 she and her husband built an ostentatious home outside Boise near family flour mills, a home that boasted carpeting, three stories, thirteen European tile fireplaces, red brick towers, and green ornamental shingles. She died in 1926 of the effects of pernicious anemia, and her castle home was sold to a man who was said to be Boise's only resident millionaire of the day, Standard Oil heir James McDonald, who razed it.

Cognizant of its status in city endeavors and the dearth of library access elsewhere in the state, the Columbian Club undertook what became its major venture and legacy: establishing traveling libraries, supported by outside club funds, described in detail earlier. The club had earlier tried for Carnegie support to build a Boise library, but failed.[64] It was clear in 1902 that the Carnegie Foundation preferred dealing with city officials rather than clubs, so Mayor Moses Alexander created an official library board. Members of the Columbian Club held three of the five seats. Getting the needed grant required city guarantees of a site and annual maintenance, a fund of 10 percent of the gift to endow the library, and proof Boise would actually support—long-term—a public library. The Carnegie grant, when finally awarded, was for $40,000, and it built a two-story white brick building. Club founder Mary Beatty became president of the library board in 1903.[65]

EXPANDING THE CIRCLE

In 1900 the club reached beyond traveling libraries to organize a district federation, the first in the state, which met at Mountain Home. Club dues, fairly typical for Pacific Northwest clubs, were $1 initially, going to $2.50 by 1900–1901 and soon to $5.[66] The club never flagged in its city betterment campaigns. It got the city council to put in watering troughs for horses and drinking fountains for humans and petitioned it to pass a measure to close saloons earlier and on Sundays. The club also established a model school room in a second grade classroom in Central School. The model room sported "suitably tinted" walls, statuary, pieces of artwork, and a flag, all "made as artistic as was possible with the $50 allotted for the purpose by the club," president Hays wrote. Hays attended the Biennial GFWC meeting in 1900 in Milwaukee, representing Idaho.[67] Like the Portland Women's Union, this club was at least on the surface egalitarian. The membership of the club was open to all women who paid the initial $1 dues, and it grew fast.[68] It totaled 200 women in the small town by 1900, only eight years after its founding, when the population of Boise was under 6,000.

Within a few years the club had developed a Program and Press Committee, a Historical Committee, an Entertainment and House Department, a Civic Improvement Department, and an Educational Department. The Educational Department took up local and statewide issues and was subdivided into sections. Idaho's elected state superintendent of public instruction, Permeal French, for years chaired the club's educational committee. In the first decade, the educational department used its influence to have an industrial or reform school built in the state, at St. Anthony in eastern Idaho (not its first choice for location), and organized a night school for young men. Its members read to the blind, put together art exhibits for schools, and established an active scholarship loan fund.[69]

The Columbian Club had a rather unusual means of filling its departmental ranks, at least initially. Members threw names into a hat and drew them for membership in departments to ensure the groups were mixed. They included the Department of Household Economics, a Building Department, a Music Department, a large Study Department with sections for art and travel, and departments on Shakespeare, parliamentary procedure, German, conservation, dramatic arts, and others as desired. Club records claim credit for causes as diverse as saving timber around Payette Lakes and securing a nine-hour day for working women. The group had honorary members (like the then-absent writer and illustrator Mary Hallock Foote) and associate members such as women interested in clubwork who were in the city temporarily.[70]

This large department club offered members a range of topics for study or activism or both by 1905. The club's departments of twelve to twenty-five members each even elected their own officers. Joint club programs included monthly parliamentary drills,

and certain days each month were devoted to particular topics
(civic day, travel day, etc.). By this time, however, the club had
grown so large and unwieldy that the open admissions policy had
ended. They held the club membership to a manageable 200.
Three club leaders held the additional title of Carnegie Library
Trustees—Beatty, Richards, and Ridenbaugh. The male advisory
committee now included a bishop and Moses Alexander and
James Hawley, men who figured prominently in politics as future
governors.[71] By 1906 the new Carnegie Library had been completed, and the club sponsored a ball and reception in 1905 in its
honor. The club from then on met in the basement room of the library and changed its name from Woman's Columbian Club to
simply Columbian Club.

The group redoubled its efforts to shape the community's culture through education and government channels. It worked to
abolish the city's red-light district, lobbied for road improvement,
and placed a memorial tablet in the capitol building in honor of
soldiers killed in the Philippines. It held night schools under Miss
Sonna and named a committee to streamline the nomenclature of
the state. It started an annual tradition of bringing city and country clubs together for a luncheon. It brought Denver's juvenile justice expert Judge Ben Lindsey to Boise, the man who earned a national reputation for his Progressive era ideas about creating a
juvenile justice system to treat children in trouble differently from
adults. Soon after his lecture, the city appointed its first probation
officer. The club also raised $100 for its scholarship fund and
bought a piano.[72]

In 1907–8 the pragmatic subjects the club studied included the
Chautauqua movement, bird protection, parks for the city, civic
improvement in small cities, good roads, play reviews, Indian history, juvenile courts, civil service, and playgrounds. In 1909 it
sponsored a concert by the renowned violinist Fritz Kreisler,
termed an artistic success but a financial failure.[73] By 1911 the
club had incorporated, adopting newer, broader objects: "To promote the standards of social and intellectual culture among its
members and the community in general along literary, social, intellectual and civic lines." It had built its own clubhouse at 817
West Franklin Street on property acquired by the club and incorporated.[74] The step of incorporation was important in the life of
an organization, because it gave such groups the right to receive
bequests, enter contracts, and act as an independent legal entity.

The construction of a clubhouse for a woman's club was perhaps the ultimate statement about personal female space. Many clubs, especially in the 1920s, pursued building clubhouses, which they used to house libraries, theaters, meeting rooms, social events, classes, community events such as lectures and exhibits, and so on. As happened with the men's clubhouses, the women's clubhouses often turned into expensive albatrosses, with costly maintenance and high taxes. Some clubhouses also tended to divert clubs from programs of social reform; for other clubs they enhanced efforts to make the women's club a true center of community service.[75] For all clubs, the acquisition of a clubhouse was a symbol both of status and of stability.

The Columbian Club leaders continued to reflect the city's oldline leadership. In the 1900–1901 yearbook, the officers included president Mary Black Ridenbaugh; vice-president Mrs. A. L. Richardson; recording secretary Mrs. Douglas W. Rossi; corresponding secretary Anna Sonna; and treasurer Mrs. H. N. Coffin.[76] Their husbands continued to come from the ranks of officials and entrepreneurs, and they lived in neighborhoods that covered the city.[77] Richardson's husband was clerk of the U.S. court, and Rossi's husband was state engineer. Anna Sonna was the daughter of Peter Sonna, vice-president of the First National Bank of Idaho, a philanthropist and founder of many businesses and the city's opera house. Sonna—like many others—did not migrate from east to west but from the California gold fields to Idaho in 1860. He was elected mayor of Boise in 1893. Coffin was wife of the cashier at the Bank of Commerce.[78] The Coffin brothers founded a hardware and sheet metal business with branch stores,[79] and Frank Coffin became Idaho's attorney general in 1890.

Boise in fact had many other women's clubs, although none were as active or for as long as the Columbian Club. Club leaders overlapped organizations. Historian Mary Ritter Beard praised another Boise group, the Good Citizenship Club, for its program of municipal entertainment, which scheduled a lecture one evening a week in the plaza in the business district. The women tapped each men's organization in the city to make it responsible for one of the evening programs. The club also took the initiative in providing a paid supervisor for the playground in the plaza in the mornings and evenings during vacations.[80]

The Lady Managers of the Columbian Exposition had their Washington counterparts too. Alice Houghton was a real-estate entrepreneur in Spokane who chaired Washington's Board of Lady Managers for the Columbian Exposition. She, like the women in Boise who started a club by calling women together to build an exhibit, found the connections lived past the exposition. In Houghton's case, her board planned the state's exhibit for the Women's Building and also a women's exhibit for the Washington State Building at the fair.[81]

THE CLUBS OF SEATTLE AND TACOMA

A few trappers, loggers, and sailors were followed by five pilgrim families from Portland (itself founded in 1844) who disembarked at Alki Point in 1851 near what became Seattle. A few years after the wagon trains began moving toward Oregon, David Blaine started a Protestant church there in October 1853. His wife Catherine Paine Blaine, a teacher, was one of the original signatories to the Seneca Falls Declaration of 1848, which called for women's legal and political rights. The following spring she was paid to open the first school in the area, with a term of three months, at a salary of $65 a month.[82] Lumberman Henry Yesler was allotted a tract of land along the south side of the settlement, where he built the first steam sawmill on Puget Sound. Slowly the settlement grew. The discovery of gold on Fraser River in Canada in 1858 brought a flood of hopefuls from California and Oregon, 20,000 of them heading north through Seattle and bringing the sound its first real business expansion—including a saloon and dance hall staffed by Native American women. By 1861 Seattle still had fewer than 200 permanent residents.

The Seattle of 1870 had grown to about 1,300 people and had a business section confined to two blocks. All travel to and from the town was by boat, and railroads were still a distant dream. Other small towns now dotted the Puget Sound, including Seattle's competitor Tacoma to the south, and the city's residents feared commercial supremacy might pass to it. If the railroad landed in Tacoma first, Seattle—despite its fine harbors—might be left stranded as a kind of forest-hidden boat landing deep in the sound, where the only industries were bringing coal from the Cascade foothills, sending lumber to San Francisco, and fishing. The University of Washington opened in 1872.[83] Its first female graduate was Clara McCarty in 1876, who taught in Tacoma and Sumner and was elected Pierce County school superintendent in 1880, the year President Rutherford B. Hayes came to town.[84]

Club activism came early to the state. A Ladies' Aid Society was listed in an 1873 Steilacoom paper.[85] Other clubs such as the temperance societies and the WCTU unions soon followed. Suffrage societies grew after Anthony's 1872 tour. Perhaps the first study club on the Sound was the exclusive Olympia Woman's Club, founded in 1883 on the heels of Willard's visit and the spread of the WCTU in Washington. Another early club was the Walla Walla Woman's Club, formed in 1886 for self-improvement and study of literature. However, this group changed its focus radically in 1887 when the women of Washington Territory lost their early right to vote through a court decision invalidating the legislative action giving them suffrage. Women as a group had first voted in the Seattle municipal election of 1884, when 759 qualified to vote.[86] The Walla Walla study club transformed itself into an Equal Suffrage League. Unsuccessful in its efforts to restore the rights, the league disbanded in 1889.[87]

During the 1880s Seattle grew ever faster and larger, and women began organizing clubs and institutions to meet burgeoning community needs. The city went from 1,300 residents in 1870 to 3,500 in 1880 to a remarkable 43,000 in 1890, nearly doubling again by 1900. By 1890 Seattle had a Ladies' Library Association that helped get a provision for a public library board in the 1890 city charter. Perhaps the first club there was a benevolent society called the Ladies' Relief Society; as happened throughout the Northwest, its leaders became founders and leaders of later women's clubs and subsequent suffrage efforts.

In 1884 fifteen of Seattle's relatively elite women—including Babette Gatzert, Sarah Yesler, Catherine Maynard, and other wives of successful Seattle businessmen—gathered in Mary Leary's living room to form the Ladies' Relief Society for "the systematic benevolent work of assisting the poor and destitute regardless of creed, nationality, or color." Catherine Maynard opened a reading room in her home and helped found the Ladies' Library Association.[88] Yesler, wife of the founder of Seattle's first industry, was one of those many leaders who worked for multiple causes. She was the first librarian. She also attended Washington's first suffrage meeting in Olympia and afterward started the Seattle suffrage association.[89] After Yesler's death, her husband Henry donated their mansion to the city for a public library.

From the work of Yesler and other women came the Seattle Children's Home, especially needed after the 1884 depression in

Seattle. Within a month the initial founders had gathered 100 more to join them. The women themselves divided the city into districts and formed visiting committees responsible for searching out the "needs of the poor."[90] In 1886 the Seattle Children's Home, on land donated by Seattle founders Louisa and David Denny, opened to thirty children. Prior to that time a woman named Jennie G. Jenkins had begun taking in orphaned children to board in 1883. She transferred the children to the Seattle Children's Home once it had been established. The home eventually moved to Queen Anne Hill and continued in operation a century later.

The women who founded the Ladies' Relief Society included Caroline M. (Kavanaugh) Sanderson, whose husband John was a merchant. Born in Vermont in 1836, she was educated at Boston Art School. She and her husband came to Seattle in 1869, from San Francisco, as had Gatzert and her husband. She was a founder of the Plymouth Congregational Church, organized at her home in 1870, and was one of the teachers in the first graded school in Seattle (Central School at Third and Marion) as well as a trustee of the first library association in Seattle. She remained a trustee of the Seattle Children's Home throughout her life.[91]

Another group established to help children through an institution was the Children's Orthopedic Hospital, founded in 1907. It was created at the urging of Anna Herr Clise, whose son had died of "inflammatory rheumatism." Seattle had no facility for long-term care of children, and Clise invited twenty-three of Seattle's wealthier women to join her in a campaign to build it. It began with a seven-bed ward at Seattle General Hospital, moving to its own facility in 1911, and eventually affiliated with the University of Washington Medical School. It was sustained and steadily expanded through the fundraising support of hundreds of statewide guilds. In subsequent years, the hospital was managed by an all-female board of trustees.[92]

SEATTLE'S OWN SETTLEMENT HOUSE

In 1900 Gatzert started another influential group. She gathered thirty-four women together to form a Seattle section of the National Council of Jewish Women, founded only seven years earlier at the Columbian Exposition in Chicago in 1893 (the Portland branch was in existence by 1896). It was preceded by the Ladies' Hebrew Benevolent Society founded in 1889, when Esther Levy called together thirty-seven women to create it.[93]

Gatzert, also known as Barbetta, was the daughter of the founder of the San Francisco–based Schwabacher Brothers firm, sister to three brothers who carried the family business into the Northwest, creating what became one of the largest wholesale grocery firms on the Pacific coast. It even owned its own wharf and mills.[94] The brothers had come to Seattle in 1869. Founded in 1861, the firm also had outlets in Walla Walla, Boise, Dayton, Seattle, Idaho Falls, and an interest in one in Colfax, Washington. They did extensive business in shipping wheat and flour to market and supplied pack trains headed for mines. Gatzert's husband Bailey became part of the firm and also Seattle's first mayor.

The Council of Jewish Women that Barbetta Gatzert pulled together decided to offer help and classes to immigrant women. By 1905 the group's impressive 280 members had created its own Education Center, soon called the Neighborhood House. It was a settlement house begun as a sewing and religious school, conducted in various locations around Seventeenth Avenue South, Main, and Yesler Way until 1916, when a building to accommodate the program was built. Classes in English and Americanization became part of the expanded program. Even the Seattle Ladies' Musical Club got involved, by funding instruction beginning in 1914 for children at what was called the Settlement Music School, serving primarily a Russian-Jewish immigrant clientele.[95]

The settlement house movement, in its heyday by the turn of the century in most large cities in the country, intersected with many of the services women's clubs established and the professionalization of service into social work. Three-fifths of the settlement workers were women, and 90 percent had been to college. Settlements frequently served as local forums for political debate and information on suffrage, child-labor reform, temperance, and women's rights issues.[96]

The Seattle women's group prided itself on ecumenical management of the center, which was designed to help young and old "live a democratic life without racial prejudice." The group offered scholarships to Jewish students, hired a district nurse for the city in 1909, had set up a baby clinic by 1912, and established a children's free clinic in 1916. Early in the decade it set up a free bath, responding to the lack of bathrooms and sanitation in the central district. Along with other clubs, members also lobbied for new buildings for the University of Washington and a juvenile court building in the city. By 1909 it had opened its first night school for instruction in English and citizenship, and its sewing classes were designed to help newcomers become self-supporting.[97] By 1910 it had constructed the Deaconess Settlement House in Rainier Valley to serve a fast-growing group of Italian immigrants.

CATT FOUNDS SEATTLE'S CENTURY CLUB

Another of Seattle's important clubs was the more traditional study club, the Century Club, created in 1891. One of its founders was Seattle resident Carrie Chapman Catt, who gained national and international fame as the head of the National American Women's Suffrage Association (NAWSA), replacing Susan B. Anthony, and later as organizer of the National League of Women Voters in 1920 and the National Conference on the Cause and Cure of War in 1925.[98]

Catt, born in 1859, had studied law at the University of Iowa and worked as high school principal and superintendent of schools in Mason City, Iowa.[99] In 1885 she married newspaper editor Leo Chapman, who died of typhoid fever a year later. She ended up in San Francisco, broke and working occasionally in journalism. A gifted speaker, she, like other female leaders, organized a tour to support herself. Catt wrote three lectures centered around the ever-popular topic of the dangers of aliens to American institutions, hired an agent, and began delivering the well-attended lectures.[100] In 1890, at thirty-one, she found herself in the Northwest and decided to settle in Seattle. There she married civil engineer George Catt, a man she met in college, who then was in charge of the Washington State operations of the San Francisco Bridge Company.

On July 31, 1891, she met with a half-dozen extraordinary women residing in Seattle. Together they founded the Seattle Woman's Century Club, out of the belief that the coming century would be the woman's century.[101] The club's initial purpose in meeting was "for intellectual culture, original research, and the solution of the altruistic problems of the day." Each member was expected to complete one original paper during the year, a terrifying prospect for some members. Catt, elected president, gave the first, "The Evolution of Woman," on the progress of "the sex out of primitive barbarism and slavery into the freedom of today."[102]

Others followed. Members addressed "The Present Status of Woman, Social, Industrial, Legal," "Working Women and Their Wages," "Women in Science, Literature and Art," "Pauper Wives

and the Remedy," "Divorce," and a half-dozen other subjects written from the distinctive viewpoint of gender. According to club
records, one paper, "Women and the Social Evil," by Julia
Kennedy, was accepted by the editor of *Arena*. The group formed
round tables, precursors of departments, on art, current literature,
education, hygiene, philanthropy, religion, politics, science, temperance, woman's progress, and the world's fair, each with reports,
papers, and meetings.[103] Study of problems, however, soon turned
to attempts to solve problems.

This club's founders formed a nexus of leaders in club activity
and in some cases social and political activism in Seattle. The first
members, with Catt, included Julia Kennedy, who had been on the
Illinois State Normal School faculty and became the first superintendent of Seattle schools; Alice Blake, reputed to be the first
woman to receive a degree from Yale University; Sarah Kendall,
one of the city's first female physicians, who later became an
officer in the General Federation of Women's Clubs; and Kate
Turner Holmes, a university graduate who later founded the Seattle Federation of Women's Clubs and was the second president of
the Washington Federation of Women's Clubs.[104] Their first meeting was at Julia Kennedy's home.

One of the club's most active leaders was Kate Holmes. When
she was president of the Century Club in 1898, she sent a letter of
invitation to other clubs in Seattle, inviting them to meet to create
a Seattle Federation of Women's Clubs. Fourteen sent delegates,
and the city federation was born.[105] She became the second president of the state federation. Like most of the other women who
founded the Century Club, she was college educated, with a 1878
degree from the University of Wisconsin.[106] Her first Century
Club paper was "The Relation of the Laborer to the Employer."

An example from the Century Club of attempts to cross class
lines was the fact that one of its first presidents, Carrie Hill,
founded and presided over the Women's Industrial Club, established in 1895 for self-supporting women. Hill also published
Washington Women, a paper devoted to club interests and later
the cause of women's suffrage. She subsequently became president of the Washington Equal Franchise Society,[107] in another example of club leaders becoming suffrage leaders in the Northwest.

The Century Club, like other women's clubs and the federations,
initially renounced political activism and claimed no devotion to
any particular philanthropy or reform, but soon became involved

in corollary political issues that affected women. One of the measures for which it proudly claimed success was its role in getting the legislature to raise the age of consent for sexual activity in Washington from twelve to fifteen. The club led a spirited but unsuccessful effort to get a woman on the Seattle school board before the turn of the century. It also helped start the Martha Washington School for Girls, paid the salary of the first librarian for a year, and took credit for starting Travelers' Aid, for the protection of newly arrived rural or immigrant girls and women.[108]

Establishing Institutions

The Century Club in 1909 continued its work to provide an institution for girls like the one for boys on Mercer Island. It established the private Girls Parental School, a charity taken over by the Seattle School Board in 1914. By 1917 it had become an institution for vocational and industrial training of girls committed there by juvenile court, in a new building south of Seward Park, with a female superintendent.[109] Clubwomen frequently applied domestic and maternal values not only to schools but also to delinquency, lobbying for programs and alternatives outside the punitive, adult-oriented court system. Their school was later criticized and closed as too large an expenditure for the district ($126,000 for twenty-five to thirty girls). The club also secured Ravenna Park for Seattle and preserved its huge trees, and members established a Daughter's Auxiliary.[110]

Although the club had connections with working women and a diverse membership later, it was at first elite in its membership, at least in terms of education if not wealth, like many Northwest clubs. Members were nominated by a "secret committee" and voted in by the membership. However, within a few years the Century Club had opened its doors to welcome hundreds of Seattle women. Members paid $1 for initiation and $2 in annual dues.[111]

The Century Club was also one of the earliest Washington clubs to affiliate with the General Federation of Women's Clubs, itself founded only in 1890 nationally and in 1896 in Washington.[112] Jane Cunningham Croly's massive 1898 history of the women's club movement described the Seattle Woman's Century Club as "a strong club, more aggressive in its methods than the purely literary clubs."[113] One of its more illustrious members, who joined in 1907 and became president of it as well as president of the

Seattle federation and a dozen other women's clubs over time, was Bertha Knight Landes.

Massachusetts-born and Indiana University–educated, Landes ran for a seat on the Seattle City Council in 1922 with the backing of Seattle's women's clubs as "the women's candidate." She won her seat by a record margin and was reelected in 1924. In 1926 she became the first woman elected mayor of a large city in the United States. She credited her experience in leadership of women's clubs for her success in politics. In her governmental roles she carried forward many of the programs and ideas fostered by clubwomen. She called the city "but a larger home" where home values—including protection of women and children and adequate social services—should prevail. She also brought professional training for police, environmental concerns, and zoning to the city's agenda. During her career she pushed women to take an interest in civic issues and use the power of their vote wisely, a right women in Washington gained in 1910 with the help of women's clubs like the Century. She founded the Women's Civic Club, a large umbrella group crossing class lines oriented to political and policy issues.[114]

Seattle also had powerful arts clubs, such as the Seattle Ladies' Musical Club established in 1891. Besides fostering classical and uniquely American music productions for all of the city's residents, the club actively promoted and supported women in the performing arts. It brought eighteen women to the city to perform between 1901 and 1930, twice as many as the male-dominated Seattle Symphony featured in seventy-five years of its existence, historian Karen Blair notes.[115]

AFRICAN-AMERICAN WOMEN'S CLUBS IN SEATTLE AND TACOMA

The African Americans who came to the area worked on railroads such as the Northern Pacific or in coal mines at Roslyn in King County, as hotel staff (as at the Rainier in Seattle), or as domestic help. The small population grew slowly, as it did in Portland. The census recorded one African American in Seattle in 1860, 22 in 1880, fewer than 300 in 1890 and about 400 in 1900, but the number had reached 2,300 by 1910. Men greatly outnumbered women in the early years.

African Americans immigrating to Seattle and Tacoma followed a pattern similar to Portland's, although a decade or two behind.

In Seattle, the first African Methodist Episcopal church came into being in 1886. By 1891 there were also congregations in Spokane, Roslyn, Franklin, Salem, and Portland.[116] The smaller cities initially had no black districts. As in Portland, their first community institutions were churches, which became community centers and sites of social and organized activism, including clubs.[117] In his study of Seattle, historian Quintard Taylor found that African Americans there had a rich mix of organizations that gave the community a sense of identity and support while tying members together in overlapping memberships. Groups included fraternal lodges, political clubs, social clubs, and a number of women's clubs. Seattle had a strong and stable black middle class with clear class divisions within the African-American population. It included several women's study clubs amid purely social clubs as well as philanthropic groups, many connected in some way to churches for support.

The first women's club for African-American women of Seattle was the Colored Ladies' Society (elsewhere called Ladies' Colored Social Circle). It was created in December 1889, when "several colored ladies of this city met at the residence of Mrs. Lawrence, on Madison street, [and] organized a social circle," said a newspaper article. The organization developed about the same time the AME church building was purchased. The women met weekly in members' homes for lunch and conversation and held literary and musical entertainments. By the turn of the century, as race relations became more problematic and the African-American community more divided, some continued social and literary club activities, while others moved toward political activism. Some later were involved in organizing the Seattle Chapter of the National Afro-American Council.[118]

One of the more active African-American clubs was the Dorcus Charity Club, spurred to action by a crisis in 1906 when twin baby girls had been abandoned. The black girls had rickets, and no one was found to adopt them. They were headed for Medical Lake, a state institution, when officials there made a last-minute call to Susie Revels Cayton. She with three other black women founded the Dorcus Charity Club (elsewhere called the Dorcas Society), which supported the girls in a foster home. It also paid rent for indigent widows, gave Christmas toys to orphaned children, and met other community needs.[119] In another case, the members sought aid from the Children's Orthopedic Hospital for a fourteen-year-old girl suffering from tuberculosis of the knee, and the club and hospital agreed to share the girl's expenses. The hospital's founders in 1907 had gone on record as accepting into the institution any child, regardless of race, religion, or parents' ability to pay, with the poor given first preference.[120]

Bent on self-improvement that was rooted in a belief in better times coming, African-American women who themselves were denied education made sure children took advantage of what learning was available and reminded children of the need to be "a credit to the race," their own version of identity formation and cultural politics. African-American women's clubs seemed concerned primarily with meeting their community's needs and protecting black women and families in the face of accusations of immorality and pressures of racism. Although more African-American women proportionately were in the work force than white women at the end of the century, the African-American women who led their clubs were, like leaders of white women's clubs, from a more middle-class background. Sensitized by racism, however, they were more diligent in their fight against that prejudice than the white women's clubs were against sexism and also may have been more closely connected to causes of working-class women.[121]

They were less concerned with national issues, such as suffrage, in the face of severe local privations and their own lack of political and social power. Nevertheless, some black women worked in the suffrage and temperance campaigns in western states.[122] African-American women generally had higher educational levels and opportunities in the Northwest states and were less subject to sexual abuse, but other forms of racism were present in the West as elsewhere.[123] While the majority of African Americans nationwide were illiterate, only 26 percent of the black women in the West were illiterate, according to census data.[124]

There were clear class divisions in the African-American population before the turn of the century. As with the rest of society, the most elaborate social functions seemed to be organized by a small, upper-income group. Seattle's African-American community also had its own touring groups and entertainment opportunities, including balls. Social and economic divisions emerged. One class contained professionals and those with steady employment, while the other contained those who worked in manual labor or were drifters. Some of the former adopted the cultural activities traditions of other advantaged groups. In 1892 a Seattle group led by Elizabeth Oxendine presented an evening of Shakespeare at the Opera House, with excerpts from *Richard III* and *Macbeth*. African-American leaders and families often took excursions by train to South King County for picnics, boarded steamships bound for Tacoma or Victoria, or played in progressive whist parties. By 1901 African-American organizations including the Music Club and Evergreen Literary Society promoted cultural activities.[125]

African-American clubs included the Lincoln Helping Hand Club, the Carter Industrial and Literary Club, and others that became members of the National Council of Colored Women.[126] In 1912 the Colored Women's Council was organized from a chapter of the Lucy Thurman Temperance Union. It established its own clubhouse in 1914, joining the National Federation of Colored Women's Clubs that same year. In 1919 the Seattle Young Women's Christian Association's Culture Club, led by Mrs. W. D. Carter, established a Phyllis Wheatley branch for African-American girls.[127] In Tacoma, one remarkable woman, active in both clubwork and musical circles, made a transition from clubwork for African-American women to the founding of what became chapters of the National Association for the Advancement of Colored People. In fact, Nettie Asberry had several notable achievements during her lifetime. She earned a doctorate in music from the Kansas State Conservatory of Music, studying there after the Civil War. She also became president of the Washington Federation of Colored Women and helped establish chapters of the National Association for the Advancement of Colored People in Tacoma, Seattle, and Portland.

Asberry, who moved to Seattle in 1890, was active in women's clubs and social causes in the region for more than a half-century. She also touched many by teaching hundreds of music students of all races in her home during that time and composed her own pieces. She married Henry Asberry, the popular proprietor of the Tacoma Hotel Barber Shop, one of the few types of businesses open to black entrepreneurs in the region. Increasingly, she became involved in what is now termed social work.

In an interview she noted the shift to professional work from what used to be unpaid rescue work or work among the poor. "Today we think of social workers as being highly trained people with fancy salaries. But some of us have given countless hours with never a cent of pay. I didn't need it."[128] She spoke for many women. She died in 1968, at the age of 103, and a study club was named after her.

CLUBS AT TACOMA

One of the most active club sites was nearby Tacoma, a port town about thirty miles south of Seattle and for a time a threat to Seattle's supremacy when the railroad got there first. In 1880 Tacoma had 1,098 people and Seattle 3,533. Early in its existence Tacoma had early fine arts clubs, the Art League and the Ladies' Musical Club. Both devoted portions of their programs to the study of women in the fine arts.

The city also had early study clubs that changed almost overnight into activist organizations. Grace Moore, the first president of the Women's Library Society, made her own home into a public reading room. In order to raise money for books, the club put on plays, musical programs, and lectures. By 1889 it had organized the Tacoma Public Library.[129] In 1890 it became a charter member of the General Federation of Women's Clubs.

Some clubs in Tacoma focused on self-improvement (the women often called it "self-culture") as a route to community improvement. For instance, in 1892 the Nesika Club formed. On the back of the club's first miniature cardboard program, each copy hand-painted with a red carnation and engraved in gold, appeared the club's improvement goals: "Reading maketh a full man; Speaking a ready man; Writing an exact man." Virginia (Mrs. J. Q.) Mason, upon her return from a visit to the East where she was inspired by going to a club meeting with her sister, organized the club at her home. Fifteen gathered and kept gathering and reading. In the first year alone, 85 papers were presented and discussed, and another 122 in 1893. Club members spent hours in the new Carnegie Library. The club joined the national federation and the state federation in 1896 and furnished a room in the YWCA building in 1905.[130]

Sometimes a piece of art like a play that challenged the prevailing culture inspired collective action. That happened with one club that became particularly important to the shape of the city. It began in 1899 with the reading of an Ibsen play. That year, Elizabeth (Mrs. J. E.) Baker sat in the home of her neighbor, Mrs. A. B. Leckenby, in the evenings and read Henrik Ibsen's plays to her, her mother, and two daughters. Gradually others became interested and dropped in—soon the English Literature Club evolved.[131]

Members began reading papers about Ibsen and his seminal work on gender and female rebellion, *A Doll's House*. At the first meeting Baker also talked about other authors, notably the women George Eliot and George Sand, dissenters "who imbue their heroines with grander character and capabilities, and commenced the work of breaking down the barriers that previously surrounded women."[132] Study of art, as it often does, started a discourse that changed the status quo.

At the third meeting members read and tabled an invitation to join the Washington federation. At the fourth they adopted a constitution and bylaws, with the stated purpose "to broaden the field for women, better the conditions for humanity, and secure concerted action in intellectual and philanthropic activities."[133] One of the charter members of the club was another physician, Nina Jolidon Croake, later one of the first two women to be elected to the Washington legislature. Croake, whose husband worked in mining, advertised herself as an osteopath physician and dermatologist.[134] Another early club president, Mary (Mrs. A. B.) Warner, came from a social welfare background, having spent fourteen years working with the inmates of a St. Paul workhouse.[135]

The backgrounds of key members of the club show the diverse economic, educational, and class backgrounds in the Pacific Northwest from which members came. Generally, the women were married to small businessmen or mid-managers.[136] Leaders were often practicing professionals, such as Croake and Alice Maude Smith (profiled in this chapter), in practice in Tacoma since 1989.[137] Ellen Swinburg Leckenby, one of those who first listened to the challenging Ibsen readings, later became a suffrage leader in Washington State.

The Tacoma group met initially in the Mathematical Room of Puget Sound University. Although the club was not yet in the federation, many members spent a week in Seattle at the federation meeting and extolled the advantages of federation, "as it brings women together and causes them to broaden out in their viewpoints."[138] They changed the name to Tacoma Woman's Study Club in July and joined the federation. The women chose lavender and white for club colors, and lavender and white sweet peas often adorned the club meetings in the summer. They established departments in photography, floriculture, Shakespeare, and French, ordered club stationery, and set an entrance fee of 25 cents.[139]

The group moved to City Hall and by October—only six months

after its founding—had decided to sponsor suffrage leader and lecturer Carrie Chapman Catt's appearance at the Tacoma Hotel. Catt, who left Seattle soon after founding the Century Club, was president of the National American Woman Suffrage Association from 1900 to 1904 and again from 1915 until her death. Her turn-of-the-century appearance cost the club $10 for use of the hotel parlor, $2.50 in hotel expenses, and only $15 for the lecture itself.[140] The October 20 lecture was filled "with an intellectual and appreciative audience," club minutes noted. At a following meeting the women voted to add a civics department and decided it would hold evening meetings under the leadership of Dr. Alice Smith, one of the Northwest's most interesting club leaders.[141]

PROFILE: DR. ALICE MAUDE SMITH

Alice Maude Smith, who combined the unlikely roles of physician and playwright, was one of the first and most active members of Tacoma's women's clubs. She arrived in Tacoma in 1898 and later called her arrival inauspicious. She found four other female physicians married to doctors who were not exactly pleased to see her. Moreover, her surgical instruments were stolen on the way, and she felt she was overcharged for transportation of her goods from Chicago.

Smith, born in Quebec in 1867, set up practice in Tacoma at age thirty-one, although other doctors there supposedly undercut her prices to keep her out. A graduate of Linn Hospital Training School for Nurses in Massachusetts, Smith had taken additional training to become a physician. By the time she moved to the West, she had already gained recognition for her public health work in the Midwest and added to it in the Northwest. She had served as vice-president of the medical board of the Jackson Park Sanitarium for Children in Chicago. At Tacoma she became the first female physician to hold a seat on the State Medical Examining Board and to hold the chair of social hygiene at a college.

Smith also gained considerable fame later as an "alienist," a specialist in the legal aspects of psychiatry, testifying in a number of criminal trials in the 1920s. She wrote on health care issues for the *Legislative Counsellor,* the newsletter of the Women's Legislative Council of Washington, a powerful joint lobbying group formed in 1917.[142]

Smith was one of the members of the Tacoma Women's Study Club who sought to move it from study to civic activism. At one of its early meetings she proposed adding a civics department, an idea she brought with her from the Midwest. Members approved it and decided that group would hold evening meetings under her leadership. She had proposed forming "a civic federation" department scheduled in the evenings so men could also join and attend.

As "superintendent" of this group Smith was "to bring before the city council any question along the lines of city reform that the club thought advisable."[143] She helped the group organize a "Civic Council" as an auxiliary, reflecting the Chicago "Civic Federation."

At one point in her long career Smith suffered serious and debilitating health problems. She was unable to walk for more than a year as the result of sciatica, a painful inflammation of nerves from the lower spine, yet she continued to meet appointments by being carried in and out of automobiles rather than become an invalid.

Smith also had an impressive creative bent. She wrote a play that was produced in New York and eventually made into a movie. *Pauline Darcy,* first produced in Tacoma, was about a woman whose easy morals drew the father of her fiancé to her. He revealed his love for the heroine to his son, who then died "from a wasting disease" and poison.

The play, retitled *The Strength of the Weak,* was ultimately produced in New York. Later it was made into a Universal film starring Mary Fuller, who in 1912 gained fame in the forerunner of movie serials called *What Happened to Mary,* appearing simultaneously in monthly installments in the magazine *McClure's Ladies' World* and on the screen. The play netted Smith $5,000 in royalties, but that was after she paid almost $25,000 in commissions to agents. In fact, she later said plagiarism, agents, and copyright technicalities dogged her career. For their part, agents complained that she shopped her plays around indiscriminately and that her handwriting was illegible.[144]

Smith became chair of the Health Department of the Washington Women's Legislative Council in 1920. She was involved in the Tacoma center of the Drama League of America and was a fellow of the Royal Society of Arts of London, as well as a member of medical associations at the county, state, and national levels, including the State Board of Medical Examiners. She died in 1938.[145]

The Tacoma club moved rapidly from Ibsen to activism and study of political culture. By December—within nine months of its founding—the club had decided to have a parliamentary procedures instructor and five minutes of drill at each meeting. It was represented at a Chicago antitrust conference by Mrs. W. L. Johnson, who spoke there and to the local club on the topic "Why Women Should Study Political Economy." In January Lola Menzines presented a paper titled "The Illogical Status of Women."[146] In March Johnson talked to members about details of city government, such as revenue sources and financial problems, focusing on saloons, gambling rooms, and betting devices. That same month Smith suggested a Mothers Club and Domestic Science Club be added as departments, but members balked at the additional commitment.[147] Within a year the club went from seven members to forty-three, and Croake was reelected president.[148]

In 1900 the group began meeting weekly and decided to work with other women's groups, notably the Mary Ball Chapter of the DAR, on city beautification projects. In April the club heard a report on sweatshops and child labor in Chicago. Meanwhile, the Civic Council continued its separate meetings, on issues such as "The School System, Its Defects and Advantages."[149] The club also, like counterparts in Seattle and Portland, went on record as favoring shorter hours for retail clerks and appointed a committee on the issue, netting a thank you letter from the Retail Clerks Union. The group named a committee to work on "women's comfort stations" in the city at the end of streetcar lines and another for the circulating library. It selected the year's study plan, focusing on Women and Economics, and elected Elizabeth Harris president. The club voted to "assist in maintaining a kindergarten school in Old Town."[150]

Croake wrote a paper, "Clubwomen along Reform Lines," which the group liked so much that it voted to publish and circulate it. In January 1901 the club voted "to use the postal card plan to agitate early closing" of saloons and to lobby the legislature on a bill appropriating $1,000 to the Washington Federation for Free Traveling Libraries.[151] When she was forty, Croake was elected to the Washington State Legislature.

One of the key members, Dr. Sarah Kendall, a Century Club founder in Seattle before coming to Tacoma, returned to Seattle. There she championed a Consumers' League and did legislative and other work for the Washington federated clubs. In 1901–2 the group held a rummage sale for the Ferry museum, netting a satisfying $1,164. In 1902 the Tacoma Woman's Study Club took up topics delving deeper into business and politics: what are industrial panics; what system of industry would you substitute to do away with these periodical industrial panics; labor and competition; what is the profit system and how does it operate.[152] Most women's clubs shied away from study of economic issues and party politics, but others took them up directly, recognizing them as structural issues that needed study and understanding in order to enact club priorities.

The following year the club went into steep decline as some officers moved away and attendance dropped to fewer than ten. The group debated whether to hold evening rather than afternoon meetings to attract working women. Clubs often faltered when they lost key leadership, and some never recovered. This club persevered—in May it named a committee of three to study and report on "all cases of cruelty, neglect and vice," calling itself the Alert Committee.[153] Membership rebounded the following year.

In 1903 members voted to study the suffrage. In February the club sent $5 to the Washington Suffrage Society. In 1904 it cut its $1 dues to 50 cents, and members voted to furnish a room for the Woman's Inn opened by the Woman's Club of Tacoma.[154] In 1905–6 modern authors and Greek philosophy became the year's study topics, and the club voted to ask the governor to put "a lady on the Board of Regents for the State University and recommend that she should be a graduate of a co-educational institution."[155]

In 1908 the members established a scholarship fund and held an open meeting at the Tacoma Municipal Hall to hear Washington suffrage leader Emma Smith DeVoe, who had moved to Tacoma in 1905. DeVoe (profiled in chapter 8) became one of the best-known lecturers and organizers in the Pacific Northwest for suffrage, a struggle won in Washington in 1910. That year the Tacoma club named a committee to investigate the city's water supply and petitioned the city council for a detention home for young girls in the city suburbs. It also passed resolutions supporting teachers' efforts to get higher salaries.[156] The detention home was established by the end of the year, and the club put together little gifts "of gloves, ribbons, hair pins and trinkets for the girls." By 1911–12 the club's activities reflected the rise of sociology and domestic science. "The Rise of Women" was the study course, and two women were appointed to interview Sheriff Longmire about putting in a matron at the county jail—he sidestepped and suggested they start a petition drive. In 1911 the club supported campaigns for pure foods laws and for correct weights and measures.[157]

The Tacoma Clubs and Protection

Pure foods and consumer rights were long-term crusades for women's clubs nationwide and in local communities. The ways that food could be cut and adulterated—and sometimes contaminated or poisoned—were many, and they went beyond the bad meat that was resold as sausage or bologna. A Washington chemist cited in a 1902 women's club publication described some of the more creative ways. Adulteration came in three forms, by direct addition of foreign material, by "abstraction" of some valuable natural ingredient from the product, or by substituting a cheaper article.

For instance, glucose or cane sugar could be added to the honey, or cottonseed oil or beef stearin to lard. Milk and mustard were particularly susceptible to adulteration by "abstraction" through removal of butter fat or mustard oil, said the state chemist. Cottonseed and peanut oil were sold for olive oil, artificial vinegar for cider vinegar, artificial coffee berries for natural ones, or syrup flavored with extract of corncob or hickory bark was artificially colored and sold as maple syrup. A mixture of alcohol, ethers, and color became lemon extract, and colored jelly made from apple cores and parings became pure fruit jellies, all sold without regulation or testing. High price, he warned, was no protection to the consumer; added to the fraud were exaggerated health claims for cereals like Grapenuts and Cream of Wheat.[158] Women's clubs like the Tacoma club were successful in getting state and federal protection for consumers, through state laws, agencies, and inspectors to enforce standards.

In 1912–13 the club's study course was titled "A Reading Journey through Our Own Land," perhaps reflecting the nationalistic fever heating up on the eve of world war and fears of radicalism in the Northwest. By 1915–16 the study plan was "Washington," and the group voted to help out Red Cross efforts two days a month.[159] The level of community activism, as happened with many women's clubs shortly before and during the war, declined.

A later and more reform-oriented club, as the outgrowth of an early alliance of Tacoma women's clubs, contrasted with the relatively typical pattern of the Tacoma Woman's Study Club. It emerged at a time when women's activism was nearing its regional height and incorporated the experiences and work of predecessors. Called the Woman's Club of Tacoma, it had three strands, each with separate organizations and minutes—a general strand with an executive board, a literary strand, and a civic strand. It was a hybrid club, an outgrowth of the City Federation of Women's Clubs, which met first in 1904. The federation had initially included the Nesika, Aloha, Browning, Yakima, and PEO groups in addition to the Tacoma Woman's Study Club. Some attendees, frustrated by the lack of action in the city federation, decided to create a new activist club. Members chose this route, modeling it like the large California Civic Club.

After selecting officers, the club floundered over purpose. One member, Mrs. B. F. Eshelman, spoke "of her sympathy for shop girls and those who had so little brightness in their lives."[160] But it was one thing to have a concern and quite another to turn it into a plan of action. The group decided to take on the issue of restrooms and a station matron first. It also set up an employment bureau, managing to get a telephone installed free. Clubs often supported projects or proposals from other clubs, adding to the strength of numbers. This club in 1905 endorsed a petition for a new juvenile court bill at the request of the Spokane federated women's clubs. Ever cognizant of the need for money to support projects, the group passed a bylaw that "any gentleman" who paid $5 would become an honorary member of the Woman's Club; $25 would buy him a life membership.[161] From twenty-five charter members the club grew to one hundred members by the end of its first year.

Nina Jolidon Croake, charter member of the Tacoma study club, was on this club's executive board as well until she left the city in 1905. In 1906 Dr. Alice Smith (profiled here) spoke to this group about the need for a detention hospital. She described a woman in what she called "acute mania" confined for many hours in the city jail with only men in attendance. Also, the president of the Arequipa Club talked to the group at the same meeting about the need for a police matron and the good that she could do among "first offenders among young girls." The club carried both measures to city officials, and the mayor promised to hire a matron.[162]

In 1906 Croake appeared again, chairing the emergency nurse committee. That year the mayor named Miss Wallace, head of the library committee, to a board of five to move public library management under state law. The group also backed a bill to make it a misdemeanor to entice anyone under eighteen from home without consent of a parent or guardian. Later in the year the club joined the federation and added literature and Mothers' Congress

departments. In 1907 the club formed a committee that successfully worked to get a separate ward for boys and girls added to the
jail, noting that in August thirty-one women had been arrested or
detained with no matron present, despite promises to the contrary from the mayor.

A New Identity—The Woman's Civic Club

The club pushed for drinking fountains, cleaner streetcars, and
garbage cans. It got the council to put cans around the city, and
its drive for cleaner streetcars elicited a promise from the superintendent to remedy the problem. In 1909 the club merged with
the Civic Department and changed its name to the Woman's Civic
Club, formalizing its shift to activism. In 1910 the club finally succeeded in getting a matron in the county jail and a detention
house. It also circulated a list of merchants who did not, in its
view, sell pure food and got a billboard ordinance passed limiting
the height of signs to six feet. It heard talks on tuberculosis, mothers, and plainer dress for schoolgirls and worked on setting up an
Emergency Home, a great need. Too often, members were told,
"men and boys spend the night in saloons, because they had no
other place to go."[163] It added a separate political science department, and seventy-five attended its "pure educational" meetings.

The Civic Club, under Mrs. James W. Brokaw, now had more
than a dozen separate committees for civic improvement, billboards, posters, advertising matter, food sanitation, streets and alleys, hospitals and schools, school lunches, short weights and
measures, streetcars, theaters and public places of amusement,
playgrounds, street improvements and paving, messenger service,
and antituberculosis work. In 1911 the club, looking at increasing
rates of unemployment in the city, started a sewing school for girls
with the idea of also helping clothe prisoners at McNeill Island. In
April Brokaw stated that juvenile courts and laws protecting newsboys would be the chief consideration for the coming years.[164]

Brokaw later noted with pride that the club could look back at
a long list of achievements. They included, first, establishing the
Women's Inn at 714 Pacific Avenue offering housing for single
working women (described in the next chapter). Others included
sanitation changes such as no more common drinking cups and
towels in schools, added ventilation, drinking fountains and garbage cans around town, and an annual clean-up day. The Mothers'
Congress committee got a visiting nurse program established for

the schools. The club finally got a cleaner streetcars ordinance passed prohibiting expectorating and smoking on cars, but had no success with getting the lower steps it sought. It also drafted a bill making it a misdemeanor for a man to desert his family and sought other structural changes benefiting women. The whole club met each month, open to all women who wanted to work on club concerns.

Legacies and Missed Opportunities

As this account of the achievements of a few clubs in the major cities of the Northwest demonstrates, organized womanhood succeeded in efforts at both self-improvement and village improvement. The most politicized clubs managed to compel changes in the legal and political framework of their states, while building support and leaders for the coming suffrage campaigns described in chapter 8.

Clubs used literature, study, and reports as a discourse to change the status quo, whether it was study of Ibsen's plays or women's legal status or the political economy. Their efforts went beyond gender debates. They protected a place in the community for the arts and created more civil towns and fairer businesses. They provided programs and services to benefit citizens, especially women and children. As part of a national social movement, they borrowed ideas and programs of action freely from one another, and from distant clubs, especially in the Northwest, as residents and club members from other regions of the country moved into new and largely unformed places.

Despite their accomplishments, the closed structure of the clubs and the level of comfort members established with one another made it difficult for them to reach very far across racial and ethnic lines, although many clubs in the Northwest made attempts to reach out to all women as sisters. In the Northwest, united clubwomen were remarkably successful at getting labor legislation passed for the benefit of working women and to end child labor, a story told in the next chapter, but initial cross-class alliances did not hold in the face of rapid expansion and changing values, creating resentment on both sides.

Unfortunately, the white clubwomen nationally, as suffragists did after the Civil War, sacrificed black clubwomen to disgruntled southern members and the racist sentiments of their own communities. In the Northwest, efforts to recognize and support

African-American women's clubs were limited by the racism of the time to organizational support rather than integration, despite the efforts of a few leaders.

Nevertheless, the activist study clubs and their cultural politics changed the Northwest's communities and the women themselves. The changes were structural, physical, and psychological. Communities were more hospitable, more ordered, and even more beautiful than they had been. Sidewalks, parks, juvenile justice systems, children's homes, police matrons, alternative schools, libraries, consumer protection, mothers' pensions, and other community goods and citizen benefits were the direct result of organized womanhood.

Their efforts also provided leaders for successful suffrage campaigns in Idaho, Washington, and Oregon. As they earned wider acceptance for women, they reordered government priorities to accommodate social welfare as a legitimate function of government, through regulation, institutions, and programs. And they moved themselves away from the artificial divisions that directed men into commerce, employment, development, and competition and relegated to women responsibility for society's social ills and policing morality and behavior, as perennial volunteers in selfless service.

CLUBWOMEN AND WORKING WOMEN

Alliances and Divisions, 1900–1920

Women's clubs wanted working women both to be protected from exploitation and to enjoy the advantages they found in club life. Yet clubwomen and working women after the turn of the century seemed to be communicating across a chasm. Sophie Reinhart, writing in a Portland newspaper in 1899, spoke for many young working women when she said they did not require help. "For this reason also the social features of a club, upon which so much stress is laid, is [sic] of hardly any importance here. Every Portland girl has access to amusement and recreation of her own, and does not stand in need of a club to furnish it to her."[1] She also complained about the protectionist legislation women's clubs had worked so hard to get passed in the Northwest as no longer necessary in this enlightened age.

Especially after the turn of the century, some clubs in the Northwest aggressively pursued improved working conditions for women and children. They did it through services, programs, and extensive labor legislation, such as bills to set minimum wage levels and maximum working hours, especially for women. They established homes for single working women, lobbied successfully for child labor laws, even surveyed conditions to compile and publicize evidence of abuses using the new social science methods, with the hope of changing conditions for all women as more and more women joined the work force.

Their successes over the long haul outnumbered their failures, but, like Sophie Reinhart and those she represented, not everyone remained grateful for their efforts. Labor laws pushed by clubwomen and others created a national model ultimately tested before the U.S. Supreme Court. Oregon in particular was at the forefront of a national movement to regulate working hours and conditions. It was in Oregon that legislation limiting women's workday to ten hours passed in 1903, despite the primacy of beliefs in individualism and legal ideas about freedom of contract. Similar but less extensive proposals passed in Washington and Idaho as well, advocated by clubwomen. Washington pioneered with minimum wage protections. Clubs in all three states joined the national movement to limit child labor. Clubs initiated some of these measures for working women and others; they also backed and legitimated campaigns initiated by workers and Progressive era alliances.

THE VALUE OF WOMEN'S WORK

Comparatively few women in the Northwest, as in the rest of the nation, worked for wages before 1900, and those who did were confined to certain jobs. But wages are only one measure of contribution to an economy. The work that women did in their homes or in clubs has seldom been viewed or measured as an economic force, and the issue of whether women could or should work for wages after marriage had only begun to be debated. The prevailing opinion was that they should not, unless it was out of economic necessity, which of course it was for many. Yet as more and more women sought higher education to be of useful service, some, married or not, sought work in the professions that had been the exclusive preserve of men. Many of these early professional women sought opportunity in the less rigid confines and higher levels of need in the Northwest and became community leaders.

The prevailing values about working women found expression in the assumption that women worked not for their economic livelihood but for "pin-money." The idea reinforced their general exclusion from men's unions and resurfaced later in the initiatives of the 1930s to end married women's employment during the adversities of the Great Depression. In 1890, out of each 100 married women, only 4.6 were employed; in 1900, 5.6; and by 1910, 10.7, at least in the list of wage-earning jobs recognized by the Bureau of the Census. Single women worked in greater proportions, reaching 40 percent by 1890. By 1910 they reached a majority—51 percent of all single women fifteen years old and over were gainfully employed, and a third of those were widowed or divorced.[2] But such wage-centered measurements failed to reflect women's work to supplement family incomes and improve living conditions or the partnership with spouses that enabled men to do paid work.

More and more women, especially single women, sought wage-work in the cities, and not as domestic help. Many of the women worked, however, in conditions that aroused the sympathies and occasional outrage that propelled clubs into pursuing services and legislation on their behalf. The clubwomen wanted to ease their lot and at the same time ensure that unattached women in the city were neither exploited nor exploiters of changing social conditions and standards of behavior for women.

Especially in Oregon and Washington, but in Idaho as well, women's clubs surveyed, mobilized, and lobbied for working hour and wage laws to protect workers, especially women and children. At the beginning, some women's clubs formed direct alliances with working women, offering classes, boarding homes, and special departments for them, especially in the larger and more industrialized cities of Portland, Seattle, and Tacoma. For instance, the Portland Woman's Union worked closely with the Portland Working Woman's Club on legislation and policies. One of the issues it and other clubs lobbied for was early business closings on Saturday, to keep women from being exploited by limiting their work hours each week.

Eventually the relationship began to irritate both sides. Working women started to drift away from the services proffered or the housing clubwomen provided and to resent their interference and standards. Clubwomen did not understand the attitude of the working women in refusing what they worked hard to provide and felt wage-earning women were becoming all too often self-centered and selfish, a complaint about the age itself. They feared for their future and the future of their communities if the ideal and standards of womanhood were tarnished by young women's cynicism and growing economic and social independence in this time of turmoil and rising radicalism.

In general, the clubs throughout the period were more sensitive to the problems of class lines and working women than they were to race. The Oregon and Washington Federated Women's Clubs worked closely with working-class groups on certain issues, as did some of the city federations. For instance, the Seattle Women's Union Card and Label League, the Washington Federation of Women's Clubs, and the Seattle Women's Trade Union League all linked arms to pursue the protective legislation such as minimum wage laws and an eight-hour workday. They also jointly sought a repeal of union policies against married women's employment, although the plea was in vain.[3] Under Seattle Waitress Union organizer Alice Lord, a coalition of the Federation of Women's Clubs, organized labor, and the Ministerial Alliance worked for the eight-hour day, beginning in 1904. It finally passed in 1911, when the Washington State Legislature took the bold step of being first in the nation to enact an eight-hour day for women, except for cannery, fruit, and domestic workers. Two years later the coalition also got a minimum-wage bill passed.[4]

Seattle Federation president Viola Crahan organized clubs for female laundry workers, who averaged $5.87 a week in pay and worked in difficult conditions. The laundry workers were on call at all times and were prohibited from joining a union.[5] In 1916 working women created a new alliance, consisting of the Federation of Union Women and Auxiliaries in Seattle, trade union women, affiliated women's auxiliaries, and the Union Card and Label League.[6] In Oregon too, a cross-class alliance of women's organizations helped gain passage of comprehensive labor laws aimed at protecting women's rights. But as labor unrest in the Northwest spilled into open conflict, strikes, and the Seattle general strike of 1919, these alliances fell apart. Women's clubs divided and retreated over this and other social issues.

CLUBS AND PROGRAMS FOR THE WORKING WOMAN

It is often assumed that clubwomen, as mostly middle-class Anglo-Saxons caught up in the study of the arts and cultural affairs, had little connection to or understanding of working women or women of color. That conception of club activity does not fit the Pacific Northwest experience. Issues related to equity, to protection of all working women and women as consumers, and to improving conditions for women were always legislative priorities for clubs, many of them realized. But beyond their policy agenda, many clubs had other involvements with working women, through organizing working women's clubs, establishing classes for working women, or even running boarding hotels for them as did the Portland Women's Union and the Woman's Club of Tacoma. Women already working as teachers or in other professional jobs were vital leaders of Northwest clubs.

For instance, in 1895 the Women's Industrial Club was founded by Carrie Hill, an early member of the influential Century Club of Seattle who was president of the state suffrage association from 1900 to 1906. Hill had an abiding concern that women's clubs represent all women, without regard for class. At the first Washington Federation of Women's Clubs meeting, Hill was one of four women named to represent the state federation at the national meeting. She made a plea for laying aside all social differences in clubwork, referring specifically to working women.

The Women's Industrial Club, with annual dues of 50 cents, had as its object "mutual improvement, bettering of physical conditions, and the elevation of tastes." Its membership included women working primarily as domestics, work that many women, especially Scandinavian immigrants in the Northwest, undertook in order to survive. In the club, working women were assumed to need and want a woman's club agenda for self-improvement. They practiced elocution, drilled in parliamentary procedure, and debated current events.[7]

Other clubs established housing or noon rest rooms for working women. As described earlier, the Woman's Club of Tacoma had as its major undertaking establishing a hotel/boarding house with a cafeteria specifically for working women. It first established a cafeteria and rest room in 1904 for both clerks and shoppers. Clerks making $3–$5 a week could ill afford lunch in public restaurants, and the women hoped to fill this need. Soon 200 girls and women were eating there each day at cost. A similar program was established in Spokane, staffed by club members, to support a Working Women's Guild there.[8] In 1905 the Tacoma club opened the Woman's Inn on Pacific Avenue. Through it, the club found women employment, offered shelter and food for the needy and sick, and helped reach friends for them.[9] They funded the enterprise through dues, cake sales, card parties, and public fundraising.

The Women's Inn reception room became the site of meetings, and the group managed to get money and furnishings donated by companies and other clubs. From one room with a cook the project grew within a year to three floors and twelve employees with sleeping rooms furnished by this and other Tacoma clubs. Although successful initially, these extensive efforts such as the Mary Washington House or the Women's Inn gradually lost their customer base, or costs grew too high for clubs to sustain, or both.

Members of the Portland Women's Union, like members of many clubs, initially viewed women working in industry, business, and the professions, absent from their parents' home and therefore vulnerable, as a misfortune. A few years later "this theory was no longer tenable. Women were firmly established in many fields of activity outside of domestic life," noted the club president.[10]

The Portland Women's Union in 1886 established a Women's Evening School, on Sixth Street between Morrison and Alder, with an initial enrollment of fifteen, as a way to give the woman wage-earner a chance for schooling. The club's board established a rather holistic program—on Monday students studied grammar and shorthand; on Tuesday writing and talks; on Wednesday spelling and shorthand; on Thursday arithmetic and reading; and on Friday bookkeeping and shorthand. The club lamented that good teachers were hard to find (and pay) and urged the public school system to absorb the program, particularly since by then boys as well as working girls wanted to be admitted to their alternative school. It was yet another example of the women's club way of creating a private program to benefit a particular population, striking a responsive chord that indicated a need for its support and expansion, then seeking public involvement to sustain the worthy program through government.

Mary Cook, superintendent of the Women's Evening School, wrote in a report to the club's board that while keeping the school going the group "should endeavor to educate public opinion to incorporate an evening school as part of our public school system," for several reasons. "First, it will give school privileges to many of both sexes, that are under the adult age. Second, it will remove the stigma of charity. Third, it will foster that feeling of independence of which we Americans are so proud. Fourth, it would insure to the school that regularity of teaching which it needs so much and place it at once upon the basis of the present school system."[11] Public authorities accepted her rationale. By 1890 the school board did assume control of the evening school the club built, at least for a while.

Nevertheless, changing values, changing interests, and changing social conditions and living standards made the clubwomen's efforts eventually seem anachronistic, maternalistic, irrelevant, or annoying to the population they were designed to help, which now had other options. Class lines still existed despite gender-based alliances, especially in a time of assault on ideas of selfless virtue and service, not to mention an explosion of options for entertainment.

Sometimes it seemed the emphasis in classes and working women's clubs was to teach traditional behavioral codes along

with the skills, such as appropriate etiquette in all things and domestic skills training. Manners and behaviors were significant de-
terminants of what historian John F. Kasson calls the "dialectics of
social classification," those rituals of everyday behavior that sent
messages about social identities, relationships, and "reality."[12] Although the Northwest was less class-oriented than many other regions, class existed. It was exacerbated by the pace of change and
development. One woman with working-class sensitivities who
worked tirelessly for women's causes had difficulty closing the
gap herself, despite being catapulted into an economic elite.

May Arkwright Hutton, boarding house cook turned wealthy
mine owner, spent her life pursuing the causes of culture and suffrage while chasing yet defying the genteel respectability that
came so easily to so many clubwomen. Because of her background, she kept a sensitivity and connection to working men and
women while at the same time aspiring to women's club circles
and "self-improvement."

PROFILE: MAY ARKWRIGHT HUTTON

May Arkwright Hutton embodied the overused word *colorful*. She
was a self-taught and independent working woman, who went from
poor to prosperous due to a partial interest in what was believed
to be a played-out mine. She used her newfound wealth to support
the causes she believed in, from orphanages to suffrage, sometimes to the irritation of her more conservative and "well-bred"
neighbors and colleagues. She was, like them, not above making a
play for power on behalf of her beliefs, and sometimes she succeeded. When she failed, it was spectacular.

Hutton came to the mining district of northern Idaho in 1883
from Ohio to work after her husband left with their savings. She ran
a boarding house, washed clothes, and cooked. She ended up in
the mining town of Wardner Junction, later called Kellogg, where
she set up a restaurant. It had a cookstove, a table covered with
oilcloth, and sleeping quarters in the back. She later took a job
cooking for a hotel, where she met her future husband.[13]

Even after striking it rich, she was never a member of the Wallace
social club set made up of wives of mine owners and managers, at
least until much later. Even then some were not exactly friendly toward her. "May's raucous voice, her gaudy taste in clothes, and her
assertive personality did much to rouse criticism from well-bred
women . . . May resented her ostracism by them," according to a

report cited by a historian of the fabulously wealthy Hercules Mine that changed May's life, taking her into regional activism and far away from Wallace.

Mary (May) Arkwright was born in 1860. Her mother was unmarried, and she was abandoned by her father. She reportedly was taken from school to care for a blind grandfather full-time. They enjoyed going to a local park and listening to soap box orators, which introduced her to social issues.[14] After coming to Idaho, she married one of her customers, railroad engineer Levi W. (Al) Hutton, in 1887. He too had been orphaned, in Iowa at age six, and had lived with various relatives, running away at fifteen. They were twenty-seven years old when they married. She continued to cook for the Wallace Hotel from then until 1901. In fact, she cooked her own wedding supper for fifty guests.

She and her husband had minor celebrity status as local characters. The chubby and dark-haired Mary, called May by all those who knew her, and her husband seldom missed a picnic, excursion, or union dance, and she particularly liked costume balls (she once went dressed as a baby, another time as a man).[15] They frequently bought mining stocks, most of them worthless, and Levi was known as an easy touch for a grubstake. He, May, and several others bought into an old mine in 1897 and worked it on their own in their spare time. Four years later the miracle all miners sought happened. They struck it rich. Out of their 3/32 piece of the wealthy Hercules mine, the Huttons made over $2 million.

Like her husband, May valued and felt deprived of an education. She compensated for her lack of formal education by extensive reading, creating her lifelong interest in literature and drama. She wrote poems and stories and sided with labor in some of the bitter labor disputes between the miners and management. She once bullied deputies until they released her husband from a Wardner bullpen during a period of martial law. May wrote a spirited but vitriolic book in defense of miners, *The Coeur d'Alenes, a Tale of the Modern Inquisition in Idaho*. It was a one-sided account of the labor revolt in north Idaho, when miners commandeered a train and blew up a mine, that pictured oppressed miners as goaded into retaliation against an evil management that then rounded them up and put them in pens through military force. She wrote several stories about atrocities by management against labor. "Read them, you curled darlings of wealth, you trifling puppets of society. These men, who have suffered such indignities, are those whose labor has made it possible for you to enjoy your present position in idleness," read one passage.[16]

Once the Huttons were wealthy mine owners themselves, they reportedly tried to buy up copies to put the book out of circulation and reduce potential embarrassment.[17] However, her sympathies remained with workers and the disadvantaged throughout her life. For years she served on the board of the Florence Crittenton Home in Spokane, among others. She tried to arrange weddings for residents and, if successful, paid their wedding expenses. She also cooked meals on holidays for the needy out of her own kitchen for years.[18]

Once she had money and more leisure time, May began organizing her own women's clubs in Wallace—a musicale, a Shakespeare Club. The latter presented her a sterling silver ice-cream knife when she held a last party for them before moving to Spokane in 1907.[19] At Spokane the Huttons, although outsiders, entertained frequently and traveled. Guests in their home over the years included Teddy Roosevelt, Clarence Darrow, and even Carrie Chapman Catt. Their move to Spokane satisfied Al's desire to invest in real estate, which he considered a proper avocation for a wealthy man. He built the Hutton Building in Spokane, and the couple moved into a nine-room apartment on its fourth floor.

As he pursued adventures in real estate she worked for charities and for women's rights, particularly for suffrage in Washington State. In this Hutton crossed paths (and swords) with Emma DeVoe, NAWSA suffrage organizer from Illinois who charmed audiences with her womanly grace. They knew each other by 1905. At a banquet they both attended honoring Susan B. Anthony when NAWSA convened in Portland, May spoke and read a poem she wrote for the occasion. Initially they worked together, and DeVoe named May organizer for eastern Washington. DeVoe meanwhile became president of the Washington Equal Suffrage League.

However, the two women became enemies in the middle of the campaign for the suffrage vote set for November 8, 1910. Hutton's letters to DeVoe were friendly and solicitous, including invitations for DeVoe to be her house guest. But as campaign tensions and divisions mounted DeVoe pulled away. She claimed to have received damaging personal information about May's past, hinting at connections to vice at Wallace. Some said May's attention from others made DeVoe jealous; others said that Devoe worried about the potential negative effects of May's methods and bulldog tenacity.

DeVoe saw victory in a quiet but persuasive campaign with workers who would offer no opinions on political issues, like workers' rights, other than suffrage and not appear radical or threatening to the men who would decide the issue. Hutton ended up miffed and insulted, especially after a damaging story appeared in the *Idaho Daily Statesman* supposedly traced back to DeVoe. Each side had its faithful followers, and the dispute turned into an East/West split.[20]

Campaign leaders generally saw Hutton as well intentioned, but crude and clumsy. For instance, at the famed Delmonico's in New York, site of the Sorosis meetings, May supposedly had tucked her napkin under her chin prior to eating her meal, only to be chastised by the maître d'. She sat upright and responded, "I am May Arkwright Hutton and I will do as I please."[21] Hutton accused DeVoe of spreading lies about her character, specifically that she had kept a bawdy-house in Wallace under the alias "Black Leg Mary," a name she supposedly gained during the mining strikes by smuggling whiskey in her stockings to imprisoned miners. Hutton's informant said the story was repeated to important club and suffrage leaders such as Leckenby, Kendall, Dr. Cora Smith Eaton, and Adella Parker. May was ousted as a presidential candidate for the suffrage organization, and DeVoe threatened to blackmail her if she persisted. Hutton, outraged, protested her innocence, more determined than ever to win.[22]

Hutton, as leader of the eastern Washington contingent, had scheduled and funded a banquet in Spokane for those who were planning to board one of the suffrage trains carrying delegates to the NAWSA national meeting set for 1909 in Seattle. The meeting had been scheduled there in conjunction with both the Alaska-Yukon-Pacific Exposition and the suffrage vote. In the showdown, the Spokane club and her delegates were denied seats amid claims the Spokane club had inflated its membership for political advantage. Never to be denied, Hutton walked across the street to another hall and her group elected Carrie Hill—founder of the Seattle Century Club and its working women's club—president pro tem. Hill had been president of the state association from 1900 to 1906. The NAWSA officers were at a bit of a loss about how to proceed. They finally decided no one from Washington State would be seated, and national president Anna Howard Shaw warned attendees about factionalism sinking the suffrage boat in Washington.

Once back in Spokane, Hutton formed the Political Equality League, her own women's suffrage organization, and as its first public event sponsored a huge dinner for the two hundred members of the Spokane Chamber of Commerce. Unlike many suffrage supporters who ignored the issue, she promoted the idea of women becoming active members of established political parties and published articles arguing that position. Flamboyant in her red touring car and ostrich-plumed hats, Hutton would never be silenced—or ignored. She worked hard throughout eastern Washington for the suffrage cause, sponsoring a high school oratorical contest on suffrage and sending dozens of letters and petitions to officials. May's campaign was not undignified, but DeVoe complained of her "aggressiveness" and "peculiar methods."23 However, after the successful 1910 vote, May was lauded at a Spokane reception as being the critical factor in the campaign, to the irritation of the mainstream camp.

May's Political Equality League then became the Non-Partisan League, and she continued her social welfare work. She became one of the first two female jurors in Spokane County. In 1912 she was one of three female delegates to the state Democratic convention and the first female delegate to the national convention in Baltimore. While in Baltimore she gave well-received talks on women's suffrage in Washington and Idaho. Back home, she drew up plans for a large home in Spokane circled by pillars, completed in 1914. There she and Al hosted a housewarming for 2,000 guests. Even William Jennings Bryan came by to pay his respects to this powerful woman.

Worsening Bright's disease made May curtail her activities. But she was in her usual box on opening night at the Liberty Theater, organized Spokane Women for World Peace, and read a poem before a Northwest Mining Association meeting. In 1915 she held a lawn party for over 1,000 women attending the Washington State Federation of Women's Clubs convention. The national president came by to see May, who sat in a wheelchair in a new gown.24 She died of the kidney disease a few years later; when she was buried, the president of the Women's Democratic Club of Spokane released a white dove of peace at her grave.25

While in Spokane, May and her husband reportedly gave $458,000 to charity. Her husband remained in their home, serving on boards of both commercial and charitable enterprises. They had donated land east of their property for Lincoln Park Playground, and he bought 112 acres east of Spokane for a new kind of or-phans' home, a plan they had often discussed. The resulting Hut-ton Settlement opened a year after May died, with a deed making it nonsectarian and stating a preference for orphaned children from Idaho since the profits to create it came out of Idaho's mines.

When Al died in 1928 at age sixty-eight, he left their $1.25 million estate to the settlement. He eventually gave the Hutton Settlement 384 acres and established the policy of putting the children into homelike individual cottages staffed with housemothers. Set up for eighty children, the orphanage also had a movie theater and swim-ming pool. He visited frequently, and the children were pleased to see him.[26] It remained a residential care center for children with exceptional needs for many decades after the Huttons died.

The rise of elaborate manners and an emphasis on appropriate behavior before the turn of the century, along with new behav-ioral codes of conduct for parks, theaters, restaurants, and con-cert halls, created class divisions as clear-cut as clothing and ac-cents did. Issues of etiquette became a part of urbanization and the protection of traditional social divisions in the face of eco-nomic, social, and industrial change.

There was more than condescending maternalism and behav-ior control involved in imparting these "codes." Learning the right behaviors was important for more than what such behaviors said about social class or conduct; they also opened opportunities for advancement, practitioners believed. The proper response and introduction, the "right" expression of emotion, control of ap-petites, and disciplined audience behavior at performances all belonged to behavioral codes and reflected cultural values and modes of expression at the same time that they reinforced class divisions.[27] Thus it is no surprise that clubwomen who reached out to working women sought to teach them their codes along with other "useful" subjects.

What happened in the Northwest and elsewhere after the turn of the century was a growing divide over such issues. It had hap-pened earlier elsewhere. Working-class women had joined with more highly educated clubwomen and reformers to form Working Girls' Clubs as early as the 1880s. The clubs typically offered ac-cess to a clubhouse, where factory or service workers could read books, talk to one another, and avail themselves of classes in cooking and sewing. Sometimes the heavy hand of reform entered the program, with advice on personal hygiene and etiquette.[28] By the end of the century, however, such clubs began to die, in part because working women began to turn toward unionization rather than self-improvement as a means to meet their economic and social needs.[29]

THE PROBLEMS OF PROTECTIONISM

Women's clubs acting alone or as parts of an alliance did manage to protect women who took jobs. But soon some women began to see the inherent dangers of such policies to women's employment and chances for advancement. They blamed the clubs rather than the system. In 1899 the president of the Working Woman's Club, Sophie Reinhart, pointed out the problem of protectionist philosophy in her bylined Portland newspaper article. "We are continually hearing the cry of equal wage for equal work; again and again we are insisting on the fact that woman's work is equal to man's and yet, here, in the face of all this growing agitation, in spite of every attempt towards a proper adjustment of the wage question, woman herself is forcing upon us the tacit admission of her incapability to compete with her brother in the struggle for existence!"[30]

She noted that more and more young women were entering the labor force, "not because they like it or choose it, but because circumstances force them there." Morever, they understand nothing of what is expected of them and enter into it "entirely unprepared . . . looking forward to the time when they can marry and throw it all aside." She added that their attention is most often focused on payday, and not on reforms or betterment. Instead, she argued for even more training and education through the women's clubs so they might improve themselves and their lot. "Instead of telling them then that they are being ill-used, teach them how to deserve better treatment, and they will get it."[31]

Reinhart was also sensitive to the cultural issues spurring the clubwomen, however. She argued that in Portland "working girls" have comparatively more culture and education "than is to be found among working girls in the same grade of labor in the East." The reason, she said, "is that here the social lines are not so strictly drawn, and the field for work is more limited." Besides that, working women did not need the club programs designed for them.[32]

The ideas of protective legislation versus "the cry of equal wage for equal work" attacked the issue of helping working women from opposite ends of the spectrum, and both were somewhat misguided. Teaching women how to deserve better treatment, as Reinhart advocated, was not an effective strategy for remedying the poor conditions, bad wages, and exploitation many working women faced in industry; however, protectionist legislation did indeed give employers a ready reason not to promote women or hire them for higher-paying positions. Clubs, unions, and courts danced around this issue then and throughout the twentieth century.

Although frictions and divisions grew between clubwomen and working women, in many cases the conflict represented two different generations with different mindsets and experiences. But both agreed on one issue—the need to eliminate child labor abuses. Clubwomen in the Northwest joined a national effort to end the practice of turning children, sometimes small children, into cheap, dispensable factory labor. A national priority for the GFWC, it led to passage of state laws and the federal Child Labor Amendment.

Getting Children
out of Factories and into School

Saved in the Portland Woman's Club records, stuffed in a book of minutes, was a pamphlet published by the National Child Labor Committee. It pictured two young girls at work in a cotton factory. "Will You Help Us Get These Little Girls out of the Factory and into the School?" asked the pamphlet, calling the use of children under sixteen in wage labor a "national disgrace." It said boys of nine and ten were employed in the coal industry and glass factories. Many of them worked all night, as did the little girls in southern cotton mills. "These are WHITE children of AMERICAN Stock," complained the brochure. Apparently finding black or "alien" children in such conditions was assumed to be less alarming.

"THOUSANDS of Little Children are working in sweatshops in our large cities," the pamphlet continued, adding that children from five to ten years of age work in tenement houses in New York all day and into the night. "The sweatshop, the coal mine, the glass factory, the silk mill, the cotton mill, the cigar shop and bottling works, invade the school and the home to capture the American child."

On the back a sad-faced boy's picture haunted the viewer. He gazed at the photographer, one sleeve of his jacket hanging limp. "This Industrial Soldier entered the coal breaker when he was twelve years old. A few months ago his arm was caught in the ma-

chinery and torn out at the shoulder. With no pension from our
government nor from the corporation that employed him, he is
now discharged from the army of wage-earning children. Is this
an honorable discharge?"

The efforts of the women's clubs and others to end child labor
met with considerable success in state after state, ultimately including the proposed federal amendment. According to one writer,
in 1900 there were 186,000 children between the ages of ten and
thirteen working in nonagricultural jobs and another 502,000
who were fourteen or fifteen. Twenty years later, after the women's
campaigns and an increase in population, only 50,000 children
ten to thirteen and 367,000 between fourteen and fifteen were at
work. By 1930 the total had fallen even further, to 30,000 children between ten and thirteen and 168,000 between fourteen and
fifteen. In 1910 a total of 12.3 percent of all children below fourteen were in the labor force, including agricultural work. By 1920
it was 4.4 percent, and by 1930, 2.4 percent.[33]

A parallel effort of clubwomen to enhance public school education for children also resulted in structural changes, another dimension of their cultural politics. As child employment was dropping, compulsory education and longer school sessions helped
put many of these children in schools. School expenditures doubled between 1900 and 1910 and again between 1910 and 1920.
The average school term length went from 135 days in 1890 to
162 days in 1920. Educational access, always a club priority, improved, as did the educational levels attained.

Protectionism through legislative remedies had negative side
effects, particularly for women's classifications of employment,
but few could argue that children were not better off in school
than in the factory working long hours at sometimes dangerous
jobs. The impact of this on family economies to which wage-earning children contributed, or on companies that used this cheap
source of labor, is less clear. But these fundamental changes in the
social landscape meant the realization of reordered social priorities that had spurred many women to join clubs in the first place.

INVESTIGATING CONDITIONS

Using the new social science methods, the Consumers' League of
Portland (founded and led by activist clubwomen including Mil-
lie Trumbull, Mrs. J. C. Card, and Sarah Evans) decided to investigate conditions for working women and whether Oregon's child

labor laws and others were being enforced. Women came to realize getting an ordinance or law passed was only part of the battle.
Fixing the problem also required enforcement of the provisions,
something more difficult to ensure than passage.

The league commissioned a massive survey of thousands of
working women inside and outside Portland.[34] They, like most
other reformers, believed that the steps of study, evidence, awareness, and publicity would lead inexorably to reform. The "Report
of the Social Survey Committee of the Consumers' League of Oregon" found that working conditions for a great many women were
substandard, inadequate, and sometimes hazardous. Investigators
found that the large majority of self-supporting women in the state
earned less than it cost them to live decently, requiring many to
live in substandard conditions or get financial help from their
homes, "which thus contributes to the profits of their employers;
that those who do not receive assistance from relatives are breaking down in health from lack of proper nourishing food and comfortable lodging quarters, or are supplementing their wages by
money received from immoral living."

The problems in businesses of filthy conditions, disease, noise,
inadequate ventilation, and unsafe fire escapes were often brushed
off by employees and employers alike as "the girls get used to it."
Even in places that paid living wages, "workshops are in such
unsanitary condition that immediate changes are necessary,"
including addressing the hours of labor required in certain industries. They also found that piece work rates frequently were
reduced once the women reached a certain level of production or
that women who worked for years were never able to earn more.[35]
Even after the women's clubs, in alliance with other groups, got
Oregon's visionary labor laws passed in the first decade of the
century, establishing the right of the state to intervene to protect
citizens by limiting work hours for women and children, the laws
were being flagrantly violated by employers in the Northwest,
women said. And even where the labor laws were followed, limiting women to ten-hour days and sixty-hour weeks, the loss of
overtime pay exacerbated the problems of low wages, the study
recognized.

Back workrooms for many industries were dark, poorly ventilated, often unheated, and bosses paid workers far below what the
study's writers indicated was a minimum subsistence level of pay
at $10 a week, itself a novel concept. Even those who worked in

the bright lights and clean conditions of department stores started
at $3 a week because they were young and inexperienced, and
overtime pay up to the legal sixty hours a week seldom existed.
Women in factories in Oregon typically began at $3 to $6 a week,
with woolen mills at the high end, but women were placed on
piece work rates after two weeks. According to a 1903 Portland
publication, average weekly wages in the East for women were
$7.52 in shops, $10.45 in shoe factories, $5.38 in restaurants,
$8.35 in textile mills, and only $3.99 in household work. The
paper added that all such wages ran lower on the West Coast.[36]

Of women working in factories, the survey found one-third
earned less than $7 a week and one-half less than $8 a week. In
fact, 75 percent of the 427 factory women surveyed earned less
than the "poverty level" pay of $10 a week. The maximum that
women who had spent their careers in the industry were ever
paid was $12–$20. Because piece work rates declined when workers gained speed, a woman "finds herself set back a year as far as
her earning power is concerned." Lowest paid were women working in hotels and restaurants ($31.65 a month), followed by tele-
phone operators ($33.07 a month). Statewide, stenographers were
paid most, at $50 a month, followed by office help ($35.50 a
month) and retail store workers ($39.01).

Oregon's child labor law prohibited employment of children
under sixteen, even during vacation months, without a permit.
And under no circumstances was a permit to be given to a child
under twelve years of age. However, the Portland Consumers'
League investigators in the summer of 1912 saw children under
eleven with their parents—sometimes alone—not only working,
but working more than the ten hours a day allowed even an adult.
The canneries opened at 6 A.M. and closed at 10:30 P.M. One-half
hour was permitted at noon for lunch, but employees were threatened with losing work if they stopped for an evening break despite
the grueling schedule.

Many women worked in laundries, which paid a meager $1.25
to $2 a day, but never any more. Worker categories included
markers, starch room, manglers, folders, stackers, body manglers,
and ironers. It was hard work, especially in summer when tem-
peratures inside soared to and stayed above 100 degrees. Those
who fainted were laid outside until they recovered and went back
to work. The study noted, however, that of the forty power laun-

dries in Portland surveyed, three managers worked with fans and awnings to make intolerable conditions tolerable.

Other women worked as chambermaids and waitresses. But 49 percent of the 213 women interviewed in this category made less than the magic $10 a week. "Both lines of work are popular with women; hotel work because the work is through in the middle of the afternoon; restaurant work because women are continually meeting new people," said the report. "Both lines of work are hard, the latter sometimes injuriously so on account of carrying the heavy trays." Women working in the trades that were open to them fared better. The survey included the categories hairdresser, "janitress," and dressmaker. "A woman who is a plain sewer only can earn $2 a day with at least two meals," while "fancy waist-makers" earned $12 to $15 a week.

Unionization—the process that improved conditions for mil-lions of workers in low-paying industries and a vital force in the Northwest as well—did not help women much, according to this study. For instance, Portland had forty-two printing shops, all of which recognized the union, the study found. Women working in the shops generally bound pamphlets and books, with a minimum wage of $6 for each apprentice, rising to $7 after one year and $8 after two. That was much below the subsistence level and also much below wages men received in the plants. Men's unions were not exactly receptive or open to including women or expanding their job opportunities and in fact often resented women's employ-ment, as a threat to either their own jobs or their salary levels.

"Girls Get Used to It"

Although the report's writers avoided the term *wage slavery,* they implied women were caught in something similar. "There are scores of girls here who are living in miserable conditions, rooms without heat in winter, who do not get a new dress once a year, but make over their old one until it becomes threadbare, and who can afford but two meals a day," one of the authors (the Reverend Edwin O'Hara) told a meeting of the Consumers' League of Ore-gon. "How long will their health stand the strain? . . . We are hor-rified at the recital of atrocities in Africa where natives are forced to work for their masters under the lash. What shall we say of leading citizens of every large American city who gather in divi-dends from industries that grind down American girls to indecent and starvation wages, and deliberately pile up profits from the earnings of their shame?"[37]

The concerns have echoed again near the end of the twentieth century over the same issues, only the setting has changed to U.S. companies employing workers outside the country. It was then as now a powerful argument for tougher wage and hour legislation and enforcement. The depth of the report and the resulting outrage led to a push for a state Industrial Commission to better enforce wage and hour laws protecting women and children, set pay scales, and suggest changes in the laws and regulations. A similar commission with a different name was also pursued by activist clubs in Washington.

The extensive analysis—making use of the new methods of sociology such as the scientific survey to amass objective evidence—was hard-hitting in its conclusions and provided a valuable snapshot of life inside the world of women's work in some of the city's businesses and industries, in Portland and everywhere. The report also argued for passage of comprehensive Welfare Legislation for Women and Minors. It set forth several points similar to arguments used decades later to establish federal minimum wage legislation and argue for comparable worth wage reform. In sum, investigators found that nearly 60 percent of the women employed in Portland's industries received less than $10 a week, the minimum weekly wage "that ought to be offered to any self-supporting woman wage-earner in this city." And it demonstrated that the working conditions for women in many industries were detrimental to their health, a problem more alarming because many were potential mothers, and concluded that "the future health of the race is menaced by these unsanitary conditions."[38]

Although successful, the club efforts to provide these protections for women were often shortsighted, as were analogous union efforts. They used laws and regulations to control working women's exploitation, instead of addressing the sexism of an economic system that segregated so many women, then as now, into low-end, routinized jobs, often with little opportunity for advancement. At the time, protection for women seemed paramount and reflected an acceptance of the consequences of industrialization and a higher standard of living for both men and women. Conditions for working women in the Pacific Northwest too often included long hours, low pay, and, for some, dreadful working conditions. In 1890 in the United States women who worked in stores for long hours had no stools and toilets with no doors. Store managers had a system of store fines for petty violations that reduced their already low pay. There was no overtime pay.[39] Similar problems existed in most cities.

The National Consumers' League grew out of the Working Women's Society in New York City as a forerunner of the Women's Trade Union League. The survey was one of its earliest tools as it was for women's clubs. Incorporated in 1898, the Consumers' League sent out speakers to women's clubs—including clubs in Portland in 1902—and used the force of public opinion to bring attention to such problems. Florence Kelley became its general secretary.[40] She also filled the position of chair of the GFWC's committee on Industry of Women and Children and spoke at Seattle during the 1909 Alaska-Yukon-Pacific Exposition at the meeting of the Washington Federation of Women's Clubs. Thus she and others were able to bring the issue forward nationally with the clubs and the federation behind them.

In 1903, after New York league president spoke in Portland, the Consumers' League was established in Oregon. The Portland Woman's Club established an influential local version of the league, led by women active in various women's clubs. The Portland League was important in the campaign for labor legislation, with its overlapping leadership, its studies, and its visible role at the point of a united front. Leaders like Sarah Evans of the Portland Women's Union and others provided the bridge.

Through an alliance with women's clubs and sympathetic legislators, the coalition was able to get the legislation passed limiting work for women to ten-hour days and sixty-hour weeks, which was extended to retail store workers in 1907. From working hours the coalition moved to the issue of consumer health and sanitation in the preparation, storage, and distribution of food and became part of a state and national drive for a Pure Food Bill. They secured its passage in Oregon in 1907. Inspections finally began in 1909 after years of diligent work.[41]

OREGON'S LABOR LANDMARK—*MULLER v. OREGON*

Oregon's labor legislation finally passed after years of work only to face a court challenge by a laundry owner and a woman who had a "contract" to work for him. The case, important for what it said about states' rights in the face of private labor contracts and economic interests, began working its way to the U.S. Supreme Court.

The law itself was simple. It said that "no female [shall] be employed in any mechanical establishment, or factory, or laundry in this State more than ten hours during any one day." The penalty was a small fine of $10–$25. The court challenge came forward when Mrs. E. Gotcher in 1905 was required to work longer than the law allowed. The law was challenged on the basis that the state had no right to interfere with a business and its legal contracts with employees. The Oregon Supreme Court upheld the law, reasoning that any labor contract was subject to "reasonable limitations." It was appealed.

The case was finally heard in 1908. It had Louis Brandeis, later a Supreme Court justice himself, as counsel representing the State of Oregon, retained by the National Consumers' League. His task was to show a compelling state interest in limiting the powerful legal concept of freedom of contract. His brief, written with Josephine Goldmark, was unique and gained much attention later in legal circles. It went beyond legal arguments to use sociological data and statistics to establish the connection between the law and conditions that gave rise to it. Goldmark and Brandeis amassed and presented 113 pages of evidence on physical differences between men and women, on the effects of long work hours on the health and morals of women workers, and on the damage this posed for future generations.

The court in a landmark decision upheld the right of government to regulate wages and hours. It found that working women, especially potential mothers, suffered deleterious effects from overwork because of their biology and/or that the jobs open to them were demeaning and potentially dangerous.[42] *Muller v. Oregon* was important for what it meant for all state economic and social regulation, but also for what it said about women as a class of workers. It reversed a judicial drift toward setting aside state economic legislation as unconstitutional because such measures were deemed to have clashed with the due process clause of the Constitution.

Justice David Brewer wrote "[that] woman's physical structure and the performance of maternal functions place her at a disadvantage in the struggle for subsistence is obvious," especially in motherhood. Medical experts said being on her feet at work day after day "tends to injurious effects upon the body, and as healthy mothers are essential to vigorous offspring, the physical well-being of woman becomes an object of public interest and care in order to preserve the strength and vigor of the race." Despite gains in equal opportunity, he wrote, women still needed protective legislation and woman "is properly placed in a class by herself. . . . It is impossible to close one's eyes to the fact that she still looks to her brother and depends upon him."[43] Even though it was upheld, enforcement was a serious problem, as the later Portland Consumers' League survey revealed, one it was hoped would be remedied through the Industrial Wage Commission. It would have sweeping legal powers to investigate and indict offending business owners and set guidelines for hours, minimum wages, and work conditions as they applied to women and children.

PROTECTION IN WASHINGTON AND IDAHO

Clubwomen and others in both Washington and Idaho also worked to pass legislation to help working women and other specific groups of workers, such as coal miners or newsboys. Early in the 1900s the Washington Federation of Women's Clubs and the Washington Federation of Labor worked to establish Washington's own landmark in labor legislation, the nation's first minimum wage law guaranteeing women the magic living wage of $10 a week, the amount cited by the Oregon federation as a minimum needed for women to survive, and the nation's first eight-hour workday. The Washington Federation of Women's Clubs was embroiled in politics and controversy by 1903 over the concept of businesses being required to pay a minimum wage, and its support helped gain acceptance of the idea.

In 1903 the federation with the Grange and the Washington State Federation of Labor took several other important reform measures through the legislature—a child labor law, an initiative law, and an eight-hour day for employees on publicly funded projects.[44] The first Industrial Welfare Commission, created by the Washington legislation, was empowered to monitor wages, never an easy task. The commission included three women.[45] In 1913 the Washington federation also backed a bill requiring an eight-hour workday limit for coal miners. The women's vote, coupled with strong Populist and farmer-labor alliances, created a climate in Washington conducive to reform measures.

In Idaho, reform was again bolstered by facts gathered through a survey. During the 1912 biennium, the Idaho Federation of Women's Clubs completed its own survey of industrial and social conditions for working women. It revealed that women frequently worked for wages ten or twelve hours a day in that state, sometimes under the same bad conditions found in Oregon or Washington. Federation bill-writer and attorney Bertha Green (profiled in chapter 9) pushed for a statute limiting women to a nine-hour work day, a compromise with those who wanted an eight-hour workday.[46]

Women's clubs in the Northwest played an important national role in pioneering labor legislation. Club committees drafted many of the bills, and members lobbied for their passage. Although their programmatic relationship with working women declined and reflected growing societal divisions over women's proper role in the twentieth century, clubwomen successfully transferred their ideals about social justice through governmental regulation and the need for intervention in the marketplace into their work on behalf of working women and children. Ideas and proposals to use the marketplace in consumer boycotts to help working men and women were less successful, however, than those initial campaigns to boycott abusive department stores before the turn of the century.[47]

Although the need for such help diminished as the century progressed, clubwomen's initial efforts to establish clubs, schools, boarding houses, and other services for working women reflected cultural politics that embraced the need to use government to improve conditions and protect those who seemed powerless and came from different classes than club members did. Some working women saw these women who did not work for wages and their efforts to help in a different light and sometimes resented what they perceived as manipulation or condescension, especially in the twentieth century. Others were grateful for the help, attention, and support of their more "privileged" sisters.

The rhetoric of motherhood and ideals of domesticity remained powerful, but began to crumble under their own proscriptive weight. Early idealistic alliances broke apart, and working women's clubs eventually failed or were superseded by different organizations. But women's club efforts to open education, professions, and organizations, and to improve the legal and political status of all women, benefited working women as well.

"THE WOMAN'S CENTURY"

A Host of Progressive Movements, 1895–1915

The women's club movement offered tens of thousands of women opportunities for improvement and achievement, prominence and power. Even social science research said so.

Using the biographies of nine thousand prominent American women of 1914 compiled in John William Leonard's *Woman's Who's Who,* historian Barbara Kuhn Campbell attempted to find patterns in their family, education, careers, religion, political activities, and clubwork. Campbell found these women shared one characteristic. They were deeply into literary, alumnae, professional, patriotic, and genealogical clubs. Of the nine thousand women, 77 percent had joined women's clubs, and 49 percent of them had become club officers. For women not working at careers, the figures were even higher—85 percent had joined clubs and 54 percent held offices. Of the professional women, 79 percent belonged to clubs, with 57 percent holding leadership positions.[1]

Clearly, whatever power and status women had collectively, it coincided with club activism. The passage of time, the momentum of the Progressive era, rapid sociological and technological change, and the maturity of the movement led clubwomen to take up other social movements such as suffrage. In the Northwest, clubwomen played a critical role in women's right to vote coming early in those states, recounted in this chapter. Theirs is an important and dramatic story, but their role in the political saga has often been overlooked. Without the leaders from the clubs, suffrage would have come much later to the Northwest. Many women recognized that because politics was fundamental to enacting lasting social change through government their right to vote was of critical importance.

In the Northwest, club leaders were often suffrage leaders, but suffrage was only one cause out of many. Not all were pleased with the women's rights movement and the changes it portended, even among clubwomen. The club movement, no stranger to criticism, continued to see challenges to the emboldened use of its collective voice and vision. The success of organized womanhood from the beginning had attracted critics, but the criticism over the years had changed.

CRITICS OF THE MOVEMENT

Club activities were viewed as harmless diversions by many and downright perverse by some. The very success and explosive growth women's clubs experienced led some to respond with alarm and to attack the clubs as pernicious at worst and silly at best. Clubs and the women who participated were chastised for venturing far from hearth and home and for taking on a "public persona." The very word *club* connoted aggressive, unwomanly women to many, and self-improvement equated to selfishness. The movement often defied prevailing cultural expectations for female behavior even while it often called upon many of those expectations to justify its existence.

Later critics looking back attacked the club movement and clubwomen for different reasons. They found them elitist, centered on social standing, prejudiced about class and race, patronizing, and even downright imperialistic in their attitudes toward literature, culture, the arts, and reform at all levels. These critics came to use *middle-class* as a broad pejorative that circumscribed clubwomen's aspirations.

Jane Croly says that the Sorosis Club was the object "of many gibes and sneers, much ridicule, and cheap attempts at wit during the first months of its existence." Members were called "sorry sisters" by critics, who said there was no place or aim or excuse for its existence. She also notes how well the club overcame initial skepticism. Twenty years after its founding, young members of Sorosis wondered "why all this fuss could have been made about a mere society of women." But at the time "it was doubted, by many good men and women, whether a secular society of women, of different tastes, habits and pursuits, and with no special object to bind them, could hang together for any length of time."[2]

Ridicule is one of the most powerful means of chastising behavior and reinforcing existing cultural codes. It induces shame and is itself invulnerable to rational arguments in response. Ridicule has often been used to reinforce gender roles, and the club movement generated its share. For example, the cartoons in the popular magazine Puck often satirized women and their clubs. One 1873 cartoon shows an unattractive woman carrying copies of speeches with the label "Sorosis" who is being chastised by a Reverend Dix in a sermon that *Puck* "condensed." "Get thee to a kitchen, To a kitchen go, and quickly too," he commands.[3] In 1869 *Harper's Weekly* attacked the same club, also in a cartoon, showing mobs of women busy gabbing, drinking tea, signing petitions, and holding meetings for committee work, all while leaving care of children and home to others or leading their baby-carrying husbands around by a leash.[4] Perhaps what is most significant in this busy drawing is an unintended effect. The women are all engaged in intellectual endeavors—reading, writing, speaking, arguing, some while holding babies, hardly proper public behavior for women in 1869.

Ten years later, as many clubs moved from study to bolder levels of activism, the taunts changed. In 1879 Puck satirized women who lobby legislators with a series of drawings of women engaged in what was then even more outlandish and outrageous public behavior than attending meetings.[5] One frame shows women chasing a senator, holding demands for jobs and other bills in hand as he tries to escape. Another frame is captioned "Eve, the First Female Lobbyist." Yet another shows a dour, unattractive woman sitting with hands folded. "Female, who can't Lobby worth a Cent," reads her caption. The implication in this and other frames was that success at lobbying depended on physical appearance, connecting seduction to support and trading of female favors for legislative favors.

In 1896—the year the national federation created state federations—*Puck* carried a cartoon titled "At the Emancipated Women's Club." It showed a man with children at the door of a meeting. His wife has been handed a calling card. "Your husband wants to see you, Mum: —he says the baby's tooth is through at last, and he had to come and show it to you, Mum!"[6] The women in their new roles were viewed as selfishly neglecting their husbands and children.

Despite the use of satire and stereotypes, the fact that these popular magazines included women in this way also reflects, in addition to resistance, a grudging recognition of their organizations. They had become parts of a movement worth satirizing. Other social movements involving women were generally ignored in this "humor." They were not yet large enough or relevant enough or perceived as a threat. What got attention was the threat the women's clubs posed to the status quo for the largely urban, middle-class men that constituted the primary readership of the magazines. Immigrant women as a group were also satirized from time to time, as were the suffrage campaigns and leaders, for the same reasons. As humor often does, it also showed where the culture's pressure points were in the distribution of power, cultural norms, and the unequal gender relationships that the clubs and their petitions challenged. Clubwomen (and suffrage leaders) were often portrayed as unnatural and undesirable, as "unwomanly."

By the end of the century, the nature of the criticism had changed again. Acceptance had turned to admiration in many quarters and then to irritation in some. Even Grover Cleveland weighed in on the issue, attacking clubwomen for neglecting their duties to their families in a 1905 *Ladies' Home Journal* article that set off a boycott of the magazine. On the positive side, ten men prominent in philanthropy and reform concluded in the 1906 *Annals of the American Academy of Political and Social Science* that women's clubs had improved both their homes and their communities as well as society at large through their collective efforts.[7]

However, even a booster of women's clubs wrote in 1902 that the nation was "club-ridden" and women were "sociomaniacs." The result was that women scattered and diffused their energies and tended to be superficial. Club studies could generate emotion without action or substitute study for achievement.[8] In 1916 historian Mary Ritter Beard compiled 344 pages chronicling women's new civic accomplishments, including club achievements in ten broad areas of reform, detailing hundreds of specific local changes along those lines.[9] Organized womanhood had successfully altered at least segments of the cultural landscape, creating new configurations that would not revert to earlier forms even when the club movement passed.

GOING CLUB-MAD

In the Pacific Northwest, the *Oregon Daily Journal* in 1902 vilified and praised the clubs at the same time. "There are women who run the club into the ground. They go club-mad, as it were, and neglect duty to family and home in the running about to perform too great a portion of the work of the public," wrote the editor. "But these are mere defects in a system that has marvelous possibilities and that has already accomplished wonders for the women of the United States." He also noted that the attention to the intellectual and cultural had put women in a different place compared to men. "The women's club movement has advanced the average member to a position ahead of the average business man in mental culture. It is rapidly making the American woman the superior of the American man in literary learning and it is also making her the equal of the man in practical affairs."[10]

Another writer of the time agreed, but saw dangers in this extended "self-improvement." Anna Garlin Spencer spoke at the Columbian Exposition. She warned that women's clubs had made it easier for women than men to achieve "intellectual and moral development," resulting in a growing gap between women and all but professional and "learned" men. She also argued that women easily aroused to activism needed to consider the effects of their causes and efforts and to make sure their goals in joining were not for prestige and selfish reasons, but out of commitment to the larger goals of the group. She added that many a woman belonged to too many literary clubs, thus thinking herself cultivated, "because she hears swiftly forgotten papers by the bushel."[11] Her warning was in part about increased growth and status, two-headed threats to any growing social movement.

Indeed, club methods were not always effective. More than one critic took aim at the many lectures. They aroused listeners, but before the women could take action another lecture came along with the same claim on the members' attention. "The indefinite process of stimulation and exhaustion, without accompanying activity, goes on until the desperate club woman listens to all causes with equal stoicism and with mechanical interest," argued a critic.[12] A related criticism was that club study seldom allowed members to follow a line of thought, but instead forced members to jump from issue to issue, with nebulous vocabulary and superficial treatment.

Using satire about typical "current events" departments and women's propensity for reforms, a writer said one might soon hear about "the necessity of having—and joining—a Society for the Protection of the Motor Men from the Severe Weather."[13] And some pointed to an important consequence of the economic arrangements that gave women time for club activities. Many clubwomen had the time on their hands to study and take action upon civic affairs, time that their husbands and other women did not have the luxury to spend in such investigation. Nevertheless, even their worst critics recognized the power of the clubs to create public opinion.

Alliances of clubs, a vehicle for extending power, sometimes broke down, especially after the turn of the century when activism was reaching new heights. The course of club life in a city did not always run smoothly. As some clubs became more active socially and politically, others sometimes rebelled. And alliances of women crossing class lines to work together in suffrage organizations or on union access did not hold for long once they met their goal.[14] Sometimes members became cynical when their efforts through city councils came to naught, or other clubs failed to support their causes, or hard-fought changes in legal codes were ignored. Sometimes the divisions came out over the issue of suffrage and whether it should be the right of women to dirty themselves in politics, "hustling with the rowdies," as one newspaper writer quoted in Susan B. Anthony's *History of Woman Suffrage* described it in connection with the national suffrage campaign.

In the Pacific Northwest, the differences surfaced in a debate in Spokane about the direction clubs in that city were taking. In the *Club Journal,* the short-lived official journal of the Oregon and Washington state federations, Mrs. F. F. Emery, treasurer of the Washington Federation and member of the Spokane Sorosis Club, wrote in 1902 about her frustrations. "What are the Spokane clubs doing? I must answer, the same old things, meaning of course that our clubs are all literary and meet simply for papers, talks, etc. The topics are full of interest and are ably handled, but there is too much of sameness in our work, and I often wish we had something to take us out of ourselves and give us more of an interest in others who do not belong to our own particular set." However, like clubwomen everywhere, Spokane clubs could agree on one cause, working together on the local library. But Emery saw problems looming there too when ownership of such projects went to women only.

"The city federation, however, is taking up the question of a different location for the city library, and I hope some needed good work will be accomplished. Our library is in the City Hall, which is in the worst district in town; women do not care to walk through the street and mothers object to allowing their sons and daughters to see the sights they are obliged to witness every time they pass these gambling houses, saloons and other disreputable places," she said, voicing the community and moral concerns of clubwomen in every community who fought these profitable and sometimes controlling interests. She also alluded to city council inaction, another problem women encountered when they tried to "improve conditions," as they called it.

"The men of Spokane have never dared to move in the matter, the merchants for fear of losing the trade of these people, the politicians on account of votes and the rest because they are indifferent. Now it is proposed that the club women see what they can do to better the conditions."[15] What the women did was start negotiations with Carnegie and a $50,000 fundraising drive to build a new library, complete with a suite of rooms for women's club meetings.

The other side of the coin—the objections to club activism— turned up in an interview in the *Walla Walla Union Bulletin* with Mrs. Charles Chant, a member of the Spokane Federation of Women's Clubs, who was visiting there at the time. "Mrs. Chant believes in womanly women's clubs, those which confine their work to their sphere of rational improvement," said the article. "And this sphere she believes to be a complement of the better home life. She does not approve of the 'advanced club woman,' she who neglects her home for the purpose of following an ideal which is more mannish than womanly," it added.

"Furthermore, she does not approve of any kind of club life that thrives at the expense of the home." However, she did believe that women's clubs were destined to exert "beneficent influence" on the cities of the Northwest. "There are now about twenty women's clubs of different kinds in Spokane, all federated together," she told the paper. "One institution maintained by the Federation which is a commendable charity is the Noonday Rest, a place were working girls may go for their meals at 10 cents each, where they may rest, where they may have access to a gymnasium and to baths."[16]

Another set of priorities common in the Northwest, less divisive socially, related to environmental concerns. For instance, the Spokane federation, like other clubs, advocated legislation to protect what was left of fast-disappearing natural scenery, which often fell victim to economic development and growth, synonymous with "progress."[17] Nationally clubwomen pursued a variety of conservation causes, such as halting the spread of ugly roadside billboards, distributing seeds and plants for beautification, and creating parks. Clubwomen of Washington lobbied for Olympic National Park in Washington, and Florida clubwomen bought in 1916 and maintained what became Everglades National Park.

Fountains and gardens blossomed as club projects in cities all over the country. Clubs supported forestry or conservation departments in federated clubs, departments particularly active in the Northwest. In Washington, a long-term effort by dozens of local clubs culminated when their amassed $25,000 was used to buy the Federation Forest from a lumber company in 1926. That forest was later destroyed by a storm, but relocated elsewhere.

A magazine writer in 1903, although critical of women's clubs, gave them credit for being able to legislate by means of public opinion and getting laws passed that improved conditions and status for women and children. In dozens of states women's clubs won passage of laws to raise standards of behavior or morality, to set up separate programs and institutions for "dependent classes" such as mentally disabled adults or delinquent children, and to secure for women jobs as factory inspectors, police matrons, and members of various governmental boards.

It is difficult to state with exactitude the role of women's clubs in passage of all this social legislation. In many cases, state federation officers actually drafted bills and lobbied them through; for other measures, petitions and "public agitation" secured approval.[18] Some came about years after women brought them up as proposals. In all cases, clubs helped legitimize as part of mainstream thought these ideas on social welfare issues.

Club legislative programs established a political stronghold for women without sanctioned political power in most states, who were forced to act through third parties and without direct participation. In fact, nationally many clubwomen eschewed traditional politics, with its negative connotations, instead favoring domestication of politics to incorporate home values, including making the state the protector. As Paula Baker found in her study of rural New York during these years, women pioneered issue-oriented, nonpartisan politics and the benefits of an expanded and more powerful state.[19]

As the new century dawned, social movements designed to create, enhance, or restore a sense of the state and the community were abroad in the land, as part of something now termed the Progressive movement, an umbrella term encapsulating ideas of governmental reform. It emerged from findings in social science, changes in science and technology, and the appeal of new political methods and leaders in place of the politics of favor and corruption. The city beautiful movement, the social gospel movement, the good government movement, suffrage, divorce reform, wage and hour laws, literacy, kindergartens and curriculum changes, and temperance—all these movements contained important messages for a reformed culture and changed standards of behavior. All were carried forward in some measure by women organized into clubs, vying for legislative and civic attention to these social and cultural issues. The Progressive era modes emphasizing managerial efficiency, social control, and bureaucratic thinking played their role too, especially later in the period.

Progressives were most often remembered for their governmental reforms in the name of efficiency, direct political participation, and governmental regulation of business, particularly at the federal level. However, as one historian notes in his sharp criticism of Gilded Age history as presented in textbooks, much of the action took place in social and political policies at local levels, in every aspect of social life, from expansion of public education and protection of public health and safety to attempts to rationalize public service through merit systems and professionalization. "Statutory innovations in education, public health, and corporative organization, for example, helped to make Americans the most literate, the healthiest, and eventually the richest people in the world," even as states used their authority "in ways less acceptable today," such as tightening vagrancy laws, writes historian Ballard Campbell.[20] Activity at the local and regional level often reflected club priorities and activism and ultimately their legislative and institutional achievements for what they perceived as the social good.

As the nature of reform and community activism often differed between East and West, so did political progressivism. In the West, according to historian Richard White and others, there was much more attention to "direct democracy and its disdain for party discipline." Indeed the Oregon system of the initiative and referendum, along with direct primaries, a corrupt practices act, and a recall amendment, came to fruition in the Northwest. This lack of party loyalty and discipline also had negative effects that led to party disarray and in turn to a lack of political consensus or ability to mediate differences.[21] The fact that women in the Northwest gained the vote early and had less sympathy for or attachment to (in fact, often expressed disdain for) parties doubtless contributed to the differences in the Northwest, a factor often ignored.

For instance, female voters in Seattle and Tacoma, under the leadership of Emma DeVoe and others, gave the edge to recall elections that threw Seattle's Mayor Hiram Gill and Tacoma's Mayor Angelo Fawcett out of office. Both men were embattled over blatant plans to allow, with tacit city approval, construction of large brothels downtown. To the consternation of many women, both men declared they had reformed and were reelected in 1914. The fact that women had the vote bolstered the use of the ballot initiative to reform government or at least express the voice of the voter more directly than did parties. In fact, Oregon became the national leader in ballot initiatives after they were created in that state in 1902, about a decade before women could vote. Since adoption, the initiative had been used 274 times in that state by 1990, an average of 3 a year. Washington, which with Idaho adopted the initiative in 1912, was sixth in the nation, with 91 issues on the ballot since adoption, followed by Idaho in nineteenth place nationally, at 16 issues.[22]

By the turn of the century women's clubs had earned broad recognition for their work. Arena magazine, addressing the future of the woman's club in 1902, credited clubs for their role in improving educational opportunity, noting that fifty years before the article was written women's colleges were almost unknown and that thirty years before coeducation was a venture. Before that, girls either "picked up crumbs of learning upon half-holidays when the schoolroom was not needed by their brothers, or not at all." It called the first women's clubs "timid affections . . . but a step removed from afternoon teas," but the twentieth-century club was a "factor in social life, federated for the progress of the world. The first 'lady speaker' was a frightened apology; the modern woman is an orator and a parliamentarian."[23]

Now women had a powerful collective voice that influenced the distribution of social resources—one definition of power—and were engaged in a struggle to redefine the culture through the lens of the intellectual, the moral, the sentimental, rather than the competitive, capitalistic, or autocratic perspectives associated with masculine values as part of the power structure. They needed another form of power to move their personal, political, and cultural agendas forward, however—the power of the ballot.

GETTING THE RIGHT TO VOTE

Women in the West won the right to vote decades before women elsewhere in the country. They gained full voting rights in

Wyoming in 1869, Utah in 1870, Colorado in 1893, Idaho in 1896, Washington in 1910, California in 1911, Oregon in 1912 (after the issue was on the ballot as an amendment no fewer than six times), and Montana and Nevada in 1914. Generally the leadership of the suffrage campaigns in the Pacific Northwest came directly out of club leadership, sometimes decades before final passage. The political participation and experiences of the women in all these states were an important factor in the final push toward passage and ratification of the suffrage amendment in 1920.

The women in the Northwest got the right to vote before most women in the country for a variety of reasons, not the least of which was the leadership certain women brought to the cause. Getting the right to vote was important for reasons that went beyond basic civil rights, important as those were; getting the right to vote would enable women to better pursue those provisions expressed as club goals and priorities. It would also bring more attention to those priorities from the political structure, they believed. Historian Richard White argues that perhaps since the western community "was so often the work of women, the moral arguments of suffragists had a stronger and more immediate appeal in the West."[24] Suffrage, however, did not come either easily or quickly, even in the West. It had a long period of proposal and retreat, and a few women spent much of their lives engaged in the effort.

Interest in suffrage for women actually began early in the territorial period. The Washington Territorial Legislature, looking in part to boost the votes that would lead to statehood, had granted women the right to vote in 1883. However, in 1887, after a series of local option prohibition elections passed where women were voting, the Washington Territorial Supreme Court declared their right to vote unconstitutional when a test case came before it. The outcome of those local elections had been blamed on women using the ballot to impose changes, and the court held that they should not have been given the right in the first place.

Since a state constitution was being written when the decision denying their rights was handed down, the provision for women's suffrage could easily have been included, and there was considerable debate by convention delegates over two central issues: suffrage and prohibition. What happened in Washington continued the trend of linking the reforms of women's rights to vote and prohibition when they came before the voter, the pairing that Abigail Scott Duniway decried for decades.[25]

Early small suffrage organizations in the Washington Territory had pushed the cause of suffrage even before 1880, as they did a few years later in Idaho and Oregon. Ultimately the constitutional convention delegates decided to let voters who would have to ratify the constitution decide the questions of both woman suffrage and prohibition. Both were defeated—women's suffrage on a two-to-one margin, and prohibition by a smaller margin. The proposed constitution passed by a four-to-one ratio, leading to the November 11, 1889, entry of Washington into the union.[26] However, Washington's first state legislature in conciliation did confer on women one right—the right to vote in school elections, limiting their participation in government to an arena traditionally deemed appropriate for them.[27] Likewise, the Idaho legislature gave women the right to vote on and even run for school offices earlier, in 1885. Idaho, however, had another factor that influenced the suffrage campaign in that state—fear of the Mormon vote.

Some of Idaho's earliest settlements in the southeast corner were there because of the followers of the Mormon faith. By the mid-1880s Idaho had disenfranchised its Mormon residents (their voting rights were restored in 1892), suspicious of the growing population spreading across the Utah border and the practice of polygamy. In fact, Congress had already disenfranchised Utah women as a condition of statehood. The action and subsequent events allayed fears about suffrage resulting in a Mormon takeover of government and led to reconsideration of the suffrage issue in 1887, the year Washington women lost their right to vote. Abigail Scott Duniway eloquently addressed the territorial legislatures in Idaho, Washington, and Oregon on the issue of suffrage—again—but the move failed. Duniway (profiled here) spent most of her life fighting for women's rights, but her role in Idaho's campaign almost a decade later became an issue of controversy in the new century.

PROFILE: ABIGAIL SCOTT DUNIWAY

Abigail Scott Duniway, editor, clubwoman, and suffrage pioneer, dedicated her life to women's rights and the cause of suffrage. After decades of unending effort throughout the Pacific Northwest, often in conflict with the WCTU or eastern suffrage leaders, she lived to see it happen in all three states. She cast her ballot in Oregon, the last, when she was nearly eighty years old.

Duniway, born in Illinois in 1834, came to Oregon in 1852, but her mother died of cholera on the journey, as did a three-year-old brother. She was the third of a dozen children.[28] Duniway at an early age learned of the hardships of being female. "I remember standing at the bedside when another little sister came to our crowded home. My mother said, through her tears, 'Poor baby, she'll be a woman some day, poor baby, a woman's life is so hard.'"

After her mother's death, her father and surviving siblings settled at Lafayette, a small settlement four miles from McMinville, where she joined the McMinville Ladies' Sanitary Aid Society. After five months at an academy, she began teaching school at Cincinnati (Eola), then married Benjamin C. Duniway in 1853. After she was married, she complained of her own lot in life as wife and mother in an adverse economic system and difficult living conditions. "To bear 2 children in 2½ years from my marriage day, to make thousands of pounds of butter every year for market, not including what was used in our free hotel at home; to sew and cook and wash and iron; to bake and clean and stew and fry, to be in short a general woman drudge, and never a penny of my own, was a hard lot."[29]

Nevertheless, in 1859, at age twenty-five, she published her first novel, *Captain Gray's Company,* to mixed reviews. A few years later, as the mother of four children, she found herself in difficult straits. She became the sole family support after her husband lost their farm and later suffered a serious accident involving a team of horses. She had watched helplessly as her husband cosigned three interest-bearing notes for a friend. Crop failures months later brought the sheriff to the door with a summons for the unpaid notes, requiring sale of their farm. Incidents like this inspired women's clubs in all three Northwest states to pursue two measures to give women legal standing in such situations—one to require the wife's signature as well as the husband's on documents like contracts and the second to give a wife the ability to own her own property. None of that helped Duniway or her family at the time.

She began to teach at Needy and Lafayette. Teachers of the era earned low pay and even that was not very secure, dependent as it was on farmers' annual fortunes. She decided to open a millinery business at Albany, one business that independent women could run successfully in the Northwest because it seemed "acceptable." Its clientele was female, and it incorporated women's traditional domestic skills. The stories of hardships her customers faced and her own led her to commit her life to empowering women, especially after she met Susan B. Anthony in 1871 and toured with her in the Northwest.

Moving to Portland in 1871, she found the family stresses eased. Her husband took a job in the Customs Service, and she was able to focus on the equal rights work that occupied the rest of her life.[30] Duniway began publishing the *New Northwest,* her newspaper arguing for women's rights, that same year. The paper had a small but influential circulation throughout the Northwest during its sixteen-year life. Besides advocating women's rights, the paper included advice and serial fiction Duniway herself wrote, including *Ellen Dowd, the Farmer's Wife* and *Judith Reid, the Plain Story of a Plain Woman,* full of domestic difficulties and idealism.[31] It also serialized work by important Northwest writers, such as Frances Fuller Victor. Her three eldest sons helped set the type. She ultimately had six children, five sons and a daughter.

Like other women in the West, Duniway initially began her activism in the causes of both temperance and women's clubs. She was one of the first members of the Oregon State Temperance Alliance that formed in Portland in 1871, becoming its vice-president. She also honed her speaking skills in the cause of temperance. An author of the period called Duniway a fine speaker. "Her large language makes her a good talker, and her excellent balance of intellect makes her a good writer; but she is a better speaker than writer," temperance advocate Louis Banks wrote.[32] Duniway wrote Banks early on that she often found her demand for the woman's ballot in temperance work a bone of contention. Some called her a disturber of the peace and left in disgust, but she persevered, sometimes the only voice heard trying to build public support for the cause of women's rights.

She described her experience in 1875 speaking at Empire City on equal rights, on a day when the launch of a schooner was followed a few hours later by the launch of casks of free beer and whiskey, followed soon by fights and mayhem.[33] For her evening lecture she had to borrow two or three lamps, fearful of "men who were yelling like Comanches all over town." Halfway through her speech a "howling band of intoxicated voters came shuffling up the stairs, ready, as I well knew, for any sort of riot, if not checkmated by a little tact," she wrote Banks. She welcomed them cheerfully. "Sorry our lights are not better, but we've had a little accident with them tonight. If you'll come forward and take seats upon my right, you will find the light better here and you'll be more comfortable," she said she told them, quelling the hostile attitude. However, others standing by the door, once she started again, rushed off, "making the night hideous with their cries of blasphemy."

Duniway was active in the early women's study clubs, including the important Portland Women's Club. She also held an office in the Oregon Federation of Women's clubs. Duniway had been that group's second vice-president from its founding in 1899 to 1902, when Mrs. C. B. Wade, Pendleton, was president. After a few years Duniway had gained a national reputation for her colorful, persuasive lectures on women's rights, among other topics, following Anthony's lead from her 1871 tour. Duniway made one of her first tours in Idaho in July 1876, when she lectured in Idaho City, Placerville, Silver City, and twice in Boise. She also spoke in Lewiston in a series of lectures in December 1879 and went back there again in 1881, also lecturing in Grangeville, Mt. Idaho, and Moscow. In 1885 she lectured in Moscow and Lewiston and in 1886 in several other towns.[34]

In 1887 she appeared by invitation before the House of Representatives. That suffrage bill lost in the House 10–14, but she kept coming back. In 1884, invited to the National Women's Suffrage Association meeting in Washington, D.C., Duniway was elected one of five NAWSA vice-presidents-at-large and in 1889 joined other national leaders in presentations to congressional committees. She lectured from 1876 to 1895.[35] In 1897 Duniway wrote that in Idaho alone she had given 140 public lectures, traveled over 12,000 miles by all kinds of conveyance, distributed over 500,000 copies of her paper in the territory, addressed the legislature and constitutional convention, and mailed out 500 copies of her address.[36]

But by the end of the century she was in direct conflict with many of the national suffrage leaders, who wanted to help organize the campaigns in the Northwest. She wanted them to stay out, fearing their interference would make matters worse, just as she saw the WCTU efforts on behalf of suffrage making matters worse when leaders linked temperance to suffrage as the region's moral guardians. She later accused the women in the temperance movement of being fanatics, pawns of Democratic (secessionist) politicians, and wealthy women who failed to adequately support her own cause.[37]

Duniway argued before the Idaho Territorial legislators drafting the state's constitution that because governments derive their just powers from the consent of the governed women who were taxed should be represented. She brought up and dismissed the old arguments against women's suffrage, by pointing to the already en-franchised "ignorant and prejudiced voting classes of men" and "foreign-born voters who cannot speak our language or compre-hend the first principles of our free institutions."

She spoke after the Idaho WCTU leader and dismissed her ap-peal for imposing temperance through suffrage. Duniway, a pol-ished suffrage speaker after more than twenty years of practice, contrasted sharply with the less sophisticated WCTU leader, in both her arguments and her persuasive force. By all accounts, she gave a powerful speech reiterating the reasons why women should have the right to vote. It was not the first time she had addressed the male-dominated legislatures of the Northwest, nor the last. And by then she felt no qualms about attacking the WCTU position directly, but she did it in the kind of language that made national suffrage leaders cringe. She argued that few believed in prohibition, realizing that liquor traffic could not be stopped, but should instead be regu-lated by high taxes.[38] However, the legislators, fearing risk to state-hood, prohibition, or women who could vote, or some combination of all three, declined Duniway's proposal—again. Idaho legislators finally heeded her arguments in 1895, but by then many other leaders and strategies came into play in the statewide campaign.

Duniway continued her efforts in Oregon, seeing the measure go down to defeat several times even after it made it to the ballot be-fore being ratified in 1912. After her endless work for women's rights she wrote an autobiographical history of the suffrage move-ment called *Pathbreaking.*

Duniway finally saw her seven decades of hope and work culmi-nate in a women's suffrage amendment being permanently affixed to the Oregon, Washington, and Idaho constitutions. Although by then ill, at the request of the governor she wrote the Woman Suf-frage Proclamation for 75,000 women in Oregon following the 1912 vote. She also was given the honor of being the first woman to register to vote in Oregon. She died in the fall of 1915. Duniway, like Anthony, had served as model and mentor for countless women, not only women who worked for the cause of suffrage, but also women who assumed independent professional roles and taught themselves to organize and speak out on public issues.

Idaho by the 1890s saw statehood increase migration. Railroad construction, such as the Oregon Short Line from Wyoming to Oregon via south Idaho, made east–west travel possible, and the

Mormon rail from Utah through the Snake River Valley to Butte
joined the Union Pacific and Northern Pacific. One of the side effects was exposure to performers and lecturers. Among them was a
tireless suffrage worker from the east, Clara Colby. She also spoke
at Mountain Home, raising the ire of attorney and constitutional
convention delegate Homer Stull, who argued that women in a
"natural division of labor" should stay home and attend to the welfare of the children.[39] Passage of suffrage was not going to be easy.

SUFFRAGE WORKERS IN IDAHO

Legislators had put off Duniway and other women by telling them
the right to vote would be an issue for initial legislative action following statehood in 1890, but not before because of fears of the
"radical" provision's effects on efforts to gain statehood status.
Idaho women (those who were single taxpayers) in 1879 gained
the right to vote in school tax elections; all women got the right to
vote in school elections in 1885, and even run for school offices,
but proposals for full suffrage failed year after year, as they did in
Washington and Oregon and the rest of the nation. The failure to
get the needed two-thirds majority vote necessary for the amendment in 1893 led to the formation of suffrage organizations, although the WCTU had organized groups to work for suffrage as
part of its plan of work for years. A schoolteacher in tiny Hager-
man, Elizabeth Ingram, called friends together and started the organization.[40] A statewide suffrage organization was launched out
of Boise in 1895.

First tier Columbian Club leaders were among the founders of
Idaho's first combined suffrage organization, which met in Boise
shortly before Thanksgiving in 1895. As Carolyn Stefanco found in
Colorado, literary clubs had provided not only intellectual stimulation but also a forum for suffrage proponents and activism. Club
membership trained women for leadership, and the outside interests represented by leaders provided political education, in
overlapping memberships. Clubs and suffrage organizations frequently found common cause with other groups, such as the
WCTU, to form the backbone of a suffrage movement.[41]

The Idaho group met on November 20, 1895, at the home of
Mary (Mrs. James) Beatty, wife of the district judge named to the
Columbian Club's first advisory board. At the meeting as a delegate from Ada County was Mary Ridenbaugh, one of the club
founders (profiled in chapter 6). Beatty, already president of the

Boise Equal Suffrage Club, became president of the combined group and with other Boise members welcomed delegates from eight counties, including WCTU organizer Rebecca Mitchell, Bingham and Cassia Counties; Ridenbaugh and Mrs. J. L. Sullivan from Ada County; Annette Bowman from Latah County; Blanche (Mrs. M. J.) Whitman from Bear Lake; Mrs. Kate Feltham from Canyon County; and a Mrs. Bearby, Elmore County.[42]

Feltham too was a study club founder. In Caldwell, Feltham, who taught school and as a lawyer herself assisted her city attorney husband, had founded the Progress Club, a forerunner of the Forward Club, which started a reading room there. As vice-president of Idaho's women's suffrage association she drafted many of its statements.[43] In a newspaper article Feltham later described the November meeting that inaugurated the state suffrage group as a quiet convention. The eight delegates were not all well acquainted and thus a bit uneasy with one another. Political leaders of other parties suspected a Republican scheme because of the involvement of *Statesman* editor William Balderston and his wife and the fact that many of the Boise representatives were wives of prominent Republicans. Some members at the meeting tried to counteract that idea, further arousing suspicions.

The group later heard an address by Mrs. Balderston (another Columbian Club leader) about women's rights. The *Statesman* editor also played a key role in helping organize the campaign itself as his paper agitated for passage. His wife told the women that "whenever important questions shall arise they [women] will be found on the side of truth and justice in greater proportion than the men."[44] They discussed strategy for the upcoming suffrage campaign. That strategy included using an executive committee of five to make quick response possible, work in every county, and an all-male advisory board for the campaign. State officers elected by the association included Emily S. (Mrs. J. H.) Richards, Boise, president; Melvina (Mrs. H. W.) Woods, Wallace, vice-president; Eunice (Mrs. W. C.) Athey, Boise, secretary; and Leah Burnsides, Shoshone, treasurer. Richards, a Relief Society officer and national suffrage leader, came to Idaho from Utah. Woods, wife of a Wallace lawyer and judge, was the daughter of Utah suffrage organizer and *Women's Exponent* editor Emmeline Wells.[45] Both Richards and Woods distributed suffrage literature and left money for local suffrage campaigns.[46]

The group adopted a model constitution sent out by the

NAWSA, and Idaho now had the attention of national leaders. The group read aloud the wired greetings and sage advice from Susan B. Anthony about the men who would decide the issue of women's vote: "Educate rank and file of voters through political party papers and meetings; woman speakers cannot reach them."[47] The idea of suffrage garnered the support of political parties in Idaho. Populists in 1894 and Republicans and Democrats later all announced support of suffrage.

In organizing for the 1896 campaign Blanche Whitman worked in the predominantly Mormon communities in the southeastern part of the state, while Wallace lawyer Helen Young organized north Idaho. NAWSA organizer Laura Johns, Salinas, Kansas, helped with the southwest part of the state. The group's secretary, Eunice Pond Athey, contacted prominent businessmen and politicians, scouting out male speakers in support of the cause, as Anthony suggested, and to amass financial and political support.

The organization's primary goal was suffrage for women, but it also sought to "effect such other changes in laws as shall recognize the equal rights of women with men." By 1896 the group had organized an impressive twenty-five suffrage clubs in the state, plus five county clubs. That summer north Idaho's Helen Young spoke at the group's summer convention in a Boise opera house on property rights of married women.[48] Young was reportedly the first woman admitted to the Idaho bar, in 1885. In 1896, as an officer of the state association, she helped extensively with lectures and the press, managing the effort in north Idaho. The campaign used several key arguments—that women voting in Wyoming, Utah, and Colorado had been a positive experience, that the republic was founded on the ideal of no taxation without representation, and that white and native-born women should at least have political parity with Native American men and native-born Chinese Americans.[49] The last argument was also used by Frances Willard and Elizabeth Cady Stanton among other national leaders.

In August Carrie Chapman Catt came to Idaho. She addressed all four party conventions (Republican, Democrat, Silver Republican, and Populist); all of them endorsed suffrage, a boost to its chances but no guarantee. Catt stressed the need to involve men from each party and do the work to convert the undecided. She even suggested that ministers in each town be polled on the amendment. Those who leaned toward suffrage were asked to preach a sermon on the subject, while the names of those opposed were sent to headquarters so they could be contacted appropriately.[50] Supporters also brought in clubwoman Mary C. C. Bradford of Denver to make dozens of speeches before the vote, helping to organize local women's clubs and speak to the success of woman suffrage in Colorado.

Abigail Scott Duniway, who wanted to work on and perhaps lead the Idaho campaign, was deflected by the national leadership and told to remain on call. She was never called and left for California to help in the campaign there, somewhat bitter about her treatment by Catt and others. Duniway, now recognized as a suffrage and women's rights heroine for her leadership in the cause over the decades, was not a favorite of national leaders, nor was she enamored of them.

Catt had strong personal opinions about the western suffrage leader. She wrote NAWSA's chief campaign organizer in the West, Emma Smith DeVoe, in 1895 that Duniway was not helpful to the cause. "It is said of her both in Idaho and Portland that she is very unpopular and without influence. She is very bitter in her opposition to the WCTU for one thing and has expressed her mind so plainly they will have nothing to do with her." Catt added that Duniway had also managed to offend labor.

Duniway had her strengths, in Catt's view, but too many detractors. She was "very pleasant to meet and talks like a woman of good judgment, intelligence and foresight. She speaks well but all the suffrage association is down on her, for they say she talks all the time, and is always making out that she is neglected." Catt added that it would be a delicate problem to handle, since Duniway might want to chair the state effort in Idaho (she did and it was).[51] Emma DeVoe (also profiled in this chapter) was called instead. DeVoe ultimately played a role in both the Idaho and Washington campaigns for the right to vote.

PROFILE: EMMA SMITH DEVOE

Emma Smith DeVoe credited a lecture she heard by Susan B. Anthony for changing her life. When Anthony in an Illinois hall asked those who favored equal rights for women to stand, young Emma was the only one to rise.[52] It was the start of a lifetime of work in the cause of women's suffrage in the West, on her own and under the direction of Carrie Chapman Catt and the National American Women's Suffrage Association.

DeVoe was born in Roseville, Illinois, in 1848. Musically gifted, she eventually joined the music staff at Eureka College and married a railroad man in 1880 at the age of thirty-two. She herself began speaking on suffrage in Illinois towns and gained a reputation for eloquence. A newspaper described her as "much more feminine than the average women's rights champion."[53]

She and her husband moved to Tacoma in 1905, and she was elected president of the Washington Equal Suffrage Association a few years later. She was paid (somewhat sporadically) by the National American Women's Suffrage Association for her work throughout the Northwest in the cause of suffrage. After the right to vote came to women of Idaho in 1896 and Washington in 1910, she continued her work in other states until it became a national right in 1920, when she was seventy-two years old.

She usually began her lectures with a statement: "There is nothing in the Constitution of the United States or the Declaration of Independence that should prevent women the right of franchise. Taxation without representation is tyranny." She gained a wide reputation for her by now well-practiced lectures. When she spoke at the Mount Vernon Baptist Church in 1907, even the veterans of the Grand Army of the Republic and their wives and the members of the Women's Relief Corps, those traditionally conservative organizations, came to hear her.[54] Despite her reputation for gentility, she attacked men who opposed suffrage as "timid" and even afraid of their wives. "For this reason he will disenfranchise women who ask nothing more than the right to pass [their] written opinion into the ballot box."

Like many women's rights leaders, DeVoe linked the cause to patriotism and women's rightful role in history. She skillfully used her musical talent, closing her lecture with a song she said her husband composed while lying wounded in a hospital during the Civil War. The lyrics praised women who cared for him and others in their time of need. "And my vote shall go to free them, for they nursed and brought me through." In the style of the sentimental songs popular at the time she sang his words to her audiences.[55]

DeVoe's years of campaigning for suffrage, despite her successes, were not always smooth, as the conflicts detailed in the profile of May Arkwright Hutton indicate. Pay was inconsistent, as was income from lectures. Personal letters to DeVoe from Catt were often apologetic about the organization's inability to always pay her what was owed or cover her expenses and full of praise for her efforts.

"No man with a mortgage about to be foreclosed on his home ever felt more so than do I when we cannot pay our bills promptly," Catt wrote her, after earlier praising her for her work for NAWSA in Montana and Idaho. "You have done splendidly and well."[56] She and Catt clearly were close allies, and Catt wrote her frankly about NAWSA's strategy for the Northwest and her opinions of various leaders, such as Abigail Scott Duniway.[57]

DeVoe went from presidency of the Washington Equal Suffrage Association to leadership of the nonpartisan National Council of Women Voters (NCWV), an influential Northwest organization, an outgrowth of club and political campaigns. It included suffrage supporters and activists from Idaho, Washington, Wyoming, Utah, and Colorado.[58] Besides working for suffrage, its purpose was "to change conditions in our own states for the betterment of men and women, of children and the home, and to claim justice for women in the political, social and economic world."[59]

Unfortunately DeVoe's effective organization was eclipsed by her old friend when Carrie Chapman Catt turned NAWSA into the League of Women Voters after 1920, creating more than a little irritation on the part of DeVoe and the NCWV members in the Northwest. It further evidenced "East-West antagonisms" that sometimes served to nullify the achievements of northwestern women.[60] DeVoe died at the age of seventy-nine, seven years after women throughout the country gained the right to vote.

Despite the well-organized strategy of the Idaho campaign, national suffrage leader Alice Stone Blackwell in the *Woman's Journal* complained of the indifference of too many women in Idaho to the issue of suffrage. She said that although there were 15,000 adult women in Idaho, no more than 1,000 were affiliated with the Idaho Equal Suffrage Association.[61] However, if this is true, getting almost 7 percent of all women in the state actively enrolled in a political organization, given the tenor of the times, was no small feat. Most of the active suffrage campaigners were community leaders involved in clubwork before becoming involved in this cause and therefore used to speaking out on issues. Suffrage even in 1895 was an old issue in Idaho.

The broad-based effort and careful political strategy paid off. Women in Idaho finally gained the right to vote in 1896 through constitutional amendment, despite confrontations and internal disputes. Committees of women clustered near the polling sites,

with yellow suffrage banners and brochures reminding men to remember the amendment. The final vote on the amendment was a
clear victory at 12,126 for and 6,282 against. Only Custer County
rejected it.[62]

By 1898 three women—Clara Campbell, Hattie Noble, and Mary
Wright—had been elected to the Idaho legislature, each representing a different political party but united on women's rights
issues. Campbell, Boise, was a member of the WCTU and the
Women's Relief Corps, the auxiliary of the Grand Army of the Republic made up of Civil War veterans. A Republican, she worked to
establish a system of free schools, maintain a state library, and educate children with multiple disabilities, among other provisions.

Hattie Noble, an Idaho City Democrat, pushed for "manual
training" in the schools.[63] She also sought laws prohibiting sale of
opium, regulating the sale of imitation butter, and stiffening qualifications for dental surgery. She was a member of the Public
Health Committee that sought safer accommodations for female
convicts and a better water and sewer system for it and the soldier's home, which housed seventy-seven people at the time.

Wright, a Populist, came from Rathdrum in the north and later
ran a business in Bonners Ferry. Born in 1868 in Missouri, she
came to Idaho and taught school from 1893 to 1899. In 1901 she
was chosen chief clerk in the House.[64]

However, all three women had short tenures in office. Their
brief legislative careers were rather uneventful. Women, once
elected, often were relegated to relatively powerless positions in
state legislatures, especially in a system that valued seniority.
Idaho voters elected dozens of women to office in the decade following suffrage. Besides the three legislators, four became county
treasurers, fifteen became county superintendents and one the
state superintendent, and three were even made deputy sheriffs.
In the next twenty years female lobbyists (most affiliated with
clubs) and legislators persuaded the legislature to pass laws prohibiting child labor, giving married women rights to own and dispose of property, establishing a library commission and support
for libraries, establishing a reform school and a domestic science
department at the university, closing saloons on Sunday, and prohibiting gambling, among other measures.[65]

Suffrage in Idaho gained national attention for Idaho's clubwomen and organizers. The National American Woman Suffrage
Association meeting in Des Moines, Iowa, in 1897 heard speeches

from Emmeline Wells, her daughter Melvina (Mell) Woods, and Eunice Athey on Idaho's success and its methods of achieving it, amid much fanfare. It had been a long dry spell in the fight for women's right to vote, and Idaho and Colorado revitalized it.

Idaho's delegates to the 1898 General Federation of Women's Clubs meeting also got attention when they noted that the change in women's status in Idaho made their lobbying work easier. Suffrage "has brought in its train a disposition to give greater consideration to women's clubs and the work they undertake."[66] The Idaho delegation told the General Federation delegates at the 1904 Biennial of the power they now held, power denied women in most other states, to influence candidates and seek commitments to club bills.[67]

CLUBS AND THE WASHINGTON CAMPAIGN

Women who got the right to vote in Idaho exercised it for over a decade before their sisters across the state line could vote, but it was not for lack of interest. Following the revocation of suffrage before the end of the 1880s, suffrage organizations in places like Walla Walla tried to get back the vote, but failed. Women's club programs frequently addressed the issue, but it seemed dormant (or impossible to pass) for a time.

In 1908 a circle of suffrage leaders met at the Seattle home of Nelle Mitchell Fick. Fick herself was no newcomer to suffrage efforts. She was listed as an usher in the program for the NAWSA meeting in Washington, D.C., in 1900. She had moved to Seattle in 1906. The women meeting in her home in 1908 included some of Seattle's prominent clubwomen and Jeanette Rankin, who became the first woman elected to Congress a few years later.[68] The group called itself the Seattle Suffrage Club, with Fick (wife of a physician) as president. One of the women present was activist Adella Parker.[69]

Parker, a Seattle high school teacher and clubwoman who graduated from the University of Washington Law School, was not new to electoral politics in Washington. She is credited with organizing a successful 1906 campaign to amend the city charter to provide for the recall of public officials, prior to state authorization of the process.[70] She was also editor of the *Western Woman Voter* and associate editor of *Votes for Women,* the official paper of the Washington Equal Suffrage Association.[71] By 1909 Fick and Parker were also officers in the King County Political Equality Club.

The media said the suffrage leaders "educated the local woman" to a desire for the right of suffrage "by discussing the matter in an attractive manner at smart teas, receptions and dinners. The animated Mrs. Fick and beautiful Mrs. Jarmouth, in their modish frocks, made irresistible lobbyists at Olympia."[72] Their strategies were actually more specific. With state suffrage leader Emma DeVoe's help, they established a speaker's bureau with the goal of creating a suffrage club in every Washington city, making sure nonmembers were invited to meetings. According to a 1909 national suffrage publication, Fick instituted a series of parlor meetings, where women "of all classes were among the guests."[73]

One of the officers of the Washington suffrage society was Elizabeth Ordway, who came to the village of Seattle in 1864 from Lowell, Massachusetts, where she was a teacher. In 1870 she became a teacher in Seattle's first tax-supported school and in 1881 was elected to an eight-year assignment as Kitsap County's school superintendent, the first elective office held by a woman in Washington. Under her leadership the number of schools grew from six to twenty. Long an advocate of women's rights, she served as secretary of the Washington Suffrage Society and helped prepare the state's educational exhibit for the Chicago World's Fair in 1893.[74]

Names of club leaders and suffrage activists showed up as members of the statewide Washington Equal Franchise Society under the leadership of a Century Club founder, Carrie (Mrs. Homer) Hill, including Nelle Mitchell Fick. Hill was also founder of Seattle's Women's Industrial Club and long active in the state club federation. Fick was named by Catt to represent Washington in the national drive for suffrage.[75] The earlier suffrage organization, Washington Equal Franchise Association, had disintegrated after 1889, when its attempt to restore to women their voting rights as a constitutional amendment went down to defeat at the hands of voters. The group, with Emma DeVoe's help, had been resurrected in 1906.

Fick—square jawed, with large pale eyes—like other club leaders was active in multiple women's organizations in a long career of service and advocacy. She chaired the building committee for the Seattle YWCA, lobbied for the Child Labor Amendment in Olympia, worked for passage of the minimum wage and eight-hour day protections for women in Washington, chaired and organized the first Mothers' Training School until it was taken over by the PTA, and later presided over the Washington League of Women Voters.

Wealthier than most of her club counterparts, Fick later spent occasional springs in London and wintered in New York City and Washington, D.C., traveling with her husband. She loved the art and drama she found there and saved most of the programs for productions she attended.[76] Other workers included women like Skagit County's Susan Currier Ornes, who organized suffrage clubs throughout the county by 1905, but who died before 1910. "One in ten thousand can revolutionize the city," she liked to say about her efforts.[77]

One month before the vote on state suffrage, Mason, writing in the Tacoma paper, made a powerful statement responding to comments that most women were not interested in being involved in politics and defined cultural politics in the process. "Many women see the need of the ballot to help them (with the good men's vote) to secure better conditions for the man, woman, child and the home," she wrote. "We are all in politics! Willy-nilly." She cited the dictionary definition of politics: Politics is the regulation and government of a nation or state, for the preservation of its safety, peace, and prosperity. "All our water, our food, our clothing, even the trees we plant in our garden, the house we build, the materials we put into it, the street cars we ride in, the schools our children attend, the detention house we build and the woman in charge, the juvenile court and the judge thereof, the police matron, the humane officer, the pure food inspector, the safeguards we would place around our children and the home—all these are in politics, and that is why women want to vote."[78]

Even after women gained the vote in Washington in 1910 by a substantial margin, their political activities were not always taken seriously. "On the whole we seemed to be something of a joke to the men of the party," writes the King County Women's Democratic Club historian. "The leaders of the Progressive Party took a different attitude and much work was done at their headquarters by the women. Their national ticket carried the state and the first women to be elected to the legislature, Mrs. Nina J. Croake of Tacoma (charter member of the first woman's study club in Tacoma) and Mrs. Frances Axtell of Bellingham (leader of the New Whatcom Ladies' Cooperative Society)."[79] The historian notes that Bill No. 1 in the house was a minimum wage law long sought by women's clubs and other groups. It was carried by

Croake and "passed after a hard fight." In the legislature Croake also worked to establish a retirement fund for teachers and the mothers' pension bill, both social welfare causes. Croake's club activity in Tacoma (described in chapter 6) was extensive.

Frances C. Axtell, born in Sterling, Illinois, in 1866, came to Washington before 1900. She also became a club leader and was elected to the statehouse at age forty-seven. She also became the first woman to receive presidential appointment to a national commission, to the U.S. Employees' Compensation Commission, 1917–21. She also had been appointed to the first Washington State committee to set minimum wages for women in retail, a bill she and the clubs helped get passed.[80]

SUFFRAGE IN OREGON

Like clubs in Washington and Idaho, Oregon's powerful and active clubs included many women who worked for women's suffrage and other legal changes affecting women's status. For instance, in 1911, Mrs. A. King Wilson, president of the Portland Women's Club, appointed the tireless consumer advocate and club leader Sarah Evans (profiled in the next chapter) to chair the group's women's suffrage committee. It maintained a downtown office and a paid secretary to promote and publicize the project. Josephine (Mrs. Solomon) Hirsch, also influential in several clubs, helped finance the movement by hosting a benefit tea.[81]

Besides the women previously mentioned, the Portland Women's Club counted in its membership suffrage leaders Dr. Mary Thompson and Abigail Scott Duniway. The group also included Dr. Mabel Akin, Mrs. Frederick Eggert, and Sadie Orr Dunbar. Dunbar was born in Missouri in 1880, coming to Oregon well before 1900. During her club career, she was secretary of the National Conference, Tuberculosis Secretaries; vice-president of the Portland Americanization Council and the Council of Social Agencies; and a member of a handful of clubs besides the Portland Women's Club.[82] Dunbar eventually took a national leadership role as president of the General Federation of Women's Clubs in 1937.

THE EXPOSITIONS AND THE CLUBWOMAN'S SACAJAWEA

In social movements symbols, images, rituals, and spectacles play a critical part. The rituals of national expositions also offered an extraordinary opportunity to make dominant discourses subversive and to create coalitions around causes. As cultural anthropologist Victor Turner describes, in events like fairs and festivals, old identities for participants fall away and new identities are tested. They focus attention on new possibilities, and individuals can enter in-between or liminal states where visions of different futures with different roles for themselves and others appear and may be tried.

In the Northwest, two national expositions, themselves liminal, transitional, and symbolic, offered opportunities to intensify suffrage campaigns. So did the construction and veneration of a symbolic historical character, a female explorer of the Northwest who aided Lewis and Clark. Thanks to club leader and regional writer Eva Emery Dye (profiled in chapter 5) she played a role in winning the sentiment of the day and motivating campaign workers as women capitalized on her image and contribution to history.

The Lewis and Clark Centennial Exposition, held in Portland in 1905, and the Alaska-Yukon-Pacific Exposition in Seattle in 1909 brought the region both national attention and a chance to display its products, its values, and its issues, from irrigation projects to suffrage, in a spectacular setting. Many counties and clubs sent special commissions to represent them at these events. Both community development and women's club activism seemed a natural outgrowth of the region's spirit and its age in this first decade of the new century.

Both the Lewis and Clark Exposition and the Alaska-Yukon-Pacific Exposition featured a Woman's Day. On that day during the Portland meeting, Susan B. Anthony spoke at the unveiling of a statue of the guide Sacajawea, the Shoshone woman exalted as leader and peacemaker. She was also represented as a woman who bridged and connected two cultures, much as happened with Pocahontas on the other side of the continent 200 years earlier. Anthony told listeners that the men of Oregon in their vote on suffrage the following year should remember the part women had in the settlement and progress of the region.

At the meeting, NAWSA president Anna Howard Shaw also praised Sacajawea and her journey west, comparing it to NAWSA's journey to progress through suffrage. "May we learn the lessons of calm endurance, of patient persistence and unfaltering courage exemplified in your life, in our efforts to lead men through the Pass of justice, which goes over the mountains of prejudice and conservatism to the broad land of the perfect freedom of a true republic."[83] Besides Anthony and Shaw, Abigail Scott Duniway spoke at the meeting about Sacajawea and her inspiration for women's rights. Their words inspired listeners, but failed to move the male voters. Suffrage in Oregon lost once again.

Even grander than the Lewis and Clark Exposition was the Alaska-Yukon-Pacific Exposition four years later, in 1909, at Seattle. Organizers hoped it would put Seattle on the same plane as those other great exposition cities, Chicago, St. Louis, and Philadelphia. It was Washington's opportunity to demonstrate its material prosperity, great resource wealth, and ability to supply the rest of the world, especially Alaska and the Pacific Rim. It was also a great chance for women to "agitate" about the cause of suffrage soon coming up for a vote in the state. The Woman's Suffrage Day coincided with the close of the National American Women's Suffrage Association (NAWSA) national meeting in Seattle.

All who entered the fair that day passed below a huge "Votes for Women" kite, and visitors received a green-ribbon badge representing the Evergreen State's Equal Suffrage Association.[84] Other groups also held conferences in Seattle in conjunction with the exposition, explicitly to push forward the cause of women, thus creating a highly visible phalanx of women's organizations allied for suffrage. They included the National Council of Women, the Washington Federation of Women's Clubs, the Washington Teachers and Washington Nurses associations, the WCTU, and even the Eastern Star.[85]

The exposition gave women a chance to claim center stage to generate momentum for suffrage and to promote the other causes clubwomen held dear. NAWSA, meeting July 1–6 during the Seattle exposition, flooded the city with speakers at the conference, at area churches, and at the exposition itself. Many of the women active in the clubs of the Pacific Northwest took part in the suffrage campaign, the NAWSA meeting, and the scheduled women's activities at the exposition.

A WHO'S WHO OF WOMEN'S CLUB ACTIVISM

Even more than at the Portland exposition, regional and national leaders came together at Seattle. The local officers for the NAWSA meeting included many club leaders previously described: Dr. Cora Smith Eaton served as general chair; in charge of press was law school graduate Adella Parker; one of the Sunday speakers was Dr. Sarah Kendall, Century Club founder; in charge of courtesies was Carrie Hill, Seattle clubwoman who also delivered the welcoming address as past president of the Washington Equal Suffrage Association; and Emma Smith DeVoe, the state association's president, was in charge of organization at the meeting.

Greetings came from Margaret Platt for the WCTU, H. W. Allen for the federated clubs, and Mrs. B. B. Lord for Woman and the Grange. Even the governor and Seattle's mayor appeared onstage to welcome the national and regional rights activists. Speakers included National Consumers' League leader Florence Kelley, writer Charlotte P. Gilman, and revered national suffrage leaders Anna Howard Shaw and Henry Blackwell.[86] Anthony by this time was in her eighties and less able to travel the land for the cause.

The NAWSA meeting included many panels on issues and strategies, including comparing the U.S. and English suffrage campaigns. Gilman's speech was entitled "Masculine, Feminine and Human," while Kelley, as secretary of the National Consumers' League, spoke on a property rights issue, "The Unjust Judge and the Importunate Widow."[87] Conscious of how close the Washington effort was to achieving its goal, Catt gave $500 and the Blackwells $300 to the Washington Equal Suffrage Association.

The exposition set up on the new University of Washington campus served to promote many interests, including the new irrigated developments opening statewide.[88] It also provided the Washington Federation of Women's Clubs an opportunity to lobby for funding of a woman's building on the campus at the fair site. Ultimately suffragists, temperance workers, the National Council of Women, and other groups held meetings there.[89]

The concerted effort prior to and at the exposition paid off. Women in Washington won the vote easily. Much of the conversation at the exposition had been about progress and reform as well as suffrage, ideas bound together in the new century.

BUREAUCRATIZING REFORM AND INVENTORYING SUCCESSES

Suffrage for women in the Pacific Northwest fit into a continuum of "progress," a progression and expansion of government that made private institutions public, created more rational state policies, imposed new civic priorities, adapted findings from the new fields of psychology and sociology, and reaped the benefits of technological change in "domestic science." Women turned to the professionalization of reform and bureaucratization of the projects they had put in place as a valuable part of that progression. They began to solidify a cultural shift from private philanthropy and unregulated economic competition to social welfare as a responsibility of government at all levels, including the protection of citizen/consumers. The package included civic reform, legal reform, political reform, government control of social services, and women's entry into professional, administrative, and even elected positions.

Historian Mary Ritter Beard's 1916 book *Woman's Work in Municipalities* surveyed contributions of women's clubs to community institutions of all sorts under the rubric of "civic improvement." Her purpose in surveying the records of hundreds of organizations was to document the extent of women's interests and achievements throughout the country, with an eye toward finding trends in their work and connections to larger social problems. She, like other chroniclers who followed, including myself, found the task daunting because of the vast amount of material and the limitations of space in which to present it. She grouped her survey findings under eleven categories of contribution: education, public health, the "social evil," recreation, the "assimilation" of races, housing, social service, corrections, public safety, civic improvement, and government and administration.[90]

The resulting book listing achievements sometimes carried a defensive tone. It frequently cited objections to women's involvement in the professions and political affairs in order to counter them, sometimes with a "yes, but" line of reasoning. For instance, in the first chapter on education she noted that women's domination of teaching ranks had been criticized at the secondary level as producing teachers who do not comprehend "the realities of modern business and political and social life, and are therefore not fitted to give a wide social training to the young, especially to boys." She granted a "certain truth in this contention," but wrote that women were responding by taking broader training and that much of the responsibility lay with the colleges and normal schools and their male-dominated curricula.[91]

However, she noted that Idaho and Washington, as well as Colorado and Wyoming, had women as heads of their state school systems, and especially in the West more county superintendents were women than ever before. It was clubwomen who established kindergartens and "household arts" classes that became part of a domestic science education movement as a result of their aggressive positions on such issues.[92] In addition, schools for "mentally defective" and "crippled" children, as well as physical education and hygiene classes, were created through their efforts. Night schools and truant and parental schools were founded by women's clubs, which also provided summer vacation schools, visiting teachers, and visiting nurses. Clubs humanized and adorned school buildings and grounds with flowers, trees, artwork, and so on.

In the area of public health, Beard noted in this woman's century that women worked with all levels of government, no matter how technical or complex. "These women have had to study the most intricate mechanical problems like municipal engineering. They have had to understand city taxation and budget making," she wrote. "Moreover they have had to work for the most part without political influence, which has meant that they have had to overcome the reluctance of public officials to take women seriously; they have had to understand and combat the political influence of contractors and businessmen of all kinds; they have had to enter political contests in order to place in office the kind of officials who had the wider vision" and monitor those elected to see that campaign promises were kept.

Even when women lost, however, good came of it, she felt. Women who faced political reverses often became ardent suffragists in order to work directly for "sanitary municipal housekeeping."[93] The issues in public health that clubs addressed ranged from tuberculosis to milk fever. Abolishing the common drinking cup in favor of fountains, prohibiting spitting in public places, improved ventilation in schools, visiting nurses, better hospitals and clinics, subsidized medical care for the poor and chronically ill, health education, food inspection, infant mortality programs, and child welfare (through programs such as school lunches)—all were pursued by women in their clubs and constituted the beginnings of a complex array of social services and regulation. They were taken for granted until near the end of the twentieth century, when voters and Congress began calling for a halt to government expansion and government costs in the face of a burgeoning federal deficit and flawed programs.

Even clean streets became a club cause, due to their connection to public health and aesthetic standards. "Clean streets" was in reality often a euphemism for garbage handling and basic sanitation practices to control less visible but more pernicious rats, flies, and disease, if not the unpleasant smells and sights. In addition to one-time clean-ups, club efforts led to results from antilittering campaigns and ordinances to establishing city sanitation departments for regular garbage removal, beginning at a time when streets and alleys were the common dumping ground for all sorts of human, animal, and vegetable waste. For instance, in 1889, the *Oregonian* complained about that city's unsanitary conditions in its sewers and gutters, calling it "the most filthy city in the Northern States."[94] Hundreds of clubs started with "sanitary surveys," followed by proposals to officials for improvement—including paid inspectors and ordinances controlling citizen behavior.

Surveys were a frequent starting point for addressing many perceived community ills, from "social evils" to dangerous intersections.[95] Sometimes officials themselves initiated action (or deflected complaints) by asking women to complete surveys of community problems from garbage to food supply sanitation to school conditions. The women happily complied and used the results to pursue their goals and remedies. They left the comfort of meeting rooms to use investigation and site visits to critique and change existing situations and systems. The organized women in many cities took on belching smokestacks (and were often squelched by manufacturers who threatened to shut down if the ordinances they pursued were imposed). They fostered eradication efforts on flies (often aimed at stables), rats (which came with garbage), mosquitoes (common with stagnant water), and excessive noise (especially bad in crowded, busy cities). Elsewhere the noise came in the form of barking dogs, church and railroad bells, even crowing roosters, and more deleteriously from factory machinery. Without direct political power, women used, in addition to the power of the investigation and the report, the power of intense lobbying, often uncharitably called "nagging." Many learned that to combat disease and crime or "vice" they had to counter what Beard called "poor housing, evil labor conditions, ignorance, and vicious interests."[96]

The survey was one of the more powerful investigative methods. The documented results of child labor abuses, violations of food safety, or salary surveys of working women offered concrete examples and evidence compiled by women who in turn created and shared solutions to change the system. It was a methodology with connections to the Progressive belief in progress and social science, faith in the rational solution of problems, the use of evidence for argument, and the role of public opinion and government to change the culture through regulation.

The bureaucratization and specialization of the large departmental women's clubs led to a different level of activism and a different kind of relationship among members and to the outside world, one that reached beyond the needs of the immediate community. Another aspect of the impact of bureaucratization and professionalization on the mature club movement was the aggregation of clubs into powerful networks. Where individual clubs had little power to affect regional or state issues, clubs of clubs used numbers and common goals to direct change in a community, state, region, or nation. Their power could make a minority view the majority view, leading to systemic and permanent changes, assuming there was acquiescence on what they should be.

"CONSCIOUS NATIONAL WOMANHOOD"

The Federations, 1905–20

Frances Willard once compared women to snowflakes. One had little influence; together they could change a landscape. She used the metaphor at the 1888 meeting of the National Council of Women, forerunner of the General and State Federations of Women's Clubs.

"And the organized attack is against this old, hoary-headed, materialistic, conservative way of doing things. And the mighty breeze that shall set them flying is the new sense of sisterhood, and it will bring in all that is good, and true and pure," she said, reiterating the domestic ideal. "It has been the curse of humanity in the past that half the wisdom, more than half the purity, and more than half the gentleness did not find any organic expression."[1] She spoke for millions of women and their faith in the movement.

If clubs had power, clubs of clubs had even more. In an era of burgeoning national organizations, it was only a matter of time until the club movement gained sufficient momentum to make women realize the potential of clubs coalesced into superorganizations. The state federations had found common connections and common projects among member clubs, and the time was ripe for them to combine forces to work on national priorities. Clubs in the Pacific Northwest wanted to be included and were, almost from the start.

As early as 1896, Washington had seven clubs represented in the General Federation of Women's Clubs, founded in 1890. Idaho had five and Oregon three. Leading the way in state participation was Massachusetts, with fifty-nine clubs signed up, far ahead of second place Pennsylvania with twenty-one.[2] However, the Pacific Northwest states, despite their late development, were on equal footing with other states with club alliances. Twenty-eight of the states with GFWC member clubs had fewer than ten clubs participating. Twenty-four of those had five or fewer clubs signed up, although the states had larger populations than the Northwest states. At this point in GFWC history, forty states were represented, including the District of Columbia.

The federations in the Northwest sought many of the reforms individual study clubs pursued and were more politically oriented than most community clubs. They often had the clout to solidify in law the shift from private to public institutions, persuading states to come up with the large-scale and long-range funding needed to support them. They also continued to pursue power for women by "agitating" for women to be placed in professional and management positions, such as university boards of regents, jail matrons, or school superintendents. However, the alliances divided over some controversial issues, regionally as well as nationally. Race, suffrage, protectionist legislation, immigration policies, and pacifism all were divisive social and political issues that made consensus difficult if not impossible in the second two decades of the woman's century.

Like the WCTU and the department clubs, the federations operated through elected officers, departments, standing and special committees, subcommittees, reports, and parliamentary procedure. They also used direct political action and voter education to reach their goals, although for most women these positions were like unpaid jobs in underfunded campaigns. Nevertheless, the women were spurred by success.

Women were elated to discover what collective action could accomplish when they reached beyond themselves and across social and class lines to begin a public life.[3] Anticipating the power of collective action beyond individual clubs, at Croly's urging an alliance of national women's clubs was created in 1890. The National Council of Women, a federation of national women's organizations, had issued its own call for formation of an umbrella organization in 1888. In its call, it said the object of the new movement in organized womanhood was "to aggregate all local societies having the same object into national societies," eligible for membership in the NCW once they were national in scope.[4] The idea of a powerful federation was hardly new.

In 1888 May Wright Sewall founded the International Conference of Women at a Washington, D.C., conference, piggybacking on the NCW call. It claimed to represent six million women affiliated with eleven national women's societies who agreed to join the conference. The alliance worked for suffrage and women's rights through a series of practical reforms, such as legal changes, higher education access, temperance, career opportunities, and charitable help.

Frances Willard in her autobiography said that Susan B. Anthony was the central figure at the Washington, D.C., meeting, which with her blessing elected Willard president of the national group only five years after her visit to the Northwest. The purpose of the National Council was sweeping and gave women a special responsibility: "We, women of the United States, sincerely believing that the best good of our homes and nation will be advanced by our own greater unity of thought, sympathy, and purpose, and that an organized movement of women will best conserve the highest good of the family and the state, do hereby band ourselves together in a confederation of workers committed to the overthrow of all forms of ignorance and injustice, and to the application of the golden rule to society, custom and law."[5]

THE GENERAL FEDERATION OF WOMEN'S CLUBS IS BORN

In this stirring environment intended to change the culture and direction of the country, the call for the General Federation of Women's Clubs came through Sorosis one year later. The federation was founded in 1889 at a meeting in Madison Square Theater. Its time actually had been coming for a decade. The Indiana Woman's Club had contacted other clubs with such an idea as early as 1882, when the club idea itself was just developing in the Pacific Northwest.[6] In 1889 Sorosis contacted ninety-three clubs throughout the nation, all the clubs it knew of. Sixty-three clubs from eighteen states sent representatives to the New York meeting. A bit of a tiff developed when the 1868 Boston club, the New England Women's Club, did not get invited, in what Croly called an "oversight."

By the time of the General Federation's first biennial meeting in 1892 in Chicago, a total of 297 delegates came, representing 192 clubs from 32 states.[7] The General Federation spawned state federations beginning in 1896, including the Northwest. By the turn of the century the state federations in the Pacific Northwest had spawned city federations as well. Initially, membership in the General Federation excluded philanthropic clubs in favor of the culture club and literary society that matched the Sorosis Club idea. But in 1896, recognizing the fuzziness of the category, the limitation disappeared. "Village improvement associations were

joined with Shakespeare clubs, and cemetery associations supplemented Monday afternoon societies. The test for admission was
no longer emphasis on 'social, literary, artistic or scientific culture,'" a chronicler of the movement wrote.[8]

By 1900, nationally as well as locally, clubs reflected a shift
from study of culture to current events, from study of social problems to recommending policies.[9] Pure food—like child labor and
to a lesser extent civil service reform—became a rallying point
and regulatory issue for federations. Direct involvement in electoral politics, however, divided rather than united the women
when it came to endorsement of women's suffrage, an issue first
brought before the convention in 1910. GFWC endorsement of
suffrage came in 1914, after virtually all the western states had
adopted it, although speeches on the issue had been heard at
many biennial conventions years prior. Nevertheless, lobbying,
often called "education" by the women as it is by contemporary
lobbyists, remained a well-recognized and broadly accepted
means of action long before most women in the United States
could vote in their states.

Marriage and divorce laws, child protection, pure food laws, libraries, forest conservation, and labor regulations were among
the issues the GFWC consistently pursued through legislative
remedy despite its waffling on suffrage and racial integration. The
federation, like other large groups, did much of its work through
committees. It established an Industrial Committee to work for
improved working conditions for women, thanks to the influence
of New York journalist Rheta Childe Dorr and other activists.
Dorr, who lived in Seattle for a time and published articles in
Seattle papers before moving to New York in 1890, eventually became women's page editor for the *New York Post*. She chaired the
GFWC committee and lectured on behalf of striking workers to
women's clubs. She also reported on the poor working conditions
affecting African-American hospital nurses and Italian and Irish
spinners and weavers.[10]

The National Association of Colored Women's Clubs was established in 1897, paralleling the General Federation and angry
about being excluded from it. The General Federation, despite ac-
rimonious debate, bowed to interests of clubs in the South and denied credentials to delegates from African-American women's organizations, although the issue came up repeatedly.[11] "The color
question" first came up in 1898 when the GFWC decided to ex-

clude an African-American delegate from the Boston's Women's Era Club, Josephine St. Pierre Ruffin, who had helped found the African-American club. Ruffin intended to bring greetings to the group from the club.[12]

In 1900 the GFWC delegates sidestepped the issue of admitting black delegates by limiting the number of delegates from Massachusetts. Ruffin, also a member of the New England Women's Club, could attend as a delegate from the New England Women's Club, but not from her Women's Era Club, despite the fact that it had already received a certificate of GFWC membership. She was reportedly even refused entrance to the convention.[13]

The question of African-American representation in the GFWC came up again at the next biennial federation meeting in Los Angeles in 1902, where delegates again argued whether integrated women's clubs could be admitted into the national organization, picking up the issue from the Milwaukee meeting in 1900. New England Women's Club founder Caroline Severance, who had since moved to Los Angeles and developed a huge civic club there, came up with a compromise. Severance, then eighty-two years old, suggested each state be permitted to decide its own policy according to state federation constitutions. That dropped the race problem into the laps of the state federations.[14]

THE PACIFIC NORTHWEST SIGNS UP

The remote, sparsely populated Northwest sought more than eastern capital to speed its development. It also sought the validation of connections to the East. The first clubs in the Northwest to join the national federation began signing up in 1892, the year of its first biennial meeting. Within a few years, dozens of Pacific Northwest Clubs were members and before 1900 coalesced into their own state federations. The national organization's biennial meetings were regularly attended by Northwest representatives, and national leaders made regular appearances in the Pacific Northwest.

In addition, clubs sought connections to others elsewhere in their states. The issue of devoting time and energy to local issues of village improvement versus changing state policy and systems elicited debate from the beginning. Saved in Sub Rosa Club records was a newspaper account describing clubwork at the meeting in Nampa of the Second District Federation of Women's Clubs of Idaho. Members reviewed the group's legislative program of the prior year and decided to take up the juvenile court bill and woman's property rights bills as special work. At that meeting, however, a Mrs. Ford of Weiser advocated clubwomen doing the work nearest to them first, such as repairing fences, rehanging gates, cutting weeds, and caring for wastepaper and garbage before beginning agitation for parks and playgrounds or other issues.

The Pacific Northwest federations, when they began meeting, provided women networking across towns and states, often spanning great distances, and collective power within their states. The federations also provided a way for women to bridge the cultural, racial, and geographical barriers in the states of the Pacific Northwest. They enabled diverse groups of women from separate, often isolated communities to fashion a course of work that extended the reach of their own influence. They found ways to work together in a democratic and cooperative fashion as delegate representatives. Goals infused federations both from the top down, instigated by the national group, and from the bottom up, as members' demands for local action on issues became state and national imperatives. Those women active at the state level, a relatively small proportion of all club members, shared the Progressive era belief that government reform and education had the power to reengineer society and redraw the political landscape.

THE OREGON FEDERATION

Oregon paralleled Washington in joining the GFWC. Clubs there first joined the General Federation in 1894, only two years behind Washington. The first three clubs to sign up were the Thursday Afternoon Club of Pendleton in 1894 and the Neighborhood Club of La Grande and the Portland Woman's Club, both in 1896. Each was a department club, and the Portland club by then had grown to 125 members. The Oregon Federation of Women's Clubs was organized in 1899, a few years behind Washington and Idaho. It initially included fifteen clubs scattered widely over the state.[15] The fast spread of women's clubs in the Pacific Northwest and their belief in alliances with clubs elsewhere in the state are reflected in the number of names and locales that were added. Twenty-four member clubs from all over the state joined the original group in the Oregon Federation only a few years later. Remarkably, all of these clubs were still in existence over fifty years later.[16]

One of the attributes that tied the clubs together was an interlocking leadership, or perhaps women already designated leaders in local clubs sought places to extend their sphere of influence. At the Oregon Federation's sixth meeting at Portland in 1905 elected officers included Sarah A. Evans, president, with Mrs. Samuel White, Baker City, first vice-president, Mrs. Frederic S. Dunn, Eugene, second vice-president, and honorary presidents Abigail Scott Duniway and Adelia (Mrs. C. B.) Wade. Duniway had been the state federation's second vice-president, from its founding in 1899 to 1902, the years when Adelia Wade, Pendleton, was president. Evans at that time was recording secretary and eventually became a powerful legislative leader for the Oregon federation.

PROFILE: SARAH ANN SHANNON EVANS

Sarah Evans was throughout her life an outspoken community leader devoted to the public welfare and the legal policies that protected it. Sarah Ann Shannon was born in 1854 in Bedford County, Pennsylvania. She graduated from Lutherville College and married William M. Evans in 1873. She came to Portland in 1893 with him and their three children, quickly becoming interested in public affairs, beginning with libraries.[17]

One of her colleagues said she began her public career out of concern for the education of her daughters, because she was used to such amenities as public libraries and found a city without them. In 1895 she assisted with the effort to obtain permanent library facilities for the city, becoming a charter member of the Portland Woman's Club in 1896. She served as its president one year, then through the Portland club helped organize the Oregon Federation of Women's Clubs. She had a long sojourn as the state's federation president, from 1905 to 1915. Under her leadership the federation pursued and Oregon adopted a host of social welfare legislation and regulation.

One of her first successes in a long career of legislative work was to help secure passage of a library law from the state legislature, commuting daily between Portland and Salem to do it. She believed strongly that libraries should be both public and free and in 1901 drafted and secured passage of a state law making use of the city library free and a free state library possible. She also worked for passage of the child labor law enacted in 1900 and was made a commissioner of the governing board asked to enforce the provision.[18]

In 1905 she moved from heading legislative work to the presidency of the state federation. She spearheaded passage of a rapid succession of laws backed by the federation, including requiring more humane treatment of the insane while in transit or in institutions and enactment of pure food laws. She also helped establish the state federation's own scholarship loan fund and pursued protective labor legislation.

She placed high value on the work she did for women. "I have endeavored," she said in a farewell address as federation president, "to make the work I have put into the past ten years a consecrated service."[19] She was also active in the cause of women's suffrage, the Lewis and Clark Exposition, and the YWCA. As chair of the press committee for the NAWSA meeting at the exposition, she arranged for many local activities for the national leadership. And she was the Portland market inspector for thirty years as a consequence of her work on consumer protection issues such as pure food and fair weights. Ever conscious of women's lack of real political power to address vital issues, she sought legislation and policies to formalize protection and equitable treatment. She also assisted in the formation of the new Federation of Colored Women's Clubs in Oregon.[20]

Mary Ritter Beard in her national survey of women's work in cities made note of Sarah Evans' accomplishments. As inspector of markets in Portland in 1909 her publication of a set of clean market requirements "was the inspiration of more than one organization of women for better civic conditions," Beard wrote. She noted that in Tacoma the food inspector was also female. "Such a clean food supply is reported from that city that other communities in the state are imitating its example."[21] She added that a housing survey by the Portland Consumers' League, in which Evans was also involved, led to the group drafting and putting forward a housing ordinance to eliminate slums, a measure supported by women's clubs and welfare organizations.[22]

After women finally gained the right to vote in Oregon in 1912, Evans addressed the Oregon federation in 1915 on the issue of women's suffrage. "We were occupying the seats of the mighty by sufferance, a make-believe body of Legislators who had the legal status of idiots, Chinese and babies. Since that day one little woman, at least, has occupied one of these chairs by legal right, and did honor to her constituency and to the women of Oregon."

Evans, who worked her way through clubwork to presidency of the Oregon federation and some national prominence, also gave a presidential address in 1910. In it she distilled what in her personal view were the important deeds women, through clubs, had accomplished in their move from study to action. Her words also spoke indirectly to the female gaze on living conditions and women's will to power.

She claimed it was the nature of the clubwoman to have a core of "wholesome discontent." She "organizes a reading circle, a study club, a Shakespeare class, and before she is comfortably seated at the round table she begins to devise means for putting her study to some practical use, either for the benefit of her family or her town, and ere she is aware of it her club has a civic section—her history class is making history." Of the movement's history and its critics, she said the club movement "measured limitless progress when it transplanted the woman's club from the funny column to the editorial page, and from *Puck* to the *Century Magazine.*"

It was clubwomen who "after ten long years' fight . . . secured our National Pure Food Law" and were now fighting "against the corporate greed that would poison and adulterate the food we eat." She added that the clubwoman was the "vanguard" in the fight against child labor in workshops, factories, and mines and "battering at the doors of government, clamoring for the merit system in all our institutions where the criminal or dependent are detained." Despite all the national societies for civic improvement, "it is the clubwomen who are winning the victory under the banner of 'The City Beautiful.'"

Despite club activism, practical work had not "dimmed the aesthetic or literary side of our life," she added, citing as evidence traveling art galleries and the thousands of libraries contributed by clubwomen. She, like other clubwomen, believed that working in clubs broke down divisions among women. The club movement equalized social relations by dissolving or minimizing the "conventionalities of society." Further, clubwork "with money, caste and ancient name has been an iconoclast; it has raised the social standard of intelligence, and purity, and is developing a social life that is uplifting, kind and truthful."[23]

Earlier, at the state federation meeting in La Grande in 1908, president Evans explained why she became so active in public regulatory issues, and it went beyond women's domestic idealism to the health threat from adulterated or spoiled foods. "When a certain city council recently, after making extravagant appropriations for city improvements, refused to appropriate money for a much-needed laboratory and chemist to examine the poisonous foods that were on the market in great quantities, some one asked, 'what difference it made whether we had handsome parks and good pavements if we were all dead?'" she told the women.

"While this was a rather startling way to put the matter, we all know that after everything is said and done, our greatest asset is good health; and as the body is sustained by food, the kind of food we take into it is of paramount importance." She was concerned in particular about dairy conditions, where milk offered the perfect vehicle for terrible bacterial diseases and contamination that unsuspecting mothers fed their children.[24]

She also continued the call for better and more appropriate treatment of the "morally or mentally defective." She included in that group half of the prostitutes. "What we need in our courts and in our jails and prisons are psychologists, or at least persons who are competent to discover mental defects so that each class may receive individual treatment."

At the end of her federation career, as the United States began sliding toward the horrors of World War I, Evans, like many other clubwomen, called for pacifism as a response. "For today we stand on the brink of a greater gulf—with ages of so-called civilization back of us and the bottomless pit of despotism, militarism and barbarism yawning before us," she said at Salem in her address to the Oregon women's clubs. "There is no club so small, no club woman so insignificant but she has her part to perform in building up this wall of resistance and providing a harbor of safety against the day of calamity, which will come as the night follows the day if we listen to the Siren voice of gain and glory through militarism."[25]

Evans asked that all the women's clubs "make the peace idea the keynote of all our club activities the coming year." She also called for a fundamental change in human behavior to end war and violence.[26] Evans asked the Oregon women to "discourage in every way possible the manufacture of toy pistols, guns and other toys calculated to inspire in children the war spirit, and that we pledge ourselves not to buy them." The gender divisions remained sharp, however. She recommended "we give our little girls dolls and dishes to foster the home and maternal spirit for the time when the real things comes in to their lives."

Although successful in many other quests, Sarah Evans failed at this one. The divisions over the issue of U.S. entry into the war, translated as patriotism amid fears of spies and radicals, eventually divided the movement and became part of a backlash against its leaders.

Another important federation officer, its first president, was Adelia D. (Mrs. Charles) Bird Wade. Born in Maine, she came to Oregon in 1880 with her husband. She founded the Thursday Afternoon Club in Pendleton, called the "mother club" of Oregon. In 1902 she wrote her view of women's club activism and its connection to aesthetics and community improvement. "It is interesting to see the growing sentiment in regard to woman's influence in civic improvement. The business men of the cities and towns are too much engaged in commercial pursuits to give the aesthetic much attention and club women are invading a field which rightfully belongs to them when they become interested in beautifying their surroundings." She added that the mayor of Pendleton had asked the clubwomen to take on city beautification.[27]

Dante Is Dead

At its meeting in 1903–4, the state group heard an evening address from General Federation president Sarah Platt Decker entitled "Club Work: Its Achievements and Its Possibilities." Decker is noted for a remark promoting club activism over study at the GFWC meeting in Denver in 1904. "Dante is dead. He has been dead for several centuries, and I think it is time that we dropped the study of his Inferno and turned our attention to our own." By 1903–4 the Oregon Federation's standing committees had grown to education, library, domestic science, civics, printing, Oregon history, and membership, with special committees for legislative action and revision of Oregon's constitution.[28]

By 1910 the Oregon Federation of Women's Clubs had grown again, to fifty-one clubs representing 4,000 women in a state population of 673,000.[29] In 1910 the federated clubs, like community clubs everywhere, encountered new kinds of social problems that threatened the community and behavior standards. The federation, at its 1910–11 meeting at The Dalles, called for each club to investigate conditions "prevailing in the moving picture shows in each community" and asked citizens and city councils to appoint censorship committees "to correct the prevailing evils, pictures of low moral standard, and the poor ventilation."

The Oregon federation remained concerned about education at both ends of the age spectrum. It called for the state to establish kindergartens as part of the public school system. It sought putting the normal schools that trained most teachers on firm footing "financially and intellectually and that the diplomas issued the graduates shall entitle them to teach in any county in Oregon without further examination." It also asked the legislative committee to draft a bill prohibiting the use of the disease-spreading public drinking cup, as it sought changes in methods of enforcing the pure food laws of the state. It especially wanted laws about the pure milk supply enforced, particularly a law requiring statewide tuberculin tests of dairy cows. The women also asked for a more efficient and professional board of health, one beyond politics, with higher standards.

The federation, which had also established a scholarship loan fund for young women, was experiencing success and failure with repayments. The yearbook's description of the repayment problems of seventeen female recipients offered insights into what recipients ended up doing. One was teaching in eastern Oregon, one studying art in the East, one graduating from the state university, one was a victim of a "get-rich-quick" educational scheme, one was teaching in Clackamas County's eighth grade, one was looking for a job, one was pursuing study at a Portland business college, one was working as a sales clerk in a department store, one's expected $100 inheritance to repay the loan fell through, and another had been bilked of money but was expected to repay.[30] Whatever the federation accomplished, it did so without much in the way of material resources. Its budget for 1910 showed $471 in total receipts and $342.55 in disbursements.

THE STATE AND SOCIAL WELFARE

At its 1912 meeting in Portland, the Oregon Federation adopted a number of new resolutions on social welfare, to force the state to regulate working conditions and to aid destitute and disadvantaged populations in the face of a nonexistent public welfare system.[31] It decided to promote bills for minimum wage boards offered by the Consumers' League of Oregon, for pensions for dependent widows from the Oregon Congress of Mothers, to provide "for the pensioning of worthy and dependent mothers," and to amend the state's pure food law to cover net weights, thus regulating the food scales that cheated thousands of buyers every year.

It voted to back a bill by Oregon clubwoman and physician

Bethenia Owens Adair recommending sterilization of "confined criminals," the "incurably insane," and the "feebleminded," with a provision that it "follow the lines of the Indiana law." It also wanted the physical exams for marriage license applicants she proposed, a bill creating a State Board of Charities and Corrections similar to an Illinois law, and for each club to investigate housing conditions in its community. The women backed sex education (called sexual hygiene) for children, funded by a $10,000 appropriation.

Many of the proposals the federation backed were outside the legislative process. Reports presented at meetings detailed the achievements of individual clubs and the results of committee work. The federation's achievements for Oregon over time, listed in committee reports presented at annual meetings, were several. They included improving sanitary conditions, establishing Mothers' Meetings, and arousing interest in cooking and manual training schools. It used a pamphlet from by the Massachusetts federation, on the "Necessity of Municipal Reform," in taking up its own civil service reform work. Clubs also distributed bulbs and seeds to children for beautification projects. The Current Literature Club invited students to lectures and recitations given by prominent actors. The Pendleton clubs put copies of "the world's most famous pictures," valued at $277, in schools.

Literacy and libraries remained on the agenda. The federation at the its beginning pushed for a State Library Law "so that the boys and girls of our country schools may have access to good library books." The committee added that women's clubs needed to help better the isolated rural conditions of Oregon. Especially active in founding reading rooms and public libraries were Alpha Club of Baker City, the Woman's Club of Union, and the clubs of Granite. Yet the federation leaders complained. Too many clubs had failed "even to try to establish free public libraries in their towns." The club report said that Oregon was behind in establishing traveling libraries to benefit the rural population. "Our neighboring state, Idaho, is such a shining example of what may be accomplished in the face of great difficulties." However, it said that it had ten of the thirty cases needed to make a beginning and was counting on free railroad transportation other clubs had been successful in obtaining.

Sometimes federation projects at both the state and national level did not elicit the response intended. The Oregon federation at one point reported that it had asked all clubs in the state to ascertain "the sanitary conditions of the green grocer's supplies in their respective towns and to send a report to the chairman before May 30. To this request there was no response." However, efforts continued and successes spurred other initiatives.

As Progressive era ideas and reforms blossomed, federation agendas flowered with a greater array of legislative proposals, with more specific targets, and with wider impact. Others modified previous measures, in the interests of efficiency, stability, or the beneficiaries. Clubs, state federations, and the national federation shared ideas, bills, methods, and priorities. The federation worked with other groups on issues as well, lending support.

In Oregon, of special significance was the report in 1912 from the state federation's legislative committee on the year's work. It claimed at least partial credit for a package of legislation that dramatically and materially improved women's legal status in that state. It included a bill requiring a wife's signature as well as the husband's on contracts; a bill creating a home for "defective children"; a bill to prohibit child labor; a bill for more humane transportation of the insane; an amendment to the library law to throw out the one-fifth mill limitation and allow each city council discretion in levying the library tax; a bill requiring that in forfeiture of property the wife's signature was necessary to make the document legal; and a bill establishing state monitoring to make sure professional care was part of the appropriation for any institution to care for the "feeble-minded." Although the institutional proposal failed, the committee's "strenuous labor" induced the legislature to name a Senate committee to look into the need for such an institution and report to the next session of the legislature.

The successes did more than bring attention—they prodded policy changes. After the child labor bill passed, the governor appointed clubwomen to the legislative committee for oversight and to the Board of Child Labor Commissioners. The club's bill for transportation of the mentally ill "provided for trained attendants being sent to convey insane patients to the asylum, and when the patient was a woman a female attendant should be also sent." The current system, the report noted, allowed the sheriff of a county to pay off political debts "by giving their deputies those little jaunts to Salem, regardless of their fitness to care for a patient suffering from mental disease, and leaving insane women unprotected in the care of men for days at a time." The sheriffs organized against the bill, but the committee vowed to bring it back next year. Persistence, an important part of "agitation" and political "inputs," often paid off in subsequent years.

Once again, however, the federation found local club support on some political issues wanting, especially during the legislative session. "Reports for approval [for legislative committee action] and frequent letters of inquiry were sent to every club in the state and rarely met with a reply. This compelled the committee to rely upon its own judgment and forge ahead not knowing the sentiment of the clubs, or whether they were being supported and endorsed." This also put more power in the hands of committee and federation leaders.

For next year the committee suggested the federation pursue school truancy problems with child-centered laws that were "humane and just, dealing with the child in positive but self-respecting terms, and which above all will elevate rather than degrade it." Further, the committee wanted woman-centered control of women in trouble. It recommended that every Board of Control with power to detain or keep women or children be surveyed, with the goal of finding female staff for each one and presenting their names to the governor and legislature.

ASSEMBLING THE BEST FROM ALL SOURCES

The federations were nonpartisan, nonpolitical, and nonsectarian, Evans said. "We gather and absorb the best from all sources and bring into our work the most desirable, regardless of creed, race or politics." The federations certainly were political in many ways, but they held themselves to being nonpartisan. That, she said, kept them from pursuing some self-serving measures. In that list she included suffrage, as a divisive issue better left to individual choice. "Avoiding inharmonious alliances with issues not germane to the work of our organizations has sometimes been criticized." But the strength of women's clubs, in her view, was the fact that women as individuals could support whatever they chose "without in the least disturbing our club relations." Her point of view also helps explain why the national federation declined to take a stand on the issue of suffrage until 1914. Clubs had as their primary responsibility to remain "the great fountain of education, training and research for world betterment."[32]

Although Evans and the federation seemed ambivalent about supporting suffrage, Evans was quick to criticize the study club that had no program of action connecting its study of life to the life lived around it. "The literary club, if it is doing conscientious work, must if for no nobler purpose than self-help, elevate and improve the character of its public library; the music club will see that something beside ragtime is given in the public park, and the art club will prevent the placing of hideous monstrosities, bequeathed by defunct citizens, or grateful councilmen." In her view that was sufficient. "In doing these things they are rendering the State as signal service as the women who war against the great white and black plagues or who fight for the conservation of our resources, or take pity upon the helpless child of the unfortunate."

By 1914–15 worries about war and war relief began to infuse club consciousness, and Evans lobbied for peace and noninvolvement. In fact, the Oregon Federation was represented among the forty-seven U.S. attendees at the Hague International Congress of Women. They attended the conference with Catt, Addams, and other activists who founded the Women's Peace Party in 1915.[33] The group joined over a thousand women from twelve nations in creating a Program for Constructive Peace. Its goal, to stop world conflict, did not succeed with world leaders, but the women spread the message of peace at home as well as abroad, getting more than a little criticism for what others saw as appeasement.

Evans called for the clubwomen to continue to work for "equal representation on all elective and appointive state boards." In a sign of the times, she also recommended that the women "consecrate ourselves to the eugenics movement, but refuse to have our babies exploited and photographed for prizes or advertisements."

THE IDAHO FEDERATION BEGINS DIVIDED

The Idaho Federation actually began with three federations. Divided by Idaho's rough topography and distance into three separate but influential district organizations, the state federation did not meld until railroads and branch lines statewide made getting together faster, cheaper, and easier in the early 1900s. Idaho was divided into north, central, and southeast regions, not the first or last time the state would be thus divided. In 1900 Mrs. L. H. Henderson led the north, Gertrude Hays the central district, and Eve (Mrs. D. W.) Standrod the southeast.[34] The central district was the first of the three parts to join the national federation at the personal invitation of a GFWC president who visited the group.

The Columbian Club of Boise had elected as its secretary

Fanny L. (Mrs. Calvin) Cobb, wife of the local newspaper publisher. Cobb, with kind eyes that turned down at the corners and hair streaked with gray, counted as a friend the second GFWC president, Ellen M. Henrotin of Chicago, with whom she corresponded about the advisability of joining the new national federation and affiliated in 1894, two years after the GFWC's first biennial meeting. Henrotin, herself a supreme organizer who doubled the number of General Federation member clubs during her presidency, at Cobb's invitation came and spoke to the Idaho group in 1898. Cobb and Laura Moore Cunningham both reciprocated by attending the biennial GFWC meeting in Denver in 1898.

At the next GFWC meeting in 1900 in Milwaukee, Hays, by then president of the Idaho federation and long a club leader, appeared as a delegate. In 1902 she was elected one of eight regional directors for the GFWC.[35] Cobb and later Mary Forney of Moscow were also elected to General Federation secretary positions (then called state chairmen of correspondence). At the biennial in Los Angeles in 1902, Idaho had sixteen delegates in attendance. There was conversation and exchange between East and West through these meetings with many ideas shared. In 1906 General Federation president Sarah Platt Decker met with the Idaho group in Boise, October 25–26.[36]

Eve Standrod, a Pocatello judge's wife, called the first formal District 1 federation meeting of the clubs in the southeast part of the state to order in 1901, in Blackfoot, where five clubs sent twelve delegates. The District 2 Idaho Federation of Women's Clubs from central and southwest Idaho first met two months earlier, in December 1900 at Mountain Home. Representatives came from the Century Club, Nampa; Outlook Club, Weiser; and Entre Nous, Mountain Home, and Columbian Club, Boise. They agreed to establish committees on education, town and village improvement, educational work, and art education. District 3, covering Idaho's panhandle to the north, met in April 1902, with a dozen women representing seven groups mostly from Moscow and Lewiston. Subjects picked there for study had a pro-female and political stance. They included critic John Ruskin, Women Noted for Benevolence, Women as Office Holders, Idaho Laws Affecting Women, and Women in Music and Sociology. By the time of its first actual convention in 1903, clubs in Wardner and Grangeville and another in Lewiston joined as well.[37]

Meetings of the initial district federations in Idaho, according to

one of the members acting as historian, were for the most part attended by young, well-educated women. Many of them came to
the Northwest from the East or Midwest. "They were wives following their husbands into this land of opportunity, or they were
teachers." A high proportion of the women were college-edu-
cated, and members sought even more education. "The club was,
indeed, the married woman's college. The civic clubs too found
plenty to do in this newly developed country."[38]

That "plenty to do" for the Idaho federations included beautification and sanitation especially. It meant projects to clean litter
from streets, plant trees along new city streets and school grounds,
and beautify city parks and cemeteries. One club established a
pound for stray animals, another worked to get better-qualified
teachers, while others worked for sanitary and well-lighted public
buildings, drinking fountains, and supervised playgrounds. They
sponsored art exhibits, established domestic science and manual
training in public schools, and raised money for causes through
food sales, entertainments, special days, and rummage sales, and,
as always, established libraries and bought books for them.[39]

After several years, Idaho finally saw all the clubs united in one
federation when it met in January 1905 in Boise's City Council
chambers. By then twenty-four clubs had joined, and sixteen from
all over the state sent delegates.[40] Planning and attending a meeting of Idaho's federation of women's clubs, even with help of the
railroad, was a difficult chore, requiring long days of travel, sometimes on routes that meandered through neighboring states, but
to be an official delegate was a prized honor. Railroad companies
were talked into giving delegates special rates to attend the statewide meetings in convention cities.

At the two-day meeting, the group of women passed a package
of progressive-minded, reform-oriented, and feminist-leaning legislative proposals. They sought juvenile court laws, child labor
laws, and property rights for married women, in bills drawn up by
a diverse committee consisting of Mrs. Susanne Wilson Bowerman
of St. Anthony, Bertha Stull Green of Mountain Home, Dr. Minnie
Howard of Pocatello, and Lillian (Mrs. Festus) Foster of Weiser.
The group also passed resolutions for more support of the educational institutions in the state, to recognize the Columbian Club
"in its work revising the nomenclature of the state," to preserve
early state history, and to include the mentally disabled in a law
governing care of "deaf, dumb and blind" residents. Foster made

a presentation to the group on a "Home for Mentally Defective Children." Foster, married to a Congregational minister turned businessman at Weiser, often promoted the interests of children.[41] This continuing work by the federation eventually led to the establishment of a home and school at Nampa as a state institution for the mentally disabled.[42] The federation, after it passed the proposals and resolutions, took one more step. It copied and forwarded these materials to each legislator after collecting $2.60 from delegates for costs (federation dues were only 5 cents a year).

The Idaho clubwomen also furnished and cared for three rooms in the Idaho building at the 1904 St. Louis World's Fair and made plans for an even grander Idaho building at the Lewis and Clark Exposition at Portland in 1905. The federation president then was Eve Van Wormer (Mrs. D. W.) Standrod, leader of the Pocatello Study League and organizer of the south Idaho district federation.

The state organizations provided a place and a structure where women could broaden their leadership skills to include large organizations, no small skill and one heretofore denied women in the Northwest except perhaps in the WCTU. And as in the early years of the movement, leaders often founded or belonged to many organizations. Idaho's Standrod, for instance, organized the Wyeth Chapter of the DAR and was its first regent and organized the Idaho American War Mothers. Born in Glenville, New York, she claimed more blue blood lineage than did most clubwomen. Her ancestors, from Holland, were said to have settled in New York in 1630.[43]

Eve Standrod was described as small, wiry, and energetic. Like other club leaders, she was also well educated. A graduate of Cornell, she taught school before going west to Malad City in Idaho's southeast corner with a younger sister in 1879, working as principal of the Presbyterian Mission School there. In 1888 she married Drew Standrod of Kentucky, then prosecuting attorney for Oneida County. Six years later they came to Pocatello. He became a district judge, a legislator, and later a wealthy banker.[44]

In 1905, at the dawn of statewide club influence in Idaho, Standrod was in her early fifties. By then she had become an extremely practical leader and organizer. For instance, as head of the legislative committee of the state federation she required each club of each county to get a written pledge on federation proposals from each candidate *before* the election. The idea was to commit the candidate to supporting federation-supported measures, in a state where women could vote.

Individual departments and committees in the Idaho federation, as in other federations, did much of the work. At the 1905 meeting, the Education Committee advised members to get involved in inspecting local schools. They were to check on sanitary conditions and whether seats were the proper size and height. They also were directed to help establish free reading rooms in communities that had none and, last, to make sure good male and female candidates ran for school boards. The committee also established a scholarship loan fund for high school graduates, awarding $100 (without interest) to seniors and $50 to juniors.[45]

Expanding the Circle

In 1906 the Idaho federation delegates heard that 124 stations in Idaho had been established for the Free Traveling Library, a record clubwomen elsewhere in the Pacific Northwest envied.[46] That year the Idaho federation again pushed bills it had promoted before, adding a child labor law that set a limit of age fourteen (except for vacations over two weeks for ages twelve to fourteen by permit), with no night work for children under sixteen. In addition, it asked for a State Home for Girls, preferably at some other place than remote St. Anthony, where the boys' institution clubwomen helped build then existed.[47]

The 1906 convention, held in Moscow, brought in ten new clubs, for a total of thirty-four clubs representing 1,400 members, out of a state population of about 300,000. A new committee was established on civil service reform, fitting the government reform agenda of the movement. Standrod was its chair, and it prepared a bill requiring adoption of a merit system in civic employment. The group also submitted a bill for a home for "feeble-minded and crippled children," in the language of the time. The federation helped gain its passage, and in 1908 a Children's Home was indeed established in Boise on land donated by Cynthia Mann, a member of the Columbian Club. She taught there for several years and paid for treats for children.[48]

Mary Butterfield of Weiser became the next president of the Idaho Federation in this critical time. She was one of the few Idaho natives in the group, born in Weiser eighteen years before Idaho gained statehood and becoming state federation president at the comparatively young age of thirty-four. She had helped organized both the Outlook Club in Weiser and the Tsceminicum Club in Lewiston in north Idaho. She was the Outlook Club's first and third president. Born Mary Galloway, she was a graduate of the State Normal School at Monmouth, Oregon, and studied at the University of California. She taught and became principal of Boise's Lincoln School. She also taught college at Lewiston's Normal School (later Lewis-Clark State College) and became president of the Idaho Teachers Association. She eventually moved to the cattle ranching center of Enterprise, Oregon, and began a magazine project called Club Echoes.[49]

In 1908–10 suffragist Mary E. Forney led the federation. She had been president of both the Pleiades and Historical clubs of Moscow, clubs that had combined efforts to get a Carnegie Library in the north Idaho college town. The daughter of an itinerant clergyman, she attended college on a scholarship. She graduated from the Santa Clara Institute in California and began teaching. She married young, and they came to Mount Idaho in 1881 to pursue mining interests. Her husband James was an attorney, judge, and also acting president of the fledgling University of Idaho as one of its first regents. They entertained often, and it was she who corresponded directly with the Carnegie Foundation for the Moscow library. She also served on the local school board and was prominent in the 1896 fight for women's suffrage in the state.[50] In 1923 a women's dormitory on the UI campus was named for her.

At the meeting the women's clubs decided to emphasize civic improvement through beautification, by planting trees, lawns, shrubs, and window boxes. Forestry, waterways, and Indian affairs were objects of study, "particularly the Indians' training along industrial lines." However, the president warned member clubs about trying to cover too much territory in their work. The federation also began an antituberculosis campaign, a public health goal for the next several decades, culminating in the Idaho Hospital for Tuberculosis at Gooding in 1947. About fifty delegates attended, representing twenty-four clubs.[51]

Standing committees, each with its own divisions, included legislative, educational, historical, and art study. Those who promoted access to art capitalized on the statewide success of the traveling libraries as a means to get art into communities. The group heard reports about three traveling art cases being sent throughout the three districts in the state. The leader of the education committee, Gertrude Hays, described Chautauqua work and women's club involvement in it. Mrs. Dubois described the educational needs of Indian children, and Miss Woods, county superintendent, spoke in favor of rural high schools.

At the 1910 meeting, Standrod presented her own Civil Service bill, which was adopted. Three hundred copies of it were ordered, including copies for every legislator. Its thrust was the same as civil service reform elsewhere—to fill jobs on the basis of merit rather than as political favors or payoffs. The resolutions adopted at this significant meeting set the future course for the organization. It decided to pursue uniform divorce laws and pure food laws for Idaho, improve working conditions for women, draft a bill for medical inspection of schools, and, last, work with Utah in its attempt to get the national federation meeting located at Salt Lake City in 1912. As with federations in other states, an ongoing goal for the Idaho federation was to establish domestic science as a valid subject in high school and college curricula.

Meeting in Boise in 1912, the federation showed substantial growth. Women came from fifty-two clubs representing 2,000 members. Added departments included uniform divorce, civics, industrial and social conditions, endowment funds, and music. The meeting was presided over by Susanne Wilson Bowerman, a native of Canada who had founded St. Anthony's Woman's Literary Club in 1899, itself a charter member of the state federation. The wife of a Fremont County banker, she managed to get the Traveling Library circulated to her town and later art exhibits to schools. She also helped establish St. Anthony's first park, carrying water herself in the evenings to keep the young trees there alive.[52]

The federation generally enjoyed legislative support for its activities and paid the expenses of a federation committee in Boise during the legislative session to lobby for federation-backed bills. It had a strong leader in Bertha Stull Green, an attorney who drafted most of the bills the federation backed.

PROFILE: BERTHA STULL GREEN

Bertha Stull Green, unlike many women of the era, was not shy about being involved in either politics or the arcane process of rewriting legal codes. She ran for one public office against her husband (and lost), but still was the first woman in her area to win and hold a seat on the school board. This longtime leader of the Idaho federation's legislative committee had a legal background and used it to draft many successful proposals over the years.

Mother of three children, she was active in all three of the women's study clubs in Mountain Home. She developed a mission of making women aware of the laws that governed them and their children. To that end, in 1909 she compiled a booklet containing all state laws affecting women and children. Then she began changing some of those laws to make their situations more equitable and enact federation priorities.

Attorney Bertha Stull (Mrs. L. B.) Green described the federation bills of 1910 in some detail at a federation meeting. Most of them were written to improve the status of and conditions for women and children in Idaho, typical of Green and the federation. The proposals included the federation's bill to amend the juvenile court law and raise the age of commitment to prison to eighteen years. She also warned attendees about child labor and the enforcement of school attendance laws. She said that even the compulsory education law was in danger "because of children employed in the beet fields in the southern part of the state."

Other bills brought to the group included proposals to improve women's position in divorce, establish equal guardianship, create pure food laws, provide for medical inspection of schools, better enforce the juvenile court law, and implement the new labor laws, in both city and rural districts. In fact, Green chaired the Legislative Committee of the Idaho Federation of Women's Clubs for nearly fifteen years. As a lawyer and activist, she was well known in public life in the region. The race she ran against her Democrat husband was as the unsuccessful Republican candidate for prosecuting attorney. Green in 1920 won another race—she was elected president of the federation in 1920, serving a two-year term.

Green was born in Illinois, the daughter of a judge. She studied law and gained her degree from the University of Nebraska. Reportedly one of her law professors said hers was "the most brilliant mind he had ever had in his classes."[53] She married attorney Leslie B. Green in 1904. They traveled to Mountain Home and practiced law together for a time. Green is called by some the first woman to be admitted to the practice of law in Idaho, while others point to a lawyer in north Idaho. She also was one of the first women in her town to hold the position of school trustee.

Green became the expert on the art of drafting legislative proposals, and many came to her for help. For instance, Permeal French, Idaho's state superintendent (profiled in chapter 3) asked the Idaho club federation to work for an appropriation for a do-

mestic science building at the University of Idaho and for enough
money to send out two women as traveling instructors in domestic
science in connection with a movable School of Agriculture. It was
Green who put the ideas into a bill, working with the Idaho Department of Education, and both bills passed in time, eventually becoming part of the university extension program.

Her fellow club leader and friend Dr. Alice Pittenger talked of
Green somewhat defensively. She described her "as tall and slen-
der and very feminine, a woman who could wear flowers in her hair
with great charm. And quite often she did wear them so with evening
attire, for she was very feminine."

The federation through legislative leader Green continued to
push for a statute limiting work to a nine-hour day.[54] Green's
committee, following the direction of the state federation, again
lobbied for a uniform divorce law, equal guardianship of children,
a medical inspection bill providing a school nurse for country
schools, and once more for a women's property rights bill. It had
managed to get the bill passed earlier, only to see it vetoed by the
governor. As Duniway had complained decades earlier in Oregon,
in Idaho like other states a husband could legally dispose of community property without the wife's signature, and this bill would
have changed that by requiring her signature too.

The federation also endorsed a national public health bill, bills
establishing university extension programs in household economics, revisions of the child labor law, and a bill requiring preparation of teachers in sex hygiene. Although the group had worked
on it for years, the civil service bill failed again to pass the legislature. The federation, in a practical move, stepped back. It abandoned the proposed legislation in favor of an education campaign
to build support for it.[55] In 1912 the legislature finally allowed
federation-backed local option decisions on prohibition. The Idaho
federation decided to add, along with thirteen new member clubs
and a state dues increase of 10 cents, another department—Literature and Library Extension. Its purpose was to work with the
Idaho State Library Commission to expand permanent library facilities throughout the state and to provide a library for children
at the State Industrial School.[56]

At the federation meeting in Lewiston in 1914, the number of
clubs had grown to fifty-seven in the years before world war
changed the organization. This meeting was presided over by

Boise's Columbian Club president, Dr. Alice Pittenger, herself a physician. She had practiced medicine for two years before her marriage and for eighteen months also had studied voice at the Boston Conservatory of Music. Born Alice Butterworth in Chicago, she had married in 1902, moving to Boise in 1905. No shrinking violet, she had a reputation for matching wits and fighting to win her point "in man fashion, with no personalities involved."[57] When her adopted daughter died, she entered what friends viewed as a permanent state of grief. She abated it through tireless work for the Girl Scouts, giving them a campsite at Payette Lakes that still bears her name. She also was one of the founders of Boise Children's Home and sat on its executive committee for years. World traveled, she was noted for a flair for style and color in her clothing.[58]

The biennium of 1914–16 ended in a convention at Twin Falls. By this time the club membership had grown dramatically again, from fifty-seven to seventy-two clubs. Federation president was Sallie E. Vollmer, of Lewiston's Tsceminicum Club, born in Kentucky. She came west as a child when her father pioneered in the Walla Walla region. She attended the Whitman Seminary (later Whitman College), then married businessman John Vollmer, living first in south Boise then in Lewiston. Like other club leaders, she found herself on a board of regents, the board of overseers of Whitman College.

Under her leadership the federation added a cultural matter—clothing—to its goals. It went on record as favoring simple and modest designs in women's clothes, including adoption of a standard business suit for women. Also added to federation goals were pure food laws, police matrons, a national prohibition amendment, and support for music study in public schools.[59] Idaho, at the urging of a coalition of groups, passed a prohibition amendment in 1916. By 1917 the region had turned its attention to the war effort, and club life changed.

Subsequent federation resolutions, as the world went to war, asked for education in hygiene, child welfare exhibits at local fairs, a national park in Idaho's beautiful alpine Stanley Basin, amending the child labor law, eliminating morally dangerous features of public streets and amusements, supporting wholesome amusements and well-lighted streets, creating parks and school grounds, social disease education with regard to red-light districts, reporting of venereal diseases to the Idaho Board of Health, and, last, keeping the missionary Spalding's grave site in repair.[60]

By the 1920s, in Idaho as elsewhere, the resolutions and bills had a changed tenor. They gradually became less challenging and less confrontational in some ways and continued past priorities. They included legislative goals of establishing co-guardianship of children, adopting a red-light district law similar to one passed in Iowa, making desertion of wife and family a felony, requiring a health check before marriage, creating a "safe and sane" July 4, requiring a prisoner's pay to go to his family, and seeking half of the annual $10,000 Smith-Lever appropriation to the university for extension work for home economics.[61]

The Legacy of the Idaho Federation

Over the years the Idaho Federation of Women's Clubs pointed proudly to the passage of eighteen laws in the state. The package of laws greatly enhanced women's legal status in the state and established important services and protections for children. Several of the laws also made domestic ideals community rules, especially regarding drinking and prostitution. All of these laws were carried to the legislature by the clubs themselves, through their representatives, and passed with the help of federation lobbying and support.

Their successes included the law establishing the State Traveling Library; a juvenile delinquency law to protect children in conflict with the law (and better control their behavior), amended three times at the request of the federation; a compulsory education law keeping children in school to fourteen years of age through completion of the eighth grade; a child labor law, with additional protections; a law prohibiting minors from entering places where liquor was sold or from entering a house of prostitution; an injunction and abatement law for red-light districts; securing an appropriation to establish the Children's Home; and establishing a maximum nine-hour workday for working women.

The list also included a number of provisions improving women's legal position, property rights, and status, including a law strengthening the wife's position in inheritances in the absence of a will; a law giving a married woman sole control of her separate estate; a law making the signature of the wife necessary to encumber or convey community property; and a law giving the wife the same right her husband has to dispose of one-half of the community property by will and, upon the death of either without a will, giving all of the community property to the survivor. The latter provision was a far-seeing measure, making Idaho a community property state, which women in most other states did not enjoy even decades later.[62]

In addition, the clubs secured appropriation measures for both the School for the Feeble-Minded and State Industrial School. Other measures introduced by others but supported vigorously by the federation were to establish a domestic science building at the University of Idaho, provisions for medical inspection of the public schools, a widows' pension law, the creation of the Idaho Historical Society, pure food laws, sanitary regulations, and educational and health measures, all reflecting an overriding and continuing concern for the welfare of women and children. Along other lines the clubs also worked for equitable taxes, good roads, workmen's compensation, public institutions, and public utilities.[63]

THE WASHINGTON FEDERATION

The Washington Federation, like the federations in Oregon and Idaho, amassed a long list of both interests and achievements in the first two decades of the century. Founded in 1896, only four years after the national federation began meeting, the Washington federation eventually included a remarkable 350 member clubs, plus another 120 affiliated clubs, representing over 13,000 women at a time when Washington's population was about 500,000. The federation counted among its first goals "social uplift, civic righteousness, public welfare, and preservation of our forests."[64]

The Washington Federation promoted both cultural and political change. Its stated object was "to unite the Women's Clubs of the State for the study of cultural and altruistic subjects, for the consideration of public issues and to secure such concerted action thereon as its members may desire."[65] Its first half-dozen presidents came from New England, where the women's study club tradition was particularly strong.

At the very first federation meeting, president Amy P. Stacy described the broad and practical nature of Washington's women's clubs: "We discuss practical questions, economics, home decoration, the care and training of children, the betterment of schools, the improvement of civic conditions, the problems of ethics, and the thousand and one questions as vital to women as to men." Increasingly, those concerns reflected community and political reform ideas later lumped together under the term *Progressive*. She added that the "flippant charge can no longer be made that we 'care only for dress and amusement.'" The clubs, she said, were necessarily "altruistic." Further, a woman "of greater culture must share her benefits with her listening, less-favored sister; and as always, the most generous giver gets greatest good." She then listed dozens of civic accomplishments of member clubs already completed in their respective cities.[66]

The federation was set up in Washington by Stacy and others to be an open organization. It accepted as members only nonsecret, nonpartisan, and nonpolitical clubs. At the 1898 conference in Spokane, she led the group into agitating for traveling libraries and conservation. Federation dues were 10 cents per capita. The maternalistic Stacy pleaded for the domestic ideal. She asked the clubwomen to be good mothers and wives, striving to be pure, true, wise, and patient, according to the federation historian.[67]

Stacy herself was born in Maine in 1839, coming to Washington in 1886. The daughter of a Presbyterian minister, she too was well educated, in unusual fields. She was a teacher of "high mathematics" in New York and sufficiently versed in Judaic, Greek, and Roman history to become a scripture teacher. Like other club leaders in the Pacific Northwest, she was a leader in the Tacoma WCTU before coming to other forms of women's club activism.[68] Stacy was often dubbed the "federation mother" by those who followed, for her work solidifying all the local clubs into an integrated organization through the Presidents' Council founded in 1908 or 1909. She later became a professor of Bible literature and history at Whitworth College, which was then in Tacoma.[69]

Stacy was followed by Kate Turner Holmes, state president in 1899. Holmes organized the Seattle Federation of Women's Clubs and was president of the Seattle Kindergarten Association. She also organized young girls' clubs and mothers' clubs, helping with the Parents and Teachers Leagues. Under her leadership, the federation began initiatives it continued for years. It sought a law to make it a crime for a man to desert his family, a state reformatory for girls, an end to capital punishment, closure of saloons, and an end to gambling, as well as support for the ever-popular traveling libraries. Holmes too came west from New England. She had represented the Century Club of Seattle at the first federation meeting.[70]

Subsequent leaders, like Serena Mathews, followed the lead of early officers yet extended federation efforts in some new directions, such as establishing a state park as a gift to the state. Serena Wallis was born in 1871 in Darlington, Wisconsin. She came to

Pullman in 1892 to attend Washington State College only a few years after it was established. She taught in Pullman's public schools, then married John W. Mathews, a local attorney who had come to Pullman from Indiana.

Mathews successfully ran for several offices. She was elected to the library board, held a seat on the school board for six years, and became president of the WFWC. Her mother had been a charter member of the Pullman Fortnightly, she was one for fifty years, and her daughter Catherine Mathews Friel became a third-generation member. She was still a member when the Fortnightly celebrated its centennial in 1994, and I addressed the group on the role of clubs in Washington as part of the year-long celebration.

Mathews was a member of the federation's Pure Food Committee, legislative chair, and president of the Washington federation in 1927, during a challenging time for women's clubs. The federation under president Esther Stark Maltby made plans for an "exhibit" forest park of virgin timber between Seattle and Ellensburg in the Cascades west of Snoqualmie Pass. It was to be a gift to the state's residents from the women's clubs as well as an environmental statement (they called it "conservation"). Clubs first identified then began fundraising to buy sixty-three acres of virgin timber on Snoqualmie Pass for the Federation Forest. Arranging the land transfer from the Snoqualmie Lumber Company to the federation came during Mathews' term. She had the privilege of turning the deed over to the state. Eventually the federation and the Washington Parks Commission got permission to sell the property and used the money to relocate the new Federation Park, now augmented to 612 acres, to a site 17 miles east of Enumclaw on the Naches Highway over Chinook Pass in the Cascades. Its management became a model for long-range forest management.[71]

In the years that she was involved in the Washington federation, it pushed for the county library bill, child welfare legislation, a western Washington institution for the mentally impaired, a labor program for prison inmates, extension of civil service to other governmental jobs, preservation of the huckleberry, strengthening of prohibition laws the clubs helped pass, and study of world peace and outlawry of war.[72]

During the first decade of its existence the Washington federation had quickly turned to a mode that pursued women's interests through direct political influence. It displayed a bold activism that had sharply diminished by the end of the 1920s, as happened with women's clubs everywhere. Early in the century its resolutions and bills called for dramatic changes in the legal and political framework of the state and attention to social rather than business concerns. One of those was public education, particularly kindergartens. As early as 1902, spurred by the Century Club, the Seattle federation began a vigorous campaign for kindergartens in public schools, a cause adopted by the state federation.[73] Kindergartens represented a new developmental view of childhood education. Proponents saw them as an important new component in a progressive education that met children's unique needs. National as well as local organizations backed kindergartens, including the GFWC and the NCW.

By 1920 there were 9,000 kindergartens in the United States, but the movement still reached only about 10 percent of children.[74] Critics of the movement complained that children were too young for this, and women who advocated it were accused of abrogating their maternal responsibilities. It was an early sign of the backlash that later stymied women's clubs and their success at cultural politics, called "social engineering" or "radicalism" in more critical settings.

The women in the Washington federation, like those in Idaho and Oregon, also initially sought uniform national divorce laws. The federation advocated boycotting businesses where women were not "paid living wages," prohibiting saloons near schools, putting officials and employees of Washington's institutions under a civil service merit system, changing legislation that had weakened the new age of consent law that the Century Club got passed, enforcing the state anticigarette sales law, putting at least one woman on every school board in the state, and adding pragmatic "domestic science" and "manual training" to what became junior high curricula.

It also called for hiring women to teach physiology "and kindred subjects" to girls and as teachers of science in high schools. It attacked a state education official's recommendation that men supersede women as high school instructors in Washington, arguing that "women are endowed equally with men in all that pertains to the making of competent teachers."[75] Pressure from the united women's clubs also led to classes being established in Seattle and elsewhere for deaf, blind, and mentally disabled children.

Like the national and the Idaho and Oregon federations, the Washington federation also successfully promoted libraries, the child labor amendment, higher standards for education, support and housing programs for all children, protective laws for women and children, and the construction of special facilities for women and children in need or in trouble, as an alternative to harsher, more punitive punishments and bleak lives and to control behavior they found unacceptable. In Washington, that included a protracted campaign for a training school for girls, which had to overcome a governor's veto even after the legislation authorizing it finally passed.

SUCCESSES IN WASHINGTON

In 1901 the federation with labor groups began lobbying for a ten-hour work day for women, which eventually passed. In 1903, in concert with the Grange and the Washington State Federation of Labor, the federation managed to get several important reform measures through the legislature—a child labor law, an initiative law, and an eight-hour day for employees on publicly funded projects.[76]

The Washington Federation's broad cultural agenda also included, from the beginning, attention to environmental issues, which they lumped under "conservation" or "beautification." Those issues included reforestation, prescient bills on environmental and species protection, and eventually highway beautification and support to establish Olympic National Park.[77]

Elvira Elwood, an officer in the Washington federation, explained why the clubs wanted legislation to protect the magnificent forests of the Pacific Northwest. "While I write, a mute appeal in the shape of dense volumes of smoke reaches me from our smitten forest sentinels." As of three in the afternoon she had to use artificial light, "so obscured were the sun's rays by the smoke from the forest fires," this time occurring in southwestern Washington. "Are we, in our women's clubs, taking up the work of forestry any too soon? Can nothing be done to secure our 'primeval forest' against these devastating fires? Oregon and Washington cannot afford to witness such widespread destruction of our timber lands. . . . Protective legislation is a necessity," she wrote. "Lumbermen will say so. Our scientific men say so. Common sense certainly affirms it. Let us all work for the protection of our beautiful and wonderful forest trees." The federation had recently named a forestry department.[78]

In 1902 the state leader from Ellensburg in her inaugural address to the federation warned members that Washington's forests were not inexhaustible. Members on what became the Conservation Committee consulted with professors from the University of Washington and Washington State University to come up with a plan of action, and the governor appointed Elwood to a Washington Conservation Commission. On this issue, the federation became an effective collective voice, working for highway beautification, protection of endangered species of birds and plants, and preservation of natural scenery.[79]

The federation also successfully lobbied for a Washington pure food bill. Jennie Whitehead Ellis, Tacoma, chaired both the General and the Washington Federation's food sanitation committees. This member of Tacoma's Aloha Club established a model for handling the issue in that city. She called the heads of other women's clubs to her home to create a Pure Food Council to enforce the provisions of the new act and monitor conditions. The result was that Tacoma had a more extensive city ordinance and enforcement, with women appointed by the mayor to food inspector positions.[80] Ellis also sat on the Tacoma Library Board and chaired the Tacoma Pure Food Council.

The Washington Federation's attention to cultural politics through governmental regulations and programs increased. In 1909 its public education priorities were public kindergartens, more playgrounds, and teachers' pensions; for children and parents, a bureau of child information to deal with issues such as disease, orphans, delinquency, and others; for economic support of women, mothers' pensions. They sought justice system changes including a tougher law on the age of consent, enforcement of the anticigarette law, paying wages to convicts, and better conditions for female prisoners. They also sought institutional changes to give women more power through appointment of a commission with two women to supervise all state institutions dealing with women and children and government reform through civil service reform, including prohibiting any influence in appointments of state institutional superintendents, and even world peace.[81]

In 1913 the Washington Federation of Women's Clubs introduced a spate of social legislation, some of it resurrected from prior years. It included a higher minimum wage for women and minors, a teachers' pension bill, a mothers' pension bill for support of destitute women, and a bill for vocational schools. It also supported bills for control of liquor and red-light districts, for an eight-hour day law for coal miners, and even to protect citizens from bogus employment agencies.[82] A number of the measures passed, although some were delayed until subsequent sessions and passed then. It was not successful, however, with its resolution adding to the chorus trying to keep the nation out of world war. The wording of the resolution spoke powerfully for women of past generations caught up in yet powerless to avert war. "We believe that the voice of women who raise sons, who help care for the home and till the fields in the absence of the bread winner, should be heard before the country is plunged into war."[83]

The federation sought better conditions for female prisoners. It also established scholarships to help young women go to college and worked to get women on the University of Washington board of regents as well as on local school boards.[84] Ruth Karr McKee joined the UW board in 1917, just as women's clubs in Idaho helped get Mary Ridenbaugh and other club leaders on the University of Idaho board of regents even earlier in the century. Ruth (Mrs. James) McKee, was born in Hoquiam, Washington, in 1874, graduating from the University of Washington in 1895. She became president of the Washington Federation, 1913–15, and a director of the General Federation in 1916. She was a regent of the university from 1917 to 1926 and belonged to a number of women's clubs, including fraternal and patriotic as well as professional groups.[85]

In the years 1915–17 the federation added a Committee on Immigration to aid "the struggling immigrant mother." It offered classes in English for foreign women and provided care for their children during the classes.[86] Later in the federation's history, the goal of the Department of American Citizenship was defined, reflecting the heightened sentiments and fears of the nativism around World War I. Its goal was creating good American citizens, whether native or immigrant, on the theory "that a spiritual transformation must take place within an immigrant and it is our duty to help him. One cannot make a German girl into an American girl by merely dressing her in American clothes."[87] Classes offered included English, meal planning, sewing, and so on, with focus later expanded to Native Americans. Clubs offered similar activities for girls on seven Indian reservations in Washington within a few decades.

The African-American clubs in Washington also used a federation to pursue their interests. The Washington African-American women's clubs federated in Spokane in 1917 under Mrs. John C. Mapps, Spokane. Under state president Nettie J. Asberry, the federation undertook a number of projects to benefit the African-American community, such as an essay contest that ultimately awarded thousands of dollars in scholarships.[88] By 1918 Mapps held a national post as statistician of the National Association of Colored Women's Clubs.[89] Mapps earlier had been instrumental in organizing the City Federation of Spokane, which included a Sojourner Truth Club. It ran a home for women and girls, which later became a broadly supported facility for elderly African-American women. The Washington State Federation of Colored Women's Clubs grew steadily, from ten clubs to forty-two from all the major cities in Washington and nearby cities in Canada.[90]

THE LEGACY OF THE FEDERATIONS

The record in Washington, Idaho, and Oregon demonstrated the power of organized womanhood to alter the priorities of government to better match their own. That included public responsibility and financial support to redress serious societal problems, especially where women and children were disadvantaged. They altered the legal, cultural, and political systems where they could to extend, enhance, or protect women's rights and, last, brought to the fore concerns about art, the environment, and aesthetics as part of their cultural politics.

Although they began with the rhetoric of maternalism and domestic ideology, they used it less after the twentieth century began. They came to rely more on the rhetoric of reform and the new social sciences, lashing it to concepts of woman's moral exceptionality, a value that seemed to link the two realms of thought. They found and used allies for legislative work where they could. Frequently it was the coalitions that made passage possible, especially where the mainstream women's club movement served to validate the proposals. The clubs extended discussion and awareness within and without their organizations.

The power of alliance on political "inputs" was demonstrated repeatedly. For instance, Washington later had another powerful alliance of women's groups beyond the federation, the nonpartisan Women's Legislative Council of Washington, which grew out of Seattle's North End Progressive Club. In 1917 it invited other women's clubs to join, and 140 eventually did. It worked in governmental circles for women's rights and welfare, operating much like the Women's Joint Congressional Committee did at the federal level for a coalition of national women's organizations including the General Federation of Women's Clubs. The Women's Legislative Council of Washington worked on child labor laws, vocational training, education, and discrimination, helping secure passage of fifty-nine measures between 1919 and 1927, according to historian Margaret Andrews.[91]

Meanwhile, the General Federation, like the state federations, had its own extensive legislative program. The resolutions passed by the General Federation of Women's Clubs biennial convention in Chicago in 1914 included equal suffrage, better fire protection, increased appropriations for city and state boards of health, university extension work for disease prevention, a federal bureau of home economics, use of schools as social centers for community betterment, better systems of birth registration, and "hostility to the liquor traffic."[92]

In the Pacific Northwest, an array of social welfare laws and programs resulted from the organized efforts of the federations in the years between 1900 and 1920, especially as they gained political sophistication and the power of the vote. Year after year, clubwomen carried forward cultural, political, and social ideals realized in the form of practical measures that enhanced their communities in the ways they valued. Sometimes getting the change in state and community priorities took years of effort and "education" on their part. Some laws and programs they established were later repealed or inadequately enforced. Institutions they helped establish changed over time. But as the record demonstrates, the women in these clubs of clubs in the Pacific Northwest shaped the cultural infrastructure of the Northwest after 1900.

Although most members agreed on the course of federation priorities, the ship did not carry everybody. Some club members were worried about the movement's relentless drive to get government to assume ever more responsibility for social welfare. They questioned the shift from private charity to public welfare, and some made note of the emerging rhetoric. "In the minds of some, 'pension' has grown to be a much more respectable word than 'charity,' and men and women who would scorn to receive the latter will use all manner of devices to secure the former—and consider it perfectly honest," Oregon federation leader Sarah Evans said. She warned about the nature of charity some women espoused, especially when it came to some groups such as the un-

employed, but agreed it was the role of government to help certain classes of citizens.

"[We must] reserve our loving ministrations of sweet charity for
the sick, the afflicted, and the helpless child," she said. "All institutions for the unfortunate of whatever character should be sustained and administered by government," she added. "To combine private benefactions with state funds for the maintenance of
any institution is pernicious, leading to a duplication of work,
with unlimited temptations for dishonesty and corruption." She
said women needed to strip the unemployment and welfare problems of "sentimentality."[93]

UNINTENDED CONSEQUENCES

Like most social movements, success in the women's club movement dragged behind it unintended effects and new problems.
Occasionally their programs had consequences that actually
worsened conditions or failed to resolve the problems as intended. The Oregon federation leader, in commenting on federation successes in her address in 1915, pointed out some of the
problems. One related to the long-sought saloon closures. They
left unemployed or homeless men without a place to go, who "for
the price of a drink could procure a comfortable chair for the
evening in a warm, cozy corner, or participate in the love and
laughter and song of debauchery," she said.

"Something must be provided for what we have taken from
him. . . . there is no shirking our duty in this; our vote was largely
responsible for creating the situation, and the women in every
community must realize their responsibility in meeting the crisis
by providing some social life for the 'down and outs' which is just
as necessary as food and raiment," she told the clubwomen, in
some ways echoing the WCTU leaders speaking a half-century
earlier.[94] In fact, by 1914 the states of Oregon, Washington, and
Idaho had all enacted laws restricting sale and consumption of alcohol. Other western states also enacted some form of prohibition, contradicting (some said responding to) the West's hard-
drinking image well before the nation ratified the Prohibition
Amendment in 1919.

President Evans noted a similar consequence with clubwomen's
attempts to deal with immigrants, reflecting the nativism of the
time even as she recognized the problems with their classist approach. The hyphen "is very pronounced in some of our half-

American societies. And why is it?" she asked. "We hold ourselves too much aloof; we throw out the challenge rather than assistance, and our attitude throws them back upon themselves for entertainment and companionship," she said. "We need these people, and as never before they need us." The immigrant must be led to "loyal American citizenship through the pathway of kindness, friendship, and love."[95]

PERSISTING CHANGES

Some of the changes the federations wrought persisted throughout the twentieth century and saw expansion as the nation accepted social welfare as a legitimate function of government. The idea that citizens needed protection through government programs, a regulated commerce, and behavior control was the guiding philosophy of the later women's club movement. Citizens saw those functions ever more centralized and federalized with social welfare policies under the New Deal, War on Poverty, and Great Society programs decades later and consumer protection under a series of federal acts, departments, and regulations on everything from the workplace to medicines to the environment, all as part of an expansion of federal authority and responsibility, undergirded by an income tax system redistributing income. It was not until the end of the century that the political realm mounted a serious challenge threatening to reverse the course set by the federations a century before.

Although these women would not have called or considered themselves feminists, their work on behalf of women's rights in the Northwest put those states ahead of much of the rest of the nation in conferring rights on women, such as suffrage, community property laws, or protective labor laws. Although the clubs certainly reflected some conservative and traditional values, they effectively extended those values.

THEIR LEGACY

Facing a Changed Future

When I was a newspaper reporter trying to succeed in what was then very much a male world, covering what previously had been "male" beats, I was frequently invited to join the Idaho Press Women. I always politely declined, feeling that to join this venerable all-female organization would be a step backward. Instead, I joined the Idaho Press Club, the mostly male professional organization that represented the field. I learned much later how important the Idaho Press Women had been to female reporters and editors throughout the state in decades when women were uniformly and unilaterally confined to certain "female" slots in newspaper work, most of them connected somehow to women's role at home and its extensions. Like other women during the twentieth century, I failed to appreciate what that all-women organization had accomplished or could offer me; instead I, like countless professional women before and after, left the support of the all-female organization behind for new professional opportunities and organizations. It was our loss.

Women's clubs in the Pacific Northwest, especially the study clubs, helped redraw the cultural, social, political, and legal landscape for the region. They adapted and put into practice new ideas about education, child behavior, criminal justice, public health, domestic science, public administration, environmental activism, women's rights and women's roles. Civic reform, like other measures they supported, carried a moral dimension. Some likened it to a purification process, a pure form of government removed from politics. As Sarah Evans, longtime leader of the Oregon Federation, put it, "It means, simply, putting all public service into the merit system, and training children to look upon public service as an honorable occupation, rather than an opportunity to graft or as a plum for political distribution."[1] Connected to ideas of merit were the objective standards supposedly embodied in professionalization and bureaucratization, those allied movements.

THE MOVEMENT MATURES

As clubs matured, so did their methods. Leaders left ideas of moral suasion to engage in a political power struggle, becoming more bold and sophisticated as their numbers grew. As years passed, the most active clubs went into the community instead of the library to research the social problems they studied. Their surveys—often spurred by state or federation directives and sustained by an emerging faith in the social sciences, reform, and the possibilities of progress—became the method of choice to gather evidence, particularly for urban activist clubs.

Such work also gave women an opportunity to use professional tools rather than simply sentiment or domestic values to amass unbiased information for each community upon which wise public opinion and courses of action might be based. Their changing "habits of study" were connected to the rise of sociology and psychology as a way to understand and direct human behavior and to utilize their own rising levels of education to affect conditions around them. Yet they sometimes naively believed that exposure compelled resolution or that understanding equated with action. Only a few understood the extent of the resistance to change.

Idaho Federation of Clubs historian Vernetta Hogsett speaks for decades of clubwork when she describes the group's experiences addressing the material conditions of life: "Women were confronted with work to be done in the high cost of living, short weights and measures, pure foods, clean water, clean milk, clean markets, clean streets through which children must go to school, honest textiles, study of child labor and its ill effects."[2] In those areas—plus enhancing the employment and professional, legal, and educational status of women—women's clubs gained ground. They also left their communities with public libraries dotting the entire Northwest, giving every resident equal access to what they viewed as the highest and best literature and the latest in information.

World War I and the turmoil in the years that followed changed the world for clubwomen as it did for America. Before and even after the clubs got caught up in the patriotism and war work precipitated by U.S. entry into World War I in 1916, the bills pushed by the federations in the Northwest leaned toward reengineering legal, cultural, and social systems. Their cultural politics through policy and revised gender roles came back to haunt them in the 1920s as part of a conservative backlash against a changing culture and fears of the future. Their programs, beneficial as they were, had not fixed the world's problems, nor had getting the vote for women, who did not vote in a block to enact club priorities. In addition, gaping tears in the social fabric of the country made their ideas about "unity" an idealistic dream.

REFORM VERSUS FEARS OF THE RADICAL

In his overview of social policy during the Progressive era, historian Morton Keller argues that traditional values and American pluralism created powerful counterforces to the development of a powerful, more intrusive state and judicious public policies, as reformers sought to use state power to establish a stable culture and in their eyes an improved social order. Further, in the 1920s, the reformers of the Progressive era did not disappear but changed their agenda from structural concerns to more "ethnocultural" concerns, still in tension with the forces opposing change. The traditional social values and beliefs of their opponents reinforced ideas of individualism, laissez-faire, and local control—and fears of the radical.[3] That tension continues today in conflicts over issues such as land use, welfare, and immigration policies. The Northwest manifested this national pattern to an even greater degree than other regions precisely because of the success of women's reform efforts and its own history of an independent citizenry in conflict with but dependent on government largesse and the whims of agencies.

Accusations, using labels like *social engineering, radical,* and *unwomanly,* swirled around some of the most notable club federation successes. The clubwomen's success in resolving some social welfare problems through government programs rather than private charity increased dissension about society's proper role when it came to charity. Mothers' pensions, institutions for special needs populations, alternative schools, kindergartens, libraries, even wages for convicts, were typical social programs developed by clubs that were eventually shifted to government responsibility.

Concerns about this shift of programs from private to public continued throughout the twentieth century, especially over who was deserving of aid. They included fears about abuse of the system by the "unworthy poor," concerns about damage to individual initiative, and a dislike of increasing taxes. Those persisting concerns welled up periodically, surfacing again in the election of 1994 and the provisions of the Republican Party's Contract with America. However, virtually nobody advocated a return to the conditions clubwomen found when the movement began—no public libraries, few public programs or pensions for the elderly or disabled, no unemployment programs, no stable forms of economic aid for destitute families with children, no health care for those without funds, no minimum wage requirement, no consumer protection, and on and on—all of them club priorities.

Even after the pivotal 1994 elections that shifted power to Republicans in Congress, a scientific poll early in 1995 showed continuing majority support for not only keeping but increasing the minimum wage (72 percent). Reflecting more than a little irony, the poll found that the public remained distrustful of the federal government, with 79 percent expressing only some or very little confidence in Congress, yet overwhelmingly supportive of basic welfare (or income redistribution) programs. The public generally opposed cutbacks to Medicaid, Medicare, Social Security, Aid to Families with Dependent Children (AFDC), or federal unemployment insurance. Yet public opinion divided evenly over whether Food Stamp programs should be cut back, and two-thirds favored requiring welfare recipients to find work after two years but guaranteeing them a public sector job if they found none in the private sector.[4]

Another 1995 poll demonstrated the power of the image of the single mother as worthy of welfare aid. Respondents were asked about which groups should have welfare benefits available to them. At the top were single mothers, at 76 percent, followed by men who cannot get work at 54 percent and teenaged mothers at 53 percent. The bottom two categories pollsters defined—illegal immigrants with children born here and "welfare mothers" who have more children—polled only 31 percent and 21 percent respectively as "entitled" to benefits.[5]

If a welfare state is defined as redistribution of income to address economic and social welfare of citizens, then the United States is a welfare state, with welfare benefits for mothers and children, medical benefits, unemployment benefits, educational benefits, retirement benefits, programs for housing and home ownership, an array of public social services, consumer protection, and many other kinds of assistance and protections for citizens. However, such programs came with a cost, even club leaders recognized, including the legacy of what later was called a permanent underclass and taxpayers who feel overburdened. In some cases the cost was clubs left saddled with the responsibility of sustaining institutions and programs where they could not be transferred to government but filled a community need and the subsequent loss of the program.

The transition from private to public programs sometimes created a new set of problems. "All institutions for the unfortunate of whatever character should be sustained and administered by government," Oregon Federation president Sarah Evans said in 1915.[6] "To combine private benefactions with state funds for the maintenance of any institution is pernicious, leading to a duplication of work, with unlimited temptations for dishonesty and corruption."

Women's club activism also came with another cost. It reinforced women's traditional responsibility for social welfare, even as women campaigned to shift some of it to government. This process underscored traditional views about women in the "helping" professions, such as teaching, nursing, and social work, which were always undervalued economically. This in turn also helped limit women's access to other fields, psychologically as well as materially.

Ideas connected to the veneration of motherhood led activism in particular directions, resulting in a structural legacy that outlasted the movement. Clubwork chronicler Mary Ritter Beard found that support for mothers' pensions—public aid to women with young children to support—was a long-lived and honorable cause for clubwomen. Such aid became institutionalized later as Aid to Families with Dependent Children. She said more women agreed upon pensions for widows or mothers than any other, despite opposition that wanted to see such aid remain in the hands of private philanthropy. Opponents accused the women who supported the idea of acting on the basis of sentiment rather than reason.

Yet by 1915 no fewer than seventeen states had mothers' pension laws, primarily at the urging of women and often administered through unsalaried boards of women.[7] By 1930 mothers' pension or aid programs existed in forty-six of the forty-eight states, and in 1935 the federal Social Security Act adopted the outlines of those programs and funded them.[8] One outcome was the resulting failure to examine the economic structure that disadvantaged mothers and children or to recognize the father's role and responsibility through policy, either as a worthy part of a family in need or as responsible for support.

Government-funded welfare was designed to benefit children first and secondarily their mothers. This came to mean single mothers as the "deserving poor" and members of a population worthy of state-sanctioned support, at least until passage of the Family Support Act of 1988 designed to stop the trend and help keep poor families intact. As welfare policy historian Theda Skocpol points out, the political origins of social policy were rooted to protecting mothers and soldiers. However, if social welfare spending were more broadly defined to include all programs aimed at poor populations, plus social security, military pensions, college loans, housing, and so on, the majority of the spending went actually not to the "poor," but to the middle class, with only a fraction of all social welfare spending aimed specifically at low-income families.

Government aid to the middle class and even rich citizens came to be called entitlement, while aid to the poor became "an undeserved and dishonorable drain on our taxes."[9] Debate about the "worthy poor" persisted, when the Social Security Act passed and beyond. The aid that went primarily to men in the form of old age pensions and unemployment benefits was seen as superior to the aid going to women and children.

THE SHIFT TO GOVERNMENT

The original 1935 Social Security Act combined three programs in which women had a management role: Aid to the Blind, Aid to the Permanently and Totally Disabled, and Old Age Assistance, all means-tested programs for the poor. Aid to the Aged, Blind, and Disabled eventually became the Supplemental Security Income (SSI) program. The Old Age Survivors and Disability Insurance became the pension plan the Social Security Administration supported with worker funds.

As it became a contributory national retirement program (some prefer the term *dedicated tax*), many of the Social Security Act's welfare components landed elsewhere in the federal framework. Social Security benefits gradually became a right while other program benefits, termed *welfare,* became a cost. Many have noted that women's housework did not qualify as productive "work" in the meaning of the act, and many groups, such as the self-employed and the largely African-American domestics and farmworkers, were excluded from benefits.

Although roundly criticized for its faults, the Social Security Act's implementation was a remarkable achievement that rescued many from destitution and poverty and provided the welfare safety net that clubwomen supported for citizens, without the economic and social or political upheaval that such changes often created. Its ability to blend interests across class lines and state borders with stable support speaks well for its design and implementation. However, historian Linda Gordon notes that because Progressive reformers—including many clubwomen—believed motherhood was sacrosanct and should be full-time work, aid for single, poor mothers as it became formalized in the 1935 act became punitive and stigmatizing, especially as compared to the old-age "pensions" and unemployment "insurance."

The women who had a role in designing the basic aid program for children and mothers, part of a new professional social work network, saw this aid program as the first step in a series of legislative provisions to guarantee social rights and maternal and child welfare benefits from the state. Provisions included protectionist labor laws and even national health insurance, but that ambitious program was never fully implemented.[10] As women's clubs foundered in the 1920s and 1930s, they abandoned many of the causes relating to aid for the poor and disadvantaged, especially as the state, at their urging, stepped in with formal programs at both the state and federal level.

By the end of the twentieth century the shift from private charity to public funding of myriad programs was stunning. In 1990, 49 percent of all households received some entitlement benefits, averaging $10,320 per family. Government benefits in fiscal 1993 included roughly $302 billion in Social Security programs, $143 billion in Medicare, $76 billion in Medicaid, $35 billion for unemployment benefits, $25 billion for Food Stamps, $21 billion for supplementary aid (SSI) to the poor elderly and disabled, $17 billion to veterans' benefits, $16 billion to welfare and family support, and $16 billion to farm price supports. Total spending on federal entitlement programs totaled $762 billion in 1993, while direct aid to the government-certified poor, in Food Stamps, Medicaid, SSI, and ADC, came to $140 billion a year—about what the federal government spent on non-means-tested Medicare alone.[11]

Indeed, by the end of the twentieth century the issue became one of access to the benefits of the welfare state, with competing interests and populations worried about declines in support programs, an issue that helped drive anti-immigration initiatives and health care reform debates. Out of President Bill Clinton's proposed 1996 budget of $1.61 trillion, direct benefit payments to or for individuals represented half the budget at 48 percent of the total, with 16 percent for reserved defense and 16 percent allocated for interest payments. Another 15 percent was allocated in grants to states and localities, and 5 percent to other federal operations, according to Office of Management and Budget figures.

Programs initiated, fostered, or monitored by women's clubs for citizens found expression in what became federally subsidized unemployment benefits, medical benefits, welfare benefits, retirement benefits, educational benefits, social services, credits for home ownership, and a wide variety of other forms of assistance. Some argued that to be a true welfare state requires full employment policies and government provision of all necessary services and benefits to citizens. Certainly the United States was much closer to that end of the spectrum by the end of the twentieth century than it was at the beginning of the club movement ten or twelve decades earlier, while still maintaining a capitalist framework and market economy.

Proponents saw the move to state-funded aid as a bold statement of policy, a needed realignment of government to protect the nation's children and their homes for the good of all, without the discrimination, instability, and inconsistency of organized private benevolence. However, the long sought Widows' Pension Law in Oregon, once implemented, was criticized as being burdened with what we would call bureaucratic attitudes and "drying up the wellsprings of human sympathy." Critics said it damaged "the old neighborly helpfulness for the widowed and fatherless." It also took private organizations off the hook and led to dumping, just as some states cut benefits to force recipients to go elsewhere.

"We found fraternal organizations referring their widowed charges to the pension committee. We found church societies taking refuge in the law. We found relatives withdrawing their support and charity organizations being relieved of their widow cases." Evans warned about this new definition of social welfare—that it could make a public charge public property, and as such the public would feel entitled "to the most intimate acquaintance with every item of expenditure in the administration of the law," she told the Oregon federation. "Taxpayers have no respect for family privacy or prejudices when they are being paid for out of the taxes and no power of sentiment or sympathy will alter their attitude."[12] It was a philosophical concern that critics of governmental social welfare programs continued to voice a hundred years later.

THE CONSERVATIVE CORE

For all its emphasis on progressive reform and self-improvement, in some important ways the women's club movement was a conservative one. The ideal many members held of womanhood and motherhood, of women's superior nature, and choosing to view the community as "but the larger home" reflected conservative and traditional values and gender roles. Their successful work to rid the country of the worst abuses of child labor fit neatly into ideas of motherhood, as did the idea of enhanced republican citizenship through libraries and education. Their later attempts to wrest control of the political and policy arenas from politics as usual through civic reform and suffrage were in part an outgrowth of those ideas of republican citizenship. Ideas of culture and the arts women promoted also were connected to their "highest and best" ideals about an enlightened citizenry and what it means to be civilized.

Along those lines, the woman's club view of the arts was therefore also a conservative one, traditional and historical for the most part, as clubs put themselves in the role of conservator of the "good, the true, and the beautiful," as one member put it. Their good works and service, combined with fears of and distaste for ostentatiousness and display, for many connected this secular movement to a conservative religious ideal and tradition. Others felt not a moral zeal, but a desire to use their education and new-found power in a productive way to revitalize their communities and surroundings.

Regardless of direction, most clubs believed in and accomplished much for women's rights in the all-important cultural sites of politics, legal status, and access to education and the professions. Their leaders, especially in the Northwest, frequently went on to hold "first woman who" positions, opening doors for other women to walk through. The leaders in the Northwest— most of them professionally trained as teachers, doctors, and lawyers—managed to influence if not compel others to view the world through their female gaze, thus institutionalizing programs and services they established as a result of this perspective.

Finding a Voice

Of critical importance and often left behind in discussions of groups, movements, trends, regions, and connections to subsequent social developments is what these clubs did for the women who belonged, especially in the movement's early years. They gave thousands of individual women access to education, to the world of ideas, and to their own abilities. They gave women a voice. They fostered individual achievement, provided social and emotional support networks, and empowered women in a most fundamental way. The clubs used rituals, practices, formats, resources, and each other in ways that both comforted and challenged women to be more and do more than many believed they could.

For all their accomplishments for women and children and the institutions, conditions, or laws that affected them, however, clubwomen would not have considered themselves what we now label feminists, with their attention to gender-based constructions like patriarchy and women's rights. That model was far too selfish and too removed from "womanly" ideals for behavior and standards to be acceptable to most of these women, at least during the period of this study. Suffrage and rights were often a means to an end for these women, and they were less interested in upending than in altering systems. That end, at least they told themselves, was less for personal power than for the best ways to protect themselves, their families, their communities, and their domestic ideology.

Given the expectations of the time and the gender roles, few dared admit they were also climbing a ladder toward personal and political power. Nevertheless, they did alter gender relationships and cultural politics in their communities and the country, sowing seeds for later movements. They used a conservative and traditional philosophy, yet sometimes acted in a radical manner to bring attention to their beliefs and practical solutions, often political, to the problems they saw around them. In a liminal fashion, they often used traditional beliefs and arguments subversively, upending them even as they argued for enlarging and extending them. They also did groundwork for the transition of government into the modern state, the New Deal, and even the later women's rights movements, despite the cultural backlash of the 1920s and the economic privations of the 1930s.

However, these women, hearkening back to tradition, were not prepared for the technological and social changes of the twentieth century (few were). As domestic ideology and ideas of reform and progress seemed to grow old-fashioned and even quaint in the new century, the club movement faltered. The new generation of leaders failed to replace the earlier ones with the same degree of fervor, cohesiveness, and single-minded purpose that earlier leaders seemed to enjoy. Nor were they ready for how quickly women of subsequent generations walked away from their organizations once they found themselves facing fewer restrictions and more open doors, whether in education, professional associations, or the job market. And in the twentieth century all women found or feared striking cultural changes as a result of the spread and commercialization of new forms of communication and entertainment.

New Diversions and Entertainments

Clubwomen with their "highest and best" standards for culture and behavior faced powerful new adversaries. Movies and their growing influence as the "people's school" concerned clubwomen in many cities early in the twentieth century, and some turned to control and censorship as the answer. Mary Ritter Beard said that studies by clubwomen all over the country led clubs to push for exhibition of, if not "uplifting" films, then "high-grade" ones. A few clubs, as in Pittsburg, Kansas, worked out "a censorship plan for moving-picture shows, which is proving successful."[13] With the cooperation of theater managers, they tried to eliminate films depicting scenes of crime, drinking scenes, and suggestive love scenes.

Volunteer boards of clubwomen in other places used "tact" to persuade, while others got city officials to create formal Boards of Censors with legal authority to control theater releases and behavior. For instance, Seattle eventually had a city-sanctioned Board of Theater Censors with mostly women as members, a board sought by the city federation of women's clubs.[14] Portland, too, had a Municipal Board of Review established in 1915, when an informal group of clubwomen reviewing movies was formalized.

Sometimes the target was racism, as with *The Night Riders,* a 1910 film about the Ku Klux Klan. It also happened in Portland and Tacoma after release of D. W. Griffith's epic and racist film *The Birth of a Nation* in 1915. The film came to Portland in 1916, and a group of African-American leaders, male and female, came before the city council to protest. They all viewed the film, and the council passed an ordinance to ban showing of any film that would stir up hatred between the races. The film resurfaced in 1923 in Portland and was banned there in 1926.[15]

African-American clubwomen in Tacoma also believed film had formidable power to influence or reinforce racist beliefs. A coalition of six of them appeared before the Tacoma city council over the same film. They spoke eloquently and with pain about a local theater's plans to show it and asked the city council to suppress it. One argued that the image left by the film was that her race was "immoral, beastly, socially degenerate, and a race to be feared and shunned." Ironically, a group of white clubwomen also appeared to defend the film and the theaters against censorship, saying opponents were overreacting.[16] The council declined action on the issue, at least at that meeting.

Beard noted, however, as in the Tacoma example, that even clubwomen did not always agree on the kind of film that should be shown. Just as women sometimes had difficulty deciding what literature should be included or omitted from collections, they also disagreed on films. According to Beard, women in New York quarreled over whether white slave films should be exhibited or prohibited, divided over the issue of whether they suggested or warned.[17]

Some advocated licensing the exhibition of films, like a public service monopoly or park concession, while others recommended a national review board as a means of control. The issue eventually became moot, an issue of social control that was out of their hands, although it resurfaced repeatedly in the twentieth century in complaints about content or calls for government or industry censorship with the diffusion of each major shift in technology, from television to the Internet.

NEW DOORS OPEN, CLUB DOORS CLOSE

After clubs accomplished many of their personal and community goals, and women walked through doors clubs helped open, members split over community priorities—especially after World War I and rising fears of radicalism. Compromise often meant choosing less compelling, less controversial study programs and plans of work. In the 1920s membership changed. Women who were leaders and most active were ready to step through other organi-

zational doors and leave the strictly female alliances in clubs behind. Some women, emboldened, took additional steps to join
working-class or social reform movements, or went into public
health work, or mobilized political groups to pressure for specific
institutional changes like Prohibition and national suffrage.[18]

In a world and time already far different from the world of the
late nineteenth century, clubs in the 1920s began to diminish as
a critical mass force even while they were enjoying unprecedented success at the federal level through alliances with other
organizations. Prohibition, suffrage, the Sheppard-Towner Act for
maternal and child health, and the federal Child Labor Amendment of 1924 all were measures that women's clubs nationally
played a role in imposing on the nation's culture. Not all groups
applauded the changes.

During World War I, the fires of international conflict that en-
gulfed the United States turned club attention to international affairs and war relief efforts. Much of it was in the form of direct aid;
some of it was in the form of a separate club movement for peace.
Pacifism conflicted with the heightened nationalism and nativis-
tic forces that the international conflict caused. Women who formerly put their differences aside to work together on domestic issues split over the issue of pacifism, especially after the United
States entered the war and in the turbulent years that followed.
The labor disputes in the Northwest and appeal of the Socialists
and the IWW (International Workers of the World) there aggra-
vated regional concerns about law and order.

The backlash against women's club activism and its domestic
agenda began to build. Its programs became symbols for subversive change and societal stress. Divisiveness grew, the membership gradually aged, and projects became much more bland and
less controversial by the end of the 1920s. The very success of the
state and national federations precipitated the revolt against
changing social conditions and gender roles. Even as the club
movement began to lose steam, a supercoalition of women's
groups emerged, including the GFWC, the WCTU, and the League
of Women Voters. In 1920, the year women's right to vote was ratified, the groups created the Women's Joint Congressional Committee (WJCC) to lobby Congress. The success of it and realization of the national goals in the 1920s, creating a panoply of
federal programs and controls, also generated stiff resistance.

When the elections of 1924 showed that women did not vote as a block, fears of their political power waned and politicians became more outspoken in their opposition at the same time that cultural debates intensified.

The list of WJCC achievements up to that point, however, included significant provisions: besides the Sheppard-Towner Act to protect women and infants and the federal child labor amendment, it included the first social security legislation, the Packers and Stockyards Control Act, the Cable Act giving independent citizenship to married women, creation of a federal prison for women, and several others prior to 1924.

The powerful WJCC dubbed its priorities the six Ps: prohibition (which came in with suffrage and went out with the Great Depression), public schools, protection of infants, physical education in the schools, peace through arms reduction, and protection of women in industry.[19] The WJCC founding members included, besides the General Federation, WCTU, and League of Women Voters, the National Consumers' League, the Congress of Mothers and Parent-Teacher Associations, National Women's Trade Union League, National Federation of Business and Professional Women's Clubs, National Council of Jewish Women, American Association of University Women, and American Home Economics Association. It indeed constituted a powerful lobby, perhaps too powerful.

Women now ran the federal Children's Bureau and implemented the public health programs of the Sheppard-Towner Maternity and Infancy Act. That led to a challenge from the male-dominated medical establishment threatened by women running a federally supported clinical public health program. The American Medical Association attacked the Sheppard-Towner Act as communistic, and the National Association Opposed to Woman Suffrage called suffrage, socialism, and feminism the three branches of the tree of social revolution even before 1920. The backlash was symbolized at the national level by the 1924 "spider web" controversy tied directly to the WJCC.

It began with circulation of a chart introduced into a congressional hearing. The chart emerged in and was circulated by the War Department, angered by the Women's International League for Peace and Freedom and its attacks on military appropriations and policies. Although the league was not part of the WJCC, many members of it—like Jane Addams—were leaders in organizations that were. The chart's lines linked leaders of feminist, peace, and socialist organizations into a conspiratorial directorate that was called subversive and destructive to the nation's moral order. Names on the list included reform leaders with long careers, such as Catt, Addams, and Kelley.

It was distorted or false, but, like many favorite anecdotes repeated by politicians, the chart was hard to repudiate. It served the purpose of further casting doubt on all politically active women's groups and their goals. All female reformers became "pink sisters." It put many clubs and their leaders in retreat and left them defensive. The slide toward more and more government intervention and responsibility for social welfare slowed, at least for the time being. Even the hard-fought Child Labor Amendment, passed by Congress, failed to get national ratification. Its critics cast it as a radical plot to destroy American families or as unwise social engineering that would coddle children, corrupt family values, and bankrupt taxpayers, as Washington's Governor Roland Hartley and others claimed. Washington, in a bitter blow to forty years of club activism, voted against ratifying the amendment prohibiting child labor. Even the Children's Bureau was challenged by patriotic women's groups and others; the agency and its programs were demonized as radical.

As the 1920s came to a close, club priorities moved away from direct political action. State and national federation convention resolutions focused increasingly on the safe issues of literacy campaigns, art projects and contests, and community beautification. Membership dropped, and clubs fell away from federation involvement. The Red scare, labor unrest, social changes, and the backlash against women all took their toll. Clubwomen's progressive zeal either evaporated or found a channel elsewhere. Increasingly society itself seemed to withdraw from contentious public issues, weary of war and world turmoil. Many retreated into a private world of entertainment, pleasure, and sensationalism. Others clung to traditional values for protective cover.

It had become a society seemingly quite removed from the selfless idealism of the turn-of-the-century clubwomen striving for uplift, self-improvement, and civic betterment. The Northwest's turbulent labor history and conflicts heightened concerns about radicalism of all sorts in the culture. Most of the programs and legislation held, ingrained by then, but the cultural shift reinforced conservatism and stalled the movement as a whole.

Lasting Changes

But during the decades on either side of 1900 women's clubs had influenced the course of the region and the nation with regard to many educational, philanthropic, and reform questions of the day. They affected culture, politics, and policies in those pivotal decades spanning the shift from an agrarian century to an industrial one and from small settlements to thriving cities. They ameliorated some of the worst effects of the shift and of the development of the Northwest.

On the national level, the General Federation played its role in the creation of some major federal programs, such as the Pure Food Bureau in 1907 (forerunner of the Food and Drug Administration), the Children's Bureau in 1912, and the Women's Bureau in 1920, all part of its legislative agenda, and the culmination of dozens of smaller community and state efforts. Indeed, the huge and influential federation itself had become the object of lobbying. "Certain groups immediately ask for our yearbook and immediately make appeal for financial or other assistance," Oregon's Evans said, adding that there were many good causes, too many. "We must protect the group and its reputation."[20]

In addition to the changes that came with world war, women's increasing entry into the work force at all levels before, during, and after the war changed the woman's study club movement irrevocably. The changes combined to spell the beginning of the end of the power the federations held statewide and nationwide, although the federations continued as umbrella organizations.

Clubs, having realized many of their political and cultural goals, found others insoluble or their remedies inadequate to meet the needs. The movement seemed to waver over what direction to follow next. The club "spirit of the age," that sense of limitless potential for self-improvement and civic improvement through organized womanhood, began to dissipate. The single-issue push for women's right to vote nationally captured some club leaders; new professional alliances and organizations captured others.

The majority of the membership seemed left behind in clubs of decreasing relevance later in the twentieth century, soon to undergo the stresses of the Great Depression, the indictment and scapegoating of the failures of Prohibition, the social and programmatic upheaval of the 1930s, and then yet another great war. The realization of maternalism and the domestic ideal, always a powerful motivator and organizing factor in society, seemed ever

more remote, yet few recognized changes the clubs had already
wrought as a social movement.

<h2 style="text-align:center">VALUE UNMEASURED</h2>

The massive 1898 history of the women's club movement by Jane
Croly, compiled when the movement was still very young and
much of the Northwest was in villages or vacant, said the club
movement had already accomplished two purposes. "It provided a
means for the acquisition of knowledge, the training of power; and
the working of a spirit of human solidarity, a comprehension of
the continuity of life, its universal character and interdepen-
dence." Further, the acceptance of the club "as a means of education and development was almost simultaneous throughout
the country." Everywhere groups of women seized the idea "and
shaped it according to their own conditions and needs."[21]

The women who helped shape communities in the deserts,
farmland, and forests of the Pacific Northwest helped create its
culture and build its material environment. They did this not in
the railroads and engines of commerce or capital favored by historians like Bancroft, but in the libraries, schools, sidewalks,
parks, programs, institutions, ordinances, and statutes that made
the communities more than hospitable; they gave them depth,
stability, and order and made humane treatment of disadvantaged
segments of the population mandatory. Their alternative vision
countered the transience, rawness, tawdriness, and predatory
commerce they found in the Northwest's towns, and they persuaded those in power to support that vision. Their political
struggle and cultural imperatives contributed more than dollars
to their communities and states, although dollars and products
were easiest to measure.

Writing of another part of the country, historian Sandra
Schackel found that the New Mexico Federation of Women's Clubs
formed in 1911 played a critical role in bringing social reform and
services to that state's population as well. She calls them "agents
of change." It is an apt label. There, as in the Northwest, she found
needs far outstripped the capacities of voluntarism. Clubwomen
soon realized they had to integrate their work into governmental
priorities, and this required political skills.[22]

In virtually every large and small knot of humanity throughout
the Northwest, women banded together for some lofty and often
personal purpose and left something behind that did not exist be-

fore, in a collection of books in a library, a row of trees, a lecture series held, scholarships awarded, or wage and hour laws passed. They did it without benefit of the political and economic power men in the communities enjoyed and engaged in a public struggle for the allocation of resources to their ideas.

The Northwest's leaders generally were not financially wealthy, but were wealthy in education and empowered by the study club process itself. Women with college degrees and professional training sometimes made clubwork their profession as well as their life's work. They moved easily from study to suffrage to reform and back again.

Collectively they brought to the Northwest an end to the worst forms of child labor, raised the age of consent to sexual activity for girls, established property rights for married women, enacted protective social controls (such as Sunday closings of saloons and bans on gambling), built and furnished libraries all over the three states (and created the commissions and taxation policies that guaranteed their survival), brought cultural events, standards, and enrichment to distant communities, supported domestic science as part of the curriculum, improved the legal treatment of juveniles, established laws and policies on food purity and standard weights and measures, established and beautified playgrounds and parks, began environmental protections through conservation, created programs for disabled populations, got institutions constructed for juveniles outside the jails, helped pass establish protective labor laws that set wage and hour limits, and helped get women the right to vote. All these provisions, later taken for granted as part of the region's culture and structure, can be counted among the legacies of women's clubs throughout the Pacific Northwest.

Clubwomen as Candidates and Leaders

Women's club leaders in the Northwest became successful candidates. They were appointed regents and elected school trustees, city council members, legislators, and even mayor of a city like Seattle. The numbers of women in elected office were never great, then or during the decades that followed, but their presence lent impetus to the changes in women's status and society's nature that many in the club movement sought. It also demonstrated women's ability to govern themselves, to be part of the public sphere, to handle the complexities of politics.

One writer in 1893 claimed that the future would see gender boundaries obliterated in associations. Although women should always maintain separate clubs as a means to "acquire courage and independence, and learn the limitation of their own personal rights and respect for those of others," she wrote, the club of the future would not be composed of either women or men only. "Together they will study political economy, municipal government, scientific charity, compulsory and universal education, the labor question or some other of the social problems that to-day are crowding aside the purely aesthetic topics. . . . A diviner ideal of national life than is presented by our splendid material civilization will compel their advance," Mary Livermore wrote over a century ago.

"They will arraign the mis-government of our demoralized cities; dissect the fallacies and falsities of demagogues and machine politicians, that would submerge the nation in dishonor; and teach that manhood and womanhood are the ultimate end of everyone's life, rather than money-making or industrial skill," she hoped. Indeed, "the Club of the Future will address itself to the great problem of living. It will question poverty, crime, disease, education, economics, religion and all that pertains to society, with the aim of lessening the dreariness of human life, enlarging its scope, and lifting its horizon."[23]

That noble vision for organized womanhood, as with most visions, is yet to be realized. By the end of the twentieth century, when the majority of women had become part of the work force, nonprofit organizations suffered from a decline in volunteer labor, and government at all levels replaced some of that loss to society. Near the year 2000 politicians in power began to call for a return to community and individual benevolence as an alternative to burgeoning government funding, with limited success. Women, already stressed by multiple roles as wife, mother, and wage-earner, and often caregiver to aging parents, were not likely to assume responsibility for community caretaking through voluntary association, even if they had the inclination to do so.

Marvin Olasky, in a book cited by Speaker of the House Newt Gingrich and others called *The Tragedy of American Compassion*,[24] argues that government programs generally perpetuated poverty. Olasky believes that providing the disadvantaged with money, food, clothes, and other basics did not lift them out of poverty like the personal and spiritual aid from private organizations that could transform their lives. Aid should be offered in exchange for pledges to change behavior, he suggests, hearkening back to the days when aid carried with it pledges of sobriety or church attendance.

Some of the rhetoric in the debates about welfare and immigration near the year 2000 sounded like it came from 1900: this time the ideas had new labels for old categories such as the "deserving poor" and the "dangerous classes." What to do about these categories and their drain on public coffers continued to be debated. While some criticized Olasky's thinking as romanticizing nineteenth-century behavior standards (and the women-run organizations devoted to charity work), others saw in it a statement of the need for citizens to turn away from government and back to the community and one another to meet societal needs.

Ideas of voluntarism and charity seemed all the more attractive in the face of a mounting deficit and perceptions of failing federal programs, failing government workers (labeled bureaucrats), and calls for major welfare reform. The gender role divisions connected to ideas of voluntarism and community welfare were unstated, but lay not very far under the surface of the arguments.

OLD PROBLEMS, NEW NAMES

Some of the concerns about work that aroused clubwomen a century ago remained concerns of women at the end of the century, although they too went by different names. Day care and vacation schools for children of working mothers, working conditions for women, intractable wage differentials, child labor and abuse, public health programs, consumer rights, equity for women in employment and education—the parallels are striking despite the changes in social programs and market regulation since 1900.

Perhaps the difference is one of degree. Women found a bleak situation outside their doors in the nineteenth century. Now no one questions the need for government regulation of working conditions or consumer protection, for laws to protect children, for educational equity and access, for sanitary food and water supplies enforced through standards, inspection, and regulation, or for programs to keep people from starving in this rich country. That in itself marks the success of organized womanhood.

One of the shortcomings of that success was a flawed assumption at the movement's core about government aid for women and children supplanting a male's absence rather than as a societal investment. Indeed, one of the primary complaints about welfare at the end of the twentieth century was that changed social policies and attitudes had removed the stigmatization of unwed mothers. Yet traditional families who were part of "the working poor" were not eligible for much aid.

The model could have been different, although it was not fully in the hands of economically and politically disadvantaged clubwomen to change the policies, especially when they collaborated by using domestic ideology to gain what power they had. The focus could have been on family benefits and the support services families needed to survive intact, focusing on children as a national resource rather than on compensating for the lack of a male breadwinner. Another factor was that our economic system placed no financial value on and offered no recognition for women's domestic toil, despite its contributions both to family and to the national economy. Women who fought for women's rights over the decades ended up fighting for women's access to men's jobs, positions, and organizations, trying to corner a seat at the table of economic and political power, rather than fighting for enhanced recognition of women's traditional work within the economy as partner and producer. They gravitated away from what was already undervalued, including women's organizations, as I did.

The future of women's organizations is far from certain. In 1994 the General Federation of Women's Clubs, a shadow of its former self, counted 350,000 members in 8,500 clubs, far from its million-member mark when the population was much smaller, but significant nonetheless.[25] An important new dimension for the national organization was its growing international focus, helping women in other countries where they could benefit greatly from the empowerment and the programs the federation provides. In many parts of the world, women are without the legal, political, educational, and other rights clubwomen helped gain in the United States many decades ago.

For women's organizations to prosper in future in the United States there perhaps will have to be less formal structures and more flexibility in terms of time demands. They will also need again to concur on a collective vision, perhaps the hardest step of all. Yet there is still much to be gained from women joining together, working collectively both for their own enrichment and to change the world or at least their communities. There are still grand possibilities for organized womanhood, and many needs to be addressed.

APPENDIX

The following list includes names, sites, and deeds not detailed
in the text of a number of women's study clubs between 1875 and
1915. Categorized by state and alphabetized by city, this list reflects extant records of the more active study clubs uncovered in
research for this project. It is therefore not to be taken as a comprehensive listing of all women's club activity in the Northwest,
nor are all cities that had influential women's clubs represented
by any means.

IDAHO CLUBS

ASHTON
In 1910 fifteen women formed the Ashton Woman's Study Club,
organized strictly as a literary club. However, it helped raise funds
for many civic projects and in 1914 established a public library.[1]

BLACKFOOT
In 1900 eight women created a study club called the Current
Event Club. It joined the federation in 1901 and started a library
staffed by clubwomen in 1916.

CALDWELL
The 1894 Progressive Club established a reading room that had
no permanent home until 1901, when it occupied a room in city
hall. In 1901 the disbanded WCTU was asked to donate its 200
books as a nucleus for the library, supplemented by donation of a
100-volume library from Captain J. M. Wells. The reading room,
financed through monthly subscriptions of 25 cents to $1, was
heated with sagebrush because coal was too expensive. The Forward Club formed about 1900; it changed its name to the Village

Improvement Society in 1907. It established a small library turned over to the Carnegie Library.

COEUR D'ALENE

The Coeur d'Alene Woman's Club, with forty-six members, started a library in 1904 after a book reception netted 234 volumes and $24. The women used shelves in a grocery store for the books and kept the library open three afternoons a week. It moved to a bank building, supported through club fundraising and subscriptions, until the city council took over operations in 1909.

IDAHO FALLS

The Round Table Club began in 1896 for study, culture, and what it called recognition of public responsibility. It also founded what became the Idaho Falls public library. Historian Mary Ritter Beard praised the Idaho Falls "city mothers" in the Village Improvement Society here, who planted hundreds of trees along streets, turning the "treeless, grassless desert village" into an oasis. The group also bought land for a town park, started a hospital, founded a library, improved the cemetery, and supplied alleys with garbage boxes. Moreover, they bought the site "of a nest of vile resorts and caused the removal of tenants," Beard wrote.[2]

KELLOGG

Fourteen women in Wardner organized the Wardner Reading Club in 1900, moving it to Kellogg in 1910. Kellogg also had a New Century Club, an outgrowth of a men's club. Members set up a reading room, studied parliamentary law, held programs and socials, and worked on a city library.

LEWISTON

The Tsceminicum Club started in 1889. Forty women joined forces for community projects "and the mental stimulus of study derived from programs presented by its members." Within a year that included work on a public library, located first in the council chambers, which became the Carnegie Library of Lewiston. It studied art, literature, music, and drama and in 1899 began a series of benefits to buy books, accumulating 4,000 volumes in five years. The Carnegie Foundation's grant of $10,000 led to a library in Pioneer Park built in 1903–4. In 1900 the Twentieth Century

Club organized. Its purpose: "To present and consider practical methods for securing to women higher physical, intellectual, and moral conditions with a view to the improvement of all social and domestic relations."[3] It had three departments, civic and current events, art and literature, and home and education. It helped create Travis Park and contributed signs and scholarships to Lewiston State Normal School, now Lewis-Clark State College.

MACKAY

The Woman's Club was organized in 1907. It began as the Matron's Thimble Club, for "mutual help in fine needlework and promotion of sociability among its members."[4] By 1909 it had outgrown that name and incorporated to buy property for a library building it gave to the city in 1916.

MALAD

In 1914 the Malad Home Culture Club began a library and reading room as part of its civic work, starting with 152 books. Used largely by children in the community, it was open twice a week.

MOSCOW

The first settlers in Moscow arrived in 1871 from Walla Walla or eastern Oregon. In 1890 it had a population of 2,000 and became the site of the University of Idaho, which by 1896 had two literary societies, the Amphictyon and Websterian. The wife of the first president, Jennie (Mrs. Franklin) Gault, invited six faculty wives to meet with her in 1892 to read and discuss books. Named the Pleiades, the group joined the General Federation of Women's Clubs in 1895 and helped create the state federation in 1905. The club generally focused on the study of Shakespeare, but developed four departments: literature, home, education, and philanthropy. It maintained a membership of about fifteen and met biweekly. The club promoted courses in domestic science and manual training for the high school and developed city beautification projects such as parks.

For the 1893 Columbian Exposition, the women created and designed a "gold and silver book" made from Idaho metals studded with rubies and opals from Latah County, which still serves a ceremonial function in the UI president's office. The Ladies' Historical Club began in 1895 with thirty members under Mary

(Mrs. J. H.) Forney while she was on the board for Pleiades. In 1901 three members of the Pleiades Club joined with three members of the Historical Club to begin a door-to-door campaign for enough pledges to create a centrally located public library in Moscow. They used the $340 they raised to turn a small upstairs reading room in the old Brown's Furniture building downtown into the city's library, managing to keep it open some afternoons and evenings. It contained 150 books, a $15 stove, a half ton of coal, a 15-cent shovel, and a table with twelve chairs.[5] In 1903 the city's first library board consisted of Pleiades members Emma Little and Frances Butterfield, Historical Club members Mary Forney and Mrs. Charles Shields, and a city council member. They began corresponding with the Carnegie foundation. In 1904 they were granted $10,000, and the public library opened in 1906. However, the very first libraries appeared in Moscow in 1885. One collection was managed by a Moscow women's reading society, later disbanded, and the other was in a law office.

MOUNTAIN HOME
Mountain Home had, besides the Entre Nous and Sub Rosa clubs described earlier, the Artemisia Club, created in 1900 with thirty members, devoted to civic improvement. A beet sugar company gave them an acre of land adjoining the school grounds for creation of a playground or park for which they raised funds. The Entre Nous literary study club, limited to twenty members for two years, maintained a free reading room and library until a city board assumed it in 1902 and sought a tax levy for its maintenance.

NEW MEADOWS
In 1908 the Woman's Club of the Meadows was founded for mutual improvement. Members consisted primarily of former teachers.

PAYETTE
The Portia Club, organized in 1895, began as a cultural club, named by a member who had belonged to women's clubs in Chicago. It focused on literature and parliamentary procedure. The club started the Payette library in 1912, building it by buying postcards to send to friends asking for donated books. They opened the library with 500 books in two rooms over the old post office, staffing it on Tuesdays and Thursdays.

POCATELLO

The Women's Study League of Pocatello began in 1896 with five women who organized it for study and mutual improvement. It bought reference works to use for programs, which in turn formed the nucleus for the public library. It helped set up and broaden the curricula of the Academy of Idaho, which ultimately became Idaho State University. It also secured speakers and set up student loans.

RATHDRUM

In 1906 the Twentieth Century Reading Circle began for self-improvement and study of literature. The club also maintained a small park and sponsored a library for the town.

RUPERT

The 1915 Pansy Club of eighteen rural women who lived north-west of Rupert sought to relieve the isolation of their lives. Rupert also had the 1908 Pioneer Social Club, which studied topics such as the problems of farm life, better schools, and raising chickens and turkeys. It also canned fruits for a children's home. A Village Improvement League put swings and chairs and planted a hundred trees in a park. In 1908 the Helping Hand Club members began convening to do handwork such as quilts and carpets. They donated supplies to the various area charities. In 1905 the Century Culture Club, a literary and social club, provided lyceum courses, sponsored an art exhibit, and started a movement for women's public restrooms. It was considered an "elite" (and stuffy) group by the other women.[6]

ST. MARIES

In St. Maries, the Women's Study Club organized in 1907 as the CCC Club (for culture, courtesy, and courage). Limited to twenty members, the group studied countries, discussed "questions of the day," and established a public library. Members raised enough money to buy the lots where the library was ultimately located.

SHOSHONE

In 1902 in Shoshone, fifteen women met to form the Liberal Thought Club. It began a small reading room with thirty volumes and from 1904 to 1914 managed a trust fund for care of the cemetery. In 1908 it began community clean-up work, planted trees, and founded parks. Ultimately the Liberal Thought Club changed its name to the Civic Club.

TWIN FALLS

The Twentieth Century Club, formed in 1906 as the Syringa Club, had a membership initially limited to ten with an initiation fee of $1 and dues of $1. Its programs focused on American history, music, art, and literature. Within five years it had one hundred members and began taking on civic causes.

WALLACE

The 1907 Wallace Study Club began with twenty-seven members. Meetings featured speakers. A benefit play in 1910 raised $110 for the new library. With two other organizations, it also established and furnished a Community Assembly Room.

WEISER

In 1899 a group of women found themselves continually irritated by mud in the streets of the small town. The Outlook Club was born to help resolve that problem and took on other civic projects. Under president Mary Butterfield's leadership it started a library the same year "to provide some place other than the saloons where men and boys might spend their evenings."[7] In a second-floor room of an office building, it was staffed from 7 to 10:30 P.M. Furniture consisted of a table, a few chairs, and a lamp, and broomsticks served as newspaper racks. Members donated old magazines and books and one current newspaper until forty books were obtained through a social in 1900 and added. The Outlook Club raised more money with plays, dinners, and baby shows.

OREGON CLUBS

ASTORIA

Beautification was the overriding civic goal of the Woman's Club. The newspaper editor wrote in 1902 that "until the Woman's Club came into active existence unsightly shacks were to be seen in many parts of the city, while here and there piles of rubbish emphasized our carelessness. The club is making a noble effort to beautify Astoria and the success of its work, thus far, is indeed encouraging." The club also sent traveling libraries "to the adjacent towns and logging camps along the river, where they are much appreciated."[8]

CORVALLIS

The purpose of the Corvallis Firemen's Coffee Club of 1883 was to procure refreshments for firemen. These community volunteers equipped with a hand pumper to draw water from cisterns were accustomed to slaking their thirst at saloons after fires, often coming home drunk. The eight charter members, identified in a club history as social and intellectual leaders and in the Oregon WCTU history as "white ribboners,"[9] decided to serve beverages paid for by collections at businesses, dues, and fines for missing club meetings. They raised additional funds through picnics, dances, and amateur theatricals.

In subsequent civic projects, the club raised $100 toward construction of the first building on the new Oregon State College campus and held a moonlight excursion on the river to raise money to buy it a flag. In 1888 the Coffee Club voted to subscribe to a magazine for a "free reading room." The women initially had provided reading material for the firemen, then allowed the public to use the materials. By 1896 the club had eighty members and supported a library. In 1899 it sought a public library. The club's library was open two days a week "to give a practical demonstration of the advantages of a free public library."[10] The club rented a house, bought more books, hired a librarian, and later purchased the property that the city eventually assumed.

In 1902 a Coffee Club committee worked to rid the City Hall of ashes and unsightly material, planted trees around public buildings and streets (even carrying water for the plants from their homes), and contacted the city attorney asking "how much liberty was allowed to neighbor's chickens." Club activism led to the founding of a separate Improvement League in 1905. The civic betterment of this club contrasted with other early Corvallis clubs, such as the 1893 Law and Order League to take care of "undesirable conditions," and perhaps the earliest club, an 1880 men's Cricket Club.

In 1914, when the City Council agreed to house the library the Coffee Club created, the club adopted a broader purpose, "to create an organized center of thought and action among women for the promotion of social educational, literary, and ethical growth and whatever relates to the best interests of our city and state."[11] It became the Woman's Club, open to all women, and bought a clubhouse, which it used for Red Cross activities during World War I. The renamed group helped develop and maintain an Arts Center, contributed a $4,500 organ to the high school, and sponsored lectures, exhibits, musicals, hobby shows, and drama groups. It backed public health programs, the war effort, and other causes.[12] Its motto became "Growth through Service."

EUGENE

Construction of the Oregon and California railroad line in 1871 brought new growth to the 1846 settlement, including the University of Oregon in 1872. The Fortnightly Club began meeting in 1893, "to bring together women interested in artistic, economic, philanthropic, literary, scientific and social pursuits, with a view of rendering them helpful to each other and useful to society."[13]

GARDINER

Organized to study art, the Gardiner Woman's Literary Club was founded by eleven women in 1905, with the motto "I seek to know." The group of twenty-one met Saturday afternoons, with members bringing a work by one of the "masters" to discuss the work of the artist. The artistic aspects of the club gradually gave way to practical questions, such as "Should ethics be taught in the public schools?"; "The substitution of steam and electricity for the labor of men and animals"; "How shall we train our daughters?"; and "Does society need a leader?" In 1895 it celebrated Christmas by producing a play, *Those Women,* written by Mildred Fuller Wallace, acted entirely by club members under the supervision of the author. The club was approached to produce the play again on behalf of several charities. Gardiner women then decided to study English history and mythology, and in 1907 they began discussing current topics, such as the danger of skyscrapers, American prisoners in Russia, the immigration of girls to America, new songbirds, and Teddy Roosevelt's popularity. Later, roll calls covered such diverse topics as use of compressed air to raise sunken ships, leaving "In God We Trust" off coins, and damage to roads by autos. In 1908 it raised money for a bandstand. Afterward money raised went for relief in China and in 1914 for cotton sent to hospitals in Austria for wounded soldiers.

GRANT'S PASS

The Woman's Club through lobbying and "agitation" made it possible for the city to get $10,000 from the Carnegie Foundation for a library building in 1903. It had earlier pushed for a special election setting up a levy of two mills for the city to raise the needed

$1,000 for the library's annual maintenance. The club produced materials for the building (which also was to contain a gymnasium) and later collected donated books for the shelves.

LA GRANDE

The Neighborhood Club, formed in the 1890s, became a social, civic, and literary force in the town. It was organized by seven women, initially for social and literary improvement. It grew to 335 members by 1920 in this small ranching town and established a lengthy record as sponsor of the city's cultural activities.

MONMOUTH

Besides the Monmouth Literary Association briefly described earlier, Monmouth had the 1914 Priscilla Club, whose object was "social intercourse." It was open to female instructors of the Oregon Normal School, with other members by invitation. Maggie Butler, secretary of the literary association, was president of this club, which began with a focus on needlecraft. However, within three months of its founding the group expanded to discussion of favorite authors, domestic science demonstrations, and so on. Two months later it sent delegates to a regional meeting and by the end of 1915 began taking up health issues. During World War I, it made bandages, socks, and handkerchiefs for the Red Cross, eventually suspending club meetings after deciding "all their time and energies should be spent on Red Cross work and all other work of importance that will help in any way to win the war."[14]

ONTARIO

In 1906 seven women founded the Work and Win Club, which later became the Ontario Study Club. Its founders wanted to establish a reading room, which eventually resulted in a public library.

PENDLETON

Pendleton, platted in 1870, became the center of east Oregon's cattle industry. One of the oldest study clubs in Oregon was the Current Literature Club here. Organized in 1894, it was a "lineal descendant" of the 1890 Tourists Club, believed to be the oldest women's study club in Pendleton, founded at the home of Maria Clopton (Mrs. C. S.) Jackson. After her publisher husband died, she and her family donated a 90-acre parcel in Portland that became Sam Jackson Park. The Tourists Club changed its name when the initial group of armchair tourists decided to turn to the literature of the countries it had studied. Besides taking up study, the club's activists also established the first city restroom for country women and with other clubs helped build the Umatilla County Library.

The 1891 Thursday Afternoon Club began when Belle Bishop invited a group of booklovers to join a social and study club. Programs focused on broad cultural concepts, such as beauty, rather than specific authors or works. It celebrated anniversaries by inviting men to a dinner for toasting and teasing. It had departments of literature, art, music, belles-lettres, and Greek history, art, and literature and claimed the title of first Oregon club to join the national federation in 1894, due to Adelia D. (Mrs. C. B.) Wade's efforts. The first biennial meeting of the state federation was in Pendleton in 1900 when Wade became federation president. Like other clubs, this club's purpose was study, but it soon added social and civic betterment. Also, the Woman's Club was organized in Pendleton as the Library Club in 1908. It raised $2,000 for books and furnishings for the county library. It became the Civic Club in 1910 and the Woman's Club in 1919.

PORTLAND

The influential Council of Jewish Women already had 260 members by 1903. Organized in 1895, its philanthropic work (described in part earlier) included establishing schools in the populous district of south Portland and running a sewing school on Monday afternoons for sixty to eighty girls, a manual training school on Tuesdays, and a domestic science program on Thursdays. "These schools are absolutely free and non-sectarian, the percentage of Jewish children seldom reaching half the attendance," wrote Blanche Blumauer in a club publication.[15] It also erected Neighborhood House, a settlement house providing social services. Some of the other Portland groups are described in chapter 6.

ROSEBURG

The town, founded in 1851, became the county seat in 1854. After the Oregon and California Railroad built southward through Roseburg, it became an important lumbering town. The Roseburg Woman's Club (formed in 1895 as the Mental Culture Club) lamented living in a city without a park. In 1903 it created one, strong-arming Cobb Real Estate Company for a site that the club fenced and improved.

SALEM

A coffee club existed as of 1882. Salem, the territorial capital in 1851, saw growth as residents returning from the gold fields brought money to invest. Paddlewheel steamers brought goods, and in 1871 the railroad came from Portland. In 1882 some Salem women, like those in the Corvallis Coffee Club, began serving coffee to Salem's volunteer firemen. The Ladies' Coffee Club later that same year appointed a committee to purchase window curtains for the hall and find a half-cord of wood. The record does not show what happened to the Ladies' Coffee Club. In 1903 a group of women formed the Marion Square Improvement League, raising $1,000 to beautify Marion Square, a tract in the center of the state capital covered with a grove of firs. The women planned to carve out space for a bandstand and a fountain and lay walks to improve and brighten the grounds.

WASHINGTON CLUBS

ABERDEEN

In 1892 a group of women organized to establish a free reading room with a few books. They had a membership fee of $1 and dues of 25 cents. Following the club tradition, they helped get a Carnegie library built in 1908.

BELLINGHAM

In 1900 the PLF Club was founded with this commanding motto: "The world is advancing, advance with it."[16] It had several study committees, including progress, civic, economics, music, and literature. In 1915 fourteen of its fifty members were single.

CENTRALIA

The Ladies of the Round Table, organized in 1895, believed that "reading should teach us how to search for the truth; meditation, how to find it." Members answered roll calls with current events, and membership was limited to twenty-five. In addition, Centralia had a Swastika Club, founded in 1910. Its programs included book reviews, the national parks, and various nations, adding social problems later.

CHENEY

In 1906 the Tillicum Club wanted to establish a city park and playground and told the city it would take responsibility for its development. Members solicited donations, not only of money, but also of labor and supplies. They created a bandstand, picnic tables, shade trees, and a playground. Named Sutton Park, it was maintained by the club for thirty years until the city took it over.[17]

CLARKSTON

The Sacajawea Club had two broad departments, intellectual and social. In 1911 its twenty-four members studied Washington Irving, William Cullen Bryant, and Oliver Wendell Holmes as representatives of American literature. Its motto was "Look forward, not back."[18]

DAYTON

Dayton had several clubs, one of them organized before 1900 to promote literary culture and the public library. That group called itself the Ladies' Educational Aid Society.

DUNGENESS

Gertie Seavey, the single bookkeeper of the Mercantile Store, discussed the lack of social contacts with Mrs. Hayes Evans, and they decided to start a club. Eight women came to their meeting and created the Women's Improvement Club in 1906. They initially called themselves the PassTime Club and set dues at 5 cents a meeting. Noting that the three narrow bridges from the creamery corner into town were dangerous to pedestrians when horses and buggies passed, their first project was practical—to build sidewalks there. The club changed its name and began hosting dinners to raise money for "further town improvements."[19] Gradually afternoon meetings became evening meetings, and husbands began accompanying members, playing cards while the women met. In 1921 the group joined the federation and acquired its own clubhouse.

ELLENSBURG

The WCTU union left a drinking fountain in the city's center. By 1900 Ellensburg had several women's clubs. One was the Ladies' Municipal Improvement Society. A member donated two lots in town for the site of the future library. The Improvement Society ran a reading room with donated newspapers and books in the 1890s and led the campaign for a public library. In 1908 the city received $100,000 for a building. Funds for books also came from the Friday and Gallina clubs.[20]

EVERETT

The Woman's Book Club emerged in 1894, and by 1898 members had organized the Everett Public Library. The club began at the home of Mrs. C. C. Brown, later a president of the state federation. The library in the old city hall received 1,000 books from the club in 1898, some 600 from other clubs, and 400 more from the Everett women themselves. The club became the Columbian Woman's Book Club. By 1916–17 the club was taking up issues such as "practical suggestions for benevolent work by a club," "foremothers' day," and "why women should register and vote." At that point it had fifty-five members, divided among the mothers', literature, science and travel, art, and language departments.

GIG HARBOR

The Ladies' Fortnightly Club by 1916–17 devoted itself entirely to social welfare issues. In September it was child welfare issues, such as open air schools, the Children's Bureau, juvenile courts, parental schools, and childhood songs. In October it was motion pictures, and in November legislation of interest to women and prison reform.

GOLDENDALE

The Women's Association began in 1912 "to stimulate the social, literary, and educational advancement of the people of Goldendale and vicinity, and to initiate, recommend, and cooperate in any beneficial movement pertaining to civic work."[21] Its membership was open, and dues were $1. In 1915 it included library, social, legislative, educational, and benevolent committees. In addition, it sponsored a library day, a welfare day, and a town civics day.

HOQUIAM

The Women's Club, founded in 1908, pushed for a city library under the terms of the Carnegie Foundation grant, but it was not approved by the city until 1911. The primary movers were Mrs. Henry Patton, Mrs. Joseph Stearns, Mary Stuart, and Ruth McKee. McKee became a statewide leader.[22]

KALAMA

The Kalama Woman's Club, founded in 1912, promoted "intellectual advancement" and "general culture." It established a city library, donated prints to it, raised money for it through producing
an annual play, and worked for a "better class of motion picture."[23]

OLYMPIA

In 1880 Olympia (formerly called Smithfield) had 1,532 people.
By contrast, Tacoma had 1,098 and Seattle 3,533. The first club
in Washington Territory recognized by the General Federation as
a member was the Olympia Woman's Club, founded in 1883, the
year Willard came calling on the Northwest. The Olympia club
had a membership of fifty. More ritualized than most women's
clubs, it had special rules of order and even a burial service, bor-
rowing from the fraternal orders. In fact, it was the first woman's
club in the country to develop initiation and installation ceremonies, according to Jane Croly, who termed the group conservative and exclusive. The club issued honorary membership and
traveling certificates under seal, the latter to vouch for the "good
standing" of the member. Character was the only stated qualification for membership, and the club said all classes and opinions
were represented, although its initiation fee of $10 and annual
dues of $3 must have deterred many. In addition to the colors and
flower, this club had an insignia, a blue enameled silver bar pin.
Its motto was "United they assist."

The Olympia Woman's Club, organized for "self-improvement,"
consisted initially of nine women studying topics like "My Idea of
a Good Dinner," "How I Clean My House," and "What Shall We Do
with Our Girls?"[24] Later, however, it devoted an entire year to
the study of Washington laws relating to women. The club's creation was inspired by Mary Shelton, who had attended a self-improvement club meeting in San Francisco. Of the dozen women
invited to the first meeting, only two could come without con-
sulting their husbands. About the same time another club began,
but it veered in a very different direction. Originally the Olympia
Woman's Literary Club, it elected suffrage leader Abigail (Mrs.
A. H.) Stuart president. Initially the group met not in a home, but
in a room rented for 50 cents a night. The club's parties became
social events, and in 1907 the club used its money to buy a small
clubhouse. By 1909 the club had amassed a library of over 1,000
volumes, which it donated to the city.

The Olympia Woman's Literary Club charter members included Universalist church pastor Sarah Whitney and Thurston County school superintendent Pamela C. Hale, who was also a founding member of the State Teacher's Association in 1889. Member Janet Shotwell Moore later became president of the state federation. She headed the primary department of Olympia's schools for thirty years. A particular concern was the unsanitary public drinking cup and towel that came with all public restrooms. She led a lobbying effort backed by the federation that persuaded the legislature to impose more sanitary conditions. Other Olympia clubs included the 1899 Eenati Club.

OMAK
The 1912 Country Club's programs and civic efforts focused on flower shows, better babies programs, health issues, and music.

PORT ANGELES
The motto of the 1893 Reading Club was "No entertainment is so cheap as reading, nor any pleasure so lasting." The Woman's Literary Club (1897) had programs ranging from the "cause of the increase of crime" to "life of Beethoven" to "jellies and pickles." Its purpose was "mental instruction and the promotion of friendship among its members." Its membership was open, and its motto came from Longfellow, "Act in the living present." Over the years its programs became increasingly more oriented to the political process and social problems.[25]

PULLMAN
White settlers first came in the 1870s, and the city incorporated in 1888. The sharply rolling hills of the Palouse offered up rich harvests. The territorial government gave the town a land-grant university that became Washington State University, first called the Washington State Agricultural College and School of Sciences, sited in Pullman in 1889, only eight miles from what became Idaho's land-grant university at Moscow. Pullman's Fortnightly Club began in 1893, when Hattie Bryan, wife of the college's president, invited a group of women together to create a club for literary study. It was limited to twenty-five members, with dues of $2 and initiation fees of $2. This club was one of the region's most long-lived, celebrating its centennial in 1994. Early Pullman groups were the Ingleside Club and Pullman Historical Club

(1904). Pullman had no permanent library until 1930. However, the Fortnightly Club gave Pullman one of its first parks early in the century. The 2.5-acre plot purchased by the club, Thatuna Park, was deeded to the city.

PUYALLUP

The forerunner of the Women's Club, the Teacup Club, helped develop Pioneer Park at the site of the homestead Ezra Meeker had donated to the city. The five-acre spot soon had a playground, picnic area, and garden. It also became the setting for the Carnegie Library, which grew out of the club's work, and a community hall.[26]

RAYMOND

The 1911 Tuesday Club had as its theme "always seeking the highest."[27] Programs were arranged in debates, with group discussions and outside speakers. Members who had reference books were asked to loan them to the club for members' use to study particular topics. Issues such as the double standard in divorce, economic independence, women in industry, prison reform, and "the Negro" dominated programs and discussions.

SEATTLE

In addition to the clubs described in chapter 6, Seattle had a Classic Culture Club, organized in 1889 to bring literature through traveling libraries to frontier areas of the state, to people who had no or few books. The club's twenty-five to thirty-five members focused on history, literature, and the arts of various countries. It got the legislature to appropriate $2,000 to support the traveling library in 1901. Seattle also had the Ladies' Musical Club, founded by twenty-one women in 1891 to foster musical activity through a concert series in 1900. Membership was by audition. It also sponsored scholarships, recitals, and concerts by members, offering a venue for female musicians in particular. More than a century later the club was still sponsoring noontime concerts open to the public in the Seattle Public Library downtown. Seattle had dozens of clubs that were part of the federation, and others that were not, many of them founded before the turn of the century.

SPOKANE

The spectacular Spokane Falls powered electric street lighting by 1886 in Spokane, one of the first cities in the West to have it for its population of 3,500, which exploded to 20,000 by 1890. By 1889 the city had six banks, four cigar factories, sixteen restaurants—and forty saloons.[28] It also had a destructive fire that year. Because of the gold, silver, and lead taken out of northern Idaho, Spokane had many wealthy families and men who became community leaders, but their wives were not at the heart of club activism in the city.

The Spokane Sorosis was created in 1889 by thirty women. They found one another in response to a call placed in the newspaper by Laura Shellabarger Hunt. She had been a member of the Decatur Sorosis in Illinois and missed it. The club's purpose was "to develop fellowship among women, and to promote the best practical methods for culture and civic progress." Meetings were held Saturday afternoon, and the literary club had a treasured authors' album containing signatures of Longfellow, Jennie June (penname of Sorosis founder Jane Croly), Harriet Beecher Stowe, Julia Ward Howe, Oliver Wendell Holmes, John Greenleaf Whittier, and others. The club worked on a free library, contributing books and money to the Union Library Association. The club also helped support a Woman's Exchange, free kindergartens, and floral missions and brought in experts in social problems as lecturers. In 1892 a Shakespeare Class was organized as an auxiliary to the group, and soon after it joined the national federation, one of the first to join. It joined the state federation in 1896. The Spokane Art League founded an art school, the city's first, with classes in various media, and members volunteered to teach art classes in the public schools. In 1914 it became the Spokane Art Exhibits.

The Spokane Sorosis Club also influenced the region through the organization of neighborhood clubs, such as the Flora Club in Kettle Falls, the Woman's Club in North Yakima, and the Neighborhood Club of La Grande Avenue. Sorosis in 1897–98 considered "Scientific Methods in Modern Education," "The Decadence of the Theoretical and Introduction of the Practical," and "Patriotic Teaching in Home and School" in its education department. In 1894 the city took over control and funding of the city's club-supported, semiprivate library. By 1901 Spokane had a citywide system of fourteen kindergartens, until they were attacked as extravagant.

Spokane also had a small but active community of African-American clubs. The oldest was the Dunbar Literary Club for the study of poetry, focusing on black writers. There was also a Grandmothers Club and Ashanti Club. Before the state had a Federation of Colored Women's Clubs, historian Frances Jones Sneed found Spokane had a Booklovers Club to encourage the reading of classics, a Spokane Negro Dramatic Club, and a Merry Matrons Club as well as others. The latter club catered dinners to raise money.

Other notable Spokane clubs included the 1892 Cultus Club, a group of women with a sense of humor. The Cultus Club, according to Croly's club history, had organized with seven charter members, which within months increased to thirty. One of the charter members, Mrs. J. J. Brown, christened the club with her tongue in her cheek. The club had no literary pretenses, and *cultus* in Chinook supposedly meant worthless, good-for-nothing, without purpose. The club's theme was "all work and no play makes dull women."[29] Nevertheless, its constitution said its object was intellectual and social improvement. It joined the federation in 1893. Spokane, like other cities, had a Twentieth Century Club, formed in 1898, with an ambitious outline of study.

There was also the Amethyst Club, organized in 1898 "to seek, to know, to enjoy," the Manito Study Club, founded in 1912, and the Spokane Athenaeum Club, formed in 1902. The City Federation of Women's Organizations was created in 1915 by twenty clubs and had its own study program that year: "New Ideals of Peace"; "Immigrant Tide's Effect on the United States"; "Vocational Education"; "Conservation of Lands, Forests, Water-rights, and Mines"; and "Woman's Industry."

STELLA

The 1913 Woman's Club was founded by the wife of a physician. The group spent a day once each week mending clothing and making layettes for the needy. It was a social and sewing club until 1929, when it changed its name to Woman's Club from Ladies' Club.

TACOMA

In addition to the clubs described in detail in chapter 6, Tacoma had several other influential clubs, including the 1892 Tacoma Art League. The members of the league elected Galusha Parsons president, who served from 1892 to 1899, and decided to call their club Aloha for the friendly warmth of the word. Their goal as women was to make "home happier, schools better, society purer, government righteous, churches consistent, and Washington worthy of its honored women." The league began a campaign in 1899 to buy reproductions of old masters' paintings to be rotated through Tacoma's schools. The Aloha Club joined the General Federation in 1893 by telegraph.[30] In 1910 Mrs. Horace G. Scott organized the Monday Civic Club of Tacoma. Two years later she was the first woman to be elected to the U.S. electoral college, shortly after the state of Washington granted women the right to vote in 1910.

WAITSBURG

The 1902 Waitsburg Progressive Club joined the federation in 1905. Its purpose was "mutual improvement of its members in literature, history, and the vital interests of the day."[31] Members were invited or could join as associate members.

WALLA WALLA

In addition to the Woman's Club that became a suffrage society, as described earlier, Walla Walla had a Women's Reading Club to support literary culture and libraries, founded in 1894. The motto of the Reading Club was "We must read, you see, before we live." Its three committees were civic improvement, music, and school. The town also had an Art Club, founded in 1898, a Woman's Education Club (1911), and a Shakespeare Club (1905).

WHITE SALMON

In 1900 the women in White Salmon found themselves in a small village, with no railroad and "no good roads."[32] Mrs. Kate Butler, whose family homesteaded in the area in the 1880s, decided to organize the White Salmon Woman's Club about 1900. In 1902, at its first bazaar, it sold a silk crazy quilt of blocks made by each member for $10. Among its projects, the club loaned $100 to help furnish the city's first high school room and bought its first dictionary. It joined the federation in 1913, with seventy members by then. It also founded the Parent-Teacher Association and a Red Cross branch.

YAKIMA

The Yakima WCTU established the first public reading room there and had plans to build a temple to house a library, lecture hall, and offices, but it fell short in raising enough funds and abandoned the project. Leader Susanna Steinweg regrouped, creating the North Yakima Library Association. The group held box socials, dances, concerts, and spelling bees to raise money for books, and members took turns acting as librarian for the reading room.[33] There were also the Twentieth Century Club and the Woman's Club, which eventually merged into the Woman's Century Club. In addition there were the PEO and Adelphian Society. Other clubs included the Portia, Coterie, and two North Yakima clubs, the 1894 Woman's Club, and the 1898 Ladies' Musical Club.

NOTES

PREFACE

1. Lawrence Levine, *Highbrow/Lowbrow: The Emergence of Cultural Hierarchy in America.*

INTRODUCTION

1. Mary Stewart (1876–1943), a high school principal in Colorado, belonged to the Longmont Fortnightly Club and became dean of women at the University of Montana. After moving to Washington, D.C., she became a charter member of the powerful lobbying group the Women's Joint Congressional Committee. She helped organize the National Federation of Business and Professional Women and also worked in the Department of Labor, the Office of Indian Affairs, and the Department of Education. D. W. Spangler, "Mary Stewart, Educator, Author, and Club Woman," *Colorado Magazine* 27 (July 1950): 218–25.

2. Karen Blair, *The Clubwoman as Feminist: True Womanhood Defined, 1868–1914,* and Anne Firor Scott, "On Seeing and Not Seeing: A Case of Historical Invisibility," *Journal of American History* 71 (June 1984): 7–21.

3. Kathryn Kish Sklar, "A Call for Comparisons," *American Historical Review* 95, 4 (Oct. 1990): 1109.

4. Sklar cites the paradigm drawn by Seth Koven and Sonya Michel in evaluating women's historical role in policy history according to the state's internal dynamics, women's political culture, and the interaction between the two. This approach avoids simple bipolar analyses about women's victimization on one end of the spectrum and naive assessments of women's achievements at the other end. Sometimes where women's historical agency was strongest policies for women "were the least generous." Sklar, "A Call for Comparisons," 1111–12, and Koven and Michel, "Womanly Duties: Maternalist Politics and the Origins of Welfare States in France, Germany, Great Britain, and the United States, 1880–1920," *American Historical Review* 95 (Oct. 1990): 593–618. See also Sklar's essay "The Historical Foundations of Women's Power in the Creation of the American Welfare State, 1830–1930," in *Mothers of a New World: Maternalist Politics and the Origins of Welfare States*, ed. Seth Koven and Sonya Michel, 31–50.

5. The literature on women at and after the turn of the century in the West is "surprisingly sparse." Karen Anderson, "Western Women," in *The Twentieth Century West*, ed. Gerald Nash and Richard Etulain, 100–101. Much of what has been written fits women into a set of stereotypes. Susan Armitage, "Women and Men in Western History: A Stereoptical Vision," *Western Historical Quarterly* (Oct. 1985): 381–91.

6. Paula Baker, "The Domestication of Politics: Women and American Political Society, 1780–1920," *American Historical Review* (June 1984): 622.

7. Almost 47 percent of the land is forested, and grazing remains the second major land use. Irrigated and dry cropland still constituted 23.5 percent of the nonfederal lands in the region near the end of the twentieth century. James Pease, "Land Use and Ownership," in *Atlas of the Pacific Northwest*, ed. Philip L. Jackson and A. Jon Kimerling, 31–33.

8. Patricia Limerick, *The Legacy of Conquest: The Unbroken Past of the American West*, 50, and Donald Worster, *Under Western Skies: Nature and History in the American West*, 14–15.

9. Susan Armitage, "The Frontier through Women's Eyes," in *Interpreting Local Culture and History*, ed. J. Sanford Rikoon and Judith Austin, 149.

10. Writers who focus on Progressivism as primarily a movement for electoral and governmental reform and on the role women played in these reforms seem to promote this view. One writer looking specifically at women's roles who sees the club movement as almost exclusively urban is Margaret Wilson Gibbons in *The American Woman in Transition: The Urban Influence 1870–1920*, 95–96.

11. Geoffrey Hughes, *Words in Time: A Social History of the English Vocabulary*, 193–94.

12. Vera Norwood, "Women's Place: Continuity and Change in Response to Western Landscapes," in *Western Women: Their Land, Their Lives*, ed. Lillian Schlissel, Vicki L. Ruiz, and Janice Monk, 157, notes

that many historians of women's lives in the West emphasize the cultural continuity and deemphasize changes caused by the radically new environments of the West. Thus they exhibit more interest in the urban West than in rural or wilderness developments.

13. Karen Blair, *The Torchbearers: Women and Their Amateur Arts Associations in America, 1890–1930.*

14. The idea that every American should have access to the fine arts came to be accepted by professionals and later taken for granted. Such clubs left us "an impressive array of permanent cultural programs and institutions." Blair, *The Torchbearers*, 4–5.

15. Harvey J. Graff, *The Legacies of Literacy: Continuities and Contradictions in Western Culture and Society*, 4.

16. Barbara Sicherman, "Sense and Sensibility: A Case Study of Women's Reading in Late-Victorian America," in *Reading in America: Literature and Social History*, ed. Cathy Davidson, 214.

17. Michael Harris, "The Purpose of the American Public Library: A Revisionist Interpretation of History," *Library Journal* 98 (Sept. 15, 1973): 2509–14. See also Harvey J. Graff, "Literacy, Libraries, Lives: New Social and Cultural Histories," *Libraries and Culture* 26, 1 (Winter 1991): 24–45, and Levine, *Highbrow/Lowbrow*, for deeper discussions of this issue.

18. Robert L. Griswold, "Anglo Women and Domestic Ideology in the American West in the Nineteenth and Early Twentieth Centuries," in *Western Women: Their Land, Their Lives*, ed. Lillian Schlissel, Vicki L. Ruiz, and Janice Monk, 25.

19. The reasons western states granted women suffrage differed in each state and depended upon the nature and extent of development in each state at the time. However, in every case, gaining passage required strong, persistent, and creative leaders, and women themselves have been given insufficient attention for their own role in the process. See, for instance, T. A. Larson, "Dolls, Vassals and Drudges: Pioneer Women in the West," *Western Historical Quarterly* 3 (Jan. 1972): 5–16.

20. Lisa Anderson, "Who Are Politicians Talking about, Anyway?" original in *Chicago Tribune*, reprinted in *Spokesman-Review* (Spokane, Washington), Dec. 28, 1994, A1, A10.

21. Mary Ritter Beard, *Woman's Work in Municipalities*, 318. A writer of women's history long before it was a recognized field, Beard also was prominent in the suffrage movement and helped organize female textile workers in New York City.

22. See Glenna Matthews on the housewife and the home economist in *Just a Housewife: The Rise and Fall of Domesticity in America*, 134–55.

CHAPTER 1. WOMEN COME TOGETHER

1. Walter Nugent, "The People of the West since 1890," in *The Twentieth-Century West*, ed. Nash and Etulain, 43, and Carlos Schwantes, *The Pacific Northwest: An Interpretive History*, 185.

2. Mark S. Hoffman, ed., *World Almanac and Book of Facts*, 552–53.

3. Michael P. Malone and Richard Etulain, *The American West*, 122.

4. Gibbons, *The American Woman in Transition*, 32.

5. For example, five Sisters of Providence arrived in Vancouver, Washington, in 1856 from headquarters in Montreal. Led by Mother Joseph (Esther Pariseau), the group relocated in Olympia and over the next half-century founded eleven hospitals, seven academies, five Indian schools, and two orphanages in the Northwest. Marci Whitney, *Notable Women*, 5–6.

6. Anne Firor Scott, *Making the Invisible Woman Visible*, 279–94.

7. "Around the World," *Club Journal* (Mar. 1903): 358.

8. Flora Northrup, *The Record of a Century, 1834–1934* (New York: American Female Guardian Society and Home for the Friendless, 1934), cited in Karen Blair, The History of American Women's Voluntary Organizations, 1810–1960: A Guide to Sources, 200.

9. The founding organization, the New England Female Moral Reform Society, raised issues of class as well as gender regarding prostitution. To them men were always culpable (although the courts seldom agreed) and frequently preyed on victims from lower and more vulnerable classes. The themes in their publications were male dominance and class exploitation. Members were not middle- and upper-class women usually identified with moral crusades and benevolence, but wives of artisans and shopkeepers, and the society was more egalitarian than other charitable institutions of the era. Barbara Meil Hobson, *Uneasy Virtue: The Politics of Prostitution and the American Reform Tradition*, 54–55.

10. Esther Yarber, *Land of the Yankee Fork*, cited in Betty Penson-Ward, *Women in Idaho History*, 192.

11. Some historians argue that the educational role of women's clubs in the context of American education needs much more attention. See Theodora Penny Martin, *The Sound of Our Own Voices: Women's Study Clubs 1860–1910*, 2.

12. Anne Firor Scott found little regional difference among women's benevolent societies of the North, Midwest, and South. A common pattern was to bring domestic skills into a larger sphere through sewing circles and selling handmade goods and to undertake community projects for the worthy poor, whether the societies were benevolent, missionary, or educational. *Natural Allies: Women's Associations in American History*, 18–19.

13. Nancy A. Hewitt, *Women's Activism and Social Change, Rochester, New York, 1822–1872*.

14. Scott, *Natural Allies*, 25.

15. Robert H. Bremner, *The Public Good, Philanthropy and Welfare in the Civil War Era*, 5.

16. Thomas J. Schlereth, *Victorian America: Transformations in Everyday Life, 1876–1915*, 13.

17. Glenda Riley initially explored the influence of Hale and this philosophical development in "The Subtle Subversion: Changes in the Traditionalist Image of the American Woman," *Historian* 32, 2 (1970): 210–27. Hale, widowed mother of five, became editor of the first magazine in 1827 and co-editor of the second in 1837.

18. See Estelle Freedman, "Separatism as Strategy: Female Institution Building and American Feminism, 1870–1930," *Feminist Studies* 5 (Fall 1979): 512–29. She notes that these organizations attracted women who believed their unique qualities obligated them to solve public problems.

19. The idea of moral superiority resurfaced in neo-Freudian feminist criticism, through analysts such as Carol Gilligan and Nancy Chodorow. Psychologist Gilligan found that women respond to a different moral voice. Where men more typically follow an ethical system connected to ideas of justice and rights, women's moral thinking gravitates to care, support, and responsibility, a sense of mutuality. The differences described resonate with nineteenth-century rhetoric about women's different and "superior" connections to issues of morality. Chodorow theorizes that gender differences are socially constructed through mothers' parenting. Women develop a concept of self that is the same as their mothers' and an ego that continues to be defined in relation to others. Men, however, in the process of separating from their mothers, define themselves, and thus masculinity, as what is not feminine. They therefore find it easier to see themselves as autonomous and competitive, which fosters social practices requiring hierarchical relations and abstract rules and causes greater difficulty than women have in seeing connectedness. See Carol Gilligan, *In a Different Voice*, and Nancy Chodorow, *The Reproduction of Mothering*.

20. Marsha Wedell found in her study of club activists in Memphis during this period that clubwomen there focused their attention on the problems connected to the industrial expansion. *Elite Women and the Reform Impulse in Memphis, 1875–1915*, 4.

21. Griswold, "Anglo Women and Domestic Ideology," 27, and Lillian Schlissel, "Women's Diaries on the Western Frontier," *American Studies* 18 (Spring 1977): 87.

22. As reformers moved away from faith in the moral transformation of American society, women focusing on institutionalizing benevolence also moved into male-dominated administration and funding of such institutions, which helps explain the clubwomen's later focus on taking administrative positions out of politics and professionalizing both administrations and staffs. See Lori Ginsberg, "'Moral Suasion Is Moral Balderdash': Women, Politics and Social Activism in the 1850s," *Journal of American History* 73 (Dec. 1986): 601–22.

23. Elaine Tyler May, "Myths and Realities of the American Family," in *A History of Private Life: Riddles of Identity in Modern Times*, ed. Antoine Prost and Gerard Vincent, 15, 541–42.

24. Ruth B. Moynihan, Susan Armitage, and Christiane Fischer Dichamp, eds., introduction to *So Much to Be Done: Women Settlers on the Mining and Ranching Frontier*, xv.

25. Winnifred Harper Cooley, "The Future of the Woman's Club," *Arena* 27, 4 (1902): 374.

26. Karen Blair, *The Clubwoman as Feminist*, 12.

27. Phebe Hanaford, *Daughters of America, or Women of the Century*, 198. Margaret Fuller, frustrated by the lack of intellectual support

or institutions for women, began her "conversations," efforts at guided learning with other women, out of anger over women's superficial educations. The practices of analysis and performance were twin tenets of later study clubs. Said Fuller of women: "When they come to the business of life, they find themselves inferior, and all their studies have not given them that practical good sense . . . men are called on, from a very early period, to reproduce all that they learn. Their college exercises, their political duties, their professional studies . . . call on them to put to use what they have learned. But women learn without any attempt to reproduce. Their only reproduction is for purpose of display." Fuller was also one of the first women to write a book about the West. Her *Summer on the Lakes* described her travels through the West and condemned the treatment of the Native Americans. That led to her job on Horace Greeley's *New York Tribune. Memoirs of Margaret Fuller Ossoli*, cited in Linda K. Kerber, "'Why Should Girls Be Learn'd and Wise?': Two Centuries of Higher Education for Women as Seen through the Unfinished Work of Alice Mary Baldwin," in *Women and Higher Education in American History*, ed. John Mack Faragher and Florence Howe, 37–38.

28.   Elizabeth Carter-Brooks, introduction to Elizabeth Davis, *Lifting as They Climb: The National Association of Colored Women*, 5.

29.   Henry Baldwin, "An Old-Time Sorosis," *Atlantic Monthly* 74, 447 (1894): 748–55.

30.   Ibid., 754.

31.   Voluntarism gained popularity with the American Revolution. One historian estimated that almost 2,000 voluntary associations were formed between 1760 and 1820, with the most growth in American religion. Richard Meckel, "Educating a Ministry of Mothers: Evangelical Maternal Associations, 1815–1860," *Journal of the Early Republic* 2 (Spring 1982): 408.

32.   See Mary P. Ryan, "A Women's Awakening: Evangelical Religion and the Families of Utica, 1800–1840," *American Quarterly* 30 (Winter 1978): 602–23.

33.   Nancy Cott, *Bonds of Womanhood: Woman's Sphere in New England, 1780–1835*.

34.   Meckel, "Educating a Ministry of Mothers," 403–23.

35.   Mary Walker's Diary, in *Mary Walker: Her Book*, vol. 1, 161–62, and vol. 2, 126, in Clifford M. Drury, *First White Women over the Rockies*.

36.   The church also founded missions and churches at Tualatin Plains near Hillsboro in 1842, Oregon City in 1844, Milwaukie in 1850, Portland in 1851, and Salem in 1852. Howard McKinley Corning, ed., *Dictionary of Oregon History*, 60.

37.   The Walkers served at Tshimakain Mission (northwest of what is now Spokane) from 1838 to 1848. They lived at Oregon City, 1848–50, and in 1848 helped establish the Tualatin Academy at Forest Grove.

38.   The Whitmans and the others were killed by a small Cayuse band who reportedly blamed the Whitmans and other settlers for bringing disease with them that devastated tribal populations yet had little effect on the whites. Diseases such as dysentery, measles, influenza, smallpox, and

venereal diseases, brought first to the area by ship's crews harbored in Columbia waters, caused a series of fatal epidemics in Oregon Country. Along the lower Columbia River entire families, villages, and even tribes died. Although the main overland trail bypassed the Whitman mission after 1844, those who were sick and destitute detoured to the mission, bringing disease to the local Cayuse tribe. Half of the Cayuse died in two months, according to one estimate, precipitating the attack. Corning, *Dictionary of Oregon History*, 80–81, and Carlos Schwantes, *In Mountain Shadows: A History of Idaho*, 36.

39. Constitution of the Columbia Maternal Association, Sept. 3, 1839, Record Book, written by Mrs. W. H. Gray, Recording Secretary, reprinted in Clifford M. Drury, "The Columbia Maternal Association," *Oregon Historical Quarterly* 39 (June 1938): 99–122.

40. Drury, "The Columbia Maternal Association," 113.

41. Ibid.

42. Mary Walker, in *Book of Walker 1811–97*, 886, Pacific University Library Rare Book Room, Forest Grove, Oregon.

43. Gray, cited in Drury, "The Columbia Maternal Association," 116–17.

44. American Association of University Women, *By the Falls: Women of Determination*, 12–13.

45. Drury, "The Columbia Maternal Association," 99–122.

46. Meckel, "Educating a Ministry of Mothers," 417–18.

47. Drury lists titles such as "On Seeing an Infant Prepared for the Grave," "The Dying Mother's Request," and "Suggestions to Bereaved Mothers" as examples. "The Columbia Maternal Association," 110.

48. Harvey Green, *The Light of the Home: An Intimate View of the Lives of Women in Victorian America*, 166.

49. Meckel, "Educating a Ministry of Mothers," 417–18.

50. *Mother's Magazine* 2, 12: 184, and 14: 313, cited in Drury, "The Columbia Maternal Association," 111.

51. Drury, "The Columbia Maternal Association," 104–5.

52. Gray, "The Constitution of the Columbia Maternal Association," in *The Record Book of the Association*, reprinted in Drury, "The Columbia Maternal Association," 113.

53. Ibid., 115–16.

54. Catherine Sager Pringle, cited in Lillian Schlissel, *Women's Diaries of the Westward Journey*, 39–41.

55. In 1842, 100 immigrants left Missouri for Oregon, followed by 875 the next year and almost 1,500 in 1844, doubling to 3,000 in 1845. The California and later Northwest gold rushes greatly spurred the overland migration. In 1849 alone, 4,000 wagons came through Nebraska.

56. Schlissel, "Women's Diaries on the Western Frontier," 87–100 (quotation on 88).

57. Paul Dorpat, *Seattle, Now and Then*, 10.

58. David Brewster and David Buerge, eds., *Washingtonians: A Biographical Portrait of the State*, 74.

59. Fred Lockley Biographies, Catherine Wails Alexander, May 23, 1932, vol. 1, Manuscripts Room, OSC, UO.

60. Corning, *Dictionary of Oregon History*, 91.

61. Diphtheria outbreaks were prevalent nationally in 1863–64, between 1874 and 1882, and in 1889. Typhoid, typhus, scarlet fever, measles, and mumps outbreaks were common in the middle decades of the century, although smallpox deaths declined. Green, *The Light of the Home*, 165–66.

62. Fred Lockley Biographies, Martha Jane Allen, July 29, 1925, 1.

63. Martha Ann Minto, "Female Pioneering" (1878), P-A 51, Manuscripts, BL.

64. Sandra Myres found that many routine activities on the frontier became opportunities to socialize, leaving settlers less isolated than is commonly believed. *Westering Women and the Frontier Experience*, 178–81.

65. "The Columbia River," *Harper's Magazine* (1882), reprinted in *The West: A Collection from Harper's Magazine*, 25.

66. Farmers began to market grain they raised in the fertile topsoil of what became the Palouse, where Washington meets Idaho north of Lewiston in a unique rolling topography. Hauled to the Snake River at Almota, Washington, the grain rode on steamboats to Portland until the railroad reached Colfax in 1883. Marvin Moore, "Palouse Hills Farmstead Architecture, 1890–1915," *Oregon Historical Quarterly* (Summer 1984): 181–93.

67. John Fahey, *The Inland Empire, Unfolding Years, 1879–1929*, 15.

68. Personal Anecdotes of Mrs. Theodore Schultze, 1879, Manuscripts, BL.

69. Schwantes, *The Pacific Northwest*, 185.

70. An 1875 ledger of accounts at a general store in Monmouth, Oregon, demonstrated what was available to these families and the relative costs in a well-stocked store. For example, a dozen eggs, 25 cents; 3 pounds sugar, 50 cents; four sacks of flour, $6.50; 3 cans oysters, $1; 10 pounds rice, $1; 2.5 pounds of butter, $1; sack of fine salt, $1. Walnuts, peanuts, and dried apples were available. Also, two pairs of wool socks, $1; one yard of flannel, 50 cents; five yards of velvet, $3.13; five yards of muslin, 63 cents; a piece of velvet ribbon, $1.50; overcoat, $14.50; white shirt, $1.84; pair of overshoes, $2; hats, $3; corsette, $2.

By 1891 both what was available and the prices had changed, as well as what was popular: tomatoes and cabbage were available for sale in August; eggs, 50 cents; a can of coal oil, $1.75; a dozen mason jars, $2. Technology of food storage led to canned foods, and more sold in the West than anywhere else. From Monmouth Polk Company Records Account Ledger, Clara Powell Manuscripts, OSC, UO.

71. Frances E. Willard, *Glimpses of Fifty Years, 1839–1889: The Autobiography of an American Woman*, 362–63.

72. In her 1882 work Phebe A. Hanaford includes a long list of female lecturers, many of them already on the lyceum circuit. *Daughters of America, or Women of the Century*, 320–30.

73. Schwantes, *The Pacific Northwest*, 93.

74. Corning, *Dictionary of Oregon History*, 144, 147, 172, 185, 198.

75. Roy Alden Atwood, *Handwritten Newspapers in North America: An Annotated Bibliography*, 55. Original December 1844 issue at OHS.

76. Minutes, 1860, Peoria Lyceum, Manuscripts Collection, Associations and Institutions, OHS.

77. In some parts of the West mining camps quickly "urbanized," developing the interests and institutions of cities after an explosive phase of growth on an isolated frontier, in a maturing process. Duane Smith, *Rocky Mountain Mining Camps: The Urban Frontier*, 160–61.

78. Lori Ginsberg, *Women and the Work of Benevolence: Morality, Politics and Class in the Nineteenth-Century United States*, 174–76. She argues that the rhetoric of selfless female benevolence obscured the power and authority some women wielded in their communities, explaining why many women were so reluctant to give up that rhetoric.

79. The Christian Commission, more loosely organized than the Sanitary Commission, created branches located in major cities as collection and distribution points for contributions of local aid societies, which were often associated with Protestant church congregations. However, substantial contributions coming in from Oregon and the Far West, notably California, strengthened the Sanitary Commission's position in the region. Bremner, *The Public Good*, 59–61.

80. McMinnville Ladies' Sanitary Aid Society Records, OSC, UO.

81. Ibid.

82. Victoria Cast, newspaper clipping, *Oregonian*, Feb. 19, 1961, 7, in McMinnville Ladies' Sanitary Aid Society Records.

83. Annual Report for 1865, Treasurer's Book, McMinnville Ladies' Sanitary Aid Society Records.

84. Ibid.

85. Alvin Josephy, Jr., *The Civil War in the American West*, 265–67.

86. Annual Report for 1865, Treasurer's Book, McMinnville Ladies' Sanitary Aid Society Records.

87. Ibid.

88. Minutes for Aug. 2, Sept. 4, and Dec. 18, 1865, McMinnville Ladies' Sanitary Aid Society Records.

89. Ibid.

90. Merle Wells, *Gold Camps and Silver Cities: Nineteenth-Century Mining in Central and Southern Idaho*, 6.

91. Minutes, 1864, Ladies' Mite Association, Idaho City, Idaho, MS, ISL.

92. Ibid., Aug. 6.

93. Janice L. Reiff, "Urbanization and the Social Structure: Seattle, Washington, 1852–1910," 132–33.

94. Beverly Beeton, *Women Vote in the West: The Woman Suffrage Movement 1869–1896*, 116.

95. Ida Hustad Harper, *Life and Work of Susan B. Anthony*, vol. 1, 387–88.

96. Ibid.

97. Ibid., 395.

98. Ibid., 397.

99. Ibid., 399.

100. Ibid., 403.

101. *Club Journal* (Feb. 1902): 411.

102. Handwritten speech, Portland Woman's Congress address, no date, Owens Adair Papers, OHS.

103. Ibid.

104. Ibid.

105. Beverly Beeton and G. Thomas Edwards, "Susan B. Anthony's Woman Suffrage Campaign in the American West," *Journal of the West* 21 (1982): 5–15. They note that Anthony's four tours of the West from 1871 to 1896, plus a Portland appearance in 1905, had a considerable effect on suffrage campaign leaders such as Duniway and the campaigns.

106. J. T. Long, "The Coming Woman," in Louis Albert Banks, *Censor Echoes*, 138–53.

CHAPTER 2. "OUR LITTLE BANDS"

1. Mary Ann Clawson, *Constructing Brotherhood: Class, Gender and Fraternalism*, 162.

2. Lucia H. F. Additon, *Twenty Eventful Years of the Oregon Women's Christian Temperance Union, 1880–1900*, 91.

3. See Ruth Bordin, "'A Baptism of Power and Liberty': The Women's Crusade of 1873–74," in *Woman's Being, Woman's Place: Female Identity and Vocation in American History*, ed. Mary Kelley, 283–95.

4. Willard was president of a women's college that merged with Northwestern University, where she became the dean of women and professor of athletics. She left that work in 1874 to become president of the Chicago union. Kirsten Olsen, *Remember the Ladies*, 163.

5. Willard biographer Ruth Bordin found her politically gifted, capable of being "an inveterate dissembler and a clever and effective insinuator," who played the role of conciliator rather than radical. *Frances Willard: A Biography*, 7–9.

6. Willard, *Glimpses of Fifty Years*, 110, 117, 176, 188.

7. Anne Firor Scott, interviewed on National Public Radio's *All Things Considered*, Jan. 13, 1995.

8. Willard speech cited on *All Things Considered.*

9. Willard, *Glimpses of Fifty Years*, 384.

10. Others elected included Mrs. T. M. Boyd, Kate Thatcher, and Rena Poe. Leta Hagedorn, "The WCTU Story—One Hundred Years in Lewiston," *Nez Perce County Historical Society Journal* (Winter 1983): 4.

11. Ruth Bordin, *Woman and Temperance: The Quest for Power and Liberty, 1873–1900.*

12. There was a similar pattern in western Canada. Nancy Sheehan, "'Women Helping Women': The WCTU and the Foreign Population in the West, 1905–1930," *International Journal of Women's Studies* 6 (Nov.– Dec. 1983): 395–441.

13. Willard, *Glimpses of Fifty Years*, 290.

14. Sheila M. Rothman, *Woman's Proper Place: A History of Changing Ideals and Practices, 1870 to the Present*, 68–69.

15. Alma Lutz, *Susan B. Anthony: Rebel, Crusader, Humanitarian*, 263.

16. In her study about Memphis clubs, Marsha Wedell found there too the WCTU acted as a bridge to the activism of the 1890s, through its focus on sisterhood and united action on behalf of the family. Formed in Memphis in 1876, the WCTU there was revitalized in 1881 with Willard's appearance. *Elite Women and the Reform Impulse in Memphis, 1875–1915*, 57.

17. Scott, *Natural Allies*, 103.

18. Minutes, Annual Meeting, Idaho WCTU, ISL.

19. The company was owner of the Nampa townsite at the junction of the Oregon Short Line and Idaho Central Railways. The land company was one of several advertisers found in the WCTU report. Minutes, Annual Meeting, Idaho WCTU.

20. Minutes, Annual Meeting, Idaho WCTU (quotation from 22), ISL.

21. Paul G. Merriam, "Urban Elite in the Far West: Portland, Oregon, 1870–1890," *Arizona and the West* 18 (1976): 41–43.

22. Banks, *Censor Echoes*, 85–89, 95, 104.

23. Woman's Temperance Prayer League, OHS.

24. In addition to writing for newspapers in San Francisco and stories and poems widely published regionally, she wrote at least six of the volumes credited to Hubert Howe Bancroft covering the history of Oregon and other states in the West. William A. Morris, "Historian of the Northwest: A Woman Who Loved Oregon," *Oregon Historical Quarterly* 3 (Dec. 1902): 429–34.

25. Additon, *Twenty Eventful Years*, 87.

26. Ibid., 1–4, 7.

27. Ibid., 10.

28. Ibid., 103–4, and Fred Lockley, *Conversations with Pioneer Women*, compiled by Mike Helm, 137.

29. Catherine Julia Adams (Mrs. Calvin H.), Diary, 1885, OHS.

30. Additon, *Twenty Eventful Years*, 15.

31. Ibid., 10.

32. *Woman's Federation* (Jan. 1903), OSC, UO.

33. Catherine Julia Adams (Mrs. Calvin H.), Diary, 1885, OHS.

34. Beaverton WCTU Minutes, 1885, OHS.

35. G. Thomas Edwards, "Dr. Ada M. Weed: Northwest Reformer," *Oregon Historical Quarterly* 78 (Mar. 1977): 5–40.

36. *Oregon Statesman*, Nov. 23, 1858, cited in Edwards, "Dr. Ada M. Weed," 15.

37. Ibid., 14–15.

38. Dorpat, *Seattle, Now and Then*, 98.

39. Mark Phinney, Historical Records Survey (WPA Project), Benton County Societies and Organizations, OSLA, and Additon, *Twenty Eventful Years*, 45.

40. Other locations included The Dalles, Albany, East Portland, Salem, Astoria (with the YMCA), Oakland, Medford, Dundee, Eugene, Milton, Roseburg, Newport, and Cottage Grove. Elsewhere there were

WCTU lending libraries and reading circles. Additon, *Twenty Eventful Years*, 46–47.

41. Ibid., 95–96.

42. Ibid., 31.

43. Ibid., 89.

44. Ibid., 70–71.

45. Katherine Aiken, "The National Florence Crittenton Mission in the Pacific Northwest," in *Northwest Women's Heritage*, ed. Karen Blair, 108.

46. Margaret Andrews, *Washington Women as Pathbreakers*, 57.

47. (Portland) *Oregonian*, May 3, 1892.

48. Additon, *Twenty Eventful Years*, 23.

49. Ibid., 27.

50. Bremner, *The Public Good*, 29.

51. Robert Ruby and John Brown, *A Guide to the Indian Tribes of the Pacific Northwest*, 54–57, and Corning, *Dictionary of Oregon History*, 251.

52. Additon, *Twenty Eventful Years*, 42–43.

53. Ibid., 43–44.

54. Ibid., 53.

55. Ibid., 65.

56. Lucy Thurman, born in Canada in 1849, taught school in Maryland and joined temperance work in 1875. In the WCTU she became "Superintendent of Temperance Work among Colored People." When the world WCTU met in England she was the guest of Lady Henry Somerset. In 1906 Thurman was elected NACW president. Davis, *Lifting as They Climb*, 168–69.

57. Hobson, *Uneasy Virtue*, 75.

58. Additon, *Twenty Eventful Years*, 50–51.

59. Ibid., 111.

60. Hagedorn, "The WCTU Story," 4.

61. Such women's clubs helped organize not only materials for the women's exhibit at the Chicago fair but also the state's exhibits there, as detailed in the history of the Columbian Club of Boise.

62. The 1855 treaty gave the Nez Perce Tribe an 11,000-square mile homeland covering central Idaho and parts of Oregon and Washington. But after the discovery of gold in central Idaho, in 1863 a new treaty signed by a Nez Perce leader (his authority later challenged by other Nez Perce leaders) reduced the reservation to 1,100 square miles. Similarly, the Fort Hall reservation in southeastern Idaho was reduced by three-fourths when the government opened the land to white settlement after the Bannock uprising in 1878. Schwantes, *In Mountain Shadows*, 47, and *The Pacific Northwest*, 122.

63. Schwantes, *In Mountain Shadows*, 92.

64. Gene Mueller, *Lewiston: A Pictorial History*, 54.

65. That year the Lewiston Independent School District received its charter, with Mrs. John P. Vollmer (wife of a merchant who founded a bank) on its board. Mueller, *Lewiston*, 47–48.

66. Ibid., 72.

67. Report of Corresponding Secretary, Idaho WCTU Meeting, 1890, 19–20, A & M, ISL.

68. "Librarians' Recollections," Idaho Public Libraries—Hitory Materials, ISL.

69. Max Binheim, *Women of the West*, "Emma F. Angell Drake," no page number, and Cort Conley, *Idaho for the Curious*, 221–23.

70. *Syracuse Herald*, cited in *What Every Young Woman Ought to Know*, no page no.

71. Cited in Green, *Light of the Home*, 119, 132.

72. Gladys Rae Swank, "Ladies of the House (and Senate): History of Idaho Women Legislators since Statehood," 9–10, MS, ISL.

73. Leonard Arrington, *History of Idaho*, 1, 389.

74. Penson-Ward, *Women in Idaho History*, 172.

75. Idaho Library History, 1919, A & M, ISL.

76. Minutes, Annual Meeting, Idaho WCTU, 1888, A & M, ISL.

77. Report, Fourth Annual Convention, Idaho WCTU, 1891.

78. Arthur A. Hart, *The Boiseans: At Home*, 28.

79. Ibid., 44–45.

80. Mary McGee, Corresponding Secretary's Report, Minutes, Annual Meeting, Idaho WCTU, 14.

81. The list included unions in Albion, Bellevue, Blackfoot, Boise City, Caldwell, Coeur d'Alene, Eagle Rock (later Idaho Falls), Franklin, Genesee, Hailey, Hope, Malad City, Montpelier, Moscow, Mountain Home, Nampa, Payette, Pocatello, Quartzburg, Rathdrum, Soda Springs, and Weiser. Report, Third Annual Convention, Woman's WCTU, Boise City, 1889, Idaho WCTU.

82. Report, Third Annual Convention, Woman's WCTU, 19.

83. Dennis Colson, *Idaho's Constitution: The Tie That Binds*, 143.

84. Report, Third Annual Convention, Woman's WCTU, 24, ISL.

85. Ibid.

86. Ibid., 21.

87. Scientific temperance tapped into the credibility attached to science to advance the cause of temperance, beginning in the 1880s in the Midwest. The WCTU successfully pressured a number of state legislatures—including Idaho's—into requiring instruction on the effects of alcohol in public schools. Their effort in part tried to counter the common practice of physicians' prescribing alcohol as medication, in another application of new scientific theories.

88. Report, Third Annual Convention, Woman's WCTU, 1889, 24, ISL.

89. Report, Fourth Annual Convention, Idaho WCTU, 1890, 19.

90. Ibid., 19. Officers elected at the 1890 state convention of the WCTU included Sarah Black, Nampa; vice-president, Mrs. E. E. Givens, Blackfoot; corresponding secretary, McGee; recording secretary, Mrs. J. H. Barton; and treasurer, Laura Moore Cunningham, Boise.

91. Ibid.

92. *Directory and Handbook, King County Women's Christian Temperance Union* (1923), Pacific Northwest Collection, University of Washington, 65, 71.

93. William Speidel, *Sons of the Profits*, 295–96.

94. Andrews, *Washington Women*, 55.

95. *Directory and Handbook, King County, Washington, WCTU*, 67, 71, 73.

96. In Washington Territory another WCTU leader who became a suffrage leader was Julia Hulburt Hawley, born in New York in 1834. After her first husband died, she married D. H. Hawley in 1874, and for two years they lived on the shore of Lake Washington. She had the rare distinction for a nineteenth-century woman of having served on grand and petit juries under Judge Roger Sherman Greene and as bailiff in federal court under Judge C. H. Hanford. Hawley also helped build Seattle's first day nursery at Broadway and Madison. Edmond Meany, "Living Pioneers of Washington," Carkeek Scrapbooks, Seattle History 1884–1917, vol. 1, Museum of History and Industry, Seattle.

97. Emma P. Ray, *Twice Sold, Twice Ransomed: Autobiography of Mr. and Mrs. L. O. Ray*, cited in De Graaf, "Race, Sex, and Region," 291.

98. Quintard Taylor, *The Forging of a Black Community: Seattle's Central District from 1870 through the Civil Rights Era*, 39; Esther Mumford, *Seattle's Black Victorians*, 151.

99. Taylor, *The Forging of a Black Community*, 20, 38–39.

100. Ibid., 46, 164.

101. Ibid., 152.

102. Hazel Carby, *Reconstructing Womanhood: The Emergence of the Afro-American Woman Novelist*, 114.

CHAPTER 3. "ORGANIZED WOMANHOOD"

1. Hart, *The Boiseans*, 7–8.

2. Mary Livermore, in "Women's Clubs—A Symposium," *Arena* 6, 33 (1893): 386.

3. Livermore organized the 1868 suffrage convention in Chicago and with Jane Hoge created a newsletter for thousands of ladies' aid societies. She edited the *Agitator*, which merged with the *Woman's Journal* in 1870. As a young woman she and five other women petitioned Harvard president Josiah Quincy for admission. Quincy acknowledged that they were "very smart girls" but said their place was in the home, infuriating Livermore. Olsen, *Remember the Ladies*, 209–10.

4. Alexis de Tocqueville, *Democracy in America*, 485.

5. Cooley, "The Future of the Woman's Club," 375–76.

6. Mina Carson, *Settlement Folk: Social Thought and the American Settlement Movement, 1885–1930*, 55.

7. Vernetta Murchison Hogsett, *The Golden Years: A History of the Idaho Federation of Women's Clubs, 1905–1955*, 6.

8. Edith H. Altbach, *Women in America*, 115–17.

9. Mrs. W. H. Mansfield, Elizabeth Lang, and Rose Mitchell, eds., *The Dalles Times-Mountaineer*, Woman's Edition (The Dalles: Ladies of The Dalles Public Library, May 17, 1898), 20.

10. Glenda Riley, *The Female Frontier: A Comparative View of Women on the Prairie and the Plains*, 180–81.

11. Clawson, *Constructing Brotherhood*, 123.

12. Ibid., 243.

13. H. E. Holmes, *Pioneer Links*, 14–15.

14. Ibid., "Chronology," no page no.

15. Ibid., 48.

16. Ibid., 61.

17. Ibid., 61–63.

18. Ibid., 67.

19. Reiff, "Urbanization and the Social Structure," 133–34.

20. Francis Gerry Fairfield, *The Clubs of New York: An Essay on New York Club Life*, 7.

21. Ibid., 13–15.

22. Ibid., 16.

23. Ibid., 21–26.

24. Ibid., 26–28.

25. Ibid., 29.

26. Ibid., 45.

27. E. K. MacColl, *The Shaping of a City: Business and Politics in Portland, Oregon, 1885–1915*, 174–75.

28. Jane C. Croly was born in Leicestershire, England, in 1829, the daughter of a Unitarian preacher. Her family emigrated to New York State in 1841. She became a teacher and produced a small newspaper for her brother's congregation. In 1855 she went to New York and began writing for the *New York Tribune*. Her ladies' column began appearing in other newspapers, making her one of the first syndicated columnists in the United States. A prolific writer, Croly also published several books, including her massive *History of the Woman's Club Movement in America* in 1898. Blair, *Clubwoman as Feminist*, 15–16.

29. Jane C. Croly, *Sorosis—Its Origin and History*, 5–7.

30. Ibid., 7.

31. Ibid., 8–9.

32. Ibid., 11–13.

33. Ibid., 17.

34. Address of the President, 1897, History and First Annual Report, Portland Woman's Club, OHS.

35. Blair, *Clubwoman as Feminist*, 63.

36. Blair, *The Torchbearers*, 182, and Thelma Lee Hubbell, "The Friday Morning Club: A Los Angeles Legacy," *Southern California Quarterly* 50 (Mar. 1968), 59–90, and Joan M. Jensen, "After Slavery: Caroline Severance in Los Angeles," *Southern California Quarterly* 48 (June 1966), 175–86, both cited in Karen Blair, *The History of American Women's Voluntary Organizations, 1810–1960: A Guide to Sources*, 133–34.

37. Croly, *Sorosis*, 22–24.

38. Croly, *The History of the Woman's Club Movement*, 60.

39. Karen Blair, in her work on women's voluntary associations, categorized clubs into thirteen types, recognizing that they frequently overlapped in purpose or over time. They included benevolent, charitable, and philanthropic organizations; culture, arts, civics, mother's clubs, recre-

ation and education clubs; fraternity, sorority, or secret societies; peace groups; organizations centered on race; patriotic organizations; religious or mission societies; suffrage; temperance; work; youth or scouts; politics; and miscellaneous. Blair, *American Women's Voluntary Organizations*, xiii.

40. Croly, *Sorosis*, 25.

41. Ibid., 40.

42. *Soldier Weekly News* (Jan. 13, 1893), photocopy in possession of Roy Atwood, School of Communication, University of Idaho, Moscow.

43. Arrington, *History of Idaho*, 399–401.

44. Hart, *The Boiseans*, 30.

45. Dick d'Easum, *Dowager of Discipline*.

46. *Advocate* (May 16, 1879), photocopy in possession of Roy Atwood, School of Communication, University of Idaho, Moscow. Original at ISL.

47. *Soldier Weekly News* (Feb. 10, 1893), photocopy in possession of Roy Atwood, School of Communication, University of Idaho, Moscow.

48. Mumford, *Seattle's Black Victorians*, 159–61.

49. Minutes, Women's Missionary Society of the Congregational Church of Albany, OSC, UO.

50. Secretary Book Number One and Minutes, Amphictyonic Council, Parma, 1897–1910, A & M, ISL.

51. Helen Lowell and Lucile Peterson, *Our First Hundred Years: A Biography of Lower Boise Valley, 1814–1914*, cited in Penson-Ward, *Women in Idaho History*, 195.

52. Henderson, "Culture in Spokane," *Spokesman-Review,* n.d., 15.

53. Andrews, *Washington Women*, 37–38.

54. Ibid., 54.

55. AAUW, *By the Falls*, 23.

56. Minutes, Feb. 18, 1903, Sub Rosa Club, Mountain Home, 1903–22, Women's Clubs, Miscellaneous, ISL.

57. Minutes, Sub Rosa Club, Apr. 1, 1903.

58. Minutes, Sub Rosa Club, 1903–4.

59. Yearbook, 1908–9, Sub Rosa Club.

60. Caroline French Benton, *The Complete Club Book for Women*, 1–2.

61. Ibid., 3–4.

62. Ibid., 8–9.

63. Ibid., 145–47.

64. Mrs. M. E. Young, "Woman's Clubs," *The Dalles Times-Mountaineer*, 13.

65. May Wright Sewall, in "Women's Clubs—A Symposium," 365.

66. Ella Dietz Clymer, "The National Value of Women's Clubs," in *Transactions of the National Council of Women*, 298.

67. Ibid., 299.

68. Hester Poole, "Difficulties and Delights of Women's Clubs," in *Transactions of the NCW*, 302.

69. Martha White, "The Work of the Woman's Club," *Atlantic Monthly* 93, 559 (1903): 620.

70. It was not unusual for African-American families to move to Oberlin for the education of their daughters. Mary Jane Patterson in 1862 was the first African American to earn a college degree. Linda M. Perkins, "The Education of Black Women in the Nineteenth Century," in *Women and Higher Education in American History*, ed. John Mack Faragher and Florence Howe, 70–71.

71. Women were ascribed a role as nurturers of the character and virtues believed necessary to republican government, although the term *republicanism* has become a catch-all term. Linda K. Kerber, *Women of the Republic: Intellect and Ideology in Revolutionary America*. The shifts in the meaning of *republicanism* are explored in Daniel Rodgers, "Republicanism: The Career of a Concept," *Journal of American History* 79, 1 (June 1992): 11–38.

72. Thomas Woody, *History of Women's Education*, 231–52.

73. Clymer, "The National Value of Women's Clubs," in *Transactions of the National Council of Women*, in 297.

74. Ibid., 239.

75. Helen L. Webster, in *Transactions of the National Council of Women*, 181.

76. Catherine Clinton, *The Other Civil War: Women in the Nineteenth Century*, 128.

CHAPTER 4. "MAKING OURSELVES ANEW"

1. Clawson, *Constructing Brotherhood*, 13.

2. Croly, *History of the Women's Club Movement in America*, 1129.

3. Croly, *Sorosis*, 24.

4. The criticism was repeated by, among others, Thomas H. MacBride, in "Culture and Women's Clubs," an address before the Minnesota Federation of Women's Clubs, Minneapolis, Feb. 12, 1916, 10.

5. Mrs. J. C. Card, President's Address, First Annual Report, Portland Women's Club Records, 1897, 7, OHS.

6. Henry M. Robert, *Robert's Rules of Order Revised*, vii.

7. Mrs. J. C. Card, President's Address, First Annual Report, Portland Woman's Club Records, 9–10.

8. The club's first officers included president Mrs. Card, first vice-president Mrs. H. L. Pittock, second vice-president Mrs. R. M. Bingham, and secretary Mrs. William J. Lehigh. First Annual Announcement, 1896–97 Yearbook, and 1901–2 Yearbook, Portland Woman's Club Records, OHS.

9. *Club Journal* (Feb. 1902): 409.

10. Yearbook, 1912–13, Fortnightly Club, Eugene, OSC, UO.

11. Yearbook, 1897–98, Fortnightly Club, Eugene.

12. "Oregon Club Reports," *Club Journal* (Oct. 1902): 169.

13. Bethenia Angelina Owens Adair, entry in Corning, *Dictionary of Oregon History*, 187–88.

14. Bethenia Owens Adair, *Dr. Owens Adair, Some of Her Life Experiences*, 51.

15. Fred Lockley, "Impressions and Observations of the Journal Man," *Oregon Journal*, no date, Bethenia Owens-Adair Papers, UO.

16. Owens-Adair, *Dr. Owens Adair, Some of Her Life Experiences*, 56–67.

17. Owens Adair, speech to Portland Woman's Congress, no date, Owens Adair Papers, OHS.

18. Andrews, *Washington Women*, 37.

19. Owens-Adair Papers, OHS.

20. Speech for Woman's Congress, Owens-Adair Papers, OHS.

21. Additon, *Twenty Eventful Years*, 23.

22. Owens Adair Papers, OHS.

23. "Woman Physician to Fight for New Marriage Laws," *Oregon Journal*, no date, Owens Adair Papers, OHS.

24. Bethenia Angela Owens Adair to Fred Lockley, Dec. 29, 1924, Owens Adair Papers, OHS.

25. Ibid.

26. Schlereth, *Victorian America*, 274.

27. Early Presidents, Columbian Club, A & M, ISL.

28. Undated clipping from *Buffalo Express*, Mason Brayman Letters, BL.

29. Annie Pike Greenwood, *We Sagebrush Folk*, 26.

30. G. Thomas Edwards, "Interpreting Eastern Washington through the Camera of a Seattle Photographer," in *Interpreting Local Culture and History*, ed. J. Sanford Rikoon and Judith Austin, 29–30. Edwards found that ninety Oregon, Washington, and Idaho communities had agreements between commercial clubs and railroad companies for production of millions of copies of these promotional brochures.

31. Schwantes, *In Mountain Shadows*, 166.

32. Madeline Buckendorf, "The Poultry Frontier: Family Farm Roles and Turkey Raising in Southwest Idaho, 1910–1940," *Idaho Yesterdays* 37, 2 (Summer 1993): 2–8.

33. Greenwood, *We Sagebrush Folk*, 198.

34. Ibid., 116.

35. "Annie Pike Greenwood," in Binheim, *Women of the West*, no page number.

36. Hogsett, *The Golden Years*, 365.

37. Ibid., 322.

38. Ibid., 6.

39. Ibid., 331.

40. Ibid., 320.

41. Greenwood, *We Sagebrush Folk*, 120–22.

42. Hogsett, *The Golden Years*, 98–100.

43. "Rural Club Conference to Observe 50th Year on Lincoln's Birthday," *Sunnyside Sun* (Yakima), Jan. 31, 1963, 1B.

44. Photo cutline, *Sunnyside Sun*, Apr. 7, 1966, Women's Clubs, WSL.

45. Alexander McGregor, *Counting Sheep: From Open Range to Agribusiness on the Columbia Plateau*, 135.

46. "Rural Club Conference," Women's Clubs, *Sunnyside Sun*, Jan. 31, 1963, 1B.

47. Benton, *The Complete Club Book for Women*, 118.

48. Ibid., 123–26.

49. Research Club Yearbook, 1923–24, Women's Clubs Yearbooks, WSL.

50. Edith L. Niles, "Scientific Training," *Club Journal* (Oct. 1902): 153–55.

51. Yearbook, 1912–13, Portland Woman's Club, OHS.

52. Martin, *The Sound of Our Own Voices*, 66–67.

53. Members included women who showed up in other organizations, such as Josephine Hirsch, Mrs. Young, and Mrs. Taft. Croly, *History of the Woman's Club Movement*, 1016–17.

54. Monmouth Literary Association Records, Clara Powell Manuscripts, and "These Are My Clubs," *Oregon Clubwoman* (Feb. 1937): 5, OSC, UO.

CHAPTER 5. LITERATURE AND LIBRARIES

1. Mrs. W. H. Mansfield, Elizabeth Lang, and Rose Mitchell, eds., "Our Library—the Object," *The Dalles Times-Mountaineer*, 1.

2. Sicherman, "Sense and Sensibility," 201–25.

3. "Idaho Library Survey," *Idaho Women's Club Courier*, 24, and Penson-Ward, *Women in Idaho History*, 32–33.

4. Sicherman, "Sense and Sensibility," 214–15 (quotation on 209).

5. Jane Tompkins, *West of Everything: The Inner Life of Westerns*, 42–44.

6. Rodman W. Paul, "When Culture Came to Boise: Mary Hallock Foote in Idaho," *Idaho Historical Series* 19, Idaho State Historical Society (Mar. 1977): 6.

7. Ibid., 4.

8. Penson-Ward, *Women in Idaho History*, 155–56.

9. Paul, "When Culture Came," 10.

10. Mary Hallock Foote to Helena de Kay Gilder, cited in ibid., 12.

11. Dana Nelson Salvino, "The Word in Black and White: Ideologies of Race and Literacy in Antebellum America," in *Reading in America*, ed. Cathy Davidson, 145, argues that this view of literacy continued a tradition of evangelical Protestantism, combining notions of allegiance to American ideals with piety and virtue.

12. Hughes, *Words in Time*, 54–55, 197.

13. Michael Denning, *Mechanic Accents: Dime Novels and Working-Class Culture in America*, 60–61.

14. Bremner, *The Public Good*, 219.

15. Ibid., 219–20.

16. Why Carnegie aimed his philanthropy in this particular direction is debated. One conclusion is that he represented the Progressive faith in education and supported diffusion of knowledge as a means of social control and governance of the masses. See Ellen Condliffe Lagemann, *The Politics of Knowledge: The Carnegie Corporation, Philanthropy, and Public Policy*.

17. "Idaho Library Survey," *Idaho Women's Club Courier*, Idaho Federation of Women's Clubs (Apr. 1952): 24.

18. Receipts, Mrs. Samuel H. Hays, 1896–99, Columbian Club Records, A & M, ISL.

19. Gertrude Hays, "History of the Columbian Club 1898–1900, during the Presidency of Mrs. S. H. Hays," 1929, Columbian Club Records.

20. Ibid., 7, and Minutes, Columbian Club Records, Mar. 2, 1895.

21. Mrs. Samuel Hays to L. B. Styles, Nampa, undated letter, Mrs. Samuel H. Hays, 1896–99, Columbian Club Records.

22. Mansfield, Lang, and Mitchell, "Our Library—the Object," 1.

23. The grants were $40,000 to Boise in 1903; $12,500 to Caldwell in 1912; $15,000 to Idaho Falls in 1909; $10,000 to Lewiston in 1903; $10,000 to Moscow in 1904; $6,000 to Mountain Home in 1907 and $10,500 that year to Nampa; $12,000 to Pocatello in 1906; $10,000 to Preston in 1914; and $12,000 to Wallace in 1910. Carnegie Foundation Corporation to Idaho State Historical Society, 1977, Idaho Libraries, A & M, ISL.

24. Others were at Potlatch, Wallace, Weiser, Nez Perce, Mountain Home, Montpelier, Idaho Falls, Twin Falls, Caldwell, Gooding, St. Anthony's, Rigby, and American Falls. Henry T. Drennan, "Public Library Development in Idaho, A Working Paper," 3, Idaho Public Libraries— History Materials, A & M, ISL.

25. "Free Reading Room and Circulating Library," *Idaho Statesman* (Boise), June 29, 1896, 1.

26. Ralph Waldo Emerson, "Man the Reformer" and "The Poet," in *Ralph Waldo Emerson: Selected Essays*, 143, 262.

27. Hogsett, *The Golden Years*, 63–64.

28. Penson-Ward, *Women in Idaho History*, 33.

29. Mary Virginia Kennedy, "A Study of Dr. Minnie F. Howard," IS. She used the extensive Howard papers at the Idaho State University Museum, Pocatello.

30. H. Leigh Gittins, *Pocatello Portrait: The Early Years, 1878 to 1928*, 191–97.

31. Jo Ann Ruckman, "Knit, Knit, and Then Knit: The Women of Pocatello and the War Effort of 1917–1918," *Idaho Yesterdays* 26 (Spring 1982): 26–30.

32. "Minnie Howard," in Binheim, *Women of the West*, no page number.

33. *Club Journal* (Feb. 1902): 421.

34. Kate Cassatt MacKnight, "Communications: Report of the Civic Committee," *Annals of the American Academy* 28, 2: 294.

35. Ibid., 294.

36. Additon, *Twenty Eventful Years*, 24.

37. Dictionary of Oregon History, WPA Project, OSL.

38. Ronald W. Taber, "Sacajawea and the Suffragettes," *Pacific Northwest Quarterly* 58 (Jan. 1967): 7–13.

39. Eva Emery Dye, *The Conquest—The True Story of Lewis and Clark*, 290.

40. Donald Epstein, "Gladstone Chautauqua: Education and Entertainment, 1893–1928," *Oregon Historical Quarterly* 80, 4 (Winter 1979): 396.

41. Ibid., 397.

42. Ibid., 400.

43. Dye to Levine, July 2, 1901, Dye Papers, cited in ibid., 395.

44. Schwantes, *In Mountain Shadows*, 142.

45. Eva Emery Dye, review of *Letters from an Oregon Ranch*, *Oregon Historical Quarterly* 7 (1906): 435.

46. Taber, "Sacajawea and the Suffragettes," 8.

47. President's Address, Handbook, Oregon Federation of Women's Clubs Convention, 1903–4, 33–34.

48. Hierarchical culture and its connection to class and America's shift from a producer to a consumer culture are explored in Joan Shelley Rubin, *The Making of Middle-Brow Culture*. She found a thread connecting Emerson's cultivation of the self to a shift from ideas of character to the focus on personality, where a certain canon of Great Books or membership in the Book-of-the-Month Club came to define and market the idea of the educated American.

CHAPTER 6. FROM LITERATURE TO LOBBYING

1. *Spokesman*, June 23, 1892, cited in Edith E. Erickson and Eddy Ng, *From Sojourner to Citizen: Chinese of the Inland Empire*, 128–29.

2. Philip Ethington, *The Public City: The Political Construction of Urban Life in San Francisco, 1850–1900*, 325–28, and "Political Participation, Gender, and the Public Sphere: A Response to Maureen Flanagan's Review of *The Public City*," circulated on H-State Internet Mailing List, June 8, 1995.

3. Elizabeth McLagan, *A Peculiar Paradise: A History of Blacks in Oregon, 1788–1940*, 89.

4. Erickson and Ng, *From Sojourner to Citizen*, 24–25.

5. Schwantes, *The Pacific Northwest*, 187.

6. Andrews, *Washington Women*, 7.

7. Quintard Taylor, "The Emergence of Black Communities in the Pacific Northwest: 1865–1910," *Journal of Negro History* 64 (Fall 1979): 346–51.

8. Quoted in *Portland Oregonian*, Jan. 21, 1917.

9. Frances Jones Sneed, "Spokane's African-American Clubs," paper presented at Pacific Northwest History Association Conference, Bellingham, Washington, Mar. 24, 1994.

10. Cathy Luchetti and Carol Olwell, *Women of the West*, 26.

11. De Graaf, "Race, Sex, and Region," 296–97.

12. Taylor, "Black Communities," 350.

13. Erickson and Ng, *From Sojourner to Citizen*, 29.

14. MacColl, *The Shaping of a City*, 3.

15. Hogsett, *The Golden Years*, 95.

16. Kate Holladay Claghorn, *The Survey*, cited in Beard, *Woman's Work in Municipalities*, 174.

17. McLagan, *A Peculiar Paradise*, 89.

18. Paul Merriam, "The 'Other Portland': A Statistical Note on the Foreign-Born, 1860–1910," *Oregon Historical Quarterly* 80 (1989): 258–68.

19. Ibid., 264.

20. Additon, *Twenty Eventful Years*, 89.

21. Patton Home officers were president Mary Knox, vice-president Mary Foster, and secretary-treasurer Eva A. Cline. It had capital of $250. Multnomah County, Societies and Social Organizations, WPA Oregon Writers Project, OSLA.

22. Merriam, "The Urban Elite," 41–43.

23. Mary A. Hodgdon obituary, Feb. 18, 1917, unidentified clipping, Portland Women's Clubs Scrapbook, OHS.

24. (Portland) *Oregonian*, Jan. 28, 1894.

25. Fourth Annual Report of Portland Women's Union, 1891, 17, President's Annual Reports 1892–1932, Portland Women's Union Records, OHS.

26. Ninth Annual Report of Portland Women's Club, 1896, Portland Women's Union Records, OHS.

27. Corning, *Dictionary of Oregon History*, 77.

28. History and First Annual Report, Portland Woman's Club, OHS.

29. Address of the President, First Annual Report, 1897, 8, Portland Woman's Club, OHS.

30. "A History of the Portland Women's Club," Pacific Northwest Collection, OHS.

31. Home Department, Portland Woman's Club, Directories and Yearbooks, OHS.

32. Corning, *Dictionary of Oregon History*, 243.

33. "A History of the Portland Women's Club," Portland Woman's Club, OHS.

34. Ibid.

35. Oregon Association of Colored Women's Clubs, unidentified clipping, Aug. 6, 1984, *Oregonian*, OHS.

36. Davis, *Lifting as They Climb*, 373–74.

37. McLagan, *A Peculiar Paradise*, 120.

38. Ibid., 121.

39. Antoinette Wheeler Strahan, ed., *Club Journal*, official organ for the Oregon and Washington State Federation of Women's Clubs (Feb. 1902): 401.

40. Hogsett, *The Golden Years*, 4.

41. Ibid., 1–3.

42. Gertrude Hays, "Columbian Club History," 1919–20, Columbian Club, 1–2, ISL.

43. Victoria Eoff, President's Report, Columbian Club, ISL.

44. Third Annual Convention, Idaho WCTU, 1889 meeting, A & M, ISL, and *Boise City Directory* (1891).

45. Hart, *The Boiseans*, 58.

46. Ibid., 58.

47. Alan Trachtenberg, *The Incorporation of America: Culture and Society in the Gilded Age*, 221.

48. Minutes, Mar. 2, 1895, Columbian Club, A & M, ISL.

49. Hays, "Columbian Club History," 4.

50. Faith Turner, "The Golden Dream," 1955 pamphlet on Boise library history, A & M, ISL.

51. Hays, "Columbian Club History," 5.

52. Columbian Club Yearbook, 1900–1901.

53. Colson, *Idaho's Constitution: The Tie That Binds*, 10.

54. *Boise City and Ada County Directory*, no page number.

55. Hays, "Columbian Club History," 5.

56. Penson-Ward, *Women in Idaho History*, 44.

57. Ibid., 124.

58. Hart, *The Boiseans*, 52.

59. d'Easum, *Dowager of Discipline*, 54–55.

60. Ridenbaugh, Report, Early Presidents Folder, Columbian Club Records, A & M, ISL.

61. Betty Penson, "Mary Ridenbaugh," in "Biographies of Idaho Women," compiled by Altrusa Club, Boise, 1979, A & M, ISL, and Penson-Ward, *Women in Idaho History*, 78–82.

62. Penson-Ward, *Women in Idaho History*, 80.

63. Matthews, *Just a Housewife*, 148.

64. Mary C. Beatty, Chairman Educational Committee, Second Annual Report, 1898–1900, Columbian Club, A & M, ISL.

65. Turner, "The Golden Dream," 6.

66. Hays, "Columbian Club History," 7–8, Columbian Club Records.

67. Ibid.

68. The membership was open. "Any woman residing in Boise or vicinity may become a member of the club by signing this constitution and paying to the Secretary each year a membership fee of one dollar, the funds so raised to be used for defraying the expenses of the club, and it being understood that the signing of this Constitution is a pledge that the person so signing will use her best efforts for promoting the objects of the club." Columbian Club (Boise) Yearbooks, 1892–1913.

69. Eoff, President's Report, Columbian Club.

70. Columbian Club Yearbooks, 1893–1900.

71. Columbian Club Yearbook, 1905–6.

72. Ridenbaugh, "Historical Data," Columbian Club, 7, and Hays, "Columbian Club History," 9–11.

73. Hays, "Columbian Club History," 10.

74. Columbian Club Yearbooks, 1905–12.

75. Blair, *The Torchbearers*, 178.

76. Columbian Club Yearbooks, 1900–1901.

77. Hart, *The Boiseans*, 52.

78. *Boise City and Ada County Directory* (1901–2), no page number.

79. Hart, *The Boiseans*, 48.

80. Beard, *Woman's Work in Municipalities*, 165.

81. Andrews, *Washington Women*, 112.

82. Ralph Bushel Potts, *Seattle Heritage*, 4.

83. Edmond Meany, "Living Pioneers of Washington," Carkeek Scrapbooks, MHI.

84. The job paid little. She commented later that she made more

money typing legal briefs for lawyers on Pierce County's first typewriter, up to $10 a day, a huge sum for a woman. Marci Whitney, *Notable Women*, 11–12.

85. Ibid., 1.

86. H. C. Pigott, *Pigott's Political Reference Book for King County*, 32.

87. Nelson Ault, "The Earnest Ladies: The Walla Walla Woman's Club and the Equal Suffrage League of 1886–1889," *Pacific Northwest Quarterly* 42 (Apr. 1951): 123–37.

88. Andrews, *Washington Women*, 125.

89. Ibid., 5.

90. Dorpat, *Seattle, Now and Then*, 63.

91. During the Spanish-American War she was president of the local Red Cross Society and was made an honorary president for life. From Edmond Meany, "Living Pioneers of Washington," Carkeek Scrapbooks, MHI.

92. Andrews, *Washington Women*, 46.

93. Ibid., 69.

94. Gatzert-Schwabacher Papers, clippings from *Walla Walla Bulletin*, Oct. 11, 1934, MS, BL.

95. Blair, *The Torchbearers*, 65.

96. Schlereth, *Victorian America*, 259.

97. Margaret Strachan, "50 Years of Community Service," *Seattle Times*, Oct. 15, 1950.

98. Nancy Cott, *The Grounding of Modern Feminism*, 57, 258.

99. Century Club History, Washington State Federation of Women's Clubs, MC, UW.

100. Jacqueline Van Voris, *Carrie Chapman Catt: A Public Life*, 11–15.

101. New Century clubs and Woman's Century clubs were founded in many places in the United States. Clinton, *The Other Civil War*, 174.

102. *History of the Woman's Century Club*, n.d. (1942 photostat), PNWC, UW.

103. Ibid.

104. Other founders included Harriet Parkhurst, a Women's Christian Temperance Union activist; Mary Barrett Hagan, a writer who had been published in Ohio; Anna Fishback, who was also president of the Seattle Board of Friendly Visitors and Chautauqua Alumni; Elizabeth MacIntosh, in 1869 the Washington territorial legislature's enrolling clerk, making her the first female in the nation to hold that position in a state legislature; and Elizabeth Lyle Saxon, a southern-born worker in temperance and social reform. Others who signed the charter included Anna M. Brown from New York, who as a physician engaged in missionary work overseas; Frances Loyhead, a graduate of Andover and Abbot Academy and later president of Seattle's Board of Friendly Visitors; Celeste Slausson, graduate of Illinois State University and Boston School of Oratory who founded and directed the Seattle Conservatory of Arts; and Elizabeth Calbert, Scottish-born writer of verse. Washington Federation of Women's Clubs, Century Club, MC, UW.

105. Clubs sending delegates included the Century, Adastra (became Woman's Tuesday), Kindergarten (became Woman's Educational), Wednesday Afternoon, Entre Nous, Alpha, Clionian, Orptec, Classic Culture, Queen Anne Fortnightly, PEO, Coterie, Single Tax, and the Current Century Club of Ballard. In "History of Seattle Federation," unidentified clipping, Carkeek Scrapbooks, MHI.

106. She and her husband moved to Seattle in 1888, founding the Stewart and Holmes Drug company, which in 1904 became wholesalers. Edmond Meany, "Living Pioneers of Washington," unidentified clipping, Carkeek Scrapbooks.

107. *Votes for Women*, ed. Mrs. M. T. B. Hanna (Aug.–Sept. 1910): 6.

108. Century Club History, WSFWC, MC, UW.

109. Carkeek Scrapbooks, 4, "Social Welfare," MHI.

110. Margaret Knowles, ed., *The Seattle Woman—The Club Woman's Annual*, 47.

111. That club initially called itself the Woman's Social Club for Mutual Improvement. The Olympia club said it was open to discussion of all questions except "religion, temperance and politics." Despite its high cost, it claimed that all classes and opinions were represented, with character and intelligence being the only qualification for membership. Croly, *History of the Woman's Club Movement*, 1133.

112. Woman's Century Club was one of eight Seattle clubs gathered in Olympia in 1897 at the first meeting of the Washington federation. The others from Seattle included the Classic Culture Club, the Nineteenth Century Literary Club, PEO Club, Woman's Industrial Club (representing working women), Kindergarten Club, Fortnightly Club, and Advance Club, according to "Classified List of Delegates to First Convention," June 22–23, 1897, Olympia, WSFWC, MC, UW.

113. Croly, *History of the Woman's Club Movement*, 1139.

114. Sandra Haarsager, *Bertha Knight Landes of Seattle: Big City Mayor*.

115. Blair, *The Torchbearers*, 18.

116. Taylor, "Black Communities," 343, and *The Forging of a Black Community*, 37–38.

117. Taylor, "Black Communities," 345.

118. The list included Barbara Davis, Hattie Reed, Alzada Collins, Mrs. J. C. Robinson, and Mrs. C. M. Scott. Mumford, *Seattle's Black Victorians*, 128, 132–33.

119. The other founders were Letitia Graves, Alice Presto, and Hester Ray. Taylor, *The Forging of a Black Community*, 140–41.

120. Andrews, *Washington Women*, 46.

121. Angela Y. Davis, *Women, Race and Class*, 129–30.

122. Several examples of such activism on the part of African-American club leaders in the West are cited in De Graaf, "Race, Sex, and Region," 309.

123. De Graaf, "Race, Sex, and Region," 311.

124. Ibid., 293.

125. Mumford, *Seattle's Black Victorians*, 136–37.

126. Taylor, *The Forging of a Black Community*, 140–\41.

127. Andrews, *Washington Women*, 65.

128. Whitney, *Notable Women*, 31.

129. Ibid., 1.

130. Caroline Kellogg, "Nesika Club Sought Individual Improvement," *Tacoma News Tribune*, Oct. 25, 1981.

131. "History," records compiled by Mrs. Hattie Koons, Historian, Tacoma Woman's Study Club, WHC, WSL. Charter members included Nina Jolidon Croake (president), Ida Mudgett, M. Bebee, Mrs. J. M. Crump, Mrs. Elizabeth Baker (study director), Ellen Leckenby (secretary), and Mrs. Leckenby.

132. Minutes, 1899–1900, Tacoma Woman's Study Club, WSHS.

133. Constitution and bylaws, Tacoma Woman's Study Club, Box 1, folder 2.

134. *Tacoma City Directory* (1908).

135. Minutes, Jan. 28, 1901.

136. Leaders were typically wives of businessmen, according to city records. Nellie B. Crassweller was the wife of an assistant purchasing agent; Mrs. James W. Brokaw's husband was vice-president of North Western Woodenware Co.; Mrs. A. H. Smith's husband was floor manager for Dege and Milner; Laura Roberts was married to a dentist, Henry V. Roberts, as was Mrs. Benjamin F. Eshelman; Mrs. H. H. Johnston's husband Harry was part of Johnston and Swindell's; Elizabeth Baker was perhaps married to the commissioner of horticulture. *Tacoma City Directory* (1908).

137. Max Binheim, "Washington," in *Women of the West*, no page no.

138. History, Tacoma Women's Study Club, 3–4.

139. Minutes, Tacoma Women's Study Club, Aug. 6, 1899.

140. History, Tacoma Woman's Study Club, 5.

141. Minutes, Nov. 20, 1899.

142. Andrews, *Washington Women*, 21.

143. History, Tacoma Woman's Study Club, 5, and Minutes, Oct. 20, 1899.

144. Whitney, *Notable Women*, 28.

145. Ibid., 28–29, and Binheim, "Washington," in *Women of the West*, no page no.

146. Minutes, Jan. 15, 1890.

147. Minutes, Mar. 12 and 19, 1900.

148. History, Tacoma Woman's Study Club, 6.

149. Minutes, Apr. 4, 1900.

150. History, Tacoma Woman's Study Club, 7.

151. Minutes, Nov. 2, 1900, and Jan. 7 and 14, 1901.

152. *Club Journal* (Feb. 1902): 418.

153. Minutes, May 12, 1902.

154. History, Tacoma Woman's Study Club, 8.

155. Minutes, Oct. 25, 1904, and Apr. 18, 1905.

156. Minutes, Mar. 13 and 29 and Apr. 26, 1910.

157. Minutes, 1911.

158. Elton Fulmer, "The Adulteration of Food," *Club Journal*, ed. Mabel Plowman (Sept. 1902): 124–27.

159. History, Tacoma Woman's Study Club, 9–15. Club presidents during these years included, besides Croake, Mary Warner, Mrs. Mark Bailey, Mrs. E. J. Ware, Addie Barlow, Mrs. C. E. Peterson, Mrs. R. E. Roberts, Effie Moore, Mrs. A. H. Smith, Mrs. A. Bruce, Mrs. Leonard Herbert, and Mrs. Harry Stuart. Several of these names show up in other clubs and causes.

160. Minutes, Woman's Club of Tacoma, WSHS.

161. Minutes, Board Meetings, Woman's Club of Tacoma, Feb. 2 and Mar. 2, 1905.

162. Minutes, Mar. 1, 1906, Woman's Club of Tacoma.

163. Minutes, 1906–10, Woman's Club of Tacoma.

164. Minutes, Mar. 2 and Apr. 11, 1911, Woman's Club of Tacoma.

CHAPTER 7. CLUBWOMEN AND WORKING WOMEN

1. Sophie Reinhart, from bylined column printed in *Portland Oregonian*, Sept. 18, 1899.

2. Sophonisba Breckinridge, *Women in the Twentieth Century: A Study of Their Political, Social and Economic Activities*, 114–16, and Matthews, *Just a Housewife*, 267.

3. Maurine Weiner Greenwald, "Working Class Feminism and the Family Wage Ideal: The Seattle Debate on Married Women's Right to Work, 1914–1920," *Journal of American History* 76, 1 (June 1989): 140, 148.

4. Andrews, *Washington Women*, 24.

5. Richard Berner, *Seattle 1900–1920: From Boomtown, Urban Turbulence, to Restoration*, 205, 236.

6. Andrews, *Washington Women*, 22.

7. Croly, *History of the Woman's Club Movement*, 1143–44, 1149.

8. Adelaide Sutton Gilbert Diary, reprinted in *Pacific Northwest Forum* 5, 1 (Winter–Spring 1992): 50, 84.

9. Helen Felker, "Women's Club Set to Fete Its 60th Year," *Tacoma News Tribune*, Feb. 26, 1964.

10. Scrapbook and President's Report of 1965–66, Portland Women's Union, OHS.

11. Mary E. Cook, report to Portland Women's Union Board, 1888, Portland Women's Union Reports, OHS.

12. John F. Kasson, *Rudeness and Civility: Manners in Nineteenth-Century Urban America*, 1–5.

13. John Fahey, *The Days of the Hercules*, 214–15; AAUW, *By the Falls*, 24.

14. Joseph C. Brown, *The Rainbow Seekers: Stories of Spokane, the Expo City, and the Inland Empire*, 102–3.

15. Fahey, *The Days of the Hercules*, 214–15.

16. Page 149, cited in Ivan Pearson, "The Hutton Settlement" (part 2), *Pacific Northwesterner* 11, 3 (Summer 1967): 35.

17. Fahey, *Days of the Hercules*, 215.

18. Pearson, "The Hutton Settlement," 36.

19. Fahey, *Days of the Hercules*, 218.

20. Robinson, Women's Democratic Club of King County, "History," 1913–36, 5.

21. AAUW, *By the Falls*, 24–25.

22. Katherine N. Smith to May Arkwright Hutton, Dec. 26, 1910, Washington Women's Suffrage Papers, WSL.

23. Emma Smith DeVoe Papers, Washington History Room, WSL.

24. James W. Montgomery, *Liberated Woman: A Life of May Arkwright Hutton*, 128.

25. Fahey, *Days of the Hercules*, 219–24.

26. Brown, *The Rainbow Seekers*, 103.

27. A rich analysis of changes in and advice about manners and social deference is found in Kasson, *Rudeness and Civility*, 1–5.

28. One of the first such clubs was established by Grace Dodge, heiress to a copper fortune, who organized a club in 1881. Her lectures used quotations from WCTU tracts, including much material on sexual behavior. Sheila M. Rothman, *Woman's Proper Place: A History of Changing Ideals and Practices, 1870 to the Present*, 77–79, and Croly, *A History of the Woman's Club Movement*, 82–83.

29. Rosalyn Baxandall, Linda Gordon, and Susan Reverby, eds., *America's Working Women: A Documentary History, 1600 to the Present*, 214.

30. Sophie Reinhart, quoted in *Portland Oregonian*, Sept. 18, 1899.

31. Ibid.

32. Ibid.

33. Rothman, *Woman's Proper Place*, 165–66.

34. "Report of the Social Survey Committee of the Consumers' League of Oregon" (Jan. 1913), directed by Caroline J. Gleason and Edwin O'Hara. The surveyors collected information over five months on 7,603 women wage earners in the city, and 1,133 outside the city, comparing their pay and working conditions with those of women elsewhere. OSC, UO.

35. "Report," 24 (quotations from 49, 33, 25).

36. *Woman's Federation* (Aug. 1903): 5, 31, OSC, UO.

37. Edwin O'Hara, address to Consumers' League of Oregon, Portland, Nov. 19, 1912, OSC, UO.

38. The report referred specifically to conditions such as the lack of ventilation in match factories, where the use of dangerous white phosphorous in a sulphur-laden atmosphere was pernicious to workers' health. Yet the windows of the basement workroom where women tipped the matches had to be closed or the sulphur would cool and they could not tip. Women fainted from the heat in laundries that sometimes reached 135 degrees in summer or developed health problems from the glue in paper box factories. Children and women worked as long as 6 A.M. to 10:30 P.M. in the canneries during the season. "Report of the Social Survey Committee," 6, 31, 34, 39, 47–48.

39. Maud Nathan, *The Story of an Epoch-Making Movement*, 1–12.

40. Ibid., 60–71. Mary Montgomery was its first president.

41. Ibid., 198–201.

42. Marlene Stein Wortman, ed., *Women in American Law from Colonial Times to the New Deal*, 333.

43. Ibid., 341–42; see also Judith Baer, *The Chains of Protection: The Judicial Response to Women's Labor Legislation*, 56–61.

44. Berner, *Seattle 1900–1920*, 51, 54.

45. Joseph Tripp, "Toward an Efficient and Moral Society: Washington's Minimum Wage Law, 1913–1925," *Pacific Northwest Quarterly* 67 (July 1976): 97–112.

46. Hogsett, *The Golden Years*, 51–52.

47. Dana Frank in her study of the Seattle labor movement concludes that consumer organizing failed in part because women had been excluded from the strategy in the first place. *Purchasing Power: Consumer Organizing, Gender, and the Seattle Labor Movement, 1919–1929.*

CHAPTER 8. "THE WOMAN'S CENTURY"

1. Barbara Kuhn Campbell, *The "Liberated" Woman of 1914: Prominent Women in the Progressive Era*, 147–76, cited in Blair, *American Women's Voluntary Organizations*, 45–46.

2. Croly, *Sorosis*, 14–16.

3. *Puck* 18 (Mar. 28, 1873).

4. *Harper's Weekly* (May 15, 1869): 312.

5. *Puck* 4 (Apr. 2, 1879): 108.

6. *Puck* 39 (Feb. 26, 1896): 990.

7. "Men's Views of Women's Clubs: A Symposium," *Annals of the American Academy of Political and Social Science* (Sept. 1906): 283–92.

8. Cooley, "The Future of the Woman's Club," 377–78.

9. Beard, *Woman's Work in Municipalities*.

10. *Oregon Daily Journal*, cited in *Club Journal* (Dec. 1902): 330.

11. Cited by Mary Kavanaugh Oldham Eagle, *The Congress of Women Held in the Women's Building, World's Columbian Exposition*, vol. 1, 175, cited in Scott, *Natural Allies*, 132.

12. White, "The Work of the Woman's Club," 616.

13. Ibid., 618.

14. Glenna Matthews, *The Rise of Public Woman: Woman's Power and Woman's Place in the United States, 1630–1970*, 205–7.

15. Letter by Mrs. F. F. Emery, under "What Clubwomen Are Doing," *Club Journal* (Feb. 1903): 341.

16. *Walla Walla Union Bulletin*, cited in *Club Journal* (May 1903): 456.

17. "What Clubwomen Are Doing," *Club Journal* (Feb. 1903): 340.

18. White, "The Work of the Woman's Club," 619.

19. Paula Baker, *The Moral Frameworks of Public Life: Gender, Politics, and the State in Rural New York, 1870–1930*.

20. Ballard Campbell, synopsis of paper presented at the Organization of American Historians, Washington, D.C., Mar. 30, 1995, circulated through H-State e-mail list. Campbell notes that for a variety of complex reasons history texts and scholars have tended to focus on laissez-faire

ideology and legal doctrines at the federal level while ignoring what was happening in more immediate sites in cities and states on social fronts outside business and commerce.

21. Richard White, *"It's Your Misfortune and None of My Own": A New History of the American West*, 381–82.

22. Tommy Neal, "The Voter Initiative," in *National Conference of State Legislatures*, 1, 38 (1993), cited by Priscilla Southwell in a paper presented at the Pacific Northwest American Studies Conference, Lincoln City, Oregon, Apr. 8, 1995.

23. Cooley, "The Future of the Woman's Club," 373–74.

24. White, *Your Misfortune*, 359.

25. G. Thomas Edwards in *Sowing Good Seeds*, and Ross Evans Paulson, *Women's Suffrage and Prohibition: A Comparative Study of Equality and Social Control*. Paulson concludes that in some ways granting women's suffrage was a conservative rather than a liberal move, to address social disorder through women's moral superiority.

26. Mary W. Avery, *History and Government of the State of Washington*, 320–21.

27. Harold Barton and Catharine Bullard, *History of the State of Washington*, 260–61.

28. Ruth Barnes Moynihan, "Let Women Vote: Abigail Scott Duniway in Washington Territory," in *Washington Comes of Age: The State in the National Experience*, ed. David H. Stratton, 96–111.

29. Abigail Scott Duniway, *Pathbreaking: An Autobiographical History of the Equal Suffrage Movement in Pacific Coast States*, 3, 8.

30. Corning, *Dictionary of Oregon History*, 77.

31. Joan Swallow Reiter, *The Women*, 221–22.

32. Banks, *Censor Echoes*, 103.

33. Ibid., 106–8.

34. They included lectures in Weiser, Payette, Caldwell, Boise, Mountain Home, Shoshone, Hailey, Ketchum, and Bellevue. T. A. Larson, "The Women's Rights Movement in Idaho," *Idaho Yesterdays* 16 (Spring 1972): 2–15, 18–19.

35. Jean M. Ward, "The Emergence of a Mentor-Protege Relationship: The 1871 Pacific Northwest Speaking Tour of Susan B. Anthony and Abigail S. Duniway," in *Northwest Women's Heritage*, ed. Karen Blair, 135–36.

36. Scrapbook 2, Duniway Papers, cited in Larson, "The Woman's Rights Movement in Idaho," 18.

37. Ruth Barnes Moynihan, *Rebel for Rights: Abigail Scott Duniway*, 137–41.

38. Larson, "The Women's Rights Movement in Idaho," 2–15, 18–19 (quotations on 6).

39. Beeton, *Women Vote in the West*, 122–23.

40. Ibid., 125.

41. Carolyn Stefanco, "Networking on the Frontier: The Colorado Women's Suffrage Movement, 1876–1893," in *The Women's West*, ed. Susan Armitage and Elizabeth Jameson, 270–71.

42. Minutes Record Book, First State Suffrage Organization, Equal Suffrage Association of Idaho, A & M, ISL.

43. Penson-Ward, *Women in Idaho History*, 176.

44. Minutes Record Book, Equal Suffrage Association of Idaho.

45. T. A. Larson, "Idaho's Role in America's Woman Suffrage Crusade," *Idaho Yesterdays* 18 (Spring 1964): 2–15.

46. Arrington, *History of Idaho*, 435.

47. The advisory board included Kate Feltham, Caldwell, Annette Bowman, Moscow, and Blanche Whitman, Montpelier. Larson, "The Women's Rights Movement in Idaho," 10.

48. County presidents named included Alice Hefling, Lincoln; Mary Gee, Bear Lake; Mrs. William Broadhead, Blaine; Mrs. R. H. Leonard, Owyhee; Daisy Babb, Nez Perce; Irima Matheson, Kootenai; Mrs. Helen Snow, Ada; Mrs. Snodgrass, Cassia; Mrs. S. B. Holdbrook, Bingham; and federated clubs leader Emma Standrod, Pocatello, for Bannock County. Minutes Record Book, Equal Suffrage Association of Idaho, 1896.

49. Arrington, *History of Idaho*, vol. 1, 436.

50. Larson, "The Women's Rights Movement in Idaho," 12.

51. Carrie Chapman Catt to Emma Smith DeVoe, Feb. 9, 1895, Emma Smith Devoe Papers, Washington History Room, Washington State Library, Olympia, Box 1.

52. Whitney, *Notable Women*, 23.

53. *Idaho Register* (Idaho Falls), cited in Larson, "The Women's Rights Movement in Idaho," 10.

54. Ibid.

55. Whitney, *Notable Women*, 24.

56. Letters from Carrie Chapman Catt to Emma S. DeVoe, July 24, 1894, and June 11, 1894, Emma S. DeVoe Papers, WSHS, WSL.

57. The letters are found in the Emma Smith Devoe Papers.

58. Larson, "Idaho's Role," 13–15.

59. Mildred Andrews, *Votes for Women—The Northwest Crusade*, brochure (Bellingham, Wash.: Whatcom Museum of History and Art), no page no.

60. Andrews, *Washington Women*, 20.

61. *Woman's Journal* (Mar. 13, 1897), 84, cited in Larson, "The Women's Rights Movement in Idaho," 13.

62. Arrington, *History of Idaho*, 436–37.

63. Elizabeth Jacox, "Exhibit Chronicles Lives of Women," *Mountain Light: Newsletter of the Idaho State Historical Society* 33, 3 (Spring 1994): 6–7.

64. Most of the information on the three legislators comes from Swank, "Ladies of the House," 1–5.

65. Arrington, *History of Idaho*, 438.

66. Biennial Convention of the General Federation of Women's Clubs, 1898, cited in Breckinridge, *Women in the Twentieth Century*, 259.

67. Biennial Convention of the General Federation of Women's Clubs, 1904, cited in Breckinridge, *Women in the Twentieth Century*, 266.

68. Riley, *The Female Frontier*, 187.

69. Meeting with her were Edith De Long Jarmouth, Mrs. J. C. Henry, Mrs. W. F. Parrish, Mrs. Carl Frost, Mrs. F. E. Palmerton, Margaret Bayne, Mary Mitchell, Adella Parker, Adelaide Belote, and Mrs. E. M. Rininger. Nelle Mitchell Fick Papers, Biographical Information, Scrapbook, MC, UW.

70. Warren B. Johnson, "Muckraking in the Northwest: Joe Smith and Seattle Reform," *Pacific Historical Review* 40 (Nov. 1971): 481–87.

71. There was more than a little dissension within the suffrage ranks, reflected in the management of the suffrage newspapers. Mrs. M. T. B. Hanna, a suffrage worker for six years in Seattle and before that in Edmonds, was editor and proprietor of *Votes for Women* in 1909–10. Carrie Hill also edited a suffrage paper called *Washington Women*. Hanna complained bitterly about the rise of *Western Woman Voter*, Parker's paper, as an imitator. Hanna felt betrayed by the woman she felt she had taught the newspaper business, which made her "mad—mad clear through." *Votes for Women* (Jan. 1910): 5.

72. Biographical Information, Nelle Mitchell Fick Papers, MC, UW.

73. *Woman's National Daily*, 1909, Fick Papers.

74. Frank L. Green, *Washington Centennial Hall of Honor*, 28, and Whitney, *Notable Women*, 19.

75. Other participants included Mrs. E. M. Rininger, Mrs. D. L. Carmichael, Mrs. F. S. Bash, Mrs. W. T. Perkins, and Phebe A. Ryan. Biographical Information, Fick Papers.

76. Obituary, Fick Papers.

77. Linda Jennings, "Skagit County Is Strong for Woman Suffrage," *Bellingham Sunday Herald Suffrage Edition*, Oct. 9, 1910, 1.

78. Cited in Alice M. Biggs, "Women Vote for President and All Other Officers in Wyoming, Utah, Idaho and Colorado—Why Not Here?" *Bellingham Sunday Herald Suffrage Edition*, Oct. 9, 1910. Biggs, a teacher and *Herald* columnist, was chair of the Whatcom County Franchise Committee.

79. Robinson, Women's Democratic Club of King County, History, 1913–36, 6.

80. "Frances C. Axtell," in Binheim, *Women of the West*, no page number.

81. "A History of the Portland Women's Club."

82. "Sadie Orr Dunbar," in Binheim, *Women of the West*, no page number.

83. Anna Howard Shaw, cited in Taber, "Sacajawea and the Suffragettes," 9.

84. Ida Hustad Harper, ed., *History of Woman Suffrage*, 5, 264.

85. Andrews, *Washington Women*, 101.

86. "41st Annual Convention of the National American Woman Suffrage Association," Nelle Mitchell Fick Papers, MC, UW.

87. Ibid., 13, 15.

88. R. S. Jones, Jr., "What the Visitor Sees at the Seattle Fair," *American Review of Reviews* 40 (1909): 68, cited in Arthur Brown, "The Promotion of Emigration to Washington, 1854–1909," *Pacific Northwest Quarterly* 36 (1945): 16–17.

89. Karen Blair wrote about the history of the women's center building in "The Limits of Sisterhood: The Women's Building in Seattle, 1907–1921," in *Women in Pacific Northwest History: An Anthology*, 65–82.

90. Beard, *Woman's Work in Municipalities*, xi.

91. Ibid., 1–3.

92. Ibid., 11.

93. Ibid., 46–47.

94. Cited by MacColl, *The Shaping of a City*, 3.

95. Beard noted that these surveys represented comparative studies on different topics and, although often made at the request of local associations and officials, were usually instigated by women. *Woman's Work in Municipalities*, 87.

96. Ibid., 221–22.

CHAPTER 9. "CONSCIOUS NATIONAL WOMANHOOD"

1. Willard, *Glimpses of Fifty Years*, 592.

2. Croly, *The History of the Woman's Club Movement*, 166.

3. Kate Gannett Wells, "Women's Clubs—A Symposium," *Arena* 6, 33 (1893): 370.

4. Sewall, in "Women's Clubs—A Symposium," 362.

5. Willard, *Glimpses of Fifty Years*, 59.

6. Sewall, in "Women's Clubs—A Symposium," 364.

7. Ibid., 363.

8. Breckinridge, *Women in the Twentieth Century*, 19.

9. Ibid., 24.

10. Zena Beth McGlashan, "Club 'Ladies' and the Working 'Girls': Rheta Childe Dorr and the New York Evening Post," *Journalism History* 8 (Spring 1981): 7–13.

11. At the initial meeting of what became the National Association of Colored Women's Clubs President Ruffin in a keynote address noted, "Year after year, southern women have protested against the admission of colored women into any national organization on the ground of the immorality of these women," which deserved refutation once and for all. Charles Harris Wesley, *The History of the National Association of Colored Women's Clubs*, 34.

12. Ruffin is credited with calling the first convention of African-American women, culminating in the National Federation of Colored Women's Clubs. Ruffin edited the *Woman's Era*, the publication of the Federation of African-American Women, founded the first African-American woman's club in Boston, and was a charter member of the Massachusetts School Suffrage Association and the Moral Education Society. A Harvard graduate whose husband became the first African-American judge in Massachusetts, she was also a member of the New England Women's Club and helped found the Massachusetts State Federation of Women's Clubs. This outstanding record of education and service was not enough to validate her presence as a delegate from an African-American club. Wesley, *The History of the NACWC*, 13–14.

13. Davis, *Women, Race and Class*, 126.

14. Blair, *Clubwoman as Feminist*, 109.

15. Thirteen are listed here with the date they were founded: Astoria Reading Club (1895), Eugene Fortnightly Club (1893), La Grande Lyle Tuesday Musicale (1895), La Grande Neighborhood Club (1894), Parliamentary Club of Pendleton (1897), Thursday Afternoon Club in Pendleton (1891), Portland Teachers Association (1898), Portland Tuesday Afternoon Club (1898), Portland Woman's Club (1895), Portland Section of the National Council of Jewish Women (1896), the '95 Mental Culture Club of Roseburg (renamed the Roseburg Woman's Club, 1895), Silverton Social Science Club (renamed the Silverton Woman's Club, 1898), and the Union Woman's Club (1899). Oregon Federation of Women's Clubs, OHS.

16. Added were the Ashland Woman's Civic Club (1908), Aurora Woman's Club (1906), Coquille Woman's Club (1902), Corvallis Woman's Club (1883), Current Literature Club (Pendleton, 1894), The Dalles Woman's Club (1911), Forest Grove Woman's Club (1905), Hillsboro Coffee Club (1894), Klamath Falls Woman's Library Club (1904), La Grande Neighborhood Club (1894), the Milton-Freewater Woman's Improvement Club (1913), Monmouth Civic Club (1914), Newport Woman's Club (1910), North Bend Woman's Club (1918), Ontario Study Club (1906), Oregon City Woman's Club (1903), Oswego Woman's Club (1906), Rogue River Civic Improvement Club (1911), Salem Woman's Club (1901), Stanfield Woman's Study Club (1911), Talent Federated Woman's Club (Talent, 1912), Wasco Woman's Study Club (Grass Valley, 1908), Weston Saturday Afternoon Club (1913), and Woodburn Woman's Club (1903). Oregon Federation of Women's Clubs, 1970–72 Directory, OHS.

17. Corning, *Dictionary of Oregon History*, 81.

18. Ibid.

19. Mrs. Leroy Mason, "A Tribute to Sarah A. Evans, One of Oregon's Pioneer Clubwomen," *Oregon Clubwoman* (Dec.–Jan. 1939–1940): 9, OSC, UO.

20. *Portland Oregonian*, Jan. 21, 1917.

21. Beard, *Woman's Work in Municipalities*, 75.

22. Ibid., 203.

23. President's Address, Oregon Federation of Women's Clubs Meeting, Oct. 25–28, 1915, Salem, Oregon; President's Address, Yearbook, Oregon Federation of Women's Clubs, 1910–11, 10–11.

24. President's Address, Yearbook, Oregon Federation of Women's Clubs, Nov. 10–12, 1908, La Grande, Oregon.

25. President's Address, Oregon Federation of Women's Clubs Meeting, Oct. 25–28, 1915, Salem, Oregon.

26. Jane Addams, Carrie Chapman Catt, and other women convened what became the controversial Women's Peace Party in 1915, a movement joined by many clubwomen but decried by others as unpatriotic. Carson, *Settlement Folk*, 154.

27. *Club Journal* (Dec. 1902): 295.

28. Handbook, Oregon Federation of Women's Clubs Convention, 1903–4, OHS.

29. Yearbook, Oregon Federation of Women's Clubs, 1910–11, 19, 10, OHS.

30. Yearbook, OFWC, 1910–11, 14–15.

31. Yearbook, OFWC, 1912–13, 30.

32. Yearbook, OFWC, 1911–12, 10.

33. Marie Louise Degen, *The History of the Woman's Peace Party*, 112.

34. Hogsett, *The Golden Years*, 10.

35. Ibid., 9.

36. Ibid., 23.

37. Nell Irion, "Third District Idaho Federation of Women's Clubs," in Hogsett, *The Golden Years*, 273–74.

38. Mrs. H. A. Wagner, "First District Idaho Federation of Women's Clubs," in Hogsett, *The Golden Years*, 231.

39. Ibid., 232.

40. Member clubs included Chautauqua of Caldwell; the Entre Nous and Sub Rosa clubs of Mountain Home; Outlook of Weiser; Fortnightly of Hailey; Tuesday History Club, Parliamentary Club, and Columbian Club of Boise; Village Improvement Club of South Boise; Current Events of Blackfoot; Study League and Civic Club of Pocatello; Woman's Literary Club of St. Anthony; Woman's Century Club of Nampa; Gem of the Mountains Club and Kymry Club of Montpelier. Added soon to the list were the Historical Society, Moscow; Tsceminicum, Twentieth Century, and Caecilian Society of Lewiston; New Century Club of Wardner (Kellogg); Woman's Club of Mullan; Coeur d'Alene Treble Clef; and the Village Improvement Society of Idaho Falls. In addition, the group had letters of support from Boise's Fortnightly Club, Moscow's Pleiades, and Grangeville's Woman's Club. Hogsett, *The Golden Years*, 13–14.

41. Ibid., 19.

42. Ibid., 16–17.

43. Ibid., 21–22.

44. Colson, *Idaho's Constitution*, 13.

45. Hogsett, *The Golden Years*, 23.

46. Ibid., 26.

47. Ibid., 27.

48. Ibid., 32–35.

49. Ibid., 31.

50. Ibid., 36–40.

51. Ibid., 42–44.

52. Ibid., 47.

53. Ibid., 86.

54. Ibid., 51–52.

55. Ibid., 52–53.

56. Ibid., 54.

57. Ibid., 59.

58. Ibid., 58.

59. Ibid., 65–69.

60. Ibid., 54–55.

61. Ibid., 60–61.

62. Ibid., 92–93.

63. Ibid., 93–94.

64. June Almquist, undated newspaper clipping, Women's Clubs, Washington History Files, Northwest Room, WSL.

65. Washington Federation of Women's Clubs, MC, UW.

66. Amy Stacy, as quoted in Croly, *The History of the Woman's Club Movement*, 1148.

67. Serena Mathews, "History of the Washington State Federation of Women's Clubs," Washington Federation of Women's Clubs Records, MC, UW (typescript, no date).

68. Ibid., 12.

69. Whitney, *Notable Women*, 3.

70. Mathews, "History," 13–14.

71. Andrews, *Washington Women*, 137.

72. "Mrs. Serena F. Mathews, Past State President, Dies," *Washington Clubwoman* 35, 1 (June 1952): 1, and newspaper clippings in possession of Mrs. Jack Friel, Pullman.

73. *Club Journal* (Oct. 1902): 175.

74. Rothman, *Woman's Proper Place*, 99.

75. Resolutions for 1907, "Minutes of the Washington State Federation of Women's Clubs, 1900–1908," WSFWC.

76. Berner, *Seattle 1900–1920*, 51, 54.

77. Initially set aside and designated Olympic National Monument, it became Olympic National Park in 1938.

78. "Washington State Federation," *Club Journal* (Oct. 1902): 173.

79. Andrews, *Washington Women*, 137.

80. Ibid., 49.

81. Mathews, "History," 39.

82. Davis, *Lifting as They Climb*, 173.

83. Mathews, "History," 51.

84. Blair, "The Limits of Sisterhood," 67.

85. Binheim, *Women of the West*, no page number.

86. Mathews, "History," 55.

87. Ibid., 118–19.

88. Wesley, *History of the NACWC*, 452–55.

89. Davis, *Lifting as They Climb*, 37.

90. Officers of the first Washington State Federation for African-American women also included Mrs. W. D. Carter, Seattle, first vice-president; Mrs. J. C. Grubbs, Spokane, recording secretary; Mrs. Holtsclaw, Spokane, Mrs. E. J. Corbin, Tacoma, Mrs. M. F. Fisher, Seattle, Mrs. Asberry, Tacoma, Mrs. A. R. Bonner, Seattle, Mrs. E. M. J. Simms, Spokane, and Mrs. W. F. Williams, Spokane, as lesser officers. Davis, *Lifting as They Climb*, 399.

91. Andrews, *Washington Women*, 20–21.

92. Beard, *Woman's Work in Municipalities*, 224–25.

93. Sarah Evans, President's Address, Oregon Federation of Women's Clubs Meeting, Oct. 25–28, Salem, 1914–15, 10, OSC, UO.

94. Ibid., 11.

95. Ibid., 11–12.

CHAPTER 10. THEIR LEGACY

1. Sarah Evans, President's Address, Oregon Federation of Women's Clubs Eighth Meeting Yearbook, Nov. 10–12, 1908–9, 10–12, La Grande, Oregon, OSC, UO.

2. Hogsett, *The Golden Years*, 59.

3. Morton Keller, *Regulating a New Society: Public Policy and Social Change in America, 1900–1933.*

4. Those answering "no" when asked whether certain federal programs should cut to reduce the deficit included 54 percent no on AFDC; 64 percent no on unemployment insurance; 73 percent no on Medicaid cuts; 86 percent no on Social Security; and 88 percent no on Medicare cuts. The Times Poll interviewed 1,353 adults nationwide, with a sampling error of plus or minus 3 percentage points. *Los Angeles Times* Poll National Survey, Jan. 19–22, 1995, distributed to H-State e-mail list on Jan. 25, 1995.

5. ABC News Survey conducted Jan. 8–9, 1995, of 1,145 adults, with error margin of plus or minus 3.5 percentage points, conducted by Chilton Research Services, Radnor, Pa.

6. President's Address, Yearbook, Oregon Federation of Women's Clubs Meeting, Oct. 25–28, Salem, Oregon, 1914–15, 9–10, OSC, UO.

7. Beard, *Woman's Work in Municipalities*, 250–51.

8. Linda Gordon, *Pitied But Not Entitled: Single Mothers and the History of Welfare, 1890–1935*, 36–37.

9. Ibid.

10. Ibid., 59–61.

11. New York Times News Service, citing figures from Congressional Budget Office, Internal Revenue Service, Congressional Research Service, Office of Management and Budget, Department of Agriculture, and Census Bureau. "Taxpayers Are Angry: They're Expensive, Too," *Idaho Statesman* (Boise), Nov. 25, 1994, 4A.

12. President's Address, Oregon Federation of Women's Clubs Meeting, Oct. 25–28, 1915, Salem, OSC, UO.

13. Beard, *Woman's Work in Municipalities*, 148–49.

14. Haarsager, *Bertha Knight Landes of Seattle*, 185–87.

15. McLagan, *A Peculiar Paradise*, 134–35.

16. "Women Lock on Fight over Film," undated clipping, Earl W. Shimmons Scrapbook, in possession of Roy Atwood, University of Idaho, Moscow.

17. Beard, *Woman's Work in Municipalities*, 148–49.

18. Ibid., 235–36.

19. Haarsager, *Bertha Knight Landes of Seattle*, 59.

20. President's Address, Yearbook, Oregon Federation of Women's Clubs Eighth Meeting, Nov. 10–12, La Grande, Oregon, 1908, OSC, UO.

21. Croly, *The History of the Woman's Club Movement*, preface.

22. Sandra Schackel, *Social Housekeepers: Women Shaping Public Policy in New Mexico, 1920–1940*, 87, 89.

23. Livermore, "Women's Clubs—A Symposium," 387–88.

24. Martin Olasky, *The Tragedy of American Compassion.* Some

complained his work on this issue was suspect because it was funded by conservative organizations anxious to reduce the size of government.

25. Judy Magid, "Join the Club," *Salt Lake City Tribune*, Oct. 30, 1994, J1.

APPENDIX

1. Hogsett, *The Golden Years*, 300.
2. Beard, *Woman's Work in Municipalities*, 313–14.
3. Hogsett, *The Golden Years*, 333.
4. "Librarians' Recollections," Idaho Public Libraries—History Materials, A & M, ISL.
5. *Idahonian* (Moscow), Mar. 18, 1958, cited in ibid.
6. Minidoka County Historical Society, *A History of Minidoka County and Its People*, 70–75.
7. Idaho Library History, entry by Olive Locey, 1919, A & M, ISL.
8. *Club Journal* (Dec. 1902): 293–94.
9. Phinney, "The Woman's Club, Formerly the Coffee Club," Benton County Societies and Organizations, OSLA, and Additon, *Twenty Eventful Years*, 69.
10. Lee Banning Morris, "The Corvallis Woman's Club: A Century of Service," *Society Record*, publication of the Benton County Historical Society (Sept.–Oct. 1982): 3.
11. Phinney, quoting club minutes.
12. Morris, "The Corvallis Woman's Club," 3.
13. Yearbook, 1921–22, Fortnightly Club, Women's Clubs Manuscripts, OHS.
14. Clara Powell Manuscripts, OSC, UO.
15. *Club Journal* (June 1903): 21.
16. Women's Clubs Yearbooks, WHC, WSL.
17. Andrews, *Washington Women*, 139.
18. Women's Clubs Yearbooks, WHC, WSL.
19. (Port Angeles) *Evening News*, Aug. 3, 1966, Women's Clubs, Washington History Files, WSL.
20. Laura Lee Appleton, "The Heritage of a Woman's Place: Women as Wives, Workers, and Wheels," in *Northwest Women's Heritage*, ed. Karen Blair, 221, and Andrews, *Washington Women*, 126.
21. Women's Clubs Yearbooks, WHC, WSL.
22. Earle C. Jameson, "Women of Grays Harbor," WHC, WSL, 29.
23. "The Columbia Digest, Historical Edition," pamphlet in Women's Clubs, WHC, WSL.
24. Women's Clubs, WHC, WSL.
25. Women's Clubs Yearbooks, WHC, WSL.
26. Andrews, *Washington Women*, 140.
27. Women's Clubs Yearbooks, WHC, WSL.
28. AAUW, *A View from the Falls*, 33.
29. Croly, *The History of the Woman's Club Movement*, 1140–41.
30. Caroline Kellogg, "Aloha Club: 85 Years Promoting the Good

Life," *Tacoma News Tribune*, Oct. 3, 1976, and Croly, *The History of the Woman's Club Movement*, 1131.

31. Women's Clubs Yearbooks, WHC, WSL.

32. Leone Hill, "History of Local Women's Club Told by Writer," (White Salmon) *Enterprise*, Sept. 29, 1960.

33. Andrews, *Washington Women*, 126.

BIBLIOGRAPHY

PRIMARY ARCHIVAL COLLECTIONS

Bancroft Library, Berkeley, California. Manuscripts Collection. Mason Brayman Letters. Martha Ann Minto, "Female Pioneering" (1878). Mrs. Theodore Schultze, Personal Anecdotes (1879). Gatzert Schwabacher Papers.

Idaho State Library, Boise. Archives and Manuscripts. Columbian Club Records. Equal Suffrage Society Records. Idaho Public Libraries— History Materials. Idaho WCTU Records. Ladies' Mite Association Minutes, Idaho City, Idaho.

Museum of History and Industry, Seattle. Carkeek Scrapbooks, Seattle History 1884–1917 (4 vols.). Edmond Meany, "Living Pioneers of Washington."

Oregon Historical Society, Portland. Associations and Institutions. Catherine Julia Adams Diary (1885). Oregon Federation of Women's Clubs Records. Bethenia Owens Adair Papers. Portland Women's Club Records. Portland Women's Union Records. Woman's Temperance Prayer League.

Oregon State Library Archives, Salem. Societies and Social Organizations. WPA Writers Project.

University of Oregon, Eugene. Manuscripts Room. Fred Lockley Biographies. Jesse Applegate Papers. McMinnville Ladies' Sanitary Aid Society Records.

University of Oregon, Eugene. Oregon Special Collections. Clara Powell Manuscripts. Clubs and Societies. Oregon Women's Club Federation Records.

University of Washington, Seattle. Manuscripts Collection. Century Club Records. Nelle Mitchell Fick Papers. Washington State Federation of Women's Clubs Records.

Washington State Historical Society, Tacoma. Woman's Club of Tacoma Records. Tacoma Women's Club Records.

Washington State Library, Olympia. Emma Smith Devoe Papers. Washington Women's Suffrage Papers. Women's Clubs Yearbooks.

BOOKS AND ARTICLES

Additon, Lucia H. F. *Twenty Eventful Years of the Oregon Women's Christian Temperance Union, 1880–1900*. Portland: Gotshall Printing Co., 1904.

Aiken, Katherine. "The National Florence Crittenton Mission in the Pacific Northwest." In *Northwest Women's Heritage,* ed. Karen Blair, 47–63. Seattle: Northwest Center for Research on Women, 1985.

Altbach, Edith H. *Women in America.* Lexington, Mass.: D. C. Heath and Co., 1974.

American Association of University Women, Spokane Branch. *By the Falls: Women of Determination.* Spokane, Wash.: AAUW, 1989.

Anderson, Karen. "Western Women." In *The Twentieth Century West,* ed. Gerald Nash and Richard Etulain, 99–122. Albuquerque: University of New Mexico Press, 1989.

Anderson, Lisa. "Who Are Politicians Talking about, Anyway?" In *Chicago Tribune,* reprinted in *Spokesman-Review* (Spokane, Washington), December 28, 1994, A1, A10.

Andrews, Margaret. *Washington Women as Pathbreakers.* Dubuque, Ia.: Kendall/Hunt Publishing Co., 1989.

Appleton, Laura Lee. "The Heritage of a Woman's Place: Women as Wives, Workers, and Wheels." In *Northwest Women's Heritage,* ed. Karen Blair, 9–20. Seattle: Northwest Center for Research on Women, 1985.

Armitage, Susan. "The Frontier through Women's Eyes." In *Interpreting Local Culture and History,* ed. J. Sanford Rikoon and Judith Austin. Boise and Moscow: Idaho Historical Society and University of Idaho Press, 1991.

———. "Women and Men in Western History: A Stereoptical Vision." *Western Historical Quarterly* (October 1985): 381–91.

"Around the World." *Club Journal* (March 1903): 358.

Arrington, Leonard. *History of Idaho.* Moscow: University of Idaho Press, 1995.

Atwood, Roy Alden. "Handwritten Newspapers in North America: An Annotated Bibliography." Moscow, Idaho. Unpublished bibliography, 1993.

Ault, Nelson. "The Earnest Ladies: The Walla Walla Woman's Club and the Equal Suffrage League of 1886–1889." *Pacific Northwest Quarterly* 42 (April 1951): 123–37.

Avery, Mary W. *History and Government of the State of Washington.* Seattle: University of Washington Press, 1961.

Baer, Judith. *The Chains of Protection: The Judicial Response to Women's Labor Legislation.* Westport, Conn.: Greenwood Press, 1978.

Baker, Paula. "The Domestication of Politics: Women and American Political Society, 1780–1920." *American Historical Review* (June 1984): 601–22.

———. *The Moral Frameworks of Public Life: Gender, Politics, and the State in Rural New York, 1870–1930.* New York: Oxford University Press, 1991.

Baldwin, Henry. "An Old-Time Sorosis." *Atlantic Monthly* 74, 447 (1894): 748–55.

Banks, Louis Albert. *Censor Echoes.* Portland: Hines Publishing, 1882.

Barton, Harold, and Catharine Bullard. *History of the State of Washington.* Boston: D. C. Heath and Co., 1953.

Baxandall, Rosalyn, Linda Gordon, and Susan Reverby, eds. *America's Working Women: A Documentary History, 1600 to the Present*. New York: Random House Vintage Books, 1976.

Beard, Mary Ritter. *Woman's Work in Municipalities*. New York: D. Appleton, 1916.

Beeton, Beverly. *Women Vote in the West: The Woman Suffrage Movement 1869–1896*. New York: Garland Publishing, 1986.

Beeton, Beverly, and G. Thomas Edwards. "Susan B. Anthony's Woman Suffrage Campaign in the American West." *Journal of the West* 21 (1982): 5–15.

Benton, Caroline French. *The Complete Club Book for Women*. Boston: Colonial Press, Page Co., 1915.

Berner, Richard. *Seattle 1900–1920: From Boomtown, Urban Turbulence, to Restoration*. Seattle: Charles Press, 1991.

Binheim, Max, ed. *Women of the West*. Los Angeles: Publishers Press, 1920.

Blair, Karen. *The Clubwoman as Feminist: True Womanhood Defined, 1868–1914*. New York: Holmes and Meier, 1980.

————. *The History of American Women's Voluntary Organizations, 1810–1960: A Guide to Sources*. Boston: G. K. Hall and Co., 1989.

————. "The Limits of Sisterhood: The Women's Building in Seattle, 1907–1921." In *Women in Pacific Northwest History: An Anthology*, 65–82. Seattle: University of Washington Press, 1988.

————. *The Torchbearers: Women and Their Amateur Arts Associations in America, 1890–1930*. Bloomington: Indiana University Press, 1994.

Boise City and Ada County Directory. Boise: Farr and Smith, 1901–2.

Boise City Directory. Boise: Leadbetter and Walterbeek, 1891 and 1899.

Bordin, Ruth. "'A Baptism of Power and Liberty': The Women's Crusade of 1873–74." In *Woman's Being, Woman's Place: Female Identity and Vocation in American History*, ed. Mary Kelley, 283–95. Boston: G. K. Hall, 1979.

————. *Frances Willard: A Biography*. Chapel Hill: University of North Carolina Press, 1986.

————. *Woman and Temperance: The Quest for Power and Liberty, 1873–1900*. Philadelphia: Temple University Press, 1981.

Breckinridge, Sophonisba. *Women in the Twentieth Century: A Study of Their Political, Social and Economic Activities*. New York: McGraw-Hill Book Co., 1933.

Bremner, Robert H. *The Public Good: Philanthropy and Welfare in the Civil War Era*. New York: Alfred A. Knopf, 1980.

Brewster, David, and David Buerge, eds. *Washingtonians: A Biographical Portrait of the State*. Seattle: Sasquatch Books, 1988.

Brown, Arthur. "The Promotion of Emigration to Washington, 1854–1909." *Pacific Northwest Quarterly* 36 (1945): 16–17.

Brown, Joseph C. *The Rainbow Seekers: Stories of Spokane, the Expo City, and the Inland Empire*. Spokane: Wescoast Publishing Co., 1974.

Buckendorf, Madeline. "The Poultry Frontier: Family Farm Roles and

Turkey Raising in Southwest Idaho, 1910–1940." *Idaho Yesterdays* 37, 2 (Summer 1993): 2–8.

Campbell, Barbara Kuhn. *The "Liberated" Woman of 1914: Prominent Women in the Progressive Era.* Ann Arbor: UMI Research Press, 1979.

Carby, Hazel. *Reconstructing Womanhood: The Emergence of the Afro-American Woman Novelist.* New York: Oxford University Press, 1987.

Carson, Mina. *Settlement Folk: Social Thought and the American Settlement Movement, 1885–1930.* Chicago: University of Chicago Press, 1990.

Carter-Brooks, Elizabeth. Introduction to Elizabeth Davis, *Lifting as They Climb: The National Association of Colored Women.* Ann Arbor, Mich.: Xerox University Microfilms, 1974.

Chodorow, Nancy. *The Reproduction of Mothering.* Palo Alto, Calif.: Stanford University Press, 1978.

Clawson, Mary Ann. *Constructing Brotherhood: Class, Gender and Fraternalism.* Princeton: Princeton University Press, 1989.

Clinton, Catherine. *The Other Civil War: Women in the Nineteenth Century.* New York: Hill and Wang, 1984.

Colson, Dennis. *Idaho's Constitution: The Tie That Binds.* Moscow: University of Idaho Press, 1991.

"The Columbia River." *Harper's Magazine* (1882). Reprinted in *The West: A Collection from Harper's Magazine.* New York: Gallery Books, 1990.

Conley, Cort. *Idaho for the Curious.* Cambridge, Idaho: Backeddy Books, 1982.

Cooley, Winnifred Harper. "The Future of the Woman's Club." *Arena* 27, 4 (1902): 374–80.

Corning, Howard McKinley, ed. *Dictionary of Oregon History.* Portland: Binford and Mort, 1956.

Cott, Nancy. *Bonds of Womanhood: Woman's Sphere in New England, 1780–1835.* New Haven: Yale University Press, 1977.

——. *The Grounding of Modern Feminism.* New Haven: Yale University Press, 1987.

Croly, Jane C. *History of the Woman's Club Movement in America.* New York: Henry G. Allen, 1898.

——. *Sorosis—Its Origin and History.* New York: J. J. Little, 1886.

Davis, Angela Y. *Women, Race and Class.* New York: Random House, 1981.

Davis, Elizabeth. *Lifting as They Climb: The National Association of Colored Women.* Ann Arbor, Mich.: Xerox University Microfilms, 1974.

d'Easum, Dick. *Dowager of Discipline.* Moscow: University of Idaho Press, 1981.

Degen, Marie Louise. *The History of the Woman's Peace Party.* Baltimore: Johns Hopkins Press, 1939.

De Graaf, Lawrence B. "Race, Sex, and Region: Black Women in the American West, 1850–1920." *Pacific Historical Review* 49, 2 (May 1980): 285–313.

Denning, Michael. *Mechanic Accents: Dime Novels and Working-Class*

Culture in America. London: Verso, imprint of New Left Books, 1987.

de Tocqueville, Alexis. *Democracy in America.* New York: New American Library, 1984.

Directory and Handbook, King County Women's Christian Temperance Union. Seattle: King County WCTU, 1923.

Dorpat, Paul. *Seattle, Now and Then.* Seattle: Tartu Publications, 1984.

Drake, Emma Angell. *What Every Young Woman Ought to Know.* Philadelphia: Vir Publishing Co.

Drury, Clifford M. "The Columbia Maternal Association." *Oregon Historical Quarterly* 39 (June 1938): 99–122.

———. *First White Women over the Rockies.* 3 vols. Glendale, Calif.: A. H. Clark Co., 1963–66.

Duniway, Abigail Scott. *Pathbreaking: An Autobiographical History of the Equal Suffrage Movement in Pacific Coast States.* Portland, 1914.

Dye, Eva Emery. *The Conquest—The True Story of Lewis and Clark.* Chicago: A. C. McClurg and Co., 1902.

———. Review of *Letters from an Oregon Ranch. Oregon Historical Quarterly* 7 (1906): 435.

Eagle, Mary Kavanaugh Oldham. *The Congress of Women Held in the Women's Building, World's Columbian Exposition.* 2 vols. Chicago, 1894.

Edwards, G. Thomas. "Dr. Ada M. Weed: Northwest Reformer." *Oregon Historical Quarterly* 78 (March 1977): 5–40.

———. "Interpreting Eastern Washington through the Camera of a Seattle Photographer." In *Interpreting Local Culture and History,* ed. J. Sanford Rikoon and Judith Austin. Boise and Moscow: Idaho State Historical Society and University of Idaho Press, 1991.

———. *Sowing Good Seeds.* Seattle: University of Washington Press, 1987.

Emerson, Ralph Waldo. "The Conduct of Life," "Man the Reformer," and "The Poet." In *Ralph Waldo Emerson: Selected Essays.* New York: Viking Penguin, 1982.

Epstein, Donald. "Gladstone Chautauqua: Education and Entertainment, 1893–1928." *Oregon Historical Quarterly* 80, 4 (Winter 1979): 391–403.

Erickson, Edith E., and Eddy Ng. *From Sojourner to Citizen: Chinese of the Inland Empire.* Colfax, Wash.: University Printing.

Ethington, Philip. "Political Participation, Gender, and the Public Sphere: A Response to Maureen Flanagan's Review of *The Public City.*" Circulated on H-State Internet Mailing List, June 8, 1995.

———. *The Public City: The Political Construction of Urban Life in San Francisco, 1850–1900.* New York: Cambridge University Press, 1994.

Fahey, John. *The Days of the Hercules.* Moscow: University of Idaho Press, 1976.

———. *The Inland Empire, Unfolding Years, 1879–1929.* Seattle: University of Washington Press, 1986.

Fairfield, Francis Gerry. *The Clubs of New York: An Essay on New York Club Life.* New York: Henry L. Hinton, 1873. Reprinted by Arno Press, 1975.

Foucault, Michel. *Archaeology of Knowledge and Discourse on Language.* New York: Random House/Pantheon, 1972.

Frank, Dana. *Purchasing Power: Consumer Organizing, Gender, and the Seattle Labor Movement, 1919–1929.* New York: Cambridge University Press, 1994.

Freedman, Estelle. "Separatism as Strategy: Female Institution Building and American Feminism, 1870–1930." *Feminist Studies* 5 (Fall 1979): 512–29.

Fulmer, Elton. "The Adulteration of Food." *Club Journal,* ed. Mabel Plowman (September 1902): 124–27.

Gibbons, Margaret Wilson. *The American Woman in Transition: The Urban Influence 1870–1920.* Westport, Conn.: Greenwood Press, 1979.

Gilligan, Carol. *In a Different Voice.* Cambridge, Mass.: Harvard University Press, 1982.

Ginsberg, Lori. "'Moral Suasion Is Moral Balderdash': Women, Politics and Social Activism in the 1850s." *Journal of American History* 73 (December 1986): 601–22.

———. *Women and the Work of Benevolence: Morality, Politics and Class in the Nineteenth-Century United States.* New Haven, Conn.: Yale University Press, 1992.

Gittins, H. Leigh. *Pocatello Portrait: The Early Years, 1878 to 1928.* Moscow: University Press of Idaho, 1983.

Gordon, Linda. *Pitied But Not Entitled: Single Mothers and the History of Welfare, 1890–1935.* New York: Free Press, 1994.

Graff, Harvey J. *The Legacies of Literacy: Continuities and Contradictions in Western Culture and Society.* Bloomington: Indiana University Press, 1991.

———. "Literacy, Libraries, Lives: New Social and Cultural Histories." *Libraries and Culture* 26, 1 (Winter 1991): 12–17.

Green, Frank L. *Washington Centennial Hall of Honor.* Tacoma: Washington State Historical Society, 1989.

Green, Harvey. *The Light of the Home: An Intimate View of the Lives of Women in Victorian America.* New York: Pantheon, 1983.

Greenwald, Maurine Weiner. "Working Class Feminism and the Family Wage Ideal: The Seattle Debate on Married Women's Right to Work, 1914–1920." *Journal of American History* 76, 1 (June 1989): 140, 148.

Greenwood, Annie Pike. *We Sagebrush Folk.* New York: D. Appleton-Century Co., 1934. Reprinted by University of Idaho Press, 1988.

Griswold, Robert L. "Anglo Women and Domestic Ideology in the American West in the Nineteenth and Early Twentieth Centuries." In *Western Women: Their Land, Their Lives,* ed. Lillian Schlissel, Vicki L. Ruiz, and Janice Monk, 132–149. Albuquerque: University of New Mexico Press, 1988.

Haarsager, Sandra. *Bertha Knight Landes of Seattle: Big City Mayor.* Norman: University of Oklahoma Press, 1994.

Hagedorn, Leta. "The WCTU Story—One Hundred Years in Lewiston." *Nez Perce County Historical Society Journal* (Winter 1983): 4.

Hanaford, Phebe. *Daughters of America, or Women of the Century.* Augusta, Maine: True and Co., 1882.

Harper, Ida Hustad. *Life and Work of Susan B. Anthony.* New York: Garland, 1925.

———, ed. *History of Woman Suffrage.* New York: National American Woman Suffrage Association, 1922.

Harris, Michael. "The Purpose of the American Public Library: A Revisionist Interpretation of History." *Library Journal* 98 (September 15, 1973): 2509–14.

Hart, Arthur A. *The Boiseans: At Home.* Boise: Historic Boise, 1984.

Hewitt, Nancy A. *Women's Activism and Social Change, Rochester, New York, 1822–1872.* Ithaca, N.Y.: Cornell University Press, 1984.

Hobson, Barbara Meil. *Uneasy Virtue: The Politics of Prostitution and the American Reform Tradition.* New York: Basic Books.

Hoffman, Mark S., ed. *World Almanac and Book of Facts.* New York: Pharos Books, 1991.

Hogsett, Vernetta Murchison. *The Golden Years: A History of the Idaho Federation of Women's Clubs, 1905–1955.* Caldwell: Idaho Federation of Women's Clubs, Caxton Printers, 1955.

Holmes, H. E. *Pioneer Links.* Seattle: Press of the Washington Odd Fellow, 1913.

Hubbell, Thelma Lee. "The Friday Morning Club: A Los Angeles Legacy." *Southern California Quarterly* 50 (March 1968): 59–90.

Hughes, Geoffrey. *Words in Time: A Social History of the English Vocabulary.* New York: Basil Blackwell, 1989.

Jacox, Elizabeth. "Exhibit Chronicles Lives of Women." *Mountain Light: Newsletter of the Idaho State Historical Society* 33, 3 (Spring 1994): 6–7.

Jennings, Linda. "Skagit County Is Strong for Woman Suffrage." *Bellingham Sunday Herald Suffrage Edition,* October 9, 1910.

Jensen, Joan M. "After Slavery: Caroline Severance in Los Angeles." *Southern California Quarterly* 48 (June 1966): 175–86.

Johnson, Warren B. "Muckraking in the Northwest: Joe Smith and Seattle Reform." *Pacific Historical Review* 40 (November 1971): 481–87.

Jones, R. S., Jr. "What the Visitor Sees at the Seattle Fair." *American Review of Reviews* 40 (1909): 68.

Josephy, Alvin, Jr. *The Civil War in the American West.* New York: Alfred A. Knopf, 1992.

Kasson, John F. *Rudeness and Civility: Manners in Nineteenth-Century Urban America.* New York: Hill and Wang, 1990.

Keller, Morton. *Regulating a New Society: Public Policy and Social Change in America, 1900–1933.* Cambridge, Mass.: Harvard University Press, 1994.

Kennedy, Mary Virginia. "A Study of Dr. Minnie F. Howard." Unpublished paper, University of Denver, 1968, Idaho State Library, Boise, Idaho.

Kerber, Linda K. "'Why Should Girls Be Learn'd and Wise?': Two Centuries of Higher Education for Women as Seen through the Unfinished Work of Alice Mary Baldwin." In *Women and Higher Education in American History,* ed. John Mack Faragher and Florence Howe, 32–42. New York: W. W. Norton and Co., 1988.

———. *Women of the Republic: Intellect and Ideology in Revolutionary America.* Chapel Hill: University of North Carolina Press, 1980.

Knowles, Margaret, ed. *The Seattle Woman—The Club Woman's Annual.* Seattle: Washington Federation of Women's Clubs, December 1924.

Koven, Seth, and Sonya Michel. "Womanly Duties: Maternalist Politics and the Origins of Welfare States in France, Germany, Great Britain, and the United States, 1880–1920." *American Historical Review* 95 (October 1990): 1076–108.

———, eds. *Mothers of a New World: Maternalist Politics and the Origins of Welfare States.* New York: Routledge, 1993.

Lagemann, Ellen Condliffe. *The Politics of Knowledge: The Carnegie Corporation, Philanthropy, and Public Policy.* Middletown, Conn.: Wesleyan University Press, 1989.

Larson, T. A. "Dolls, Vassals and Drudges: Pioneer Women in the West." *Western Historical Quarterly* 3 (January 1972): 5–16.

———. "Idaho's Role in America's Woman Suffrage Crusade." *Idaho Yesterdays* 18 (Spring 1964): 2–15.

———. "The Women's Rights Movement in Idaho." *Idaho Yesterdays* 16 (Spring 1972): 2–15, 18–19.

Levine, Lawrence. *Highbrow/Lowbrow: The Emergence of Cultural Hierarchy in America.* Boston: Harvard University Press, 1988.

Limerick, Patricia. *The Legacy of Conquest: The Unbroken Past of the American West.* New York: W. W. Norton, 1987.

Lockley, Fred. *Conversations with Pioneer Women.* Compiled by Mike Helm. Eugene, Ore.: Rainy Day Press, 1993.

Luchetti, Cathy, and Carol Olwell. *Women of the West.* New York: Orion Press, 1982.

Lutz, Alma. *Susan B. Anthony: Rebel, Crusader, Humanitarian.* Boston: Beacon Press, 1959.

MacBride, Thomas H. "Culture and Women's Clubs." An address before the Minnesota Federation of Women's Clubs, Minneapolis, February 12, 1916. University of Iowa Extension Bulletin No. 20. Iowa City: University of Iowa, 1916.

MacColl, E. K. *The Shaping of a City: Business and Politics in Portland, Oregon, 1885–1915.* Portland: Georgian Press Co., 1976.

MacKnight, Kate Cassatt. "Communications: Report of the Civic Committee." *Annals of the American Academy* 28, 2 (1906): 293–96.

Magid, Judy. "Join the Club." *Salt Lake City Tribune,* October 30, 1994, J1.

Malone, Michael P., and Richard Etulain. *The American West: A Twentieth-Century History.* Lincoln: University of Nebraska Press, 1989.

Martin, Theodora Penny. *The Sound of Our Own Voices: Women's Study Clubs 1860–1910.* Boston: Beacon Press, 1987.

Mathews, Serena F. "Washington Women Must Take Place in World Affairs." *Spokane Woman* 8, 37 (June 20, 1929): 1.

Matthews, Glenna. *Just a Housewife: The Rise and Fall of Domesticity in America.* New York: Oxford University Press, 1987.

———. *The Rise of Public Woman: Woman's Power and Woman's Place in the United States, 1630–1970.* New York: Oxford University Press, 1992.

May, Elaine Tyler. "Myths and Realities of the American Family." In *A History of Private Life: Riddles of Identity in Modern Times,* ed. Antoine Prost and Gerard Vincent, 539–594. Cambridge and London: Belknap Press of Harvard University Press, 1991.

McGlashan, Zena Beth. "Club 'Ladies' and the Working 'Girls': Rheta Childe Dorr and the New York Evening Post." *Journalism History* 8 (Spring 1981): 7–13.

McGregor, Alexander. *Counting Sheep: From Open Range to Agribusiness on the Columbia Plateau.* Seattle: University of Washington Press, 1989.

McLagan, Elizabeth. *A Peculiar Paradise: A History of Blacks in Oregon, 1788–1940.* Portland: Oregon Black History Project, Georgian Press, 1980.

Meckel, Richard. "Educating a Ministry of Mothers: Evangelical Maternal Associations, 1815–1860." *Journal of the Early Republic* 2 (Spring 1982): 403–23.

"Men's Views of Women's Clubs: A Symposium." *Annals of the American Academy of Political and Social Science* (September 1906): 283–92.

Merriam, Paul G. "The 'Other Portland': A Statistical Note on the Foreign-Born, 1860–1910." *Oregon Historical Quarterly* 80 (1989): 258–68.

———. "Urban Elite in the Far West: Portland, Oregon, 1870–1890." *Arizona and the West* 18 (1976): 41–52.

Minidoka County Historical Society. *A History of Minidoka County and Its People.* Dallas: Taylor Publishing Co., 1985.

Montgomery, James W. *Liberated Woman: A Life of May Arkwright Hutton.* Spokane: Gingko House Publishers.

Moore, Marvin. "Palouse Hills Farmstead Architecture, 1890–1915." *Oregon Historical Quarterly* (Summer 1984): 181–93.

Morris, Lee Banning. "The Corvallis Woman's Club: A Century of Service." *Society Record,* publication of the Benton County Historical Society (September–October 1982): 3.

Morris, William A. "Historian of the Northwest: A Woman Who Loved Oregon." *Oregon Historical Quarterly* 3 (December 1902): 429–34.

Moynihan, Ruth. "Let Women Vote: Abigail Scott Duniway in Washington Territory." In *Washington Comes of Age: The State in the National Experience,* ed. David H. Stratton, 96–111. Pullman: Washington State University Press, 1992.

———. *Rebel for Rights: Abigail Scott Duniway.* New Haven: Yale University Press.

Moynihan, Ruth B., Susan Armitage, and Christiane Fischer Dichamp, eds. Introduction to *So Much to Be Done: Women Settlers on the Mining and Ranching Frontier.* Lincoln: University of Nebraska Press, 1990.

Mueller, Gene. *Lewiston: A Pictorial History.* Lewiston, Idaho: Western Printing and Lewiston Chamber of Commerce, 1986.

Mumford, Esther. *Seattle's Black Victorians.* Seattle: University of Washington Press. 1969.

Myres, Sandra. *Westering Women and the Frontier Experience.* Albuquerque: University of New Mexico Press, 1982.

Nathan, Maud. *The Story of an Epoch-Making Movement.* Garden City: Doubleday, 1926. Reprinted New York: Garland Publishing, 1986.

Niles, Edith L. "Scientific Training." *Club Journal* (October 1902): 153–55.

Norwood, Vera. "Women's Place: Continuity and Change in Response to Western Landscapes." In *Western Women: Their Land, Their Lives,* ed. Lillian Schlissel, Vicki L. Ruiz, and Janice Monk. Albuquerque: University of New Mexico Press, 1988.

Nugent, Walter. "The People of the West since 1890." In *The Twentieth-Century West,* ed. Gerald Nash and Richard Etulain. Albuquerque: University of New Mexico Press, 1989.

Olasky, Martin. *The Tragedy of American Compassion.* Crossway Books, 1992.

Olsen, Kirsten. *Remember the Ladies.* Pittstown, N.J.: Main Street Press, 1988.

Owens Adair, Bethenia. *Dr. Owens Adair, Some of Her Life Experiences.* Portland: Owens Adair, 1906.

Paulson, Ross Evans. *Women's Suffrage and Prohibition: A Comparative Study of Equality and Social Control.* Glenview, Ill.: Scott, Foresman and Co., 1973.

Pearson, Ivan. "The Hutton Settlement" (part 2). *Pacific Northwesterner* 11, 3 (Summer 1967): 35.

Pease, James. "Land Use and Ownership." In *Atlas of the Pacific Northwest,* ed. Philip Jackson and A. Jon Kimerling, 31–33. Corvallis: Oregon State University Press, 1993.

Penson-Ward, Betty. *Women in Idaho History: Big and Little Biographies and Other Gender Stories.* Boise: Legendary Publishing, 1991.

Perkins, Linda M. "The Education of Black Women in the Nineteenth Century." In *Women and Higher Education in American History,* ed. John Mack Faragher and Florence Howe. New York: W. W. Norton and Co., 1988.

Pigott, H. C. *Pigott's Political Reference Book for King County.* Seattle: Pigott, 1928.

Poole, Hester. "Difficulties and Delights of Women's Clubs." In *Transactions of the National Council of Women,* 302. Philadelphia: J. B. Lippincott, 1891.

Potts, Ralph Bushel. *Seattle Heritage.* Seattle: Superior Publishing Co., 1955.

Ray, Emma P. *Twice Sold, Twice Ransomed: Autobiography of Mr. and*

Mrs. L. O. Ray. Chicago, 1926. Reprint, Freeport, N.Y.: Books for Libraries Press, 1971.

Reiff, Janice L. "Urbanization and the Social Structure: Seattle, Washington, 1852–1910." Dissertation. Seattle, University of Washington, 1981.

Reinhart, Sophie. Bylined column printed in *Portland Oregonian,* September 18, 1899.

Reiter, Joan Swallow. *The Women.* Alexandria, Va.: Time-Life Books, Old West Series, 1968.

Riley, Glenda. *The Female Frontier: A Comparative View of Women on the Prairie and the Plains.* Lawrence: University Press of Kansas, 1988.

———. "The Subtle Subversion: Changes in the Traditionalist Image of the American Woman." *Historian* 32, 2 (1970): 210–27.

Robert, Henry M. *Robert's Rules of Order Revised.* New York: William Morrow and Co., 1971; reprint of 1915 edition.

Rodgers, Daniel. "Republicanism: The Career of a Concept." *Journal of American History* 79, 1 (June 1992): 11–38.

Rodman, W. Paul. "When Culture Came to Boise: Mary Hallock Foote in Idaho." *Idaho Historical Series* 19, Idaho State Historical Society (March 1977).

Rothman, Sheila M. *Woman's Proper Place: A History of Changing Ideals and Practices, 1870 to the Present.* New York: Basic Books, 1978.

Rubin, Joan Shelley. *The Making of Middle-Brow Culture.* Chapel Hill: University of North Carolina Press, 1992.

Ruby, Robert, and John Brown. *A Guide to the Indian Tribes of the Pacific Northwest.* Norman: University of Oklahoma Press.

Ruckman, Jo Ann. "Knit, Knit, and Then Knit: The Women of Pocatello and the War Effort of 1917–1918." *Idaho Yesterdays* 26 (Spring 1982): 26–30.

Ryan, Mary P. "A Women's Awakening: Evangelical Religion and the Families of Utica, 1800–1840." *American Quarterly* 30 (Winter 1978): 602–23.

Salvino, Dana Nelson. "The Word in Black and White: Ideologies of Race and Literacy in Antebellum America." In *Reading in America: Literature and Social History,* ed. Cathy Davidson, 145. Baltimore: Johns Hopkins University Press, 1989.

Schackel, Sandra. *Social Housekeepers: Women Shaping Public Policy in New Mexico, 1920–1940.* Albuquerque: University of New Mexico Press, 1992.

Schlereth, Thomas J. *Victorian America: Transformations in Everyday Life, 1876–1915.* New York: HarperCollins, 1991.

Schlissel, Lillian. *Women's Diaries of the Westward Journey.* New York: Schocken, 1982.

———. "Women's Diaries on the Western Frontier." *American Studies* 18 (Spring 1977): 87–100.

Schwantes, Carlos. *In Mountain Shadows: A History of Idaho.* Lincoln: University of Nebraska Press, 1991.

————. *The Pacific Northwest: An Interpretive History.* Lincoln: University of Nebraska Press, 1989.

Scott, Anne Firor. Interview on National Public Radio's *All Things Considered,* January 13, 1995.

————. *Making the Invisible Woman Visible.* Urbana: University of Illinois Press, 1984.

————. *Natural Allies: Women's Associations in American History.* Urbana: University of Illinois Press, 1991.

————. "On Seeing and Not Seeing: A Case of Historical Invisibility." *Journal of American History* 71 (June 1984): 7–21.

Sheehan, Nancy. "'Women Helping Women': The WCTU and the Foreign Population in the West, 1905–1930." *International Journal of Women's Studies* 6 (November–December 1983): 395–441.

Shimmons, Earl W. Scrapbook. In possession of Roy Atwood, University of Idaho, Moscow.

Sicherman, Barbara. "Sense and Sensibility: A Case Study of Women's Reading in Late-Victorian America." In *Reading in America: Literature and Social History,* ed. Cathy Davidson, 201–25. Baltimore: Johns Hopkins University Press, 1989.

Sklar, Kathryn Kish. "A Call for Comparisons." *American Historical Review* 95, 4 (October 1990): 1109.

————. "The Historical Foundations of Women's Power in the Creation of the American Welfare State, 1830–1930." In *Mothers of a New World: Maternalist Politics and the Origins of Welfare States,* ed. Seth Koven and Sonya Michel. New York: Routledge, 1993.

Skocpol, Theda. *Protecting Soldiers and Mothers: The Political Origins of Social Policies in the United States.* Cambridge, Mass.: Belknap Press of Harvard University, 1992.

Smith, Duane. *Rocky Mountain Mining Camps: The Urban Frontier.* Lincoln: University of Nebraska Press, 1974.

Sneed, Frances Jones. "Spokane's African-American Clubs." Paper presented at Pacific Northwest History Association Conference, Bellingham, Washington, March 24, 1994.

Spangler, D. W. "Mary Stewart, Educator, Author, and Club Woman." *Colorado Magazine* 27 (July 1950): 218–25.

Speidel, William. *Sons of the Profits.* Seattle: Nettle Creek Publishing Co., 1967.

Stefanco, Carolyn. "Networking on the Frontier: The Colorado Women's Suffrage Movement, 1876–1893." In *The Women's West,* ed. Susan Armitage and Elizabeth Jameson, 270–71. Norman: University of Oklahoma Press, 1987.

Swank, Gladys Rae. "Ladies of the House (and Senate): History of Idaho Women Legislators since Statehood." Unpublished MS. Idaho State Library, Boise, Idaho.

Taber, Ronald W. "Sacajawea and the Suffragettes." *Pacific Northwest Quarterly* 58 (January 1967): 7–13.

Tacoma City Directory. Tacoma: R. L. Polk and Co., 1908.

Taylor, Quintard. "The Emergence of Black Communities in the Pacific

Northwest: 1865–1910." *Journal of Negro History* 64 (Fall 1979): 346–51.

———. *The Forging of a Black Community: Seattle's Central District from 1870 through the Civil Rights Era.* Seattle: University of Washington Press, 1994.

"These Are My Clubs." *Oregon Clubwoman* (February 1937): 5. Oregon Special Collections, University of Oregon, Eugene, Oregon.

Tompkins, Jane. *West of Everything: The Inner Life of Westerns.* New York: Oxford University Press, 1992.

Trachtenberg, Alan. *The Incorporation of America: Culture and Society in the Gilded Age.* New York: Hill and Wang, 1982.

Transactions of the National Council of Women. Philadelphia: J. B. Lippincott, 1891.

Tripp, Joseph. "Toward an Efficient and Moral Society: Washington's Minimum Wage Law, 1913–1925." *Pacific Northwest Quarterly* 67 (July 1976): 97–112.

Turner, Victor. *From Ritual to Theatre: The Human Seriousness of Play.* New York: Performing Arts Journal Publications, 1982.

Van Voris, Jacqueline. *Carrie Chapman Catt: A Public Life.* New York: Feminist Press, 1987.

Votes for Women, ed. Mrs. M. T. B. Hanna (August–September 1910): 6.

Ward, Jean M. "The Emergence of a Mentor-Protegé Relationship: The 1871 Pacific Northwest Speaking Tour of Susan B. Anthony and Abigail S. Duniway." In *Northwest Women's Heritage,* ed. Karen Blair, 135–36. Seattle: Northwest Center for Research on Women, 1985.

Wedell, Marsha. *Elite Women and the Reform Impulse in Memphis, 1875–1915.* Knoxville: University of Tennessee Press, 1991.

Wells, Kate Gannett. "Women's Clubs—A Symposium." *Arena* 6, 33 (1893): 370.

Wells, Merle. *Gold Camps and Silver Cities: Nineteenth-Century Mining in Central and Southern Idaho.* Moscow: Idaho Department of Lands, 1983.

Wesley, Charles Harris. *The History of the National Association of Colored Women's Clubs.* Washington, D.C.: NACWC, 1984.

White, Martha. "The Work of the Woman's Club." *Atlantic Monthly* 93, 559 (1903): 616–621.

White, Richard. *"It's Your Misfortune and None of My Own": A New History of the American West.* Norman: University of Oklahoma Press, 1991.

Whitney, Marci. *Notable Women.* Tacoma, Wash.: Tacoma News Tribune.

Willard, Frances E. *Glimpses of Fifty Years, 1839–1889: The Autobiography of an American Woman.* Chicago: Woman's Temperance Publication Association, 1889.

Woman's Edition, *The Dalles Times-Mountaineer.* The Dalles: Ladies of the Dalles Public Library, May 17, 1898.

"Women's Clubs—A Symposium." *Arena* 6, 33 (1893): 362–65.

Woody, Thomas. *History of Women's Education.* New York: Science Press, 1929. Reprinted New York: Octagon Books, 1966.

Worster, Donald. *Under Western Skies: Nature and History in the American West.* New York: Oxford University Press, 1992.

Wortman, Marlene Stein, ed. *Women in American Law from Colonial Times to the New Deal.* New York: Holmes and Meier Publishers, 1990.

INDEX